My Heavenly Hockey Club

7

Ai Morinaga

Translated and adapted by Athena Nibley and Alethea Nibley

Lettered by North Market Street Graphics

DEL
REY

BALLANTINE BOOKS • NEW YORK

My Heavenly Hockey Club volume 7 is a work of fiction. Names, characters, places, and incidents are the products of the author's imagination or are used fictitiously. Any resemblance to actual events, locales, or persons, living or dead, is entirely coincidental.

A Del Rey Manga/Kodansha Trade Paperback Original

Published in the United States by Del Rey, an imprint of The Random House Publishing Group, a division of Random House, Inc., New York.

DEL REY is a registered trademark and the Del Rey colophon is a trademark of Random House, Inc.

Publication rights arranged through Kodansha Ltd.

First published in Japan in 2007 by Kodansha Ltd., Tokyo, as *Gokurako Seishun Hockeybu.*

ISBN 978-0-345-50200-1

Printed in the United States of America

www.delreymanga.com

9 8 7 6 5 4 3 2 1

Translators/Adapters—Athena Nibley and Alethea Nibley
Lettering—North Market Street Graphics

Contents

Shanghai Zoo Part 2!! Here we have the wolf, Hogeo-kun.
It looks like he's just a head, but he actually does have a body, too.
Princess Tenko is ghastly pale, too. This is Princess Hogeo. Oh, I
guess he's a prince. I made him a girl. Sorry, Hogeo. —Ai Morinaga

Honorifics Explained

Throughout the Del Rey Manga books, you will find Japanese honorifics left intact in the translations. For those not familiar with how the Japanese use honorifics and, more important, how they differ from American honorifics, we present this brief overview.

Politeness has always been a critical facet of Japanese culture. Ever since the feudal era, when Japan was a highly stratified society, use of honorifics—which can be defined as polite speech that indicates relationship or status—has played an essential role in the Japanese language. When addressing someone in Japanese, an honorific usually takes the form of a suffix attached to one's name (example: "Asuna-san"), is used as a title at the end of one's name, or appears in place of the name itself (example: "Negi-sensei," or simply "Sensei!").

Honorifics can be expressions of respect or endearment. In the context of manga and anime, honorifics give insight into the nature of the relationship between characters. Many English translations leave out these important honorifics and therefore distort the feel of the original Japanese. Because Japanese honorifics contain nuances that English honorifics lack, it is our policy at Del Rey not to translate them. Here, instead, is a guide to some of the honorifics you may encounter in Del Rey Manga.

-san: This is the most common honorific and is equivalent to Mr., Miss, Ms., or Mrs. It is the all-purpose honorific and can be used in any situation where politeness is required.

-sama: This is one level higher than "-san" and is used to confer great respect.

-dono: This comes from the word "tono," which means "lord." It is an even higher level than "-sama" and confers utmost respect.

-kun: This suffix is used at the end of boys' names to express familiarity or endearment. It is also sometimes used by men among friends, or when addressing someone younger or of a lower station.

-chan: This is used to express endearment, mostly toward girls. It is also used for little boys, pets, and even among lovers. It gives a sense of childish cuteness.

Bozu: This is an informal way to refer to a boy, similar to the English terms "kid" and "squirt."

Sempai/Senpai: This title suggests that the addressee is one's senior in a group or organization. It is most often used in a school setting, where underclassmen refer to their upperclassmen as "sempai." It can also be used in the workplace, such as when a newer employee addresses an employee who has seniority in the company.

Kohai: This is the opposite of "sempai" and is used toward underclassmen in school or newcomers in the workplace. It connotes that the addressee is of a lower station.

Sensei: Literally meaning "one who has come before," this title is used for teachers, doctors, or masters of any profession or art.

-[blank]: This is usually forgotten in these lists, but it is perhaps the most significant difference between Japanese and English. The lack of honorific means that the speaker has permission to address the person in a very intimate way. Usually, only family, spouses, or very close friends have this kind of permission. Known as *yobisute*, it can be gratifying when someone who has earned the intimacy starts to call one by one's name without an honorific. But when that intimacy hasn't been earned, it can be very insulting.

My Heavenly Hockey Club

7

Ai Morinaga

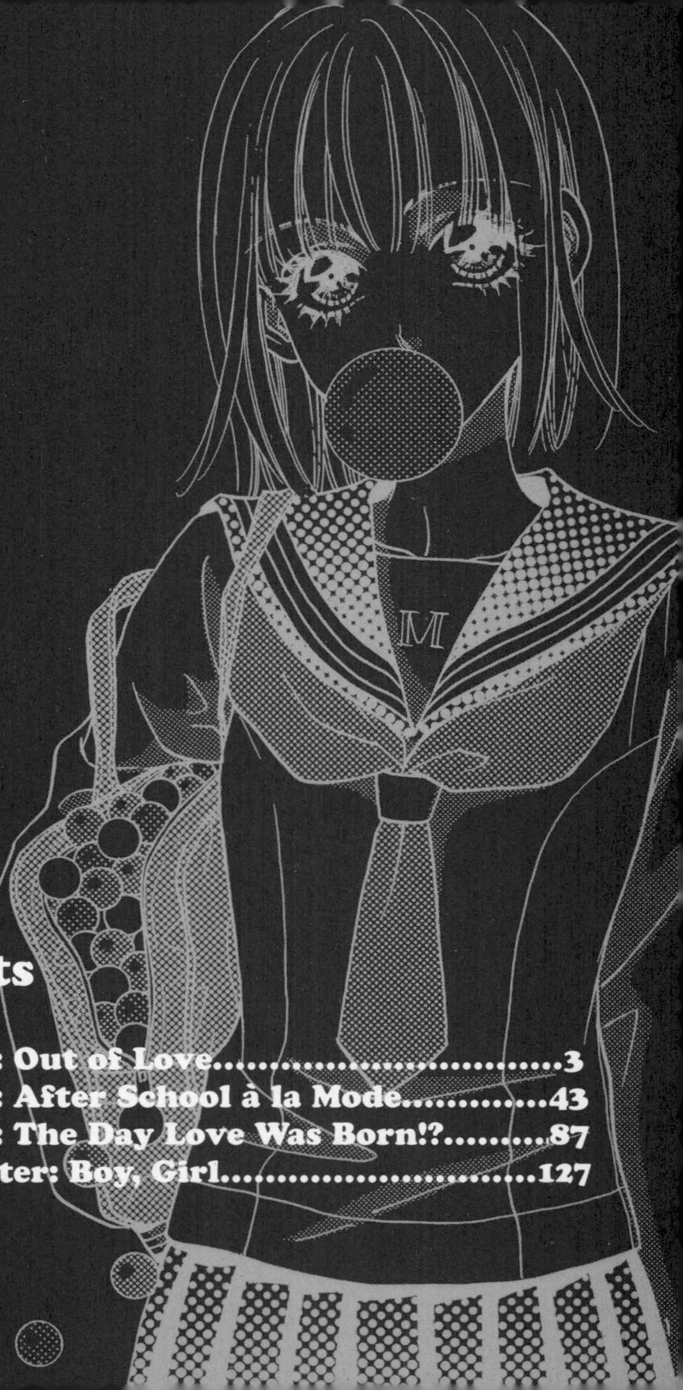
M

Contents

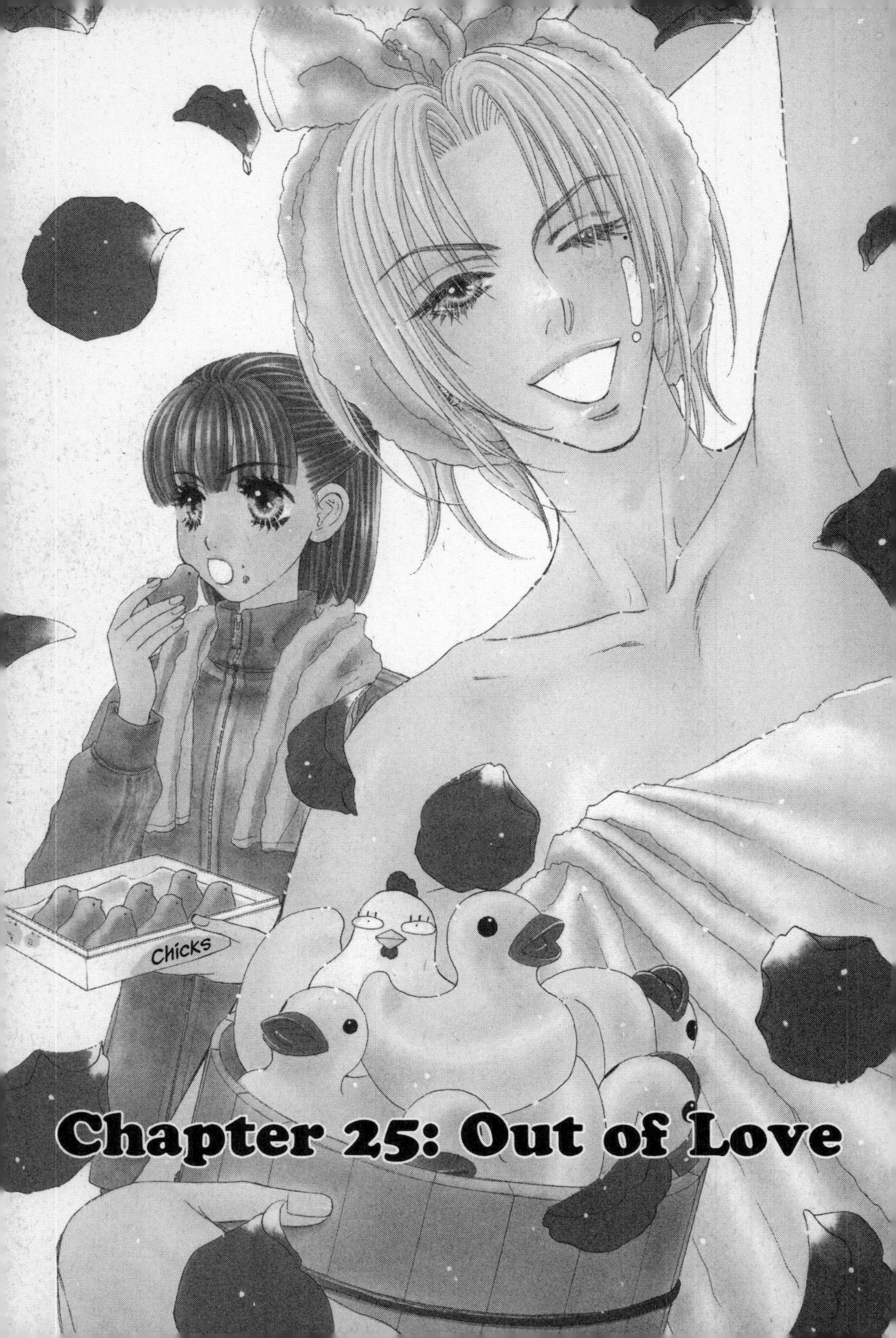
Chicks

Chapter 25: Out of Love

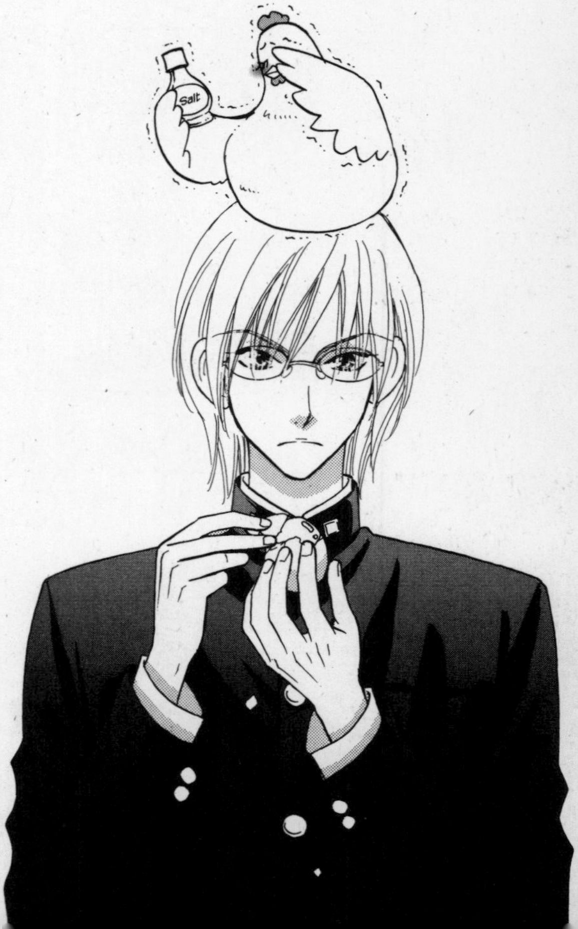
Salt

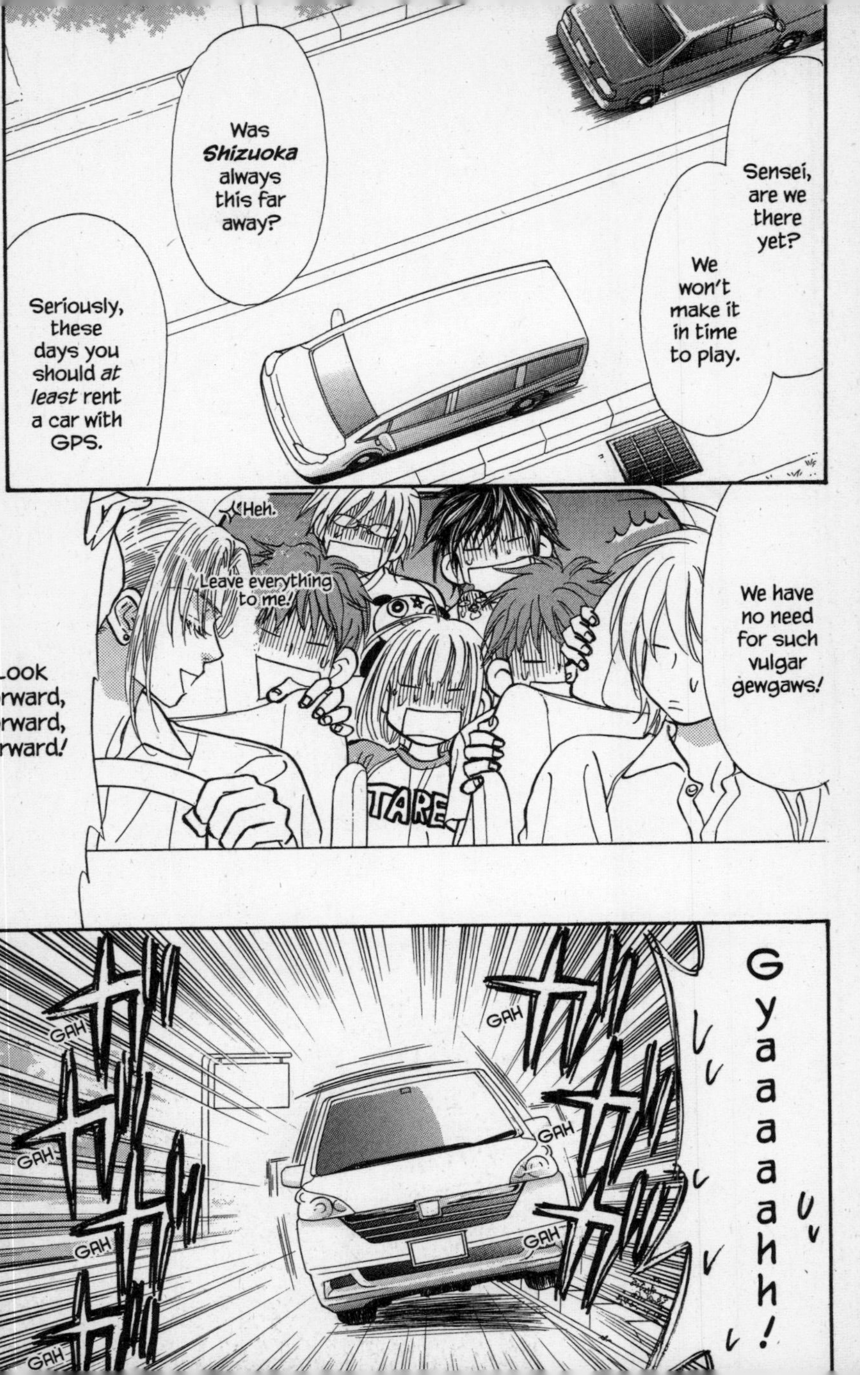
Sensei, are we there yet?
We won't make it in time to play.
Was *Shizuoka* always this far away?
Seriously, these days you should *at least* rent a car with GPS.
We have no need for such vulgar gewgaws!
Heh.
Leave everything to me!
Look forward, forward, forward!
Gyaaaaaahh!
GAH
GAH
GAH
GAH
GAH
GAH
GAH
TARE

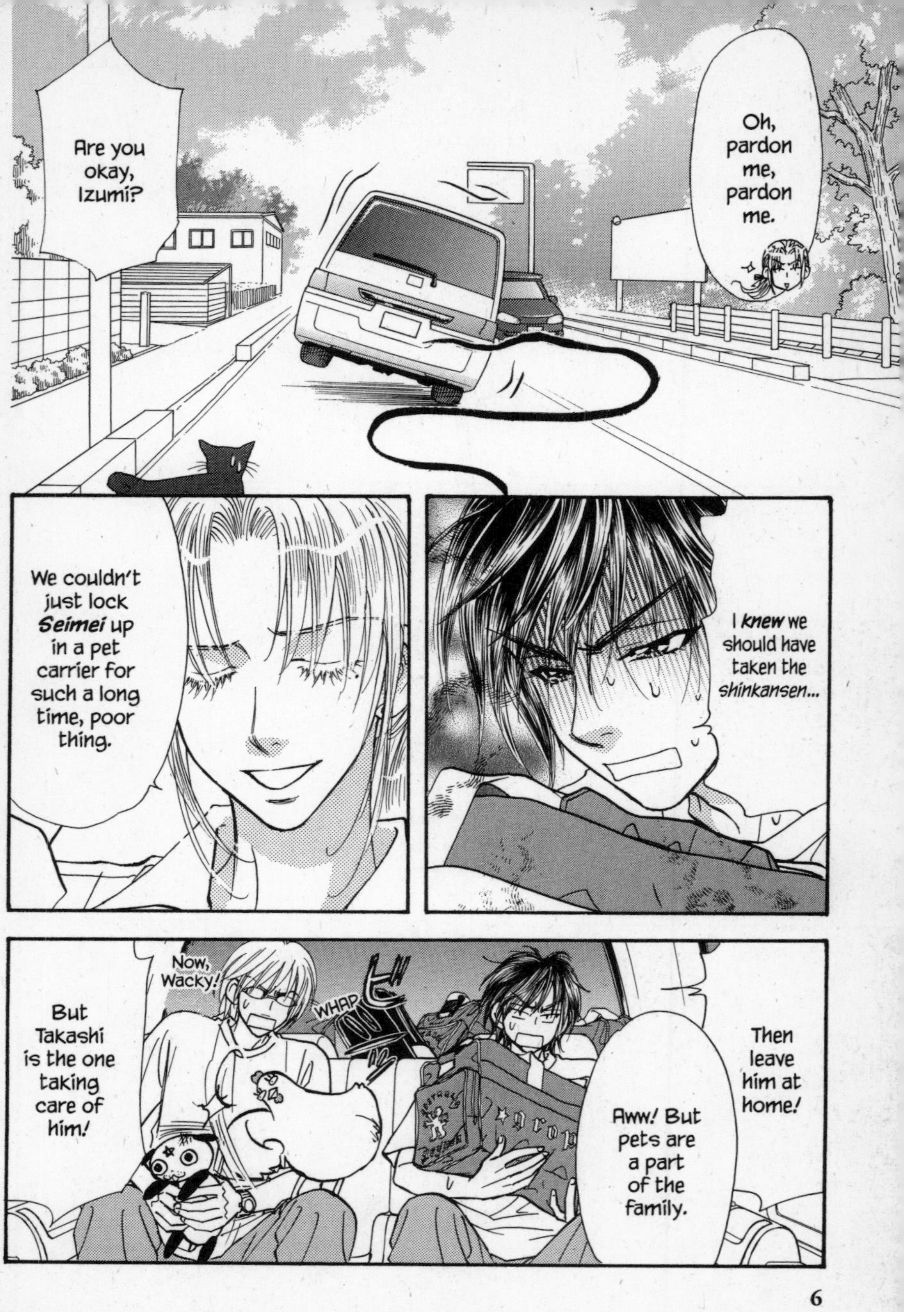
Oh, pardon me, pardon me.
Are you okay, Izumi?
I knew we should have taken the shinkansen...
We couldn't just lock Seimei up in a pet carrier for such a long time, poor thing.
Then leave him at home!
Aww! But pets are a part of the family.
WHAP
Now, Wacky!
But Takashi is the one taking care of him!

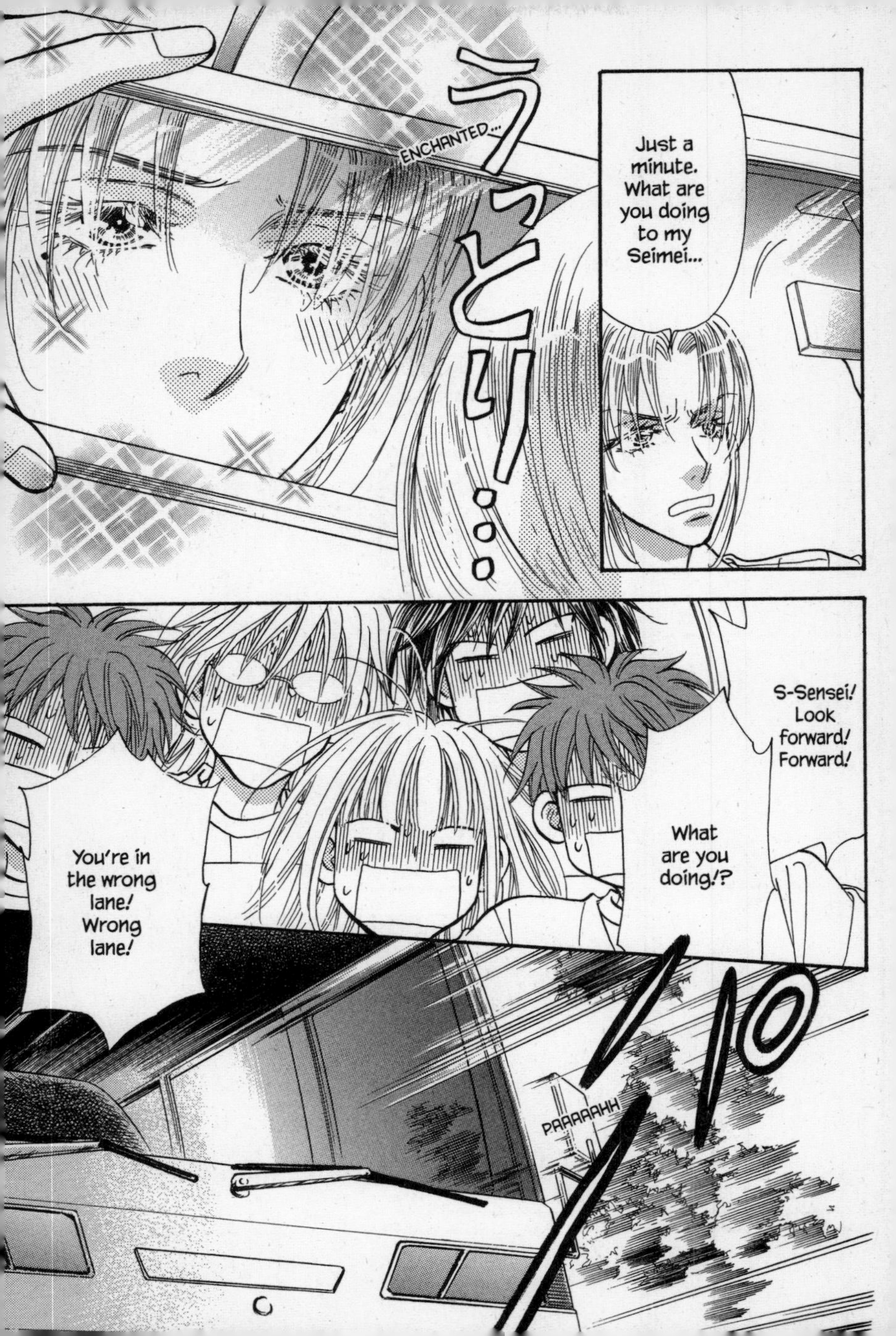
Just a minute. What are you doing to my Seimei...
ENCHANTED...
うっとり…
S-Sensei! Look forward! Forward!
What are you doing!?
You're in the wrong lane! Wrong lane!
PAAAAAHH

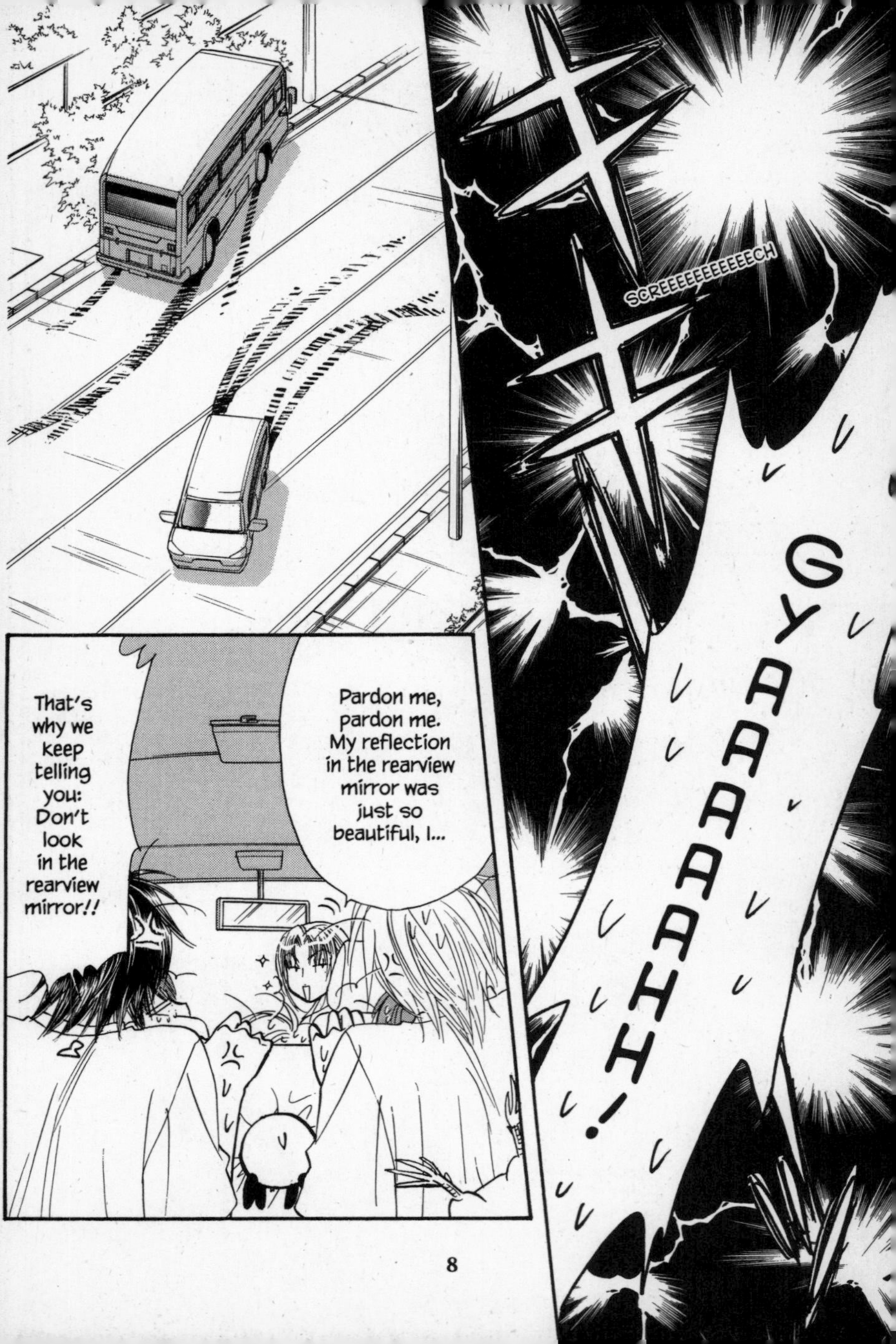
SCREEEEEEEEEEEECH
GYAAAAAHH!
Pardon me, pardon me. My reflection in the rearview mirror was just so beautiful, I...
That's why we keep telling you: Don't look in the rearview mirror!!

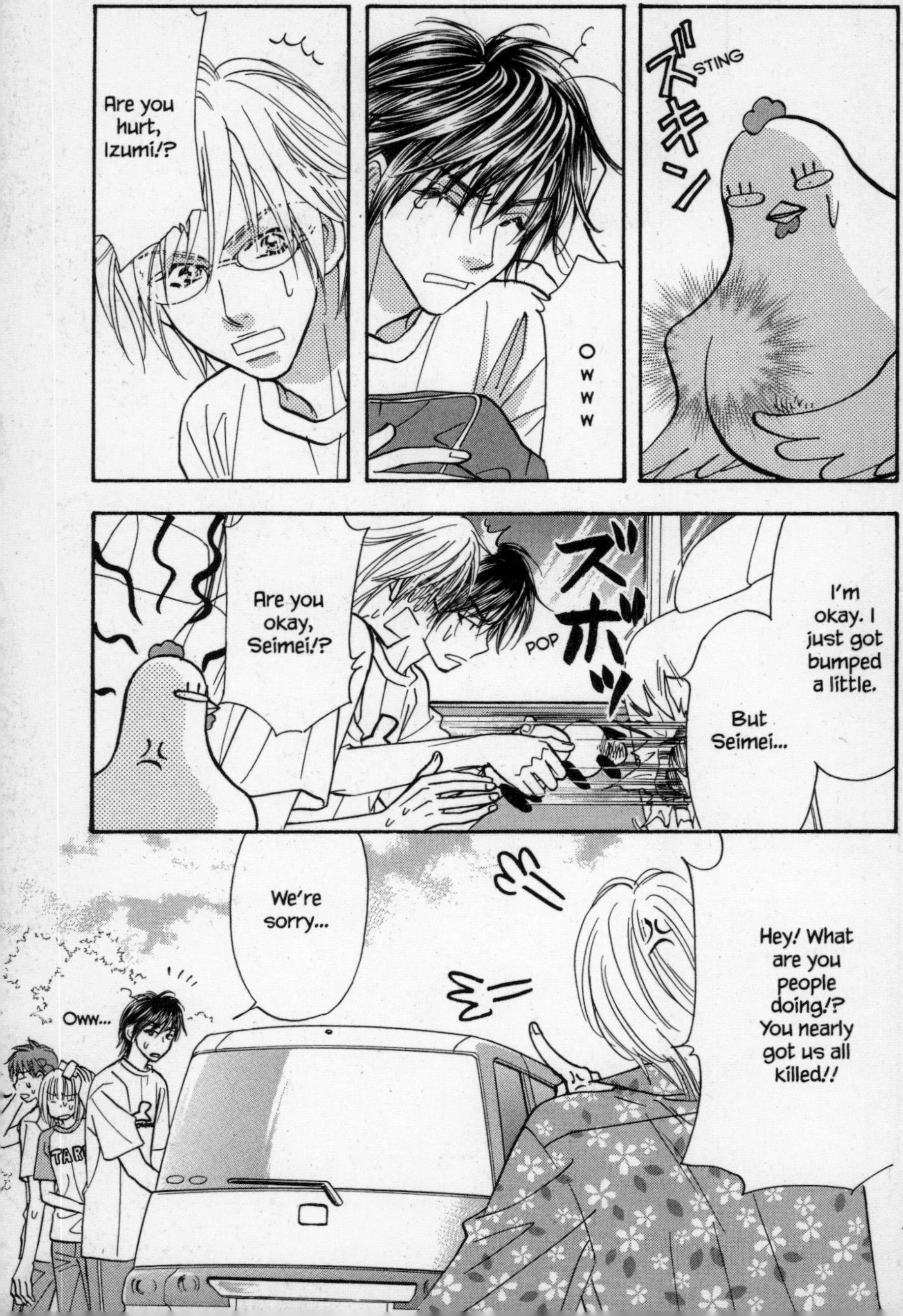

ズキン
STING
OWWW
Are you hurt, Izumi!?
I'm okay. I just got bumped a little.
But Seimei...
ズボッ
POP
Are you okay, Seimei!?
Hey! What are you people doing!? You nearly got us all killed!!
We're sorry...
Oww...

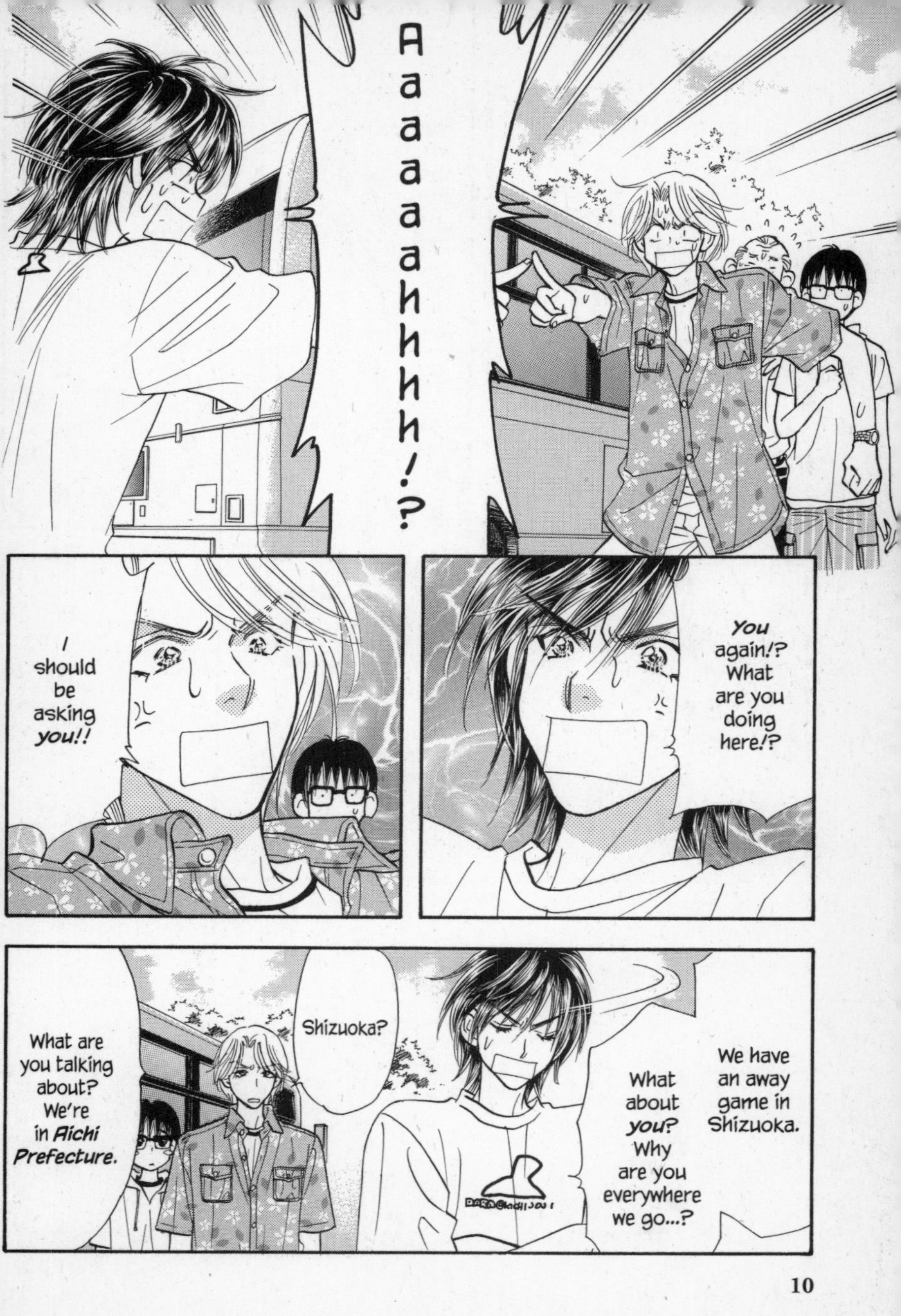
Aaaaaahhhh!?
You again!? What are you doing here!?
I should be asking you!!
We have an away game in Shizuoka.
What about you? Why are you everywhere we go...?
Shizuoka?
What are you talking about? We're in Aichi Prefecture.

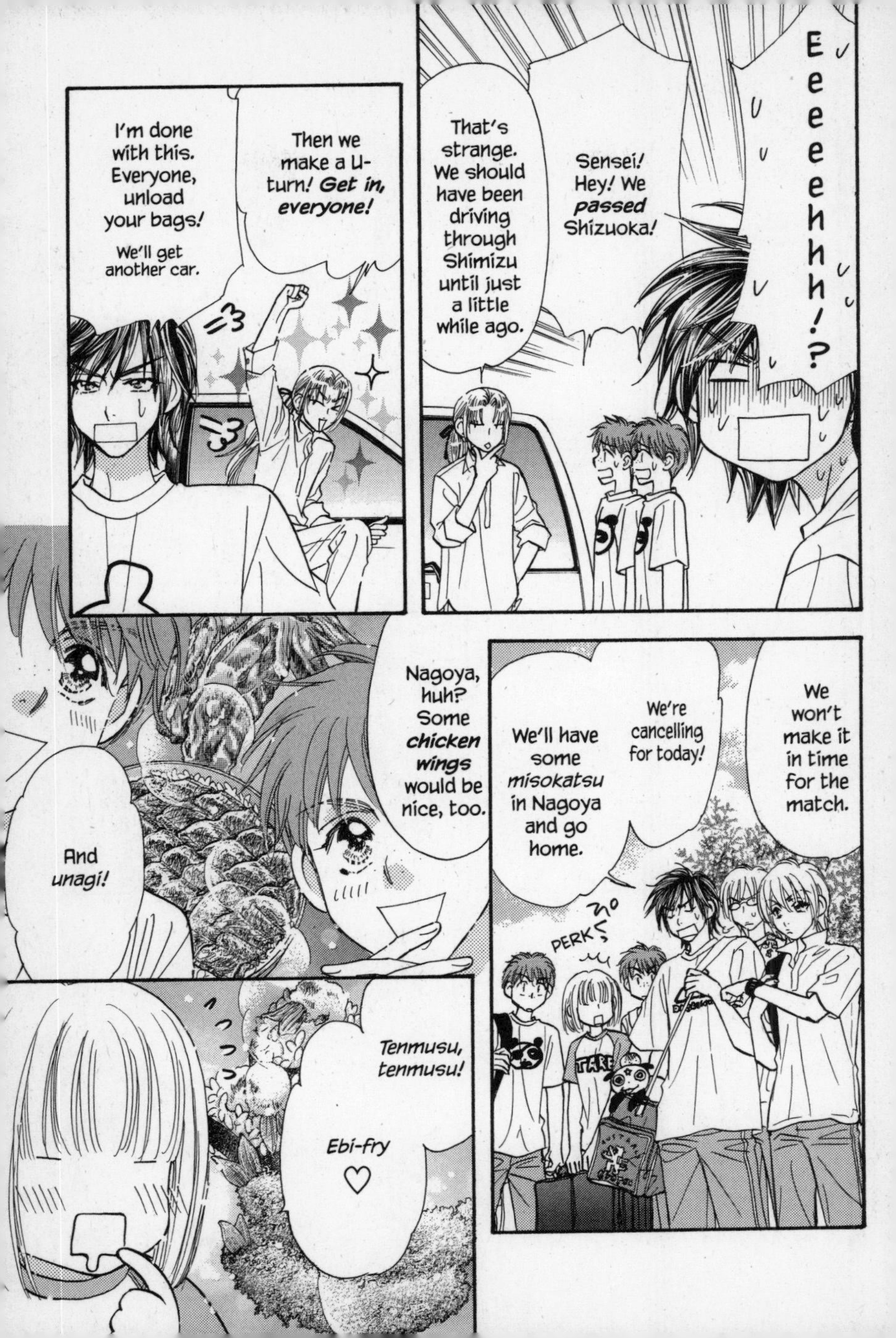
Eeeeehhh!?
Sensei! Hey! We passed Shizuoka!
That's strange. We should have been driving through Shimizu until just a little while ago.
Then we make a U-turn! Get in, everyone!
I'm done with this. Everyone, unload your bags!
We'll get another car.
We won't make it in time for the match.
We're cancelling for today!
We'll have some misokatsu in Nagoya and go home.
PERK
Nagoya, huh? Some chicken wings would be nice, too.
And unagi!
Tenmusu, tenmusu!
Ebi-fry ♡

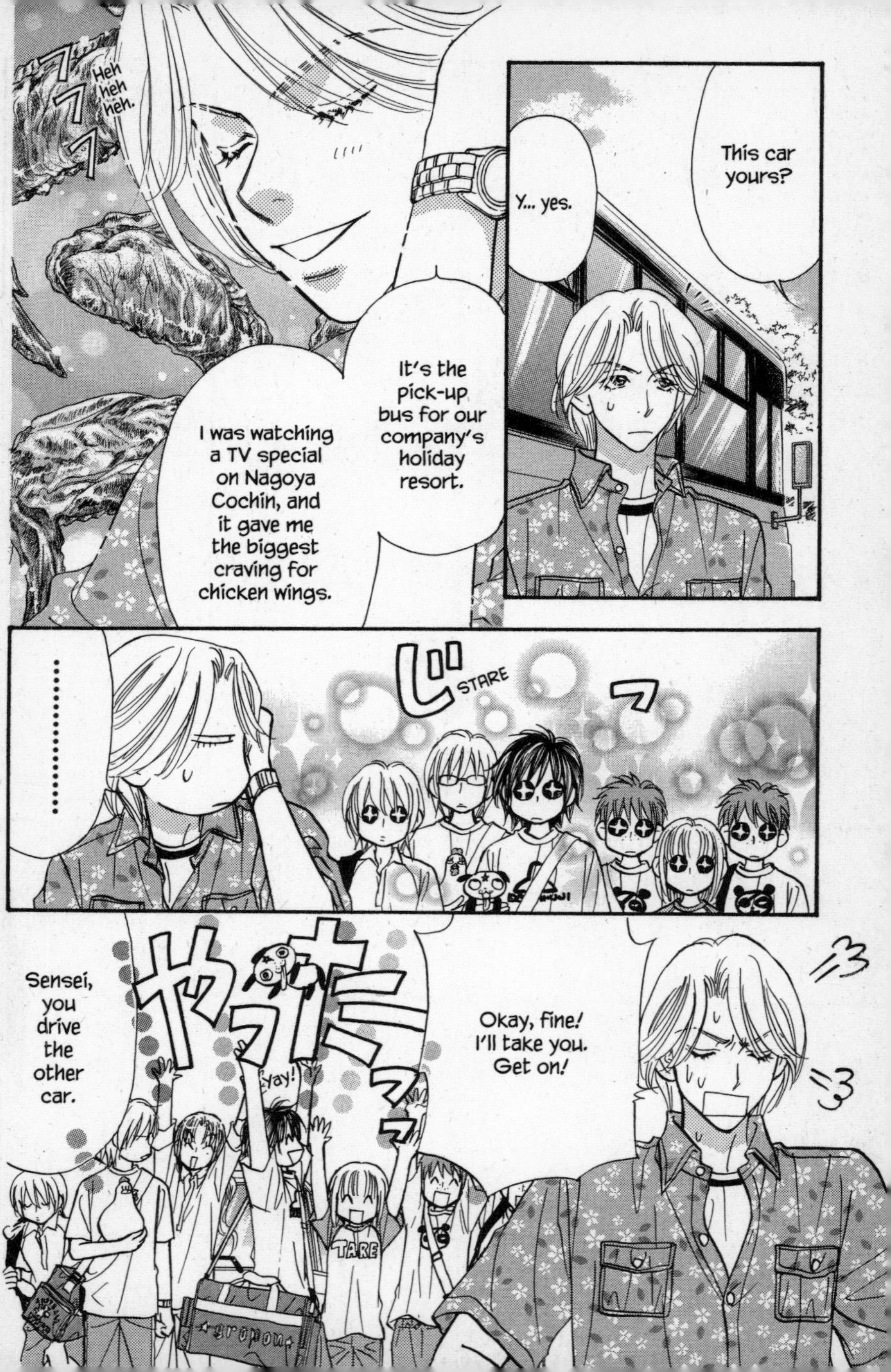
This car yours?
Y... yes.
フフフ
Heh heh heh.
It's the pick-up bus for our company's holiday resort.
I was watching a TV special on Nagoya Cochin, and it gave me the biggest craving for chicken wings.
......
じっ
STARE
Okay, fine! I'll take you. Get on!
やったーっっ
Yay!
Sensei, you drive the other car.

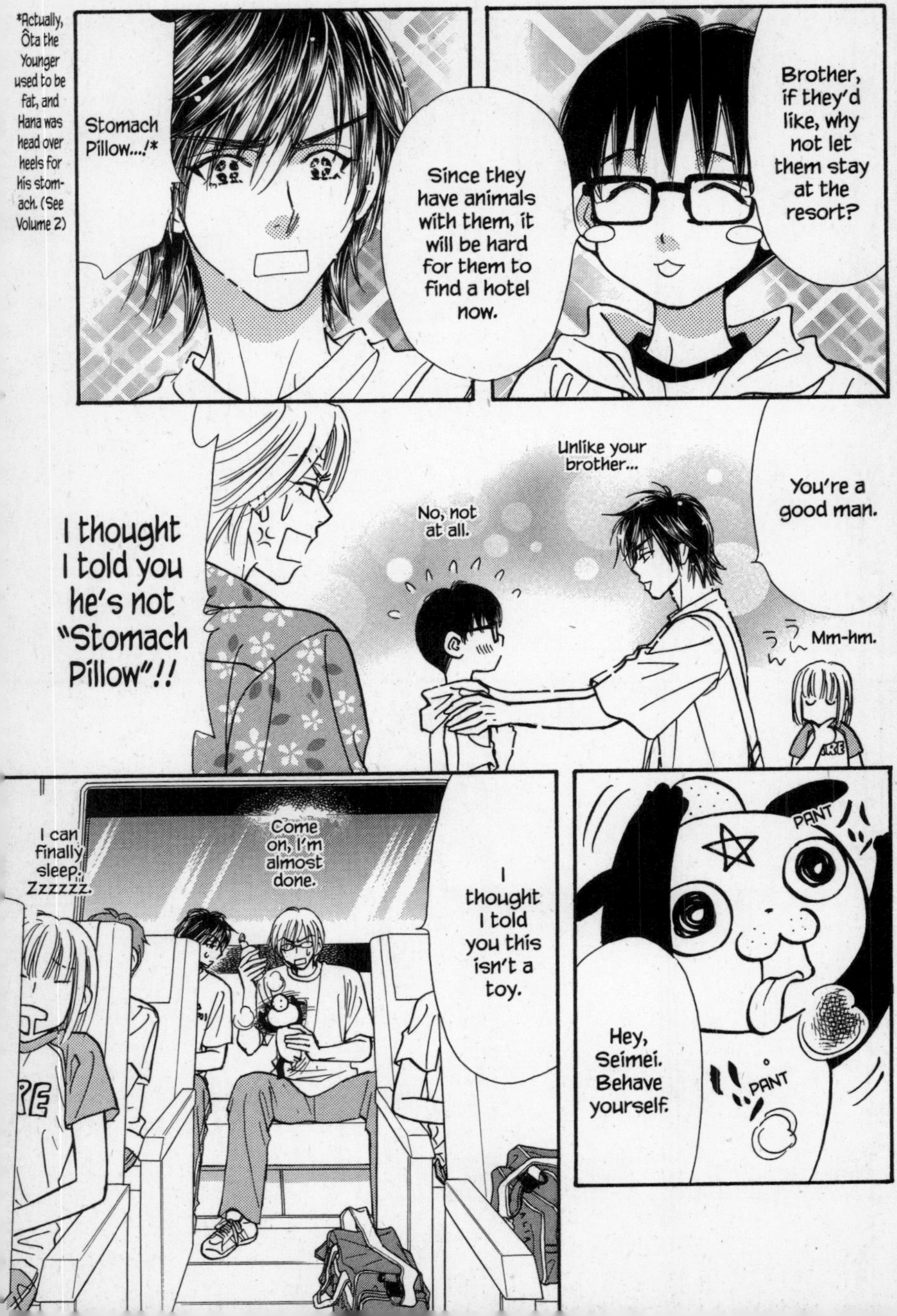
Brother, if they'd like, why not let them stay at the resort?
Since they have animals with them, it will be hard for them to find a hotel now.
Stomach Pillow...!*
You're a good man.
Unlike your brother...
Mm-hm.
No, not at all.
I thought I told you he's not "Stomach Pillow"!!
PANT
Hey, Seimei. Behave yourself.
PANT
I thought I told you this isn't a toy.
Come on, I'm almost done.
I can finally sleep. Zzzzzz.

*Actually, Ôta the Younger used to be fat, and Hana was head over heels for his stomach. (See Volume 2)

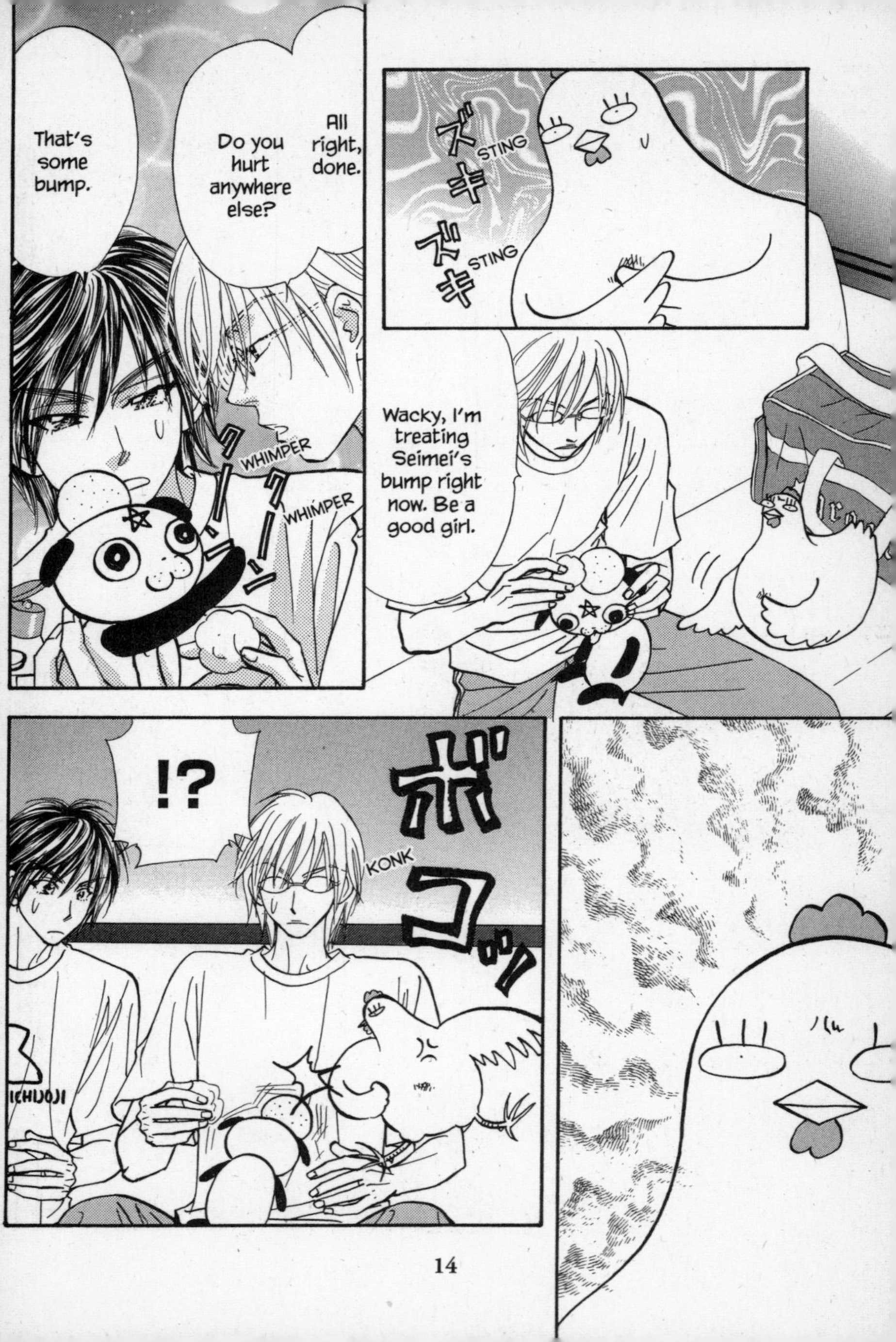
ズキ STING
ズキ STING
Wacky, I'm treating Seimei's bump right now. Be a good girl.
All right, done.
Do you hurt anywhere else?
That's some bump.
WHIMPER
WHIMPER
ボコッ
KONK
!?
ICHIJOJI

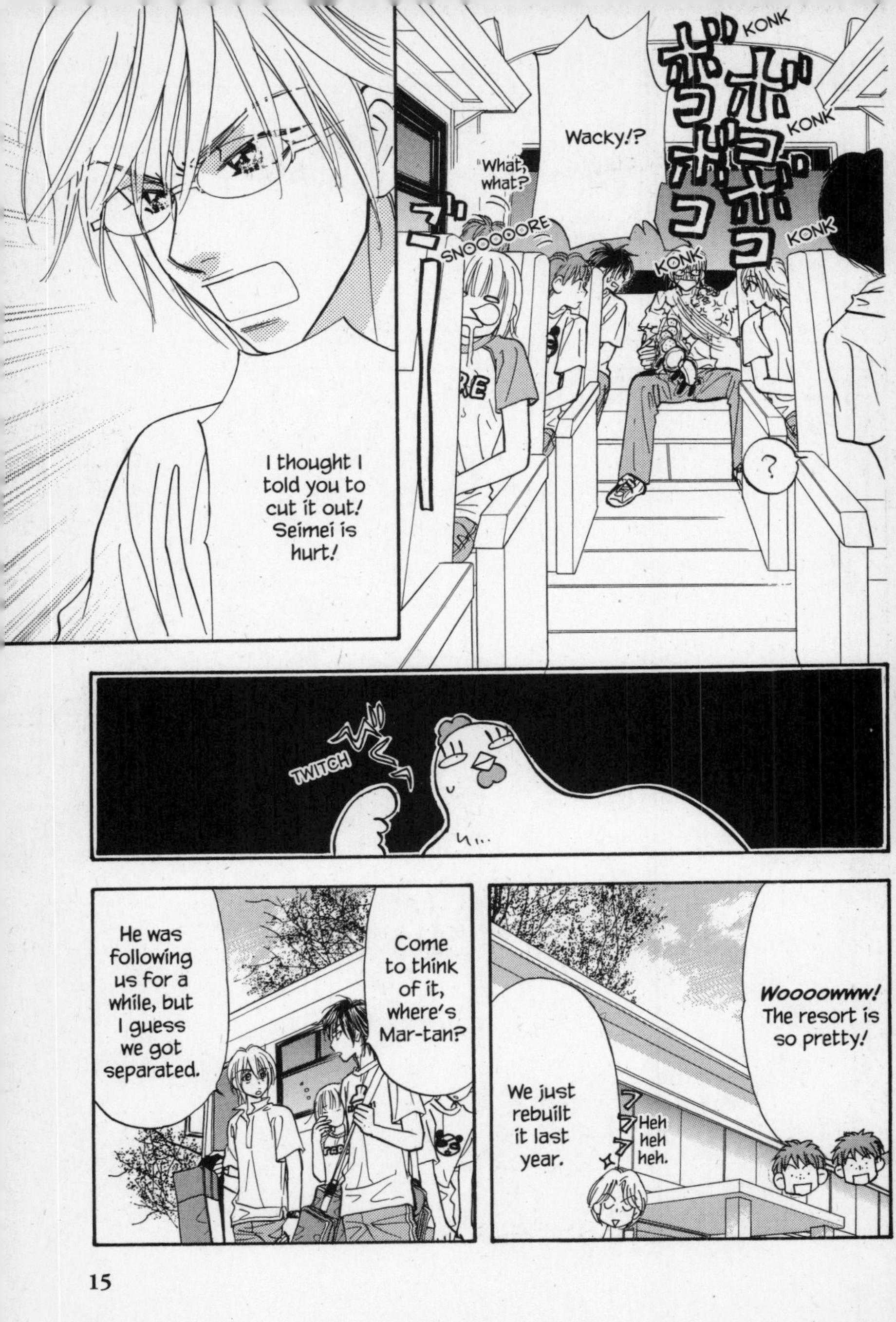
KONK
KONK
Wacky!?
"What, what?
KONK
KONK
SNOOOOORE
?
I thought I told you to cut it out! Seimei is hurt!
TWITCH
Woooowww! The resort is so pretty!
We just rebuilt it last year.
Heh heh heh.
Come to think of it, where's Mar-tan?
He was following us for a while, but I guess we got separated.

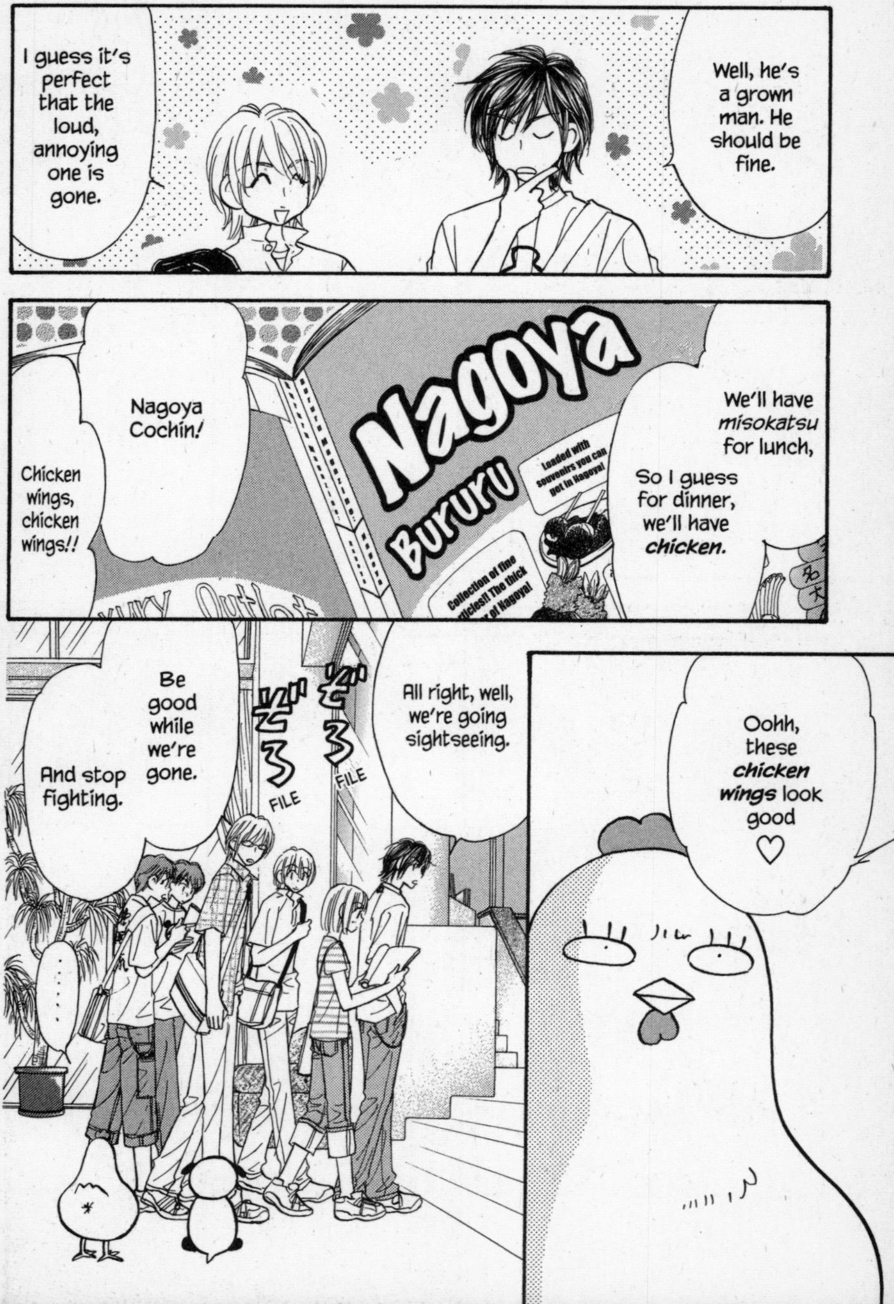

Well, he's a grown man. He should be fine.
I guess it's perfect that the loud, annoying one is gone.
We'll have misokatsu for lunch,
So I guess for dinner, we'll have chicken.
Nagoya
Bururu
Loaded with souvenirs you can get in Nagoya!
Nagoya Cochin!
Chicken wings, chicken wings!!
Oohh, these chicken wings look good ♡
All right, well, we're going sightseeing.
ぞろ FILE
ぞろ FILE
Be good while we're gone.
And stop fighting.
……

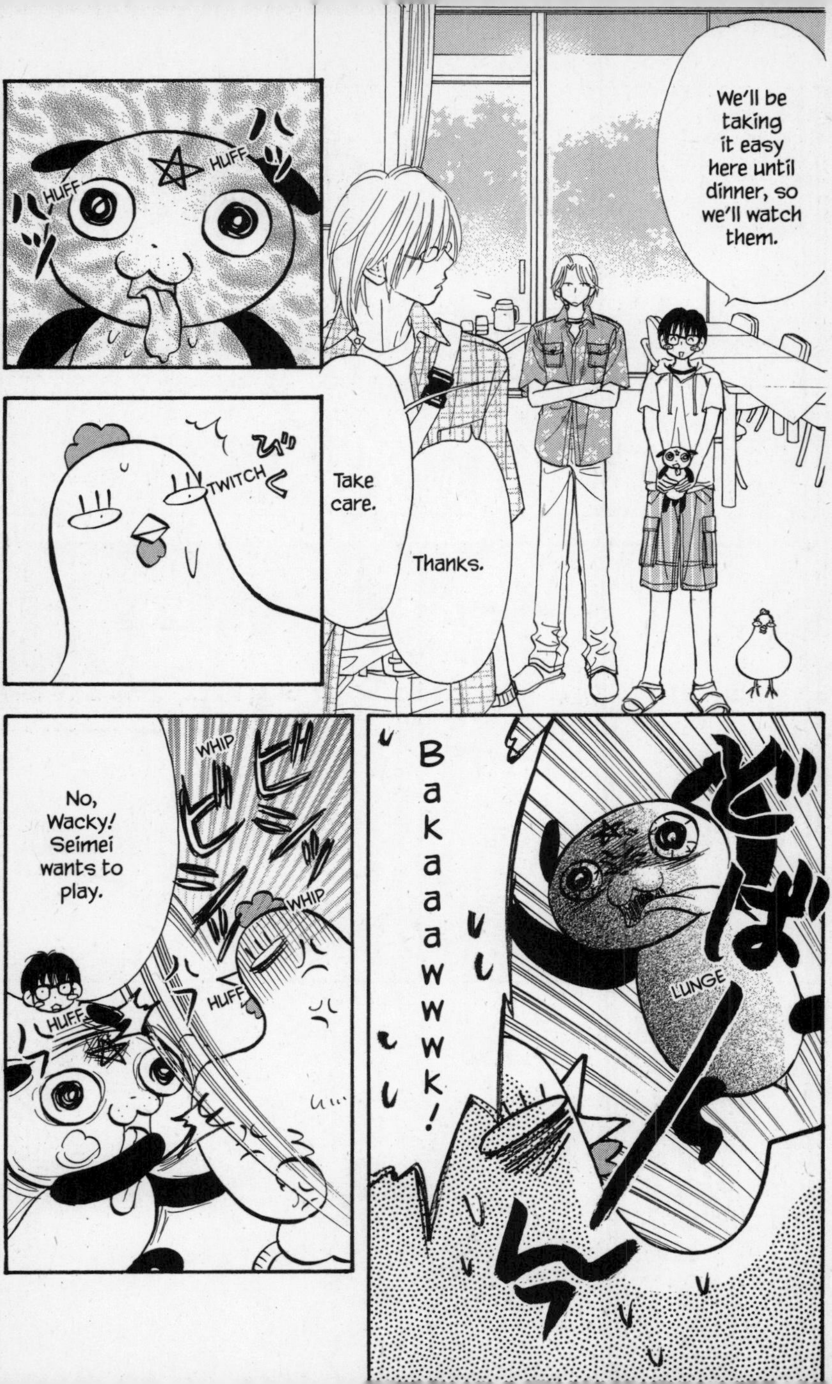
We'll be taking it easy here until dinner, so we'll watch them.
Thanks.
Take care.
HUFF
HUFF
TWITCH
Bakaaawwwk!
LUNGE
WHIP
WHIP
No, Wacky! Seimei wants to play.
HUFF
HUFF

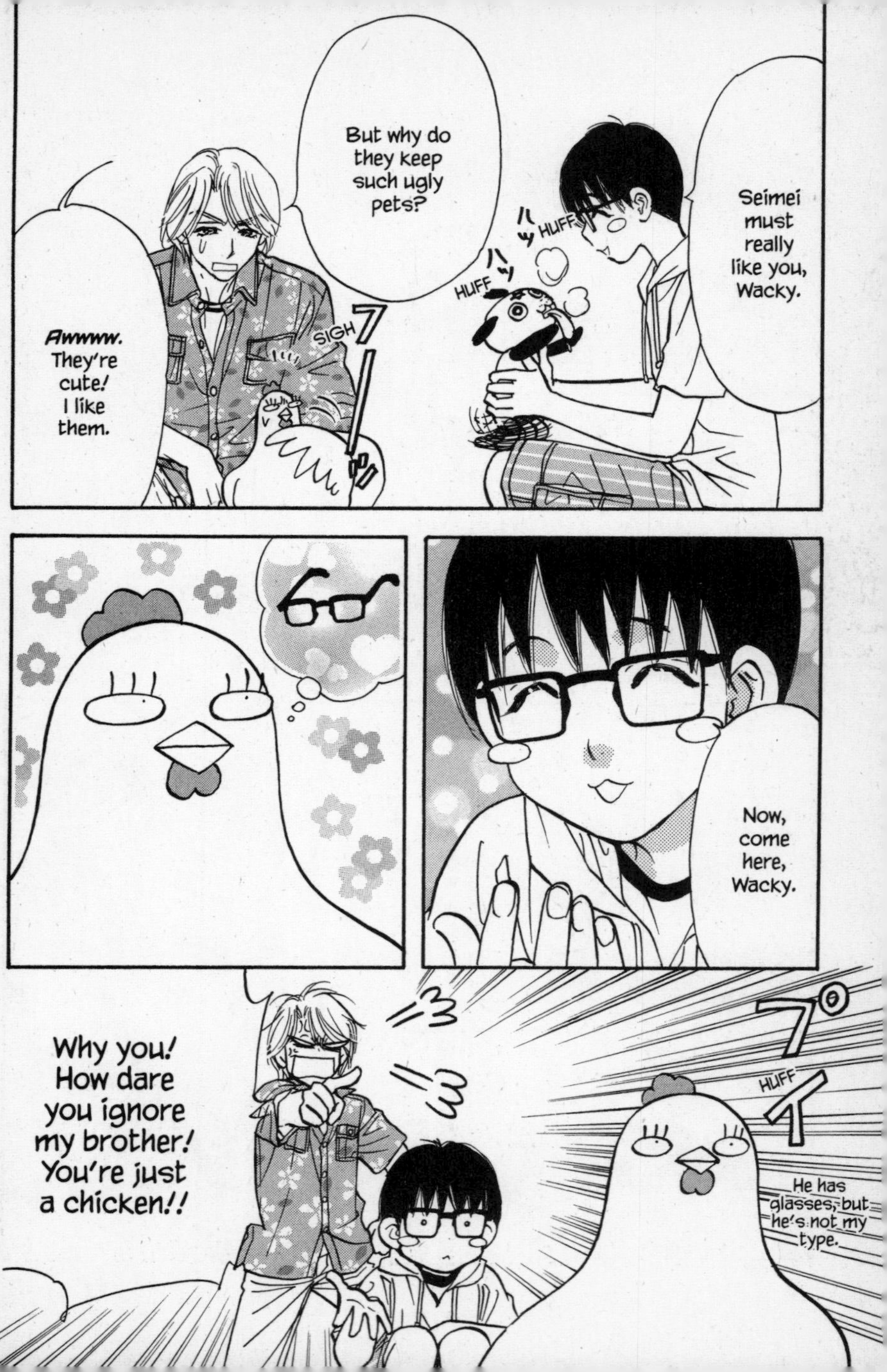
Seimei must really like you, Wacky.
HUFF
HUFF
But why do they keep such ugly pets?
SIGH
Awwww. They're cute! I like them.
Now, come here, Wacky.
He has glasses, but he's not my type.
HUFF
Why you! How dare you ignore my brother! You're just a chicken!!

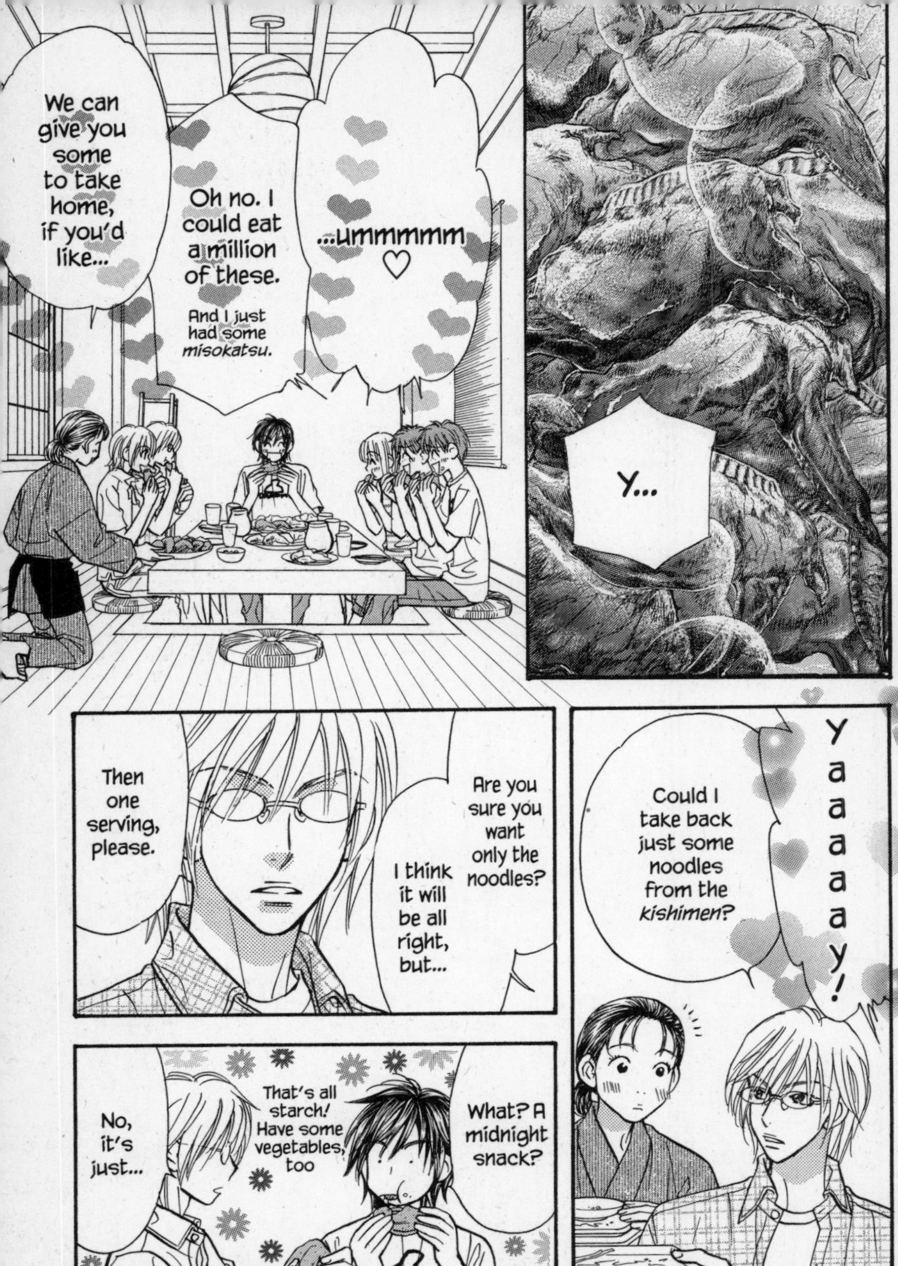
Y...
...ummmmm ♡
Oh no. I could eat a million of these.
And I just had some *misokatsu*.
We can give you some to take home, if you'd like...
Yaaaaay!
Could I take back just some noodles from the *kishimen*?
Are you sure you want only the noodles?
I think it will be all right, but...
Then one serving, please.
What? A midnight snack?
That's all starch! Have some vegetables, too
No, it's just...

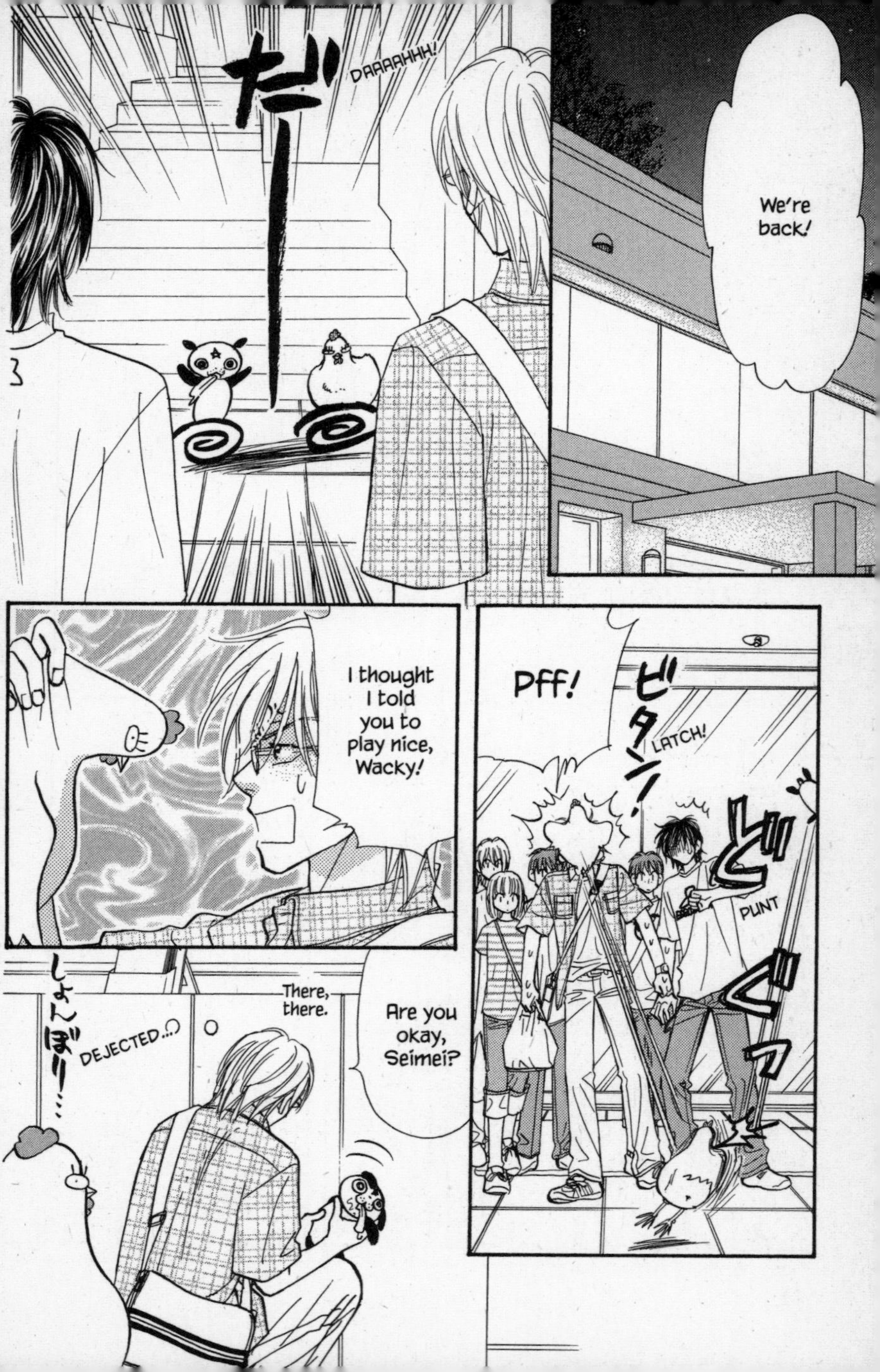
We're back!
DARAAAHHH!
Pff!
ビタン！
LATCH!
PUNT
I thought I told you to play nice, Wacky!
Are you okay, Seimei?
There, there.
しょんぼり…
DEJECTED...

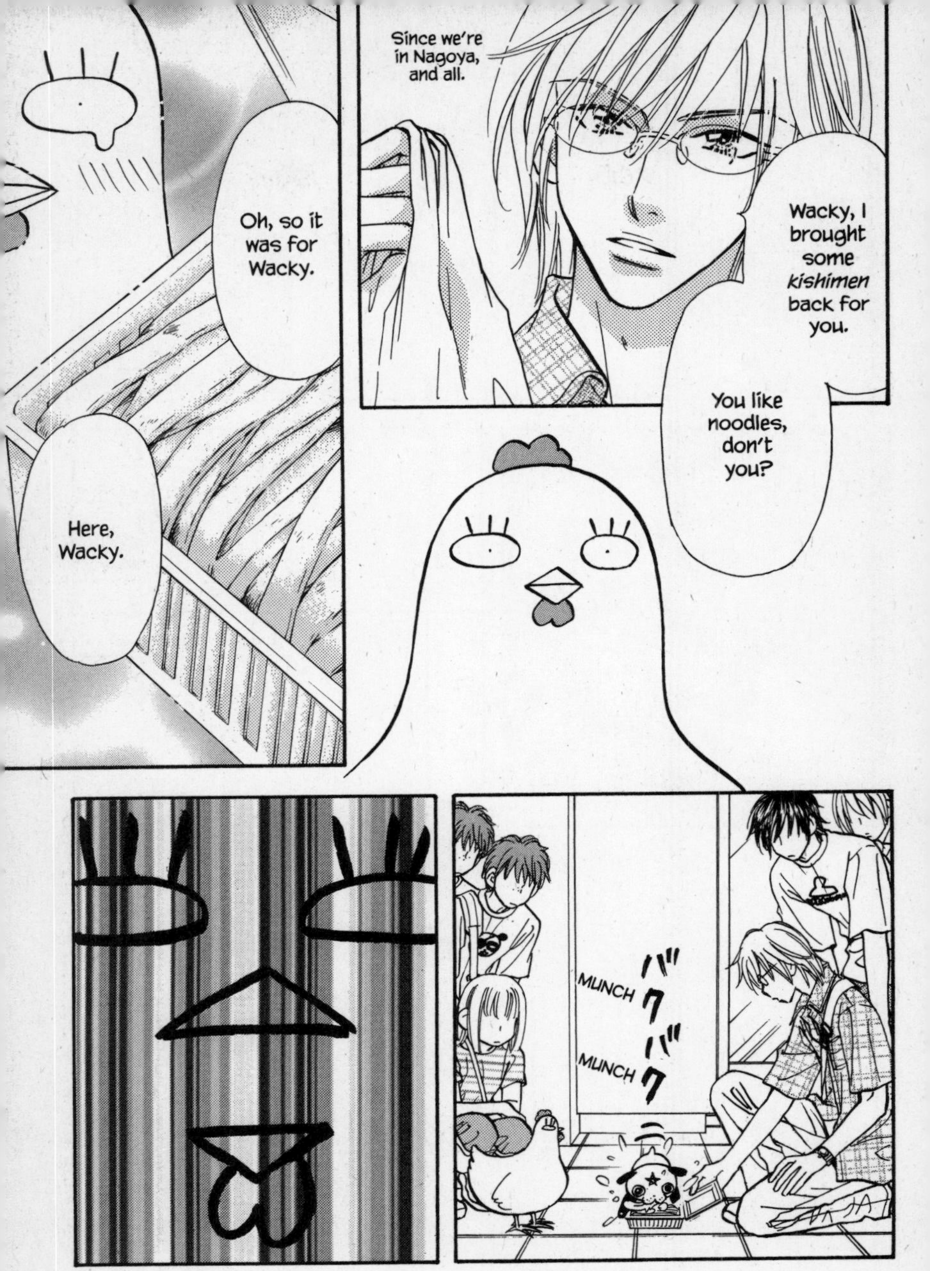
Since we're in Nagoya, and all.
Wacky, I brought some *kishimen* back for you.
You like noodles, don't you?
Oh, so it was for Wacky.
Here, Wacky.
MUNCH バク
MUNCH バク

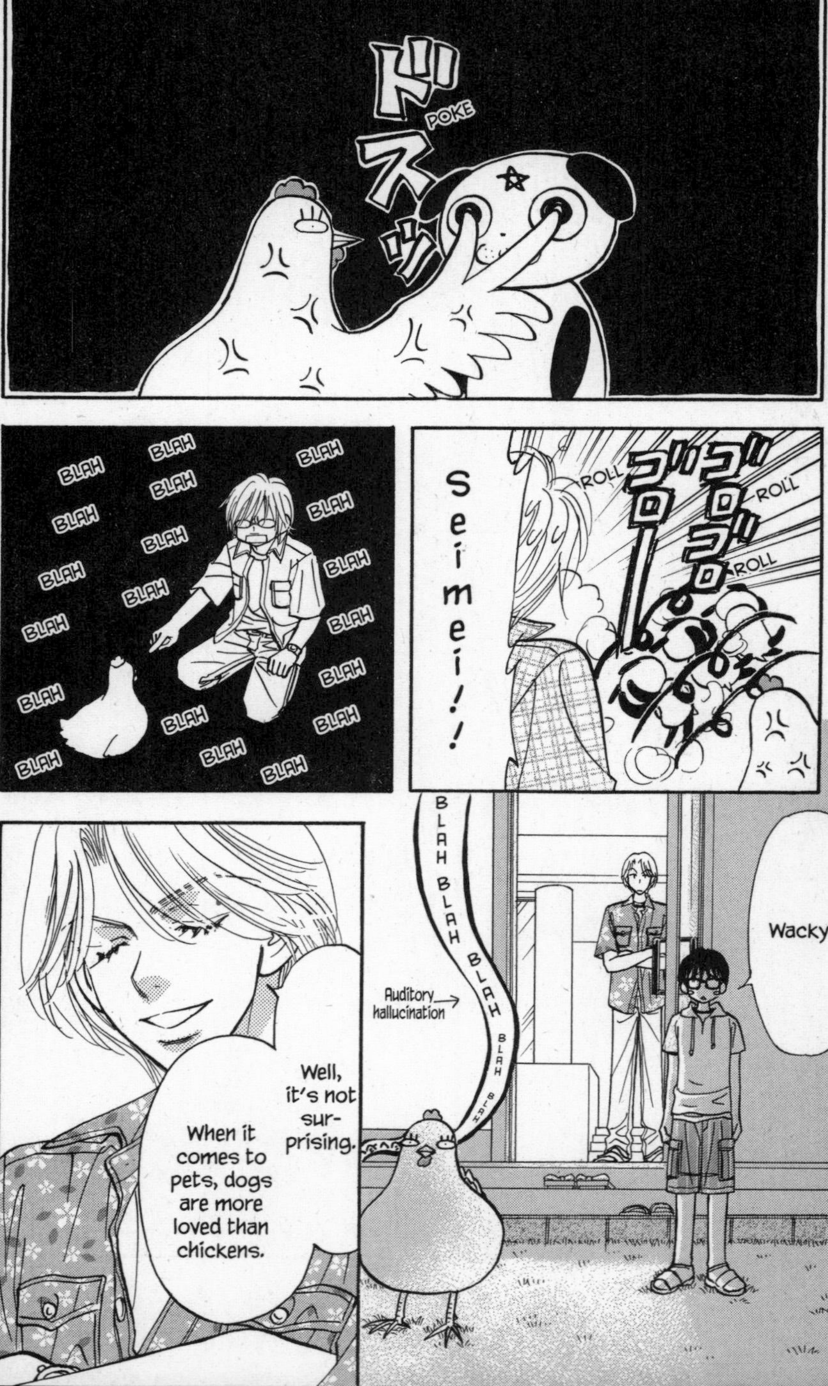
ドスッ
POKE
ゴロゴロゴロ
ROLL
ROLL
ROLL
Seimei!!
BLAH BLAH BLAH BLAH BLAH BLAH BLAH BLAH BLAH BLAH BLAH BLAH BLAH BLAH BLAH BLAH BLAH
Wacky...
BLAH BLAH BLAH BLAH BLAH BLAH
Auditory hallucination
Well, it's not surprising.
When it comes to pets, dogs are more loved than chickens.

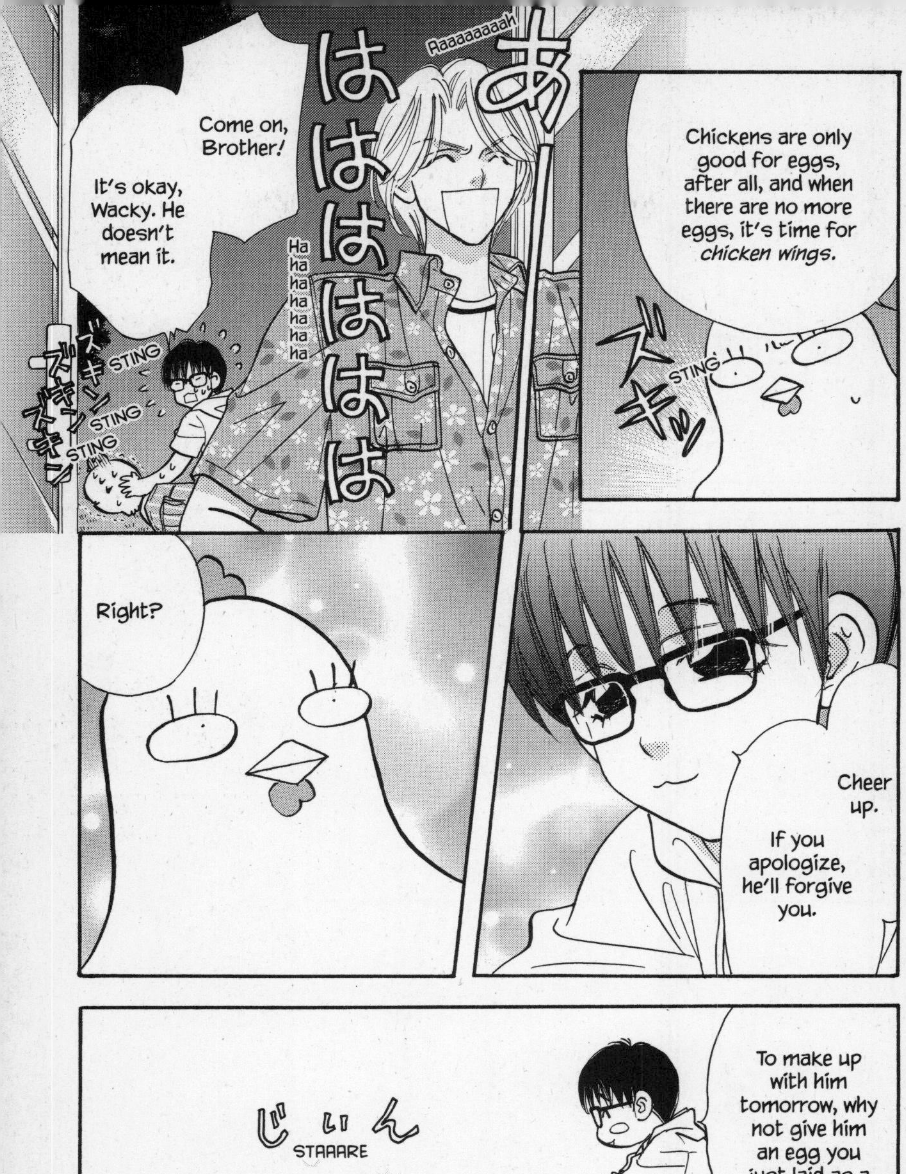

Chickens are only good for eggs, after all, and when there are no more eggs, it's time for *chicken wings.*
ズキッ
STING
あはははははは
Aaaaaaaaah
Ha ha ha ha ha ha ha
Come on, Brother!
It's okay, Wacky. He doesn't mean it.
ズキン
STING
ズキン
STING
ズキン
STING
Cheer up.
If you apologize, he'll forgive you.
Right?
To make up with him tomorrow, why not give him an egg you just laid as a present?
じいん
STAAARE

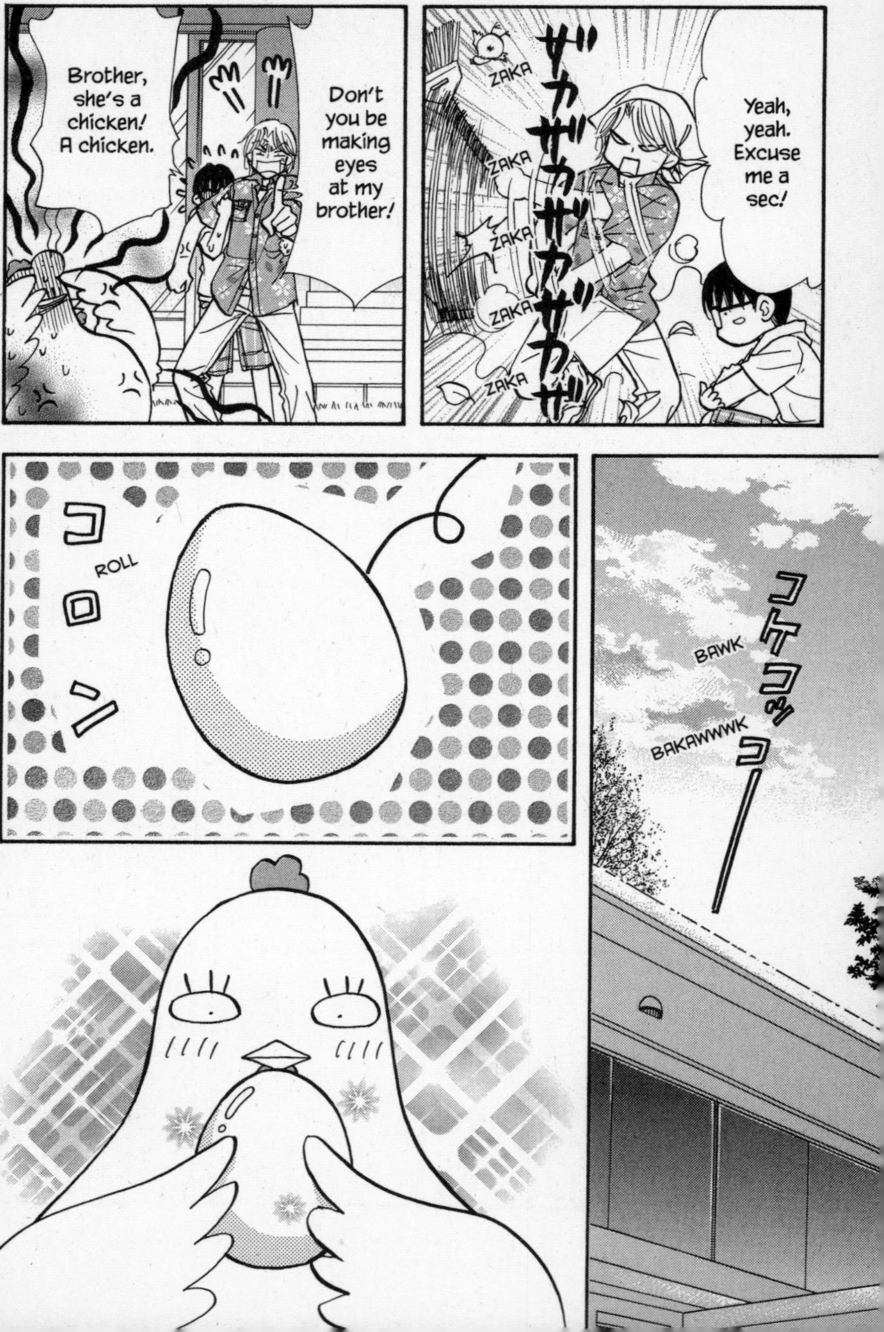
Yeah, yeah. Excuse me a sec!
ZAKA
ZAKA
ZAKA
ZAKA
ZAKA
Don't you be making eyes at my brother!
Brother, she's a chicken! A chicken.
コケコッコー
BAWK
BAKAWWWK
コロン
ROLL

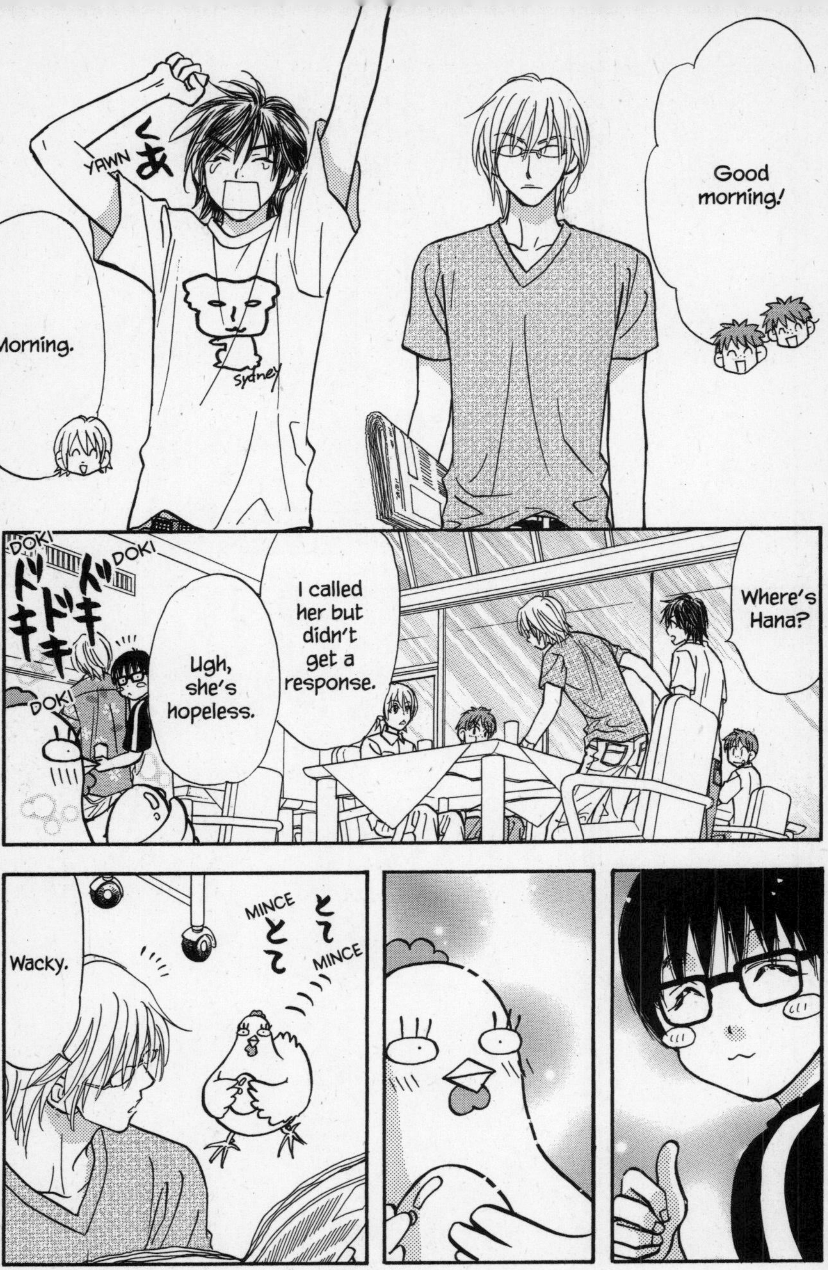

Good morning!
YAWN
くあ
'Morning.
Where's Hana?
I called her but didn't get a response.
Ugh, she's hopeless.
DOKI
DOKI
DOKI
ドキドキドキ
とて
とて
MINCE
MINCE
Wacky.

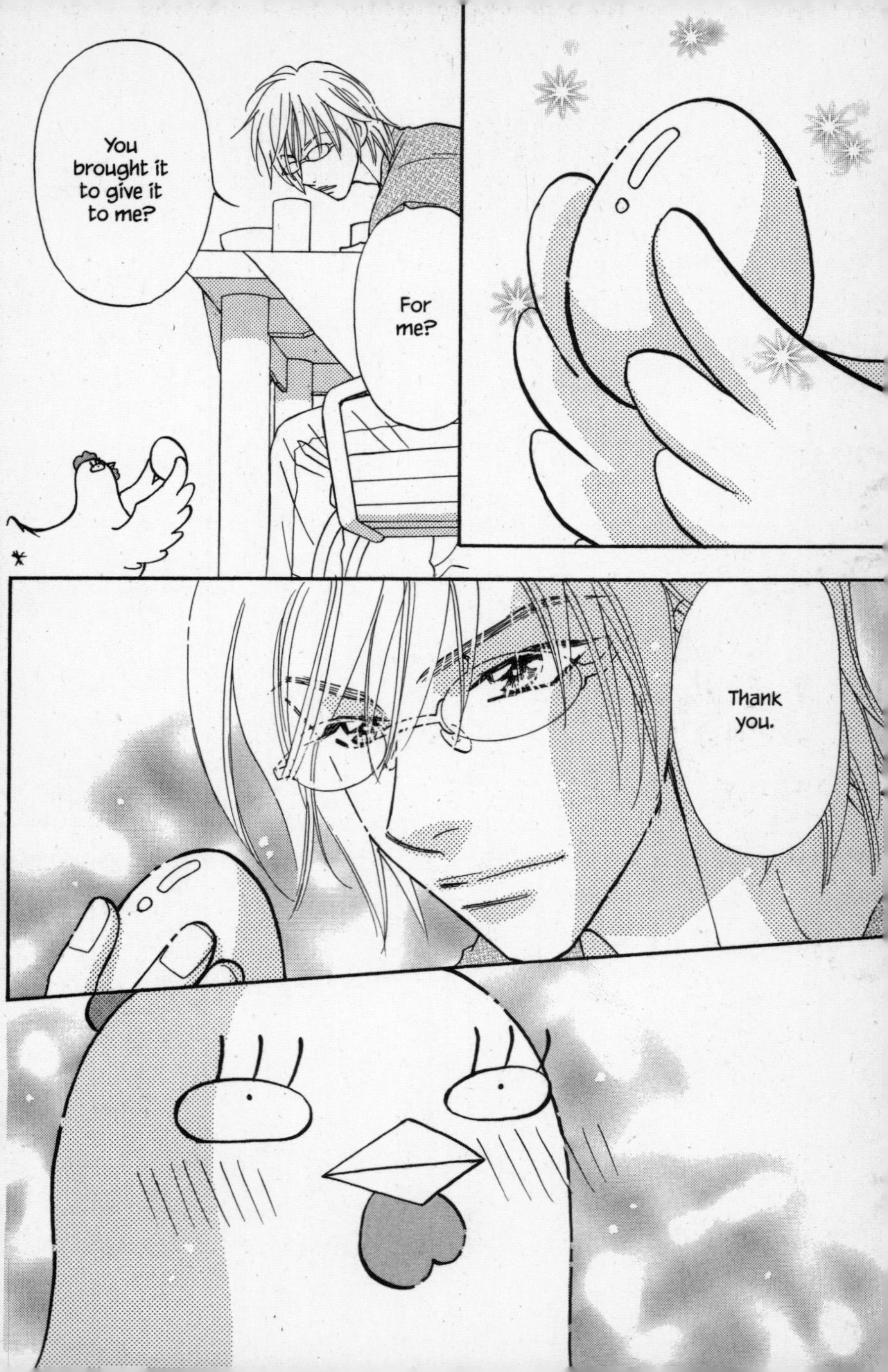
You brought it to give it to me?
For me?
Thank you.

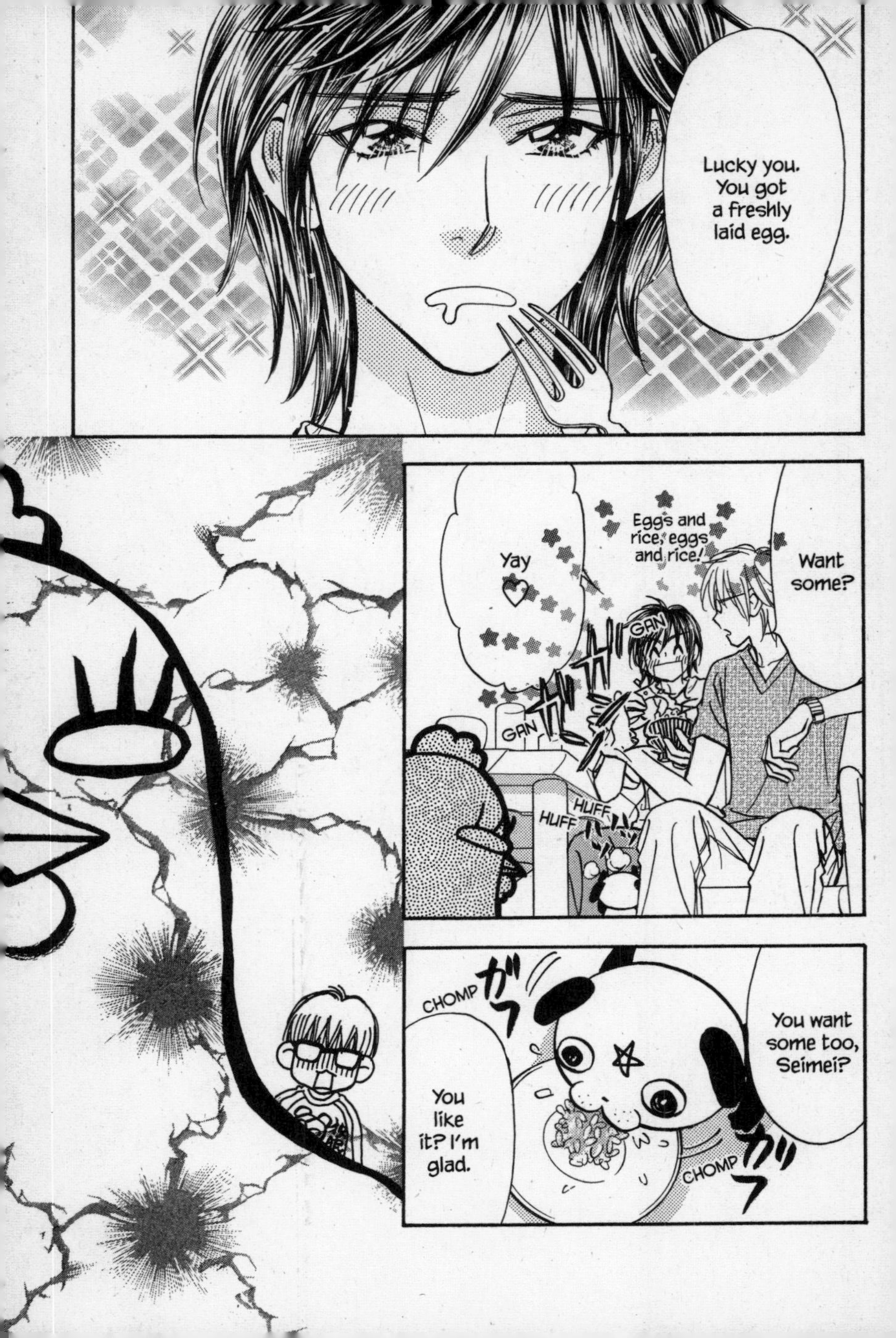
Lucky you. You got a freshly laid egg.
Want some?
Eggs and rice, eggs and rice!
GAN
Yay ♡
GAN
HUFF HUFF
You want some too, Seimei?
CHOMP
You like it? I'm glad.
CHOMP

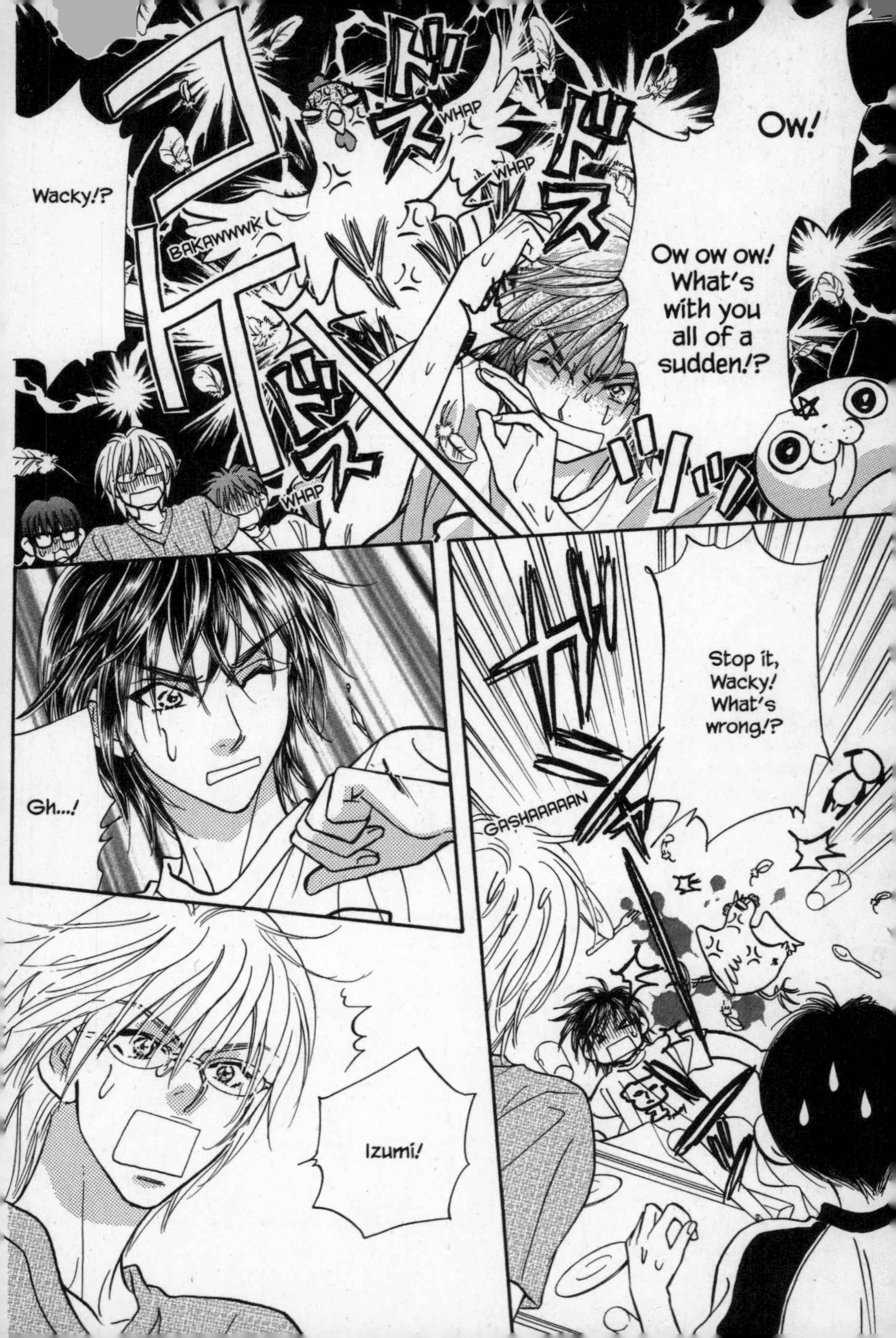
Ow!
WHAP
WHAP
Ow ow ow! What's with you all of a sudden!?
BAKAWWWK
Wacky!?
WHAP
Stop it, Wacky! What's wrong!?
GASHAAAAAN
Gh...!
Izumi!

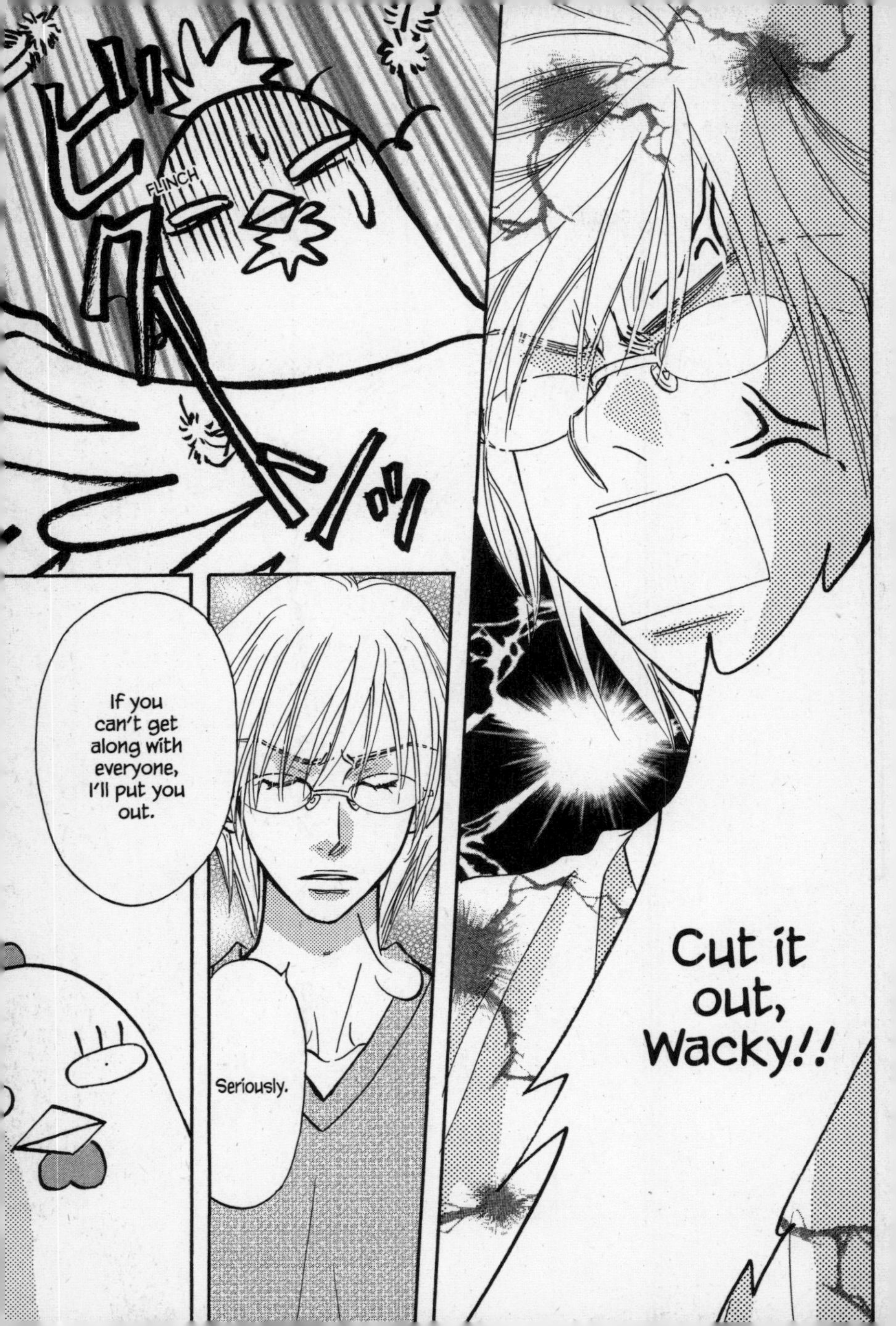
Cut it out, Wacky!!
FLINCH
Seriously.
If you can't get along with everyone, I'll put you out.

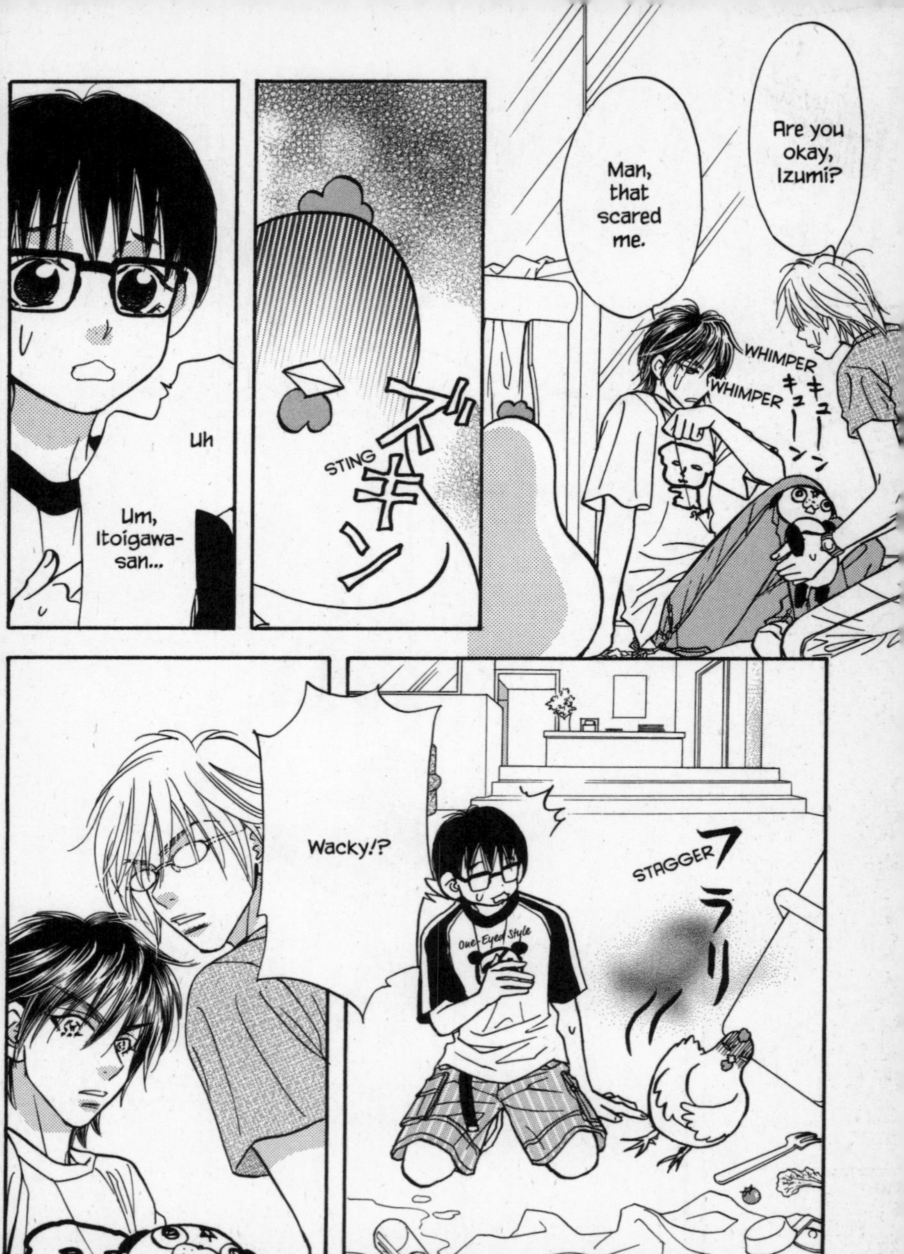
Are you okay, Izumi?
Man, that scared me.
WHIMPER
WHIMPER
キューン
キューン
STING
ズキーン
Uh
Um, Itoigawa-san...
STAGGER
フラリ
Wacky!?
One-Eyed Style

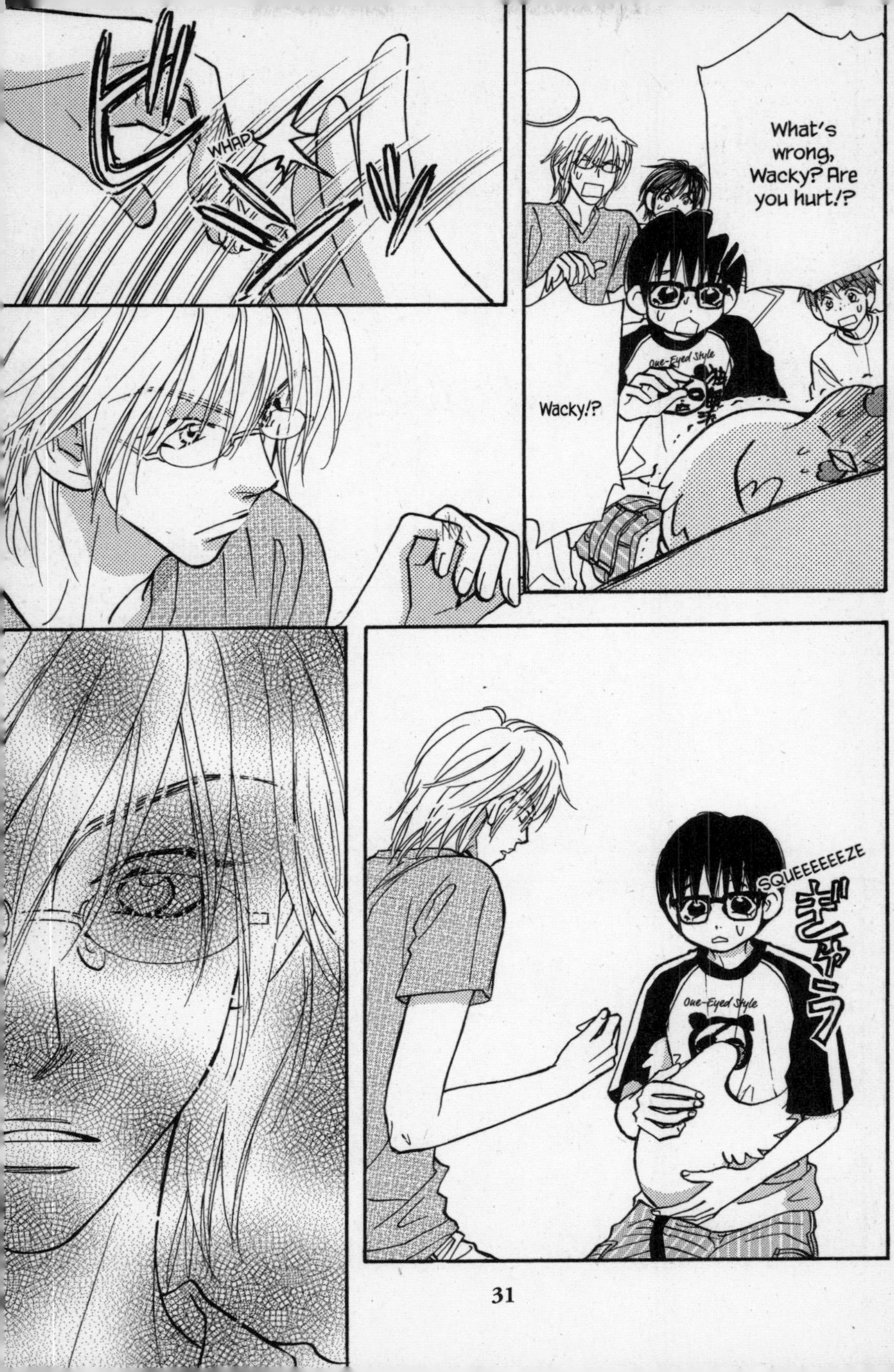
What's wrong, Wacky? Are you hurt!?
Wacky!?
WHAP!
One-Eyed Style
SQUEEEEEEEZE
One-Eyed Style

I feel so bad that we didn't notice.

So Wacky got hurt yesterday.

Sorry to have troubled you.

But it seems the emotional trauma was the worst part.

She's all right now, but apparently she was very badly hurt.

．．．．．．．．．．

I'm sorry, Wacky.

I'm sorry I didn't realize.

I wonder if you'd let me adopt Wacky.

Eh...?

Um...

If you don't mind,

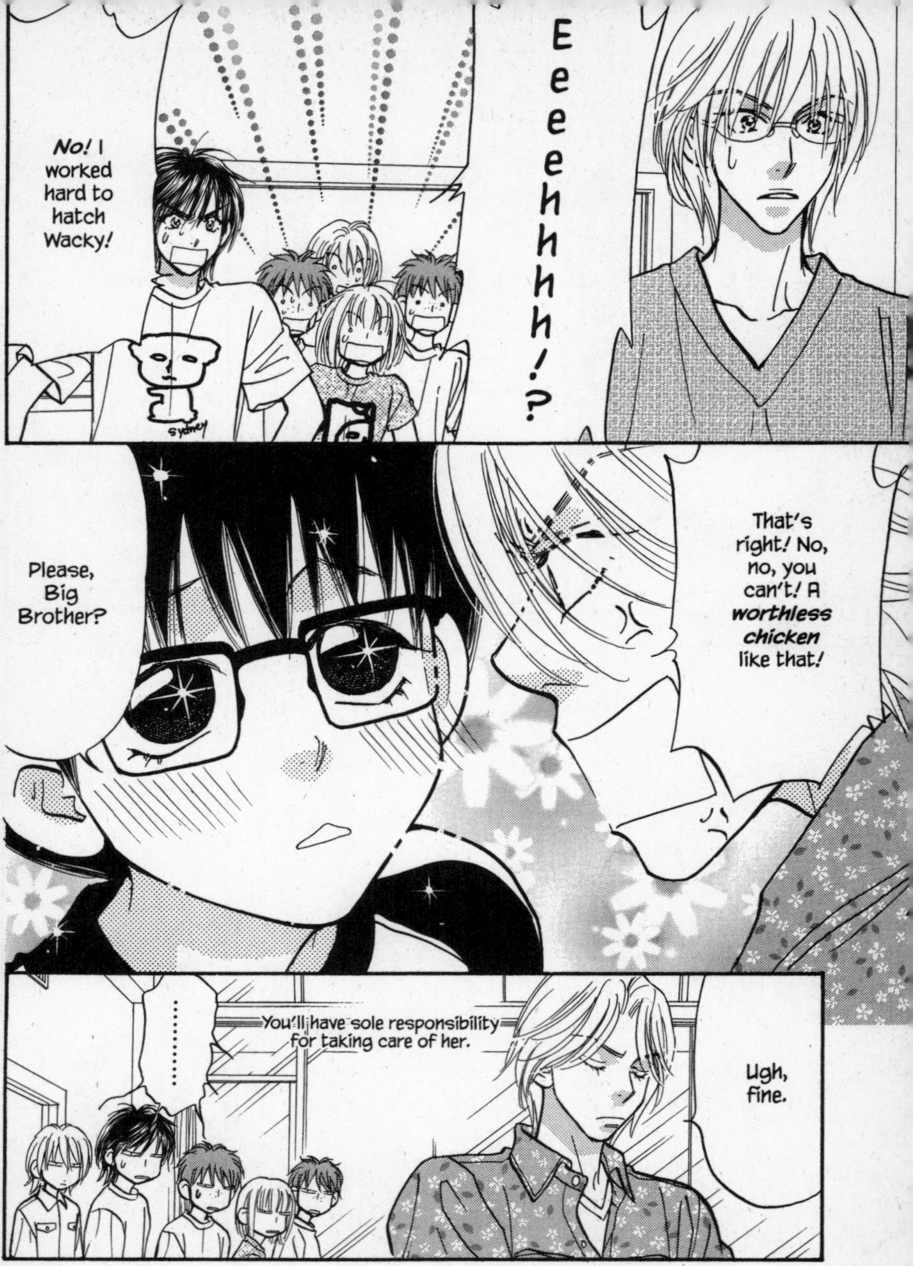
Eeeehhhh!?
No! I worked hard to hatch Wacky!
That's right! No, no, you can't! A worthless chicken like that!
Please, Big Brother?
Ugh, fine.
You'll have sole responsibility for taking care of her.
......

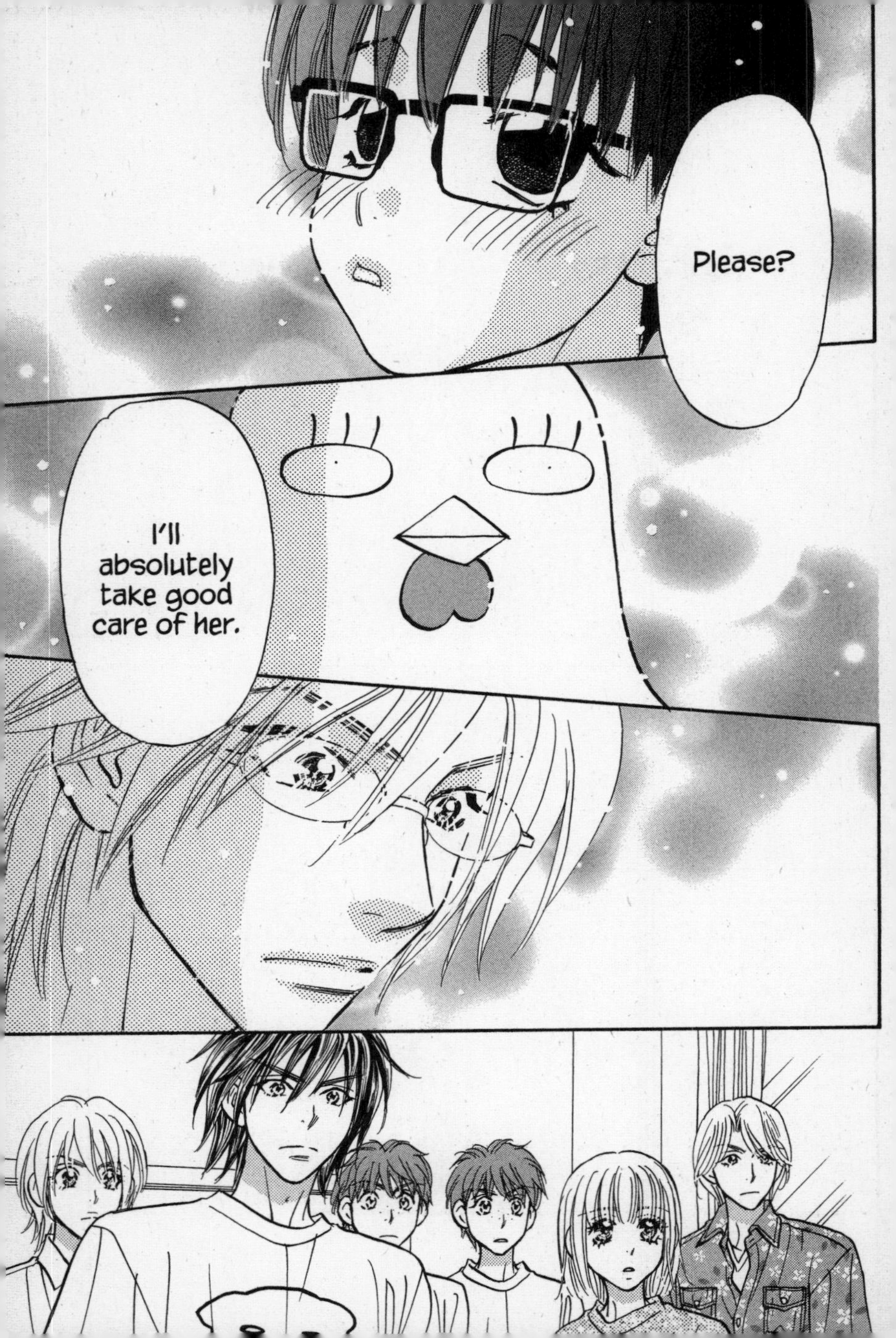
Please?
I'll absolutely take good care of her.

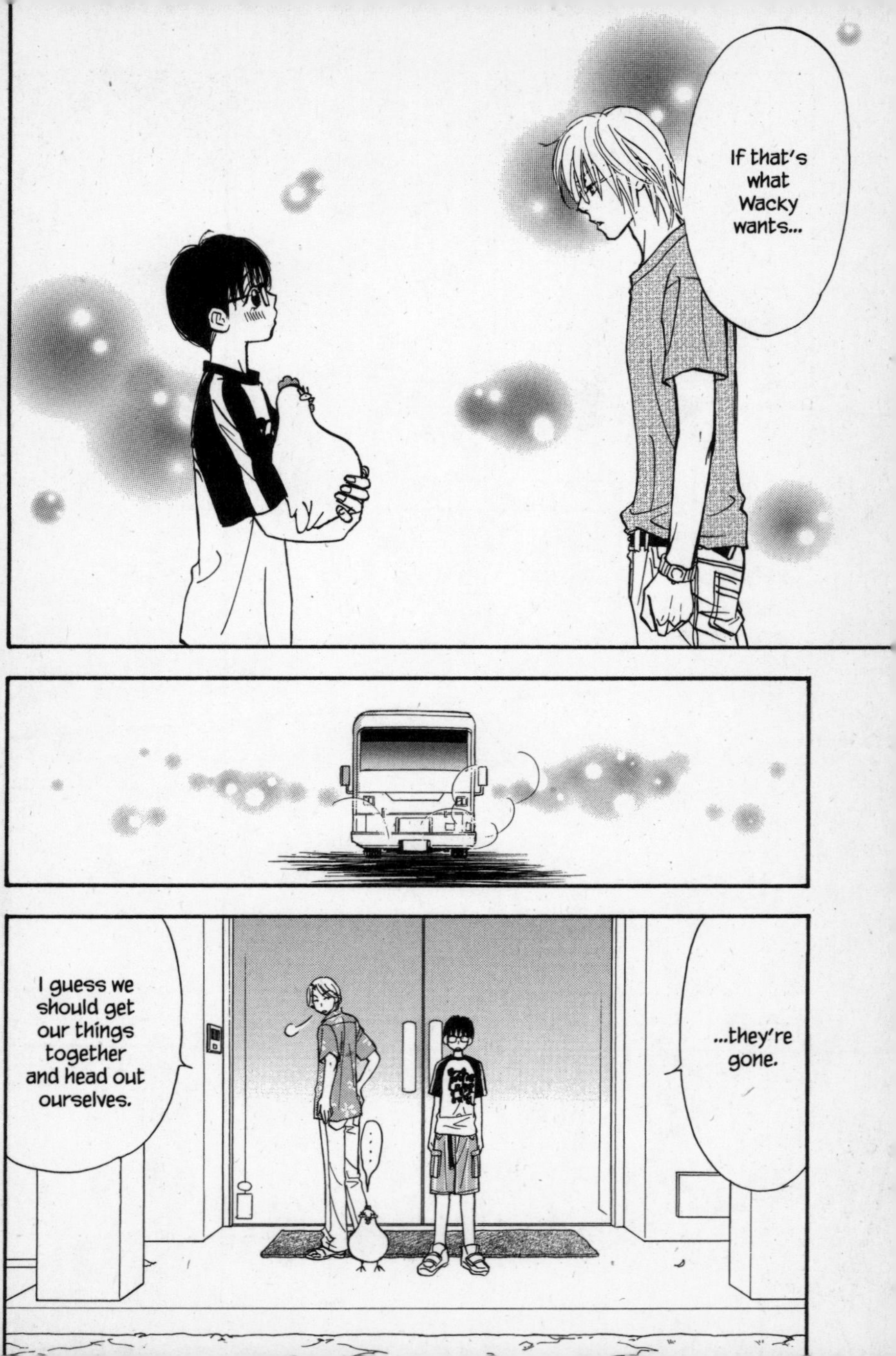
If that's what Wacky wants...
...they're gone.
...
I guess we should get our things together and head out ourselves.

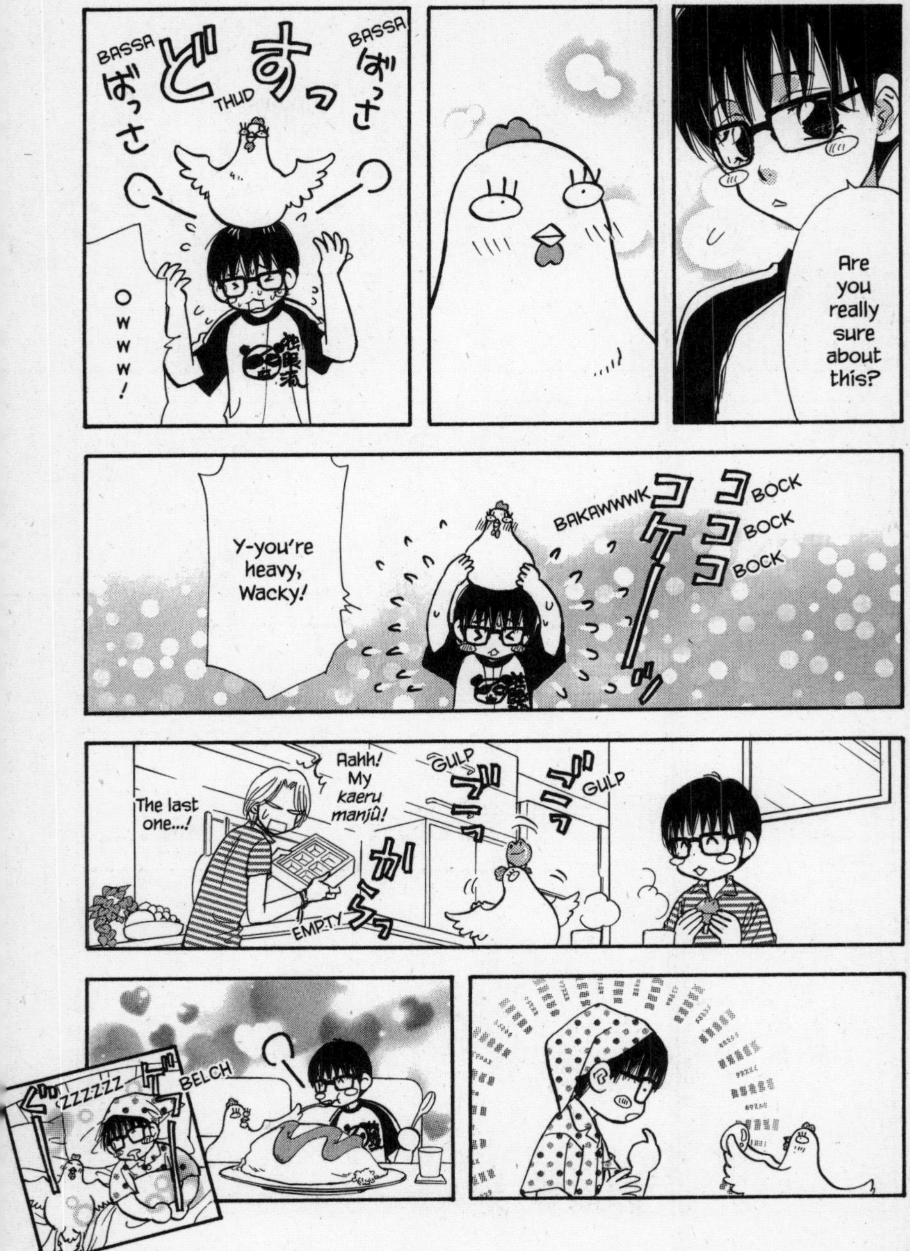
Are you really sure about this?
BASSA
ばっさ
THUD
どすっ
BASSA
ばっさ
OWWW!
BAKAWWWK
コケーーッ
BOCK BOCK BOCK
コココ
Y-you're heavy, Wacky!
GULP
ゴクッ
GULP
ゴクッ
Aahh! My kaeru manjû!
The last one...!
EMPTY
からっ
BELCH
ゲプ
ZZZZZZ

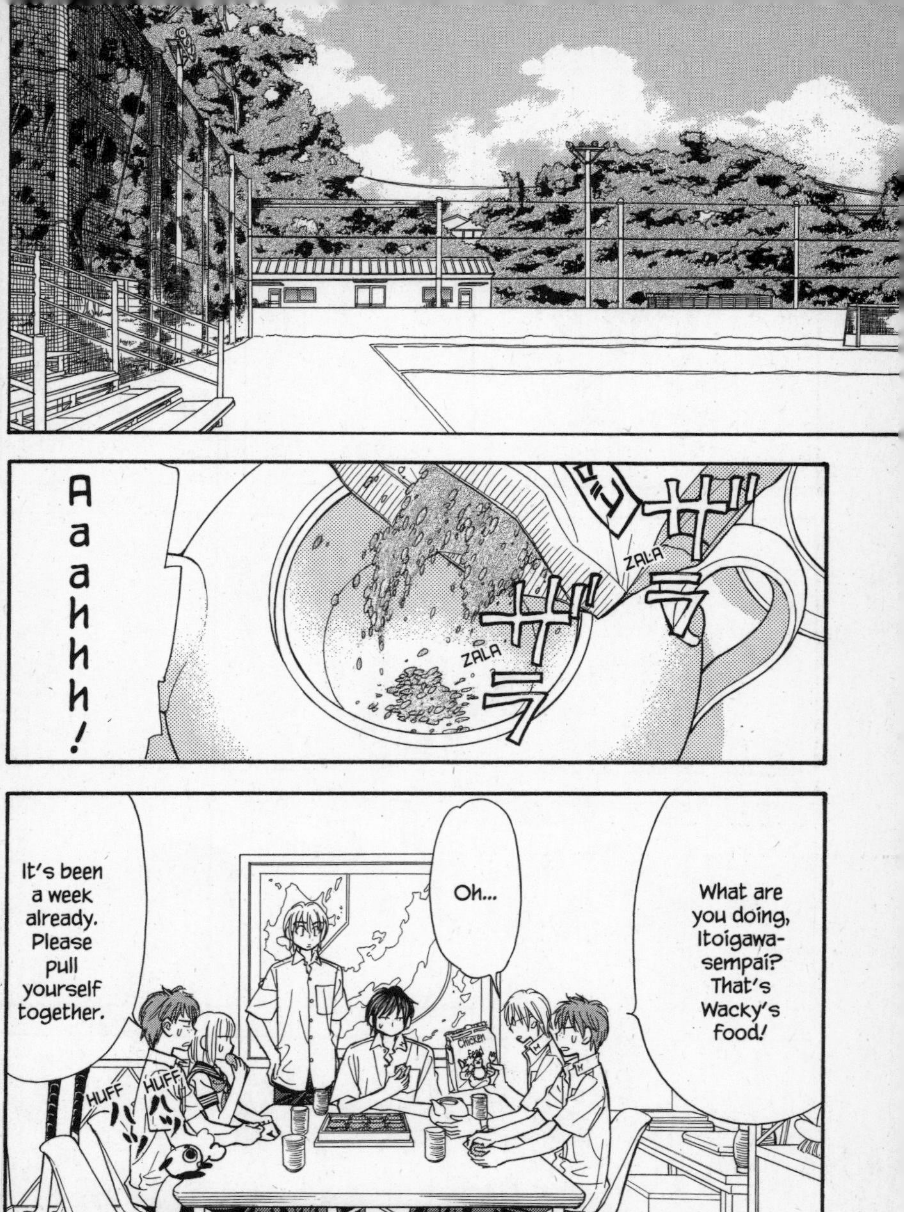
ザラ
ZALA
ザラ
ZALA
Aaahhh!
What are you doing, Itoigawa-sempai? That's Wacky's food!
Chicken Food
Oh...
It's been a week already. Please pull yourself together.
HUFF
HUFF
ハッ
ハッ

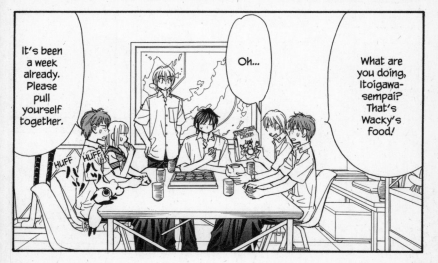

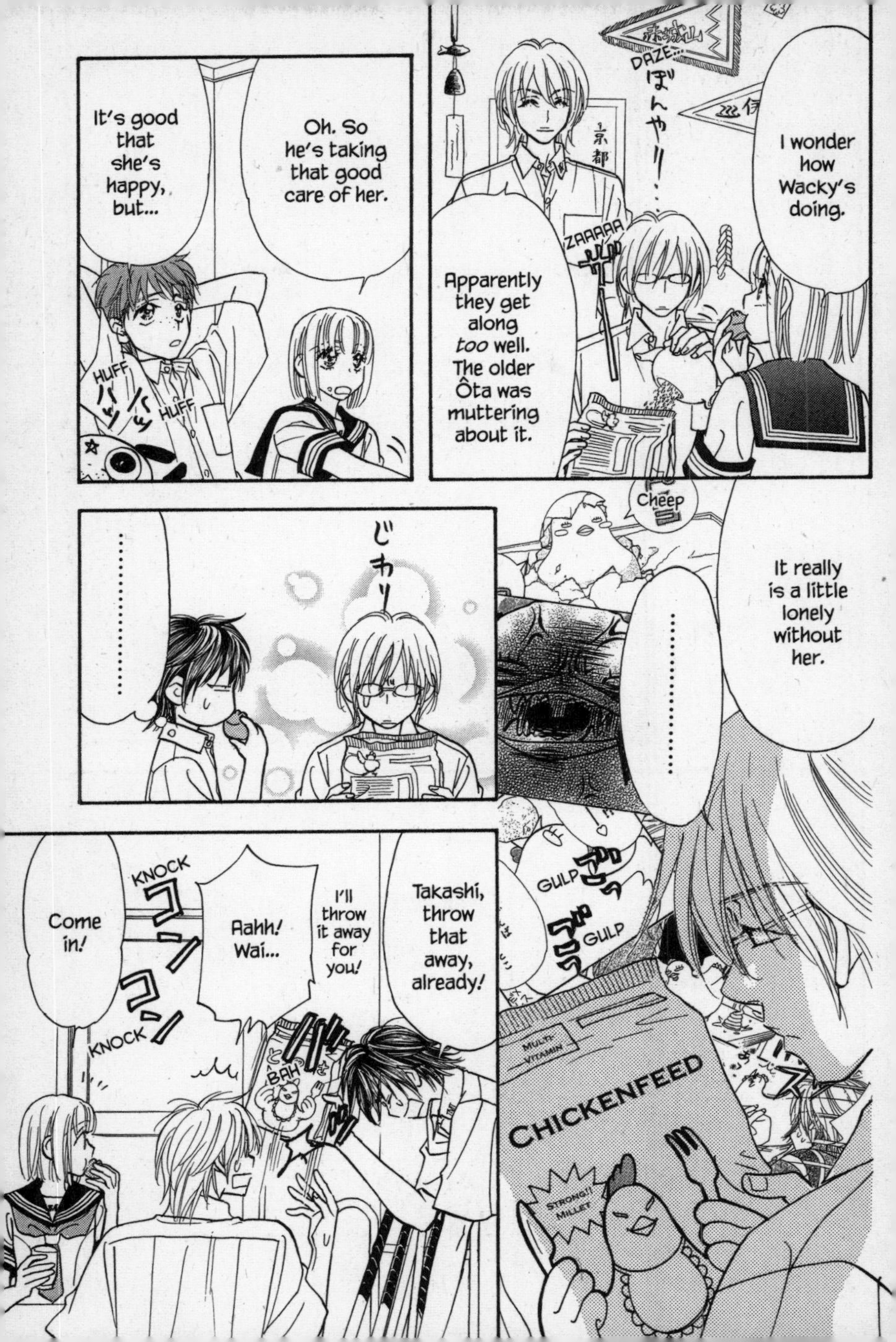
DAZE...
ぼんやり・・
I wonder how Wacky's doing.
ZAAAAA
Apparently they get along *too* well. The older Ôta was muttering about it.
Oh. So he's taking that good care of her.
It's good that she's happy, but...
HUFF
HUFF
Cheep
It really is a little lonely without her.
......
GULP
GULP
MULTI-VITAMIN
CHICKENFEED
STRONG!! MILLET
じわり
......
Takashi, throw that away, already!
I'll throw it away for you!
Aahh! Wai...
BAH
KNOCK
KNOCK
Come in!

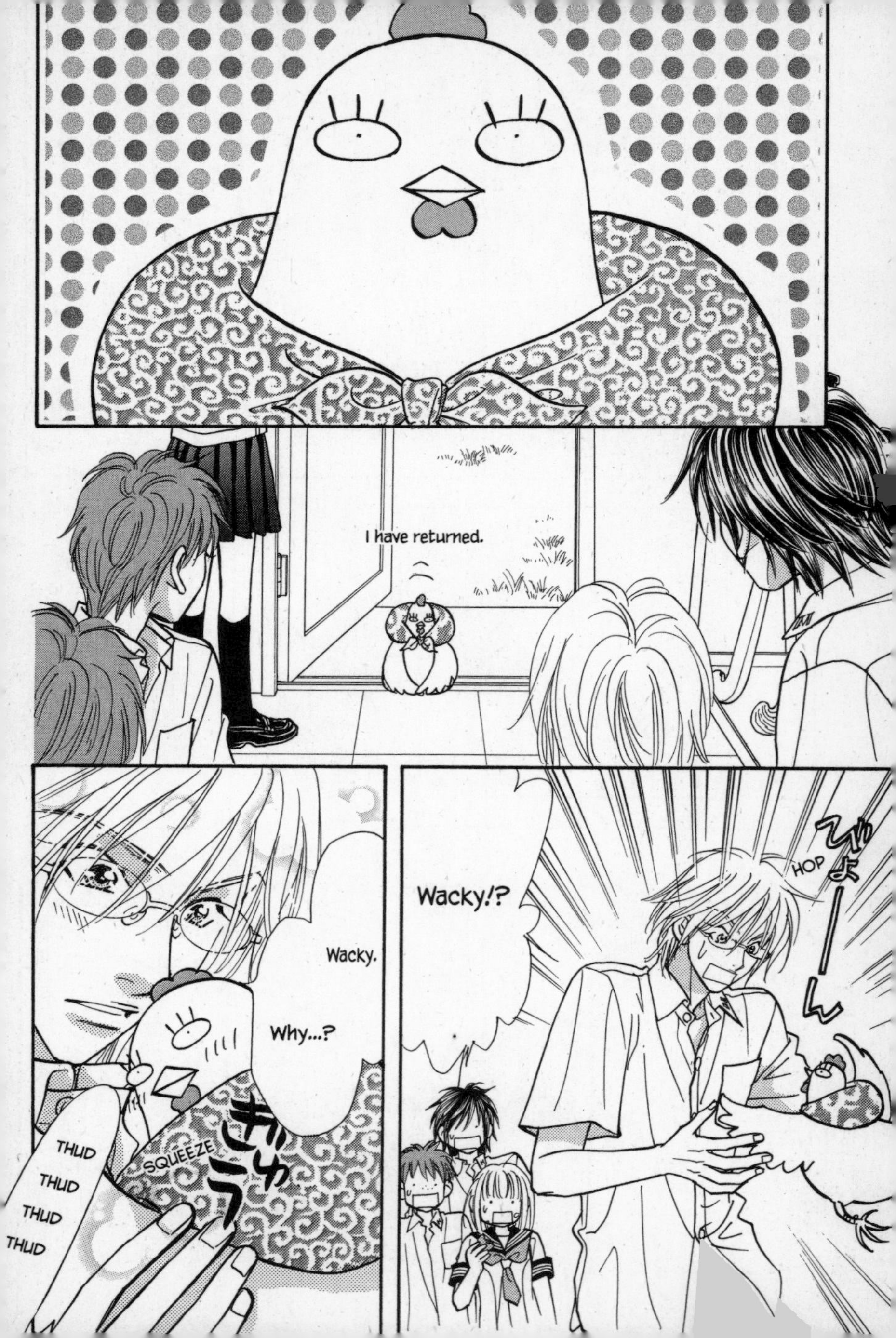
I have returned.
Wacky!?
HOP
Wacky.
Why...?
SQUEEZE
THUD
THUD
THUD
THUD

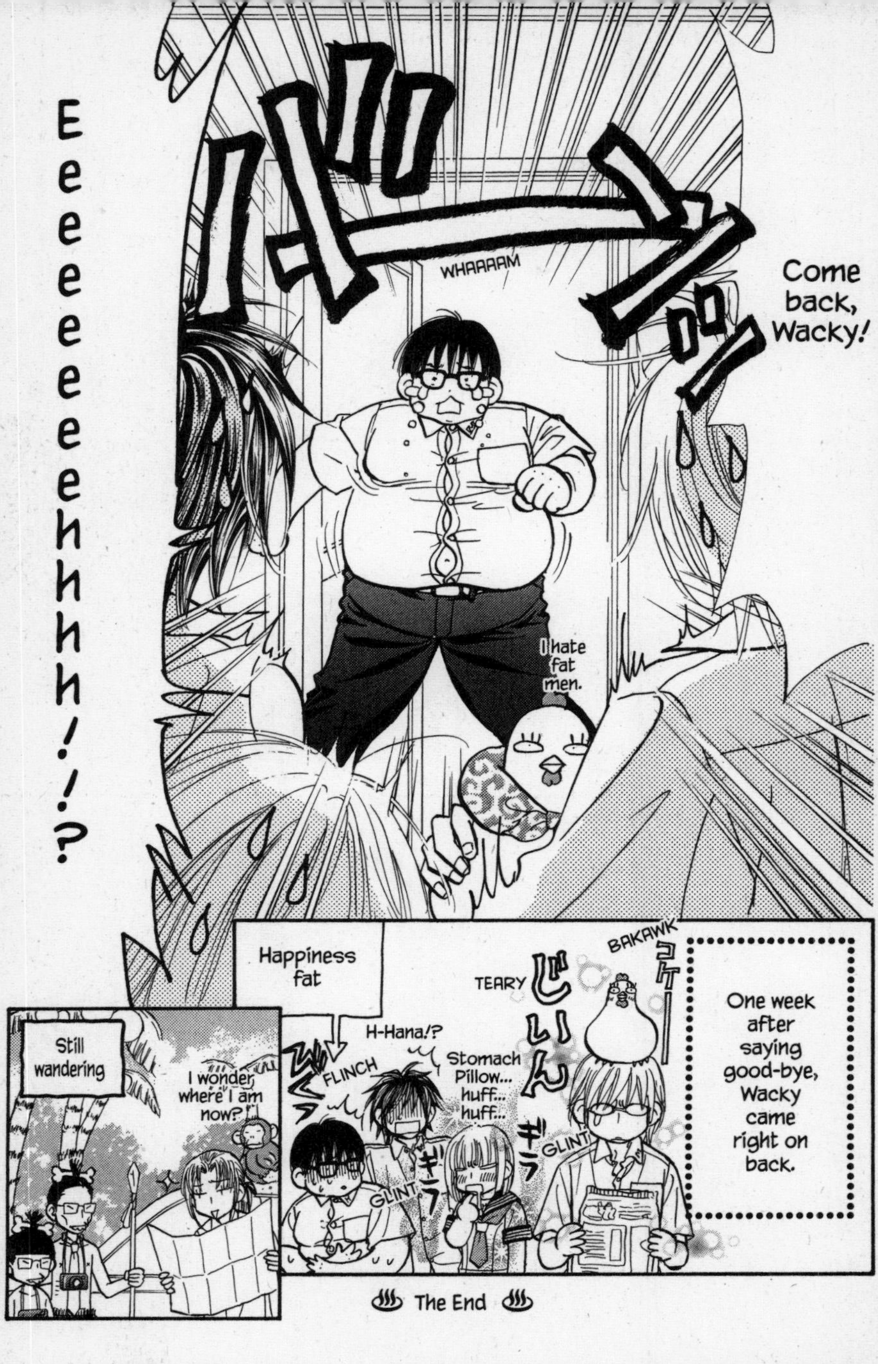
Come back, Wacky!
WHAAAAM
Eeeeeeeeehhhh!!?
I hate fat men.
One week after saying good-bye, Wacky came right on back.
BAKAWK
TEARY
GLINT
Stomach Pillow... huff... huff...
H-Hana!?
FLINCH
GLINT
Happiness fat
I wonder where I am now?
Still wandering
The End

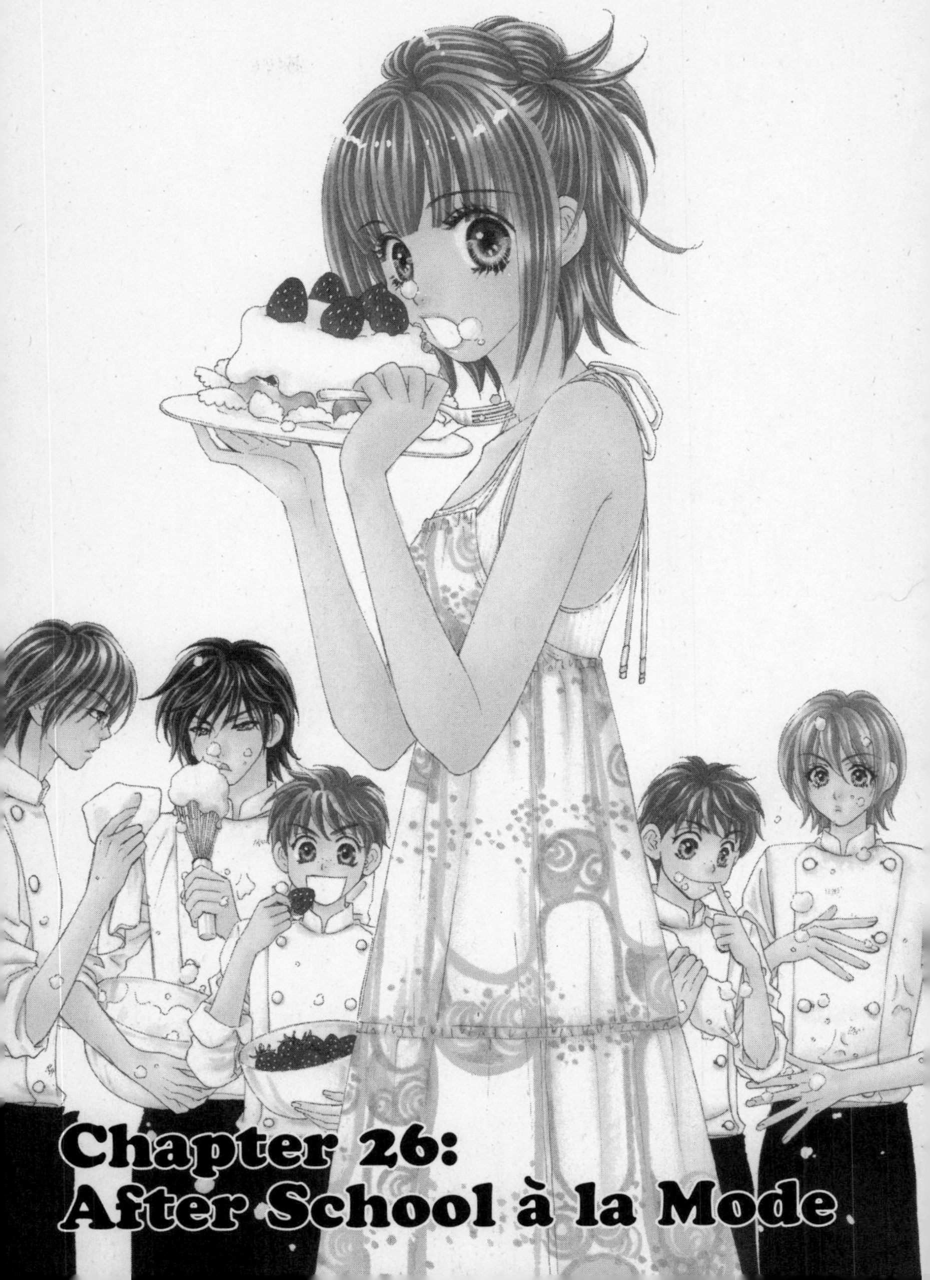

Chapter 26: After School à la Mode

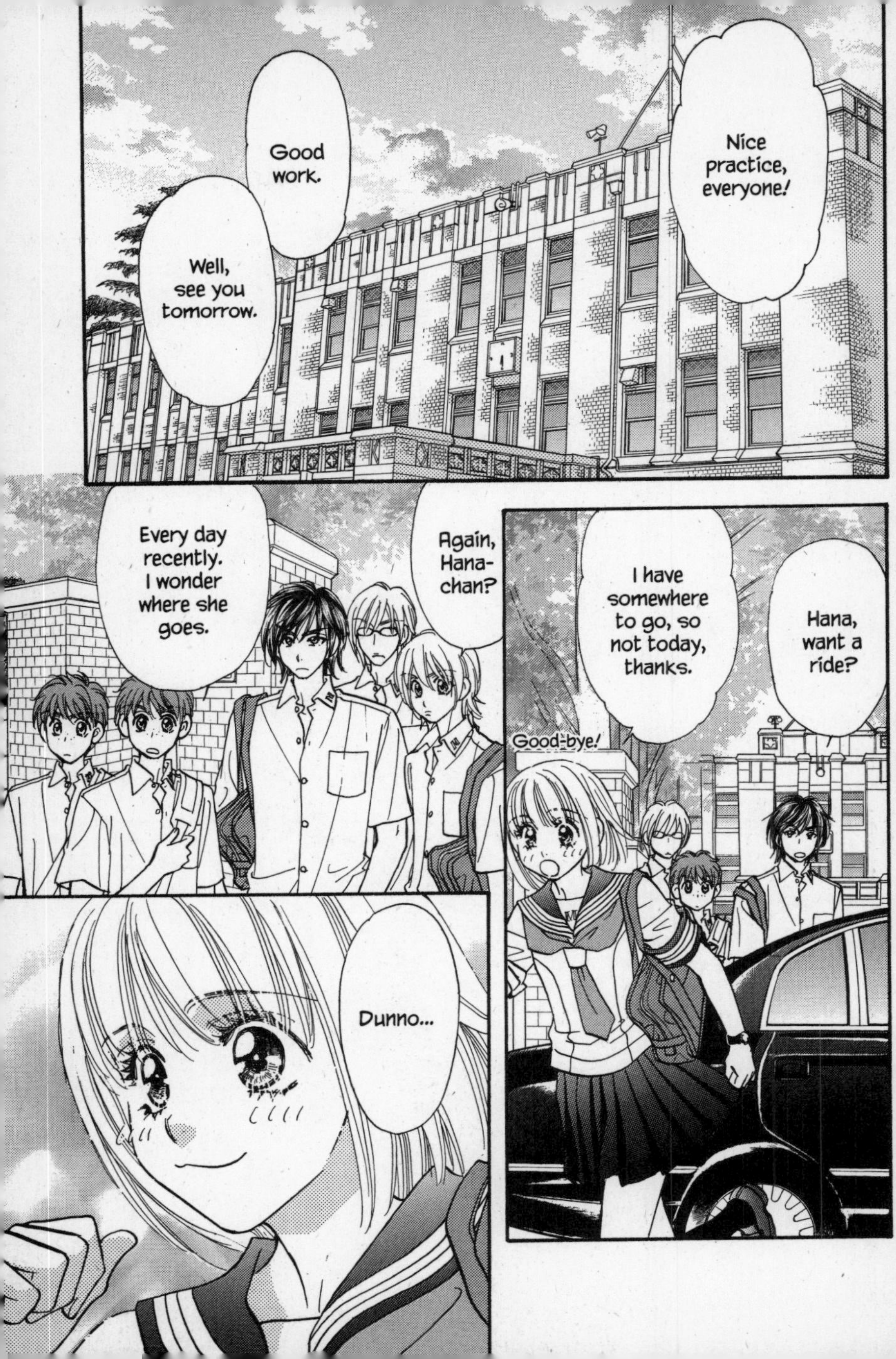
Nice practice, everyone!
Good work.
Well, see you tomorrow.
Hana, want a ride?
I have somewhere to go, so not today, thanks.
Good-bye!
Again, Hana-chan?
Every day recently. I wonder where she goes.
Dunno...

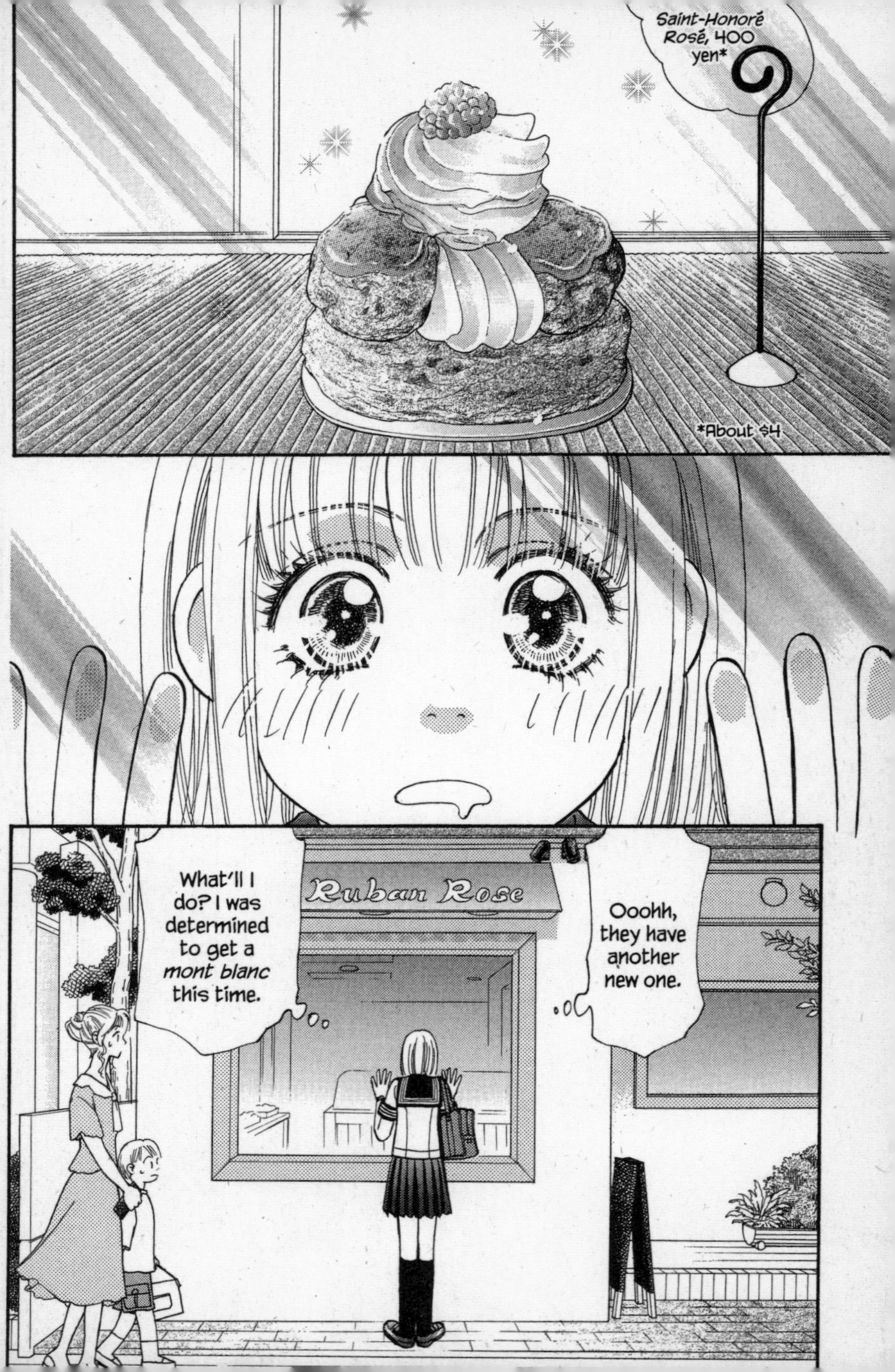
Saint-Honoré Rosé, 400 yen*
*About $4
Ruban Rose
Ooohh, they have another new one.
What'll I do? I was determined to get a *mont blanc* this time.

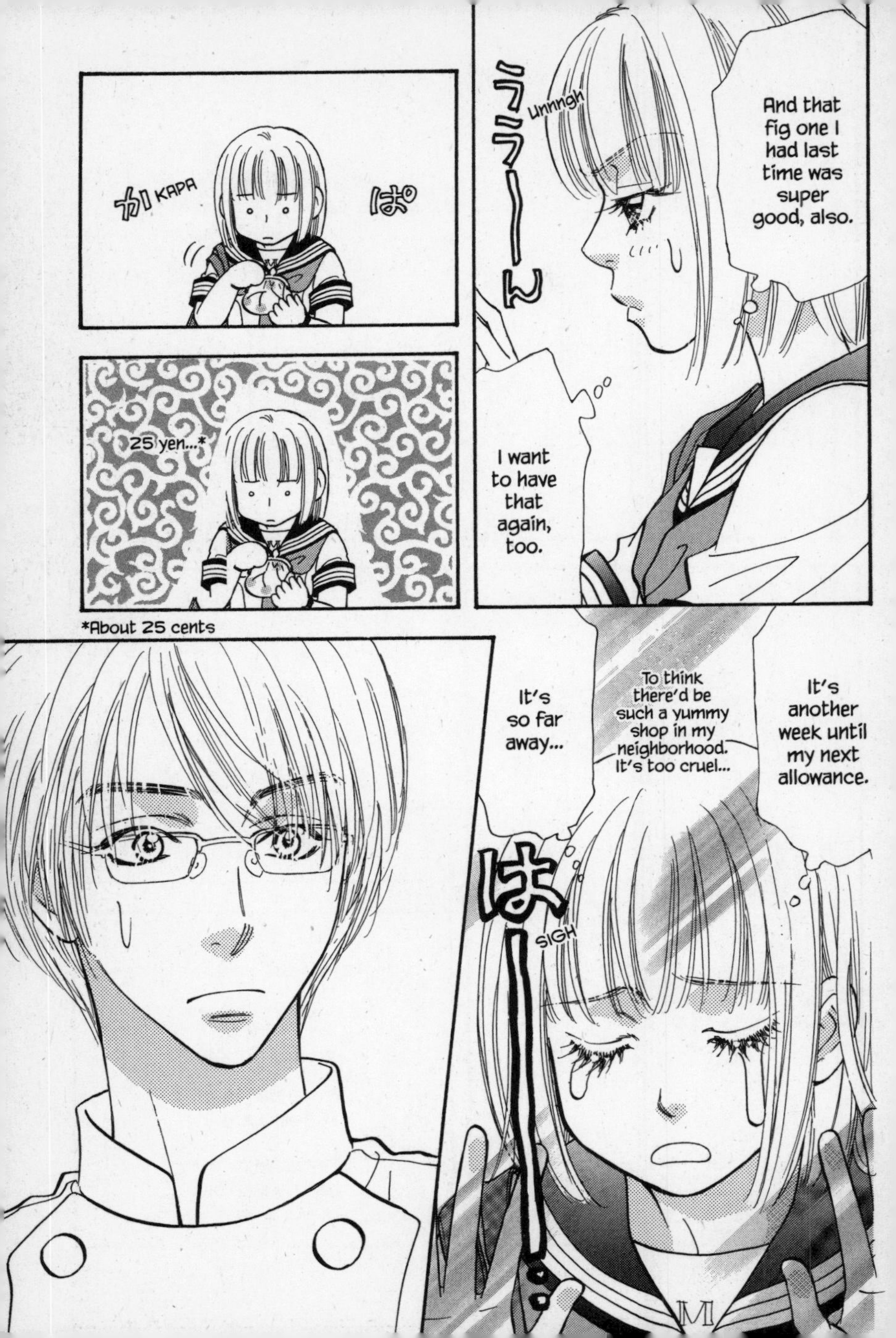
ううーーん
Unnnngh
And that fig one I had last time was super good, also.
I want to have that again, too.
か KAPA ぱ
25 yen...*
It's another week until my next allowance.
To think there'd be such a yummy shop in my neighborhood. It's too cruel...
It's so far away...
はー
SIGH

*About 25 cents

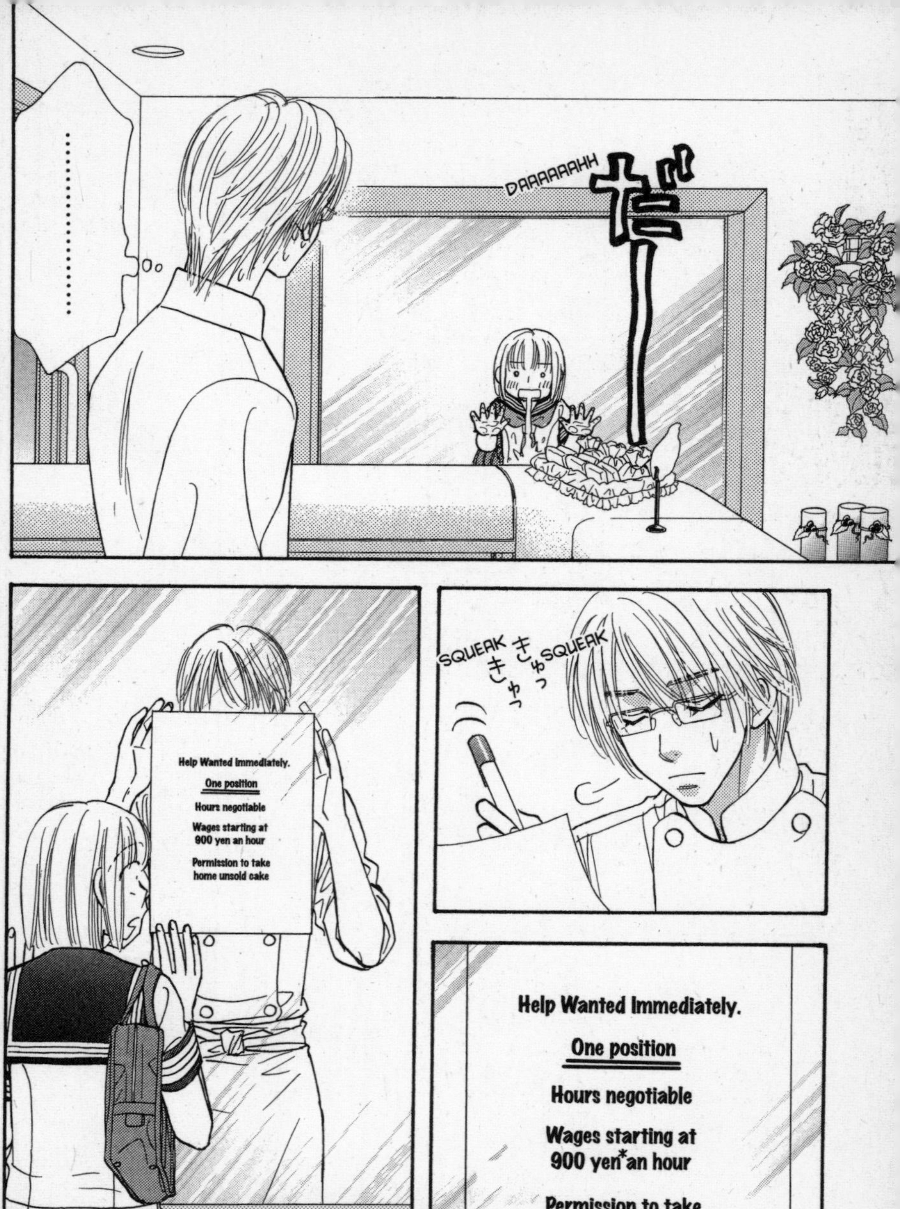
……
だー
DAAAAAAAHH
きゅっ
SQUEAK
きゅっ
SQUEAK
Help Wanted Immediately.
One position
Hours negotiable
Wages starting at
900 yen* an hour
Permission to take
home unsold cake
Help Wanted Immediately.
One position
Hours negotiable
Wages starting at
900 yen an hour
Permission to take
home unsold cake

*About $9

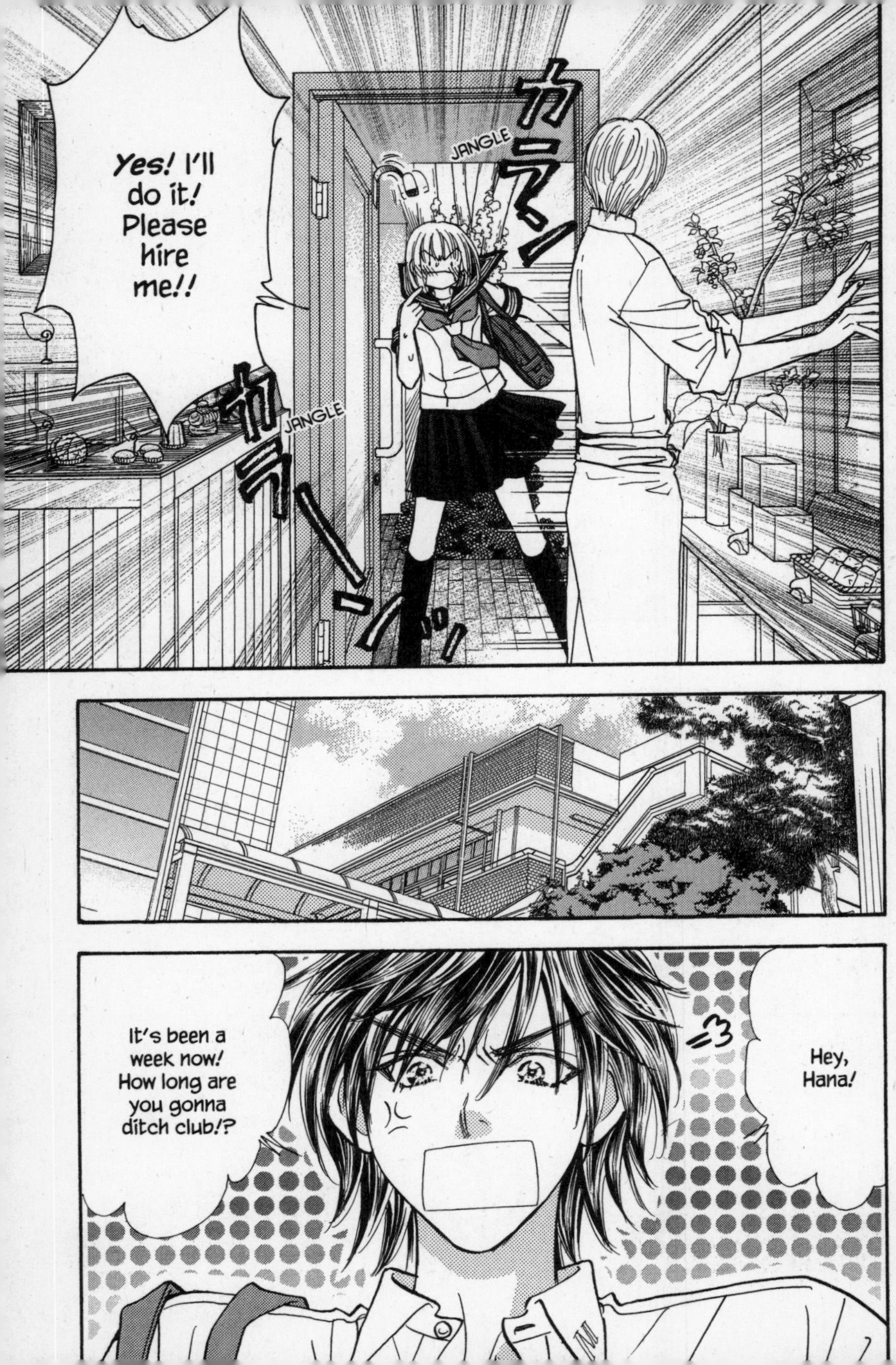
JANGLE
Yes! I'll do it! Please hire me!!
JANGLE
Hey, Hana!
It's been a week now! How long are you gonna ditch club!?

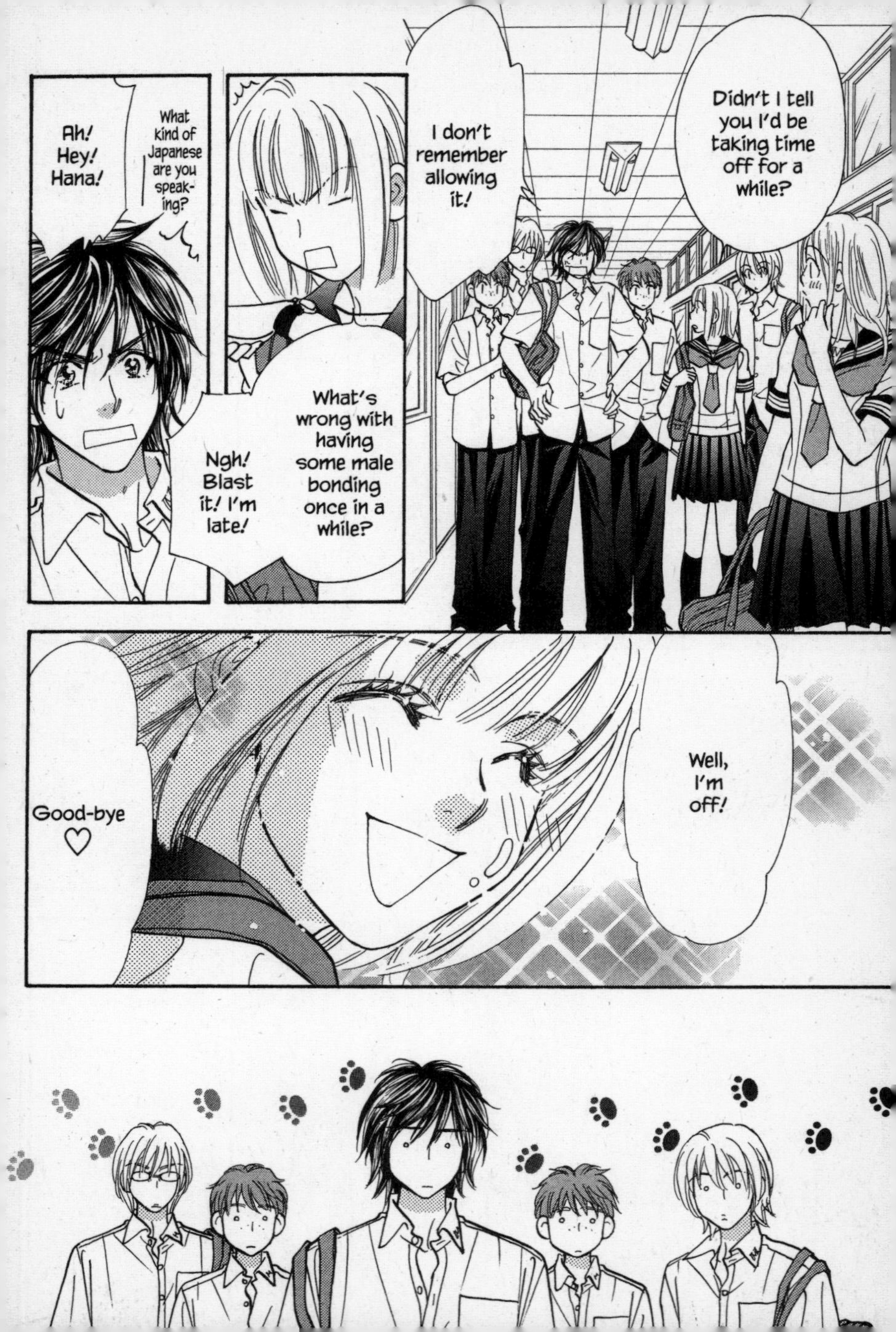
Didn't I tell you I'd be taking time off for a while?
I don't remember allowing it!
What's wrong with having some male bonding once in a while?
Ngh! Blast it! I'm late!
What kind of Japanese are you speak-ing?
Ah! Hey! Hana!
Well, I'm off!
Good-bye ♡

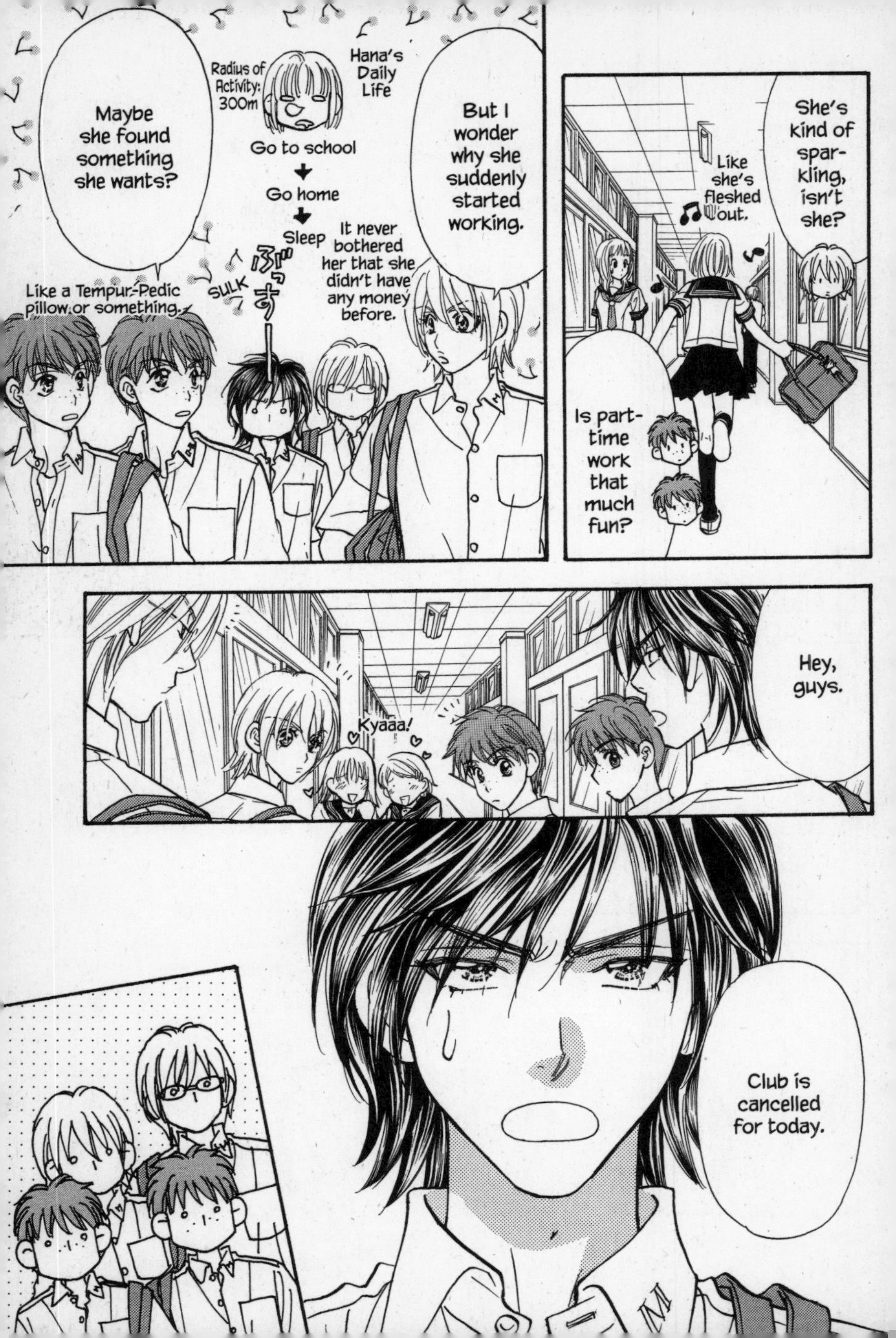
She's kind of spar-kling, isn't she?
Like she's fleshed out.
Is part-time work that much fun?
But I wonder why she suddenly started working.
Hana's Daily Life
Radius of Activity: 300m
Go to school
Go home
Sleep
It never bothered her that she didn't have any money before.
ぶす
SULK
Maybe she found something she wants?
Like a Tempur-Pedic pillow or something.
Hey, guys.
Kyaaa!
Club is cancelled for today.

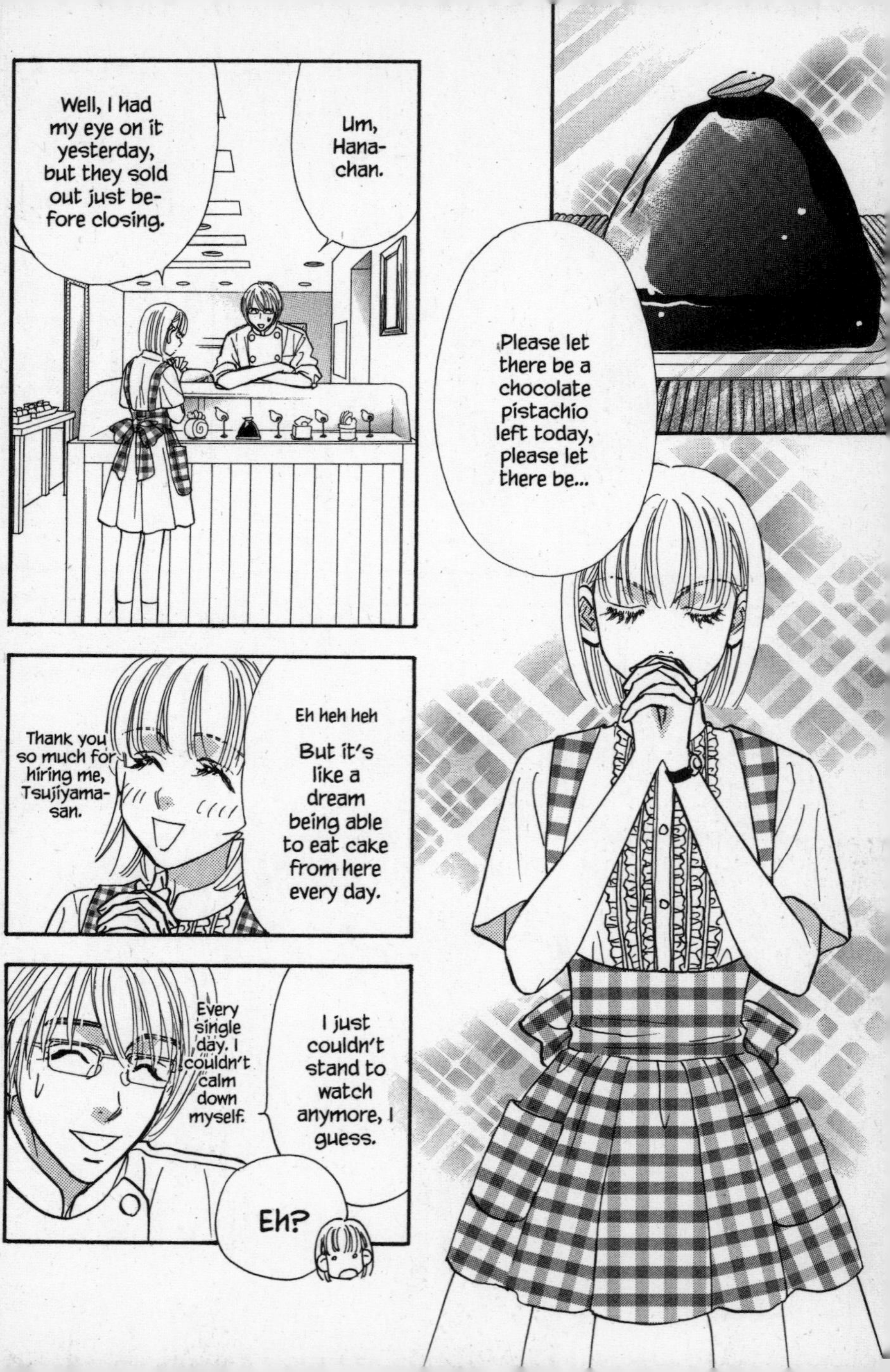
Please let there be a chocolate pistachio left today, please let there be...
Um, Hana-chan.
Well, I had my eye on it yesterday, but they sold out just before closing.
Eh heh heh
But it's like a dream being able to eat cake from here every day.
Thank you so much for hiring me, Tsujiyama-san.
I just couldn't stand to watch anymore, I guess.
Every single day. I couldn't calm down myself.
Eh?

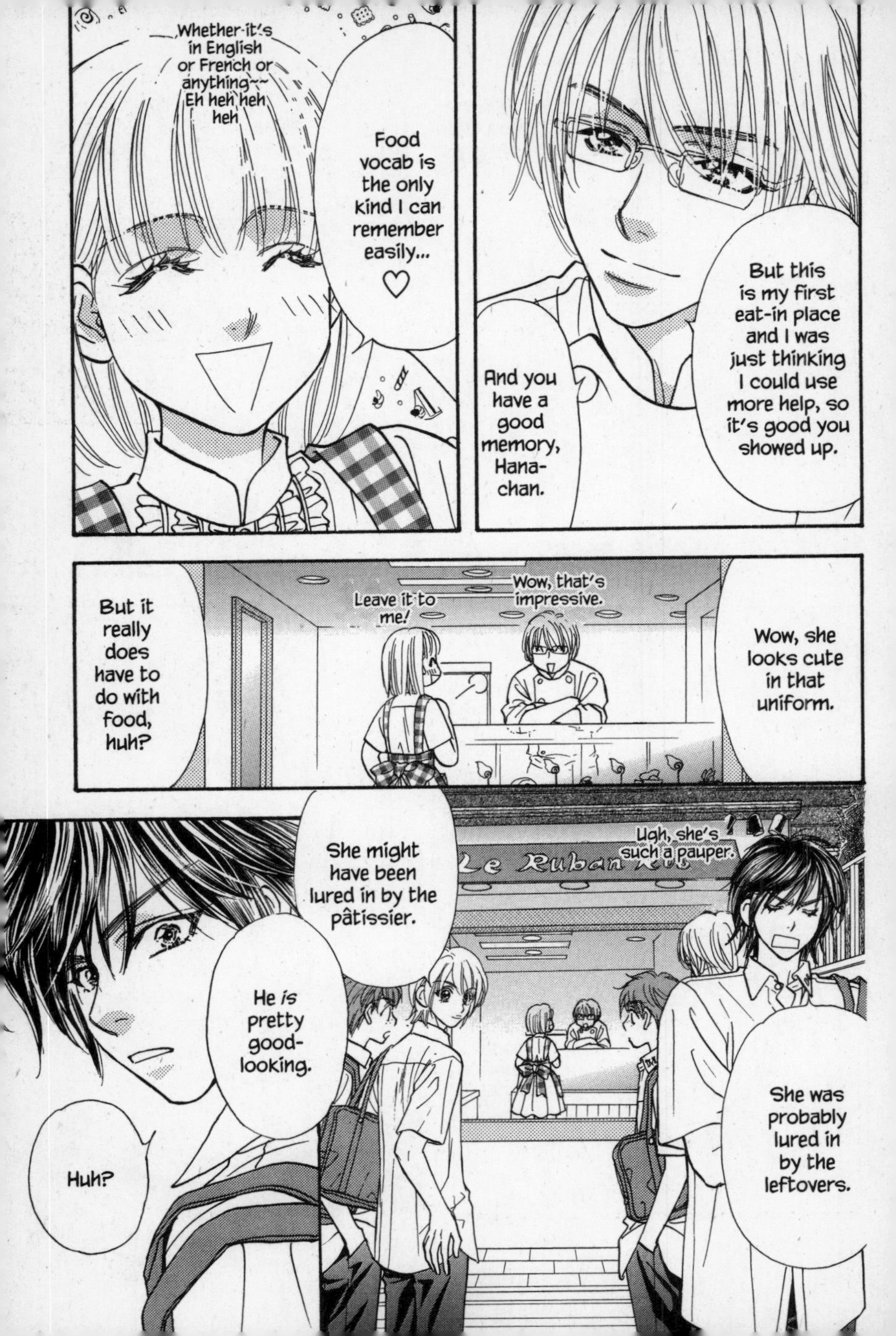
But this is my first eat-in place and I was just thinking I could use more help, so it's good you showed up.
And you have a good memory, Hana-chan.
Food vocab is the only kind I can remember easily... ♡
Whether it's in English or French or anything~~ Eh heh heh heh
Wow, she looks cute in that uniform.
Wow, that's impressive.
Leave it to me!
But it really does have to do with food, huh?
She was probably lured in by the leftovers.
Ugh, she's such a pauper.
Le Ruban
She might have been lured in by the pâtissier.
He *is* pretty good-looking.
Huh?

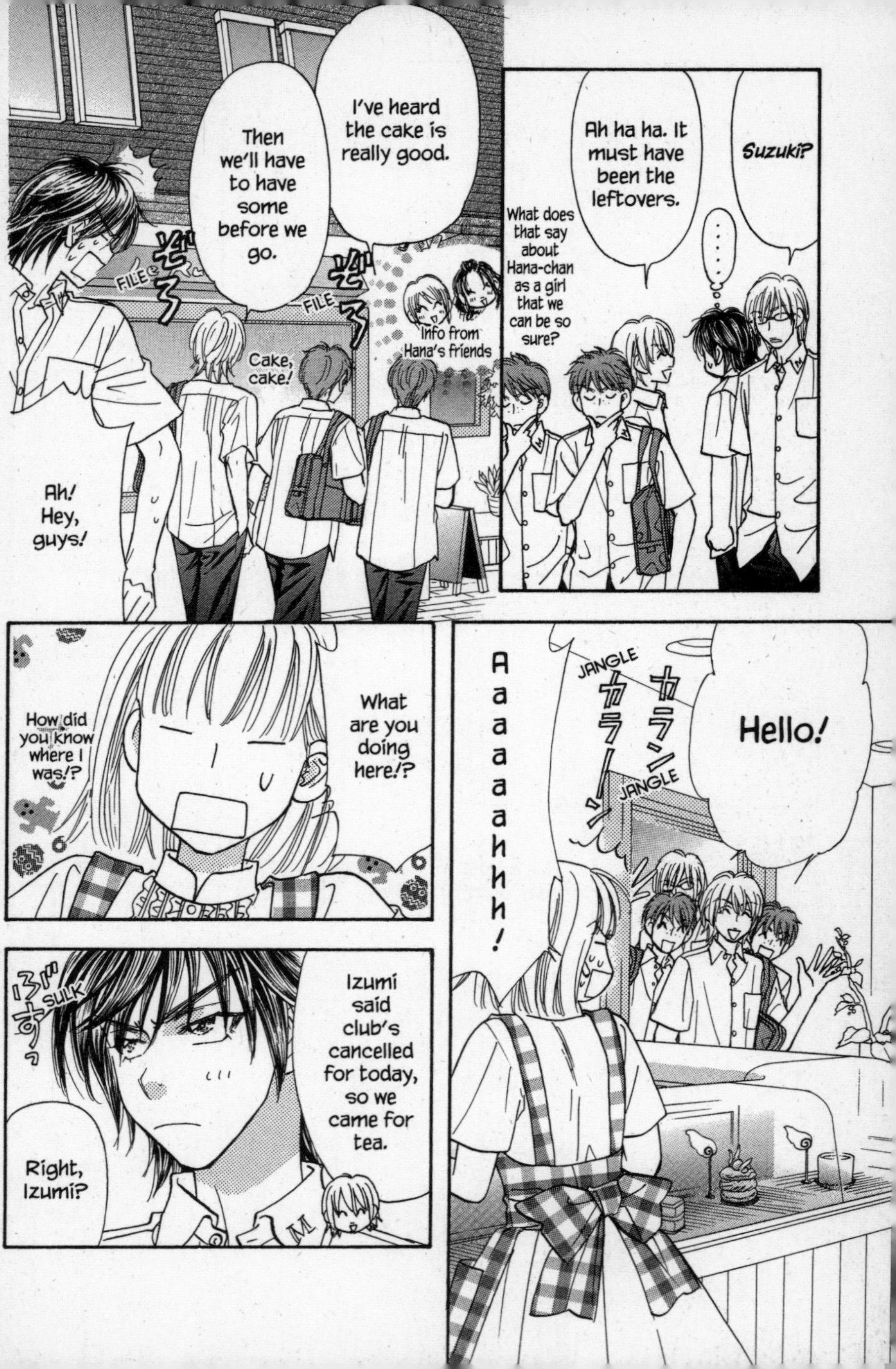
Suzuki?
Ah ha ha. It must have been the leftovers.
. . . . . .
What does that say about Hana-chan as a girl that we can be so sure?
I've heard the cake is really good.
Then we'll have to have some before we go.
Info from Hana's friends
FILE
FILEE
Cake, cake!
Ah! Hey, guys!
Hello!
JANGLE
カランカラーン
JANGLE
Aaaaaahhh!
What are you doing here!?
How did you know where I was!?
Izumi said club's cancelled for today, so we came for tea.
SULK
Right, Izumi?

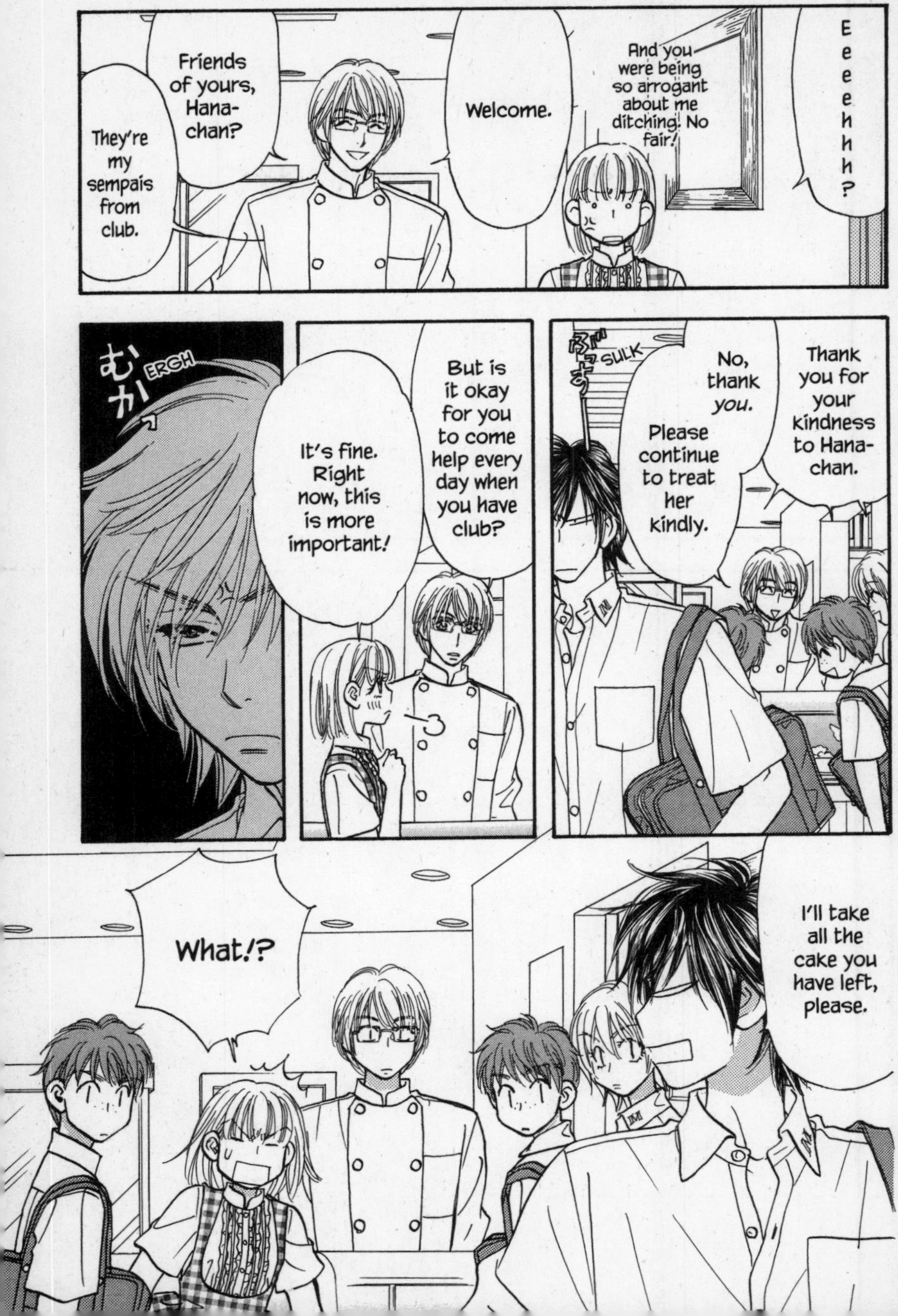
Eeeehhh?
And you were being so arrogant about me ditching. No fair!
Welcome.
Friends of yours, Hana-chan?
They're my sempais from club.
Thank you for your kindness to Hana-chan.
No, thank *you*.
Please continue to treat her kindly.
ぶす SULK
But is it okay for you to come help every day when you have club?
It's fine. Right now, this is more important!
むか ERGH
I'll take all the cake you have left, please.
What!?

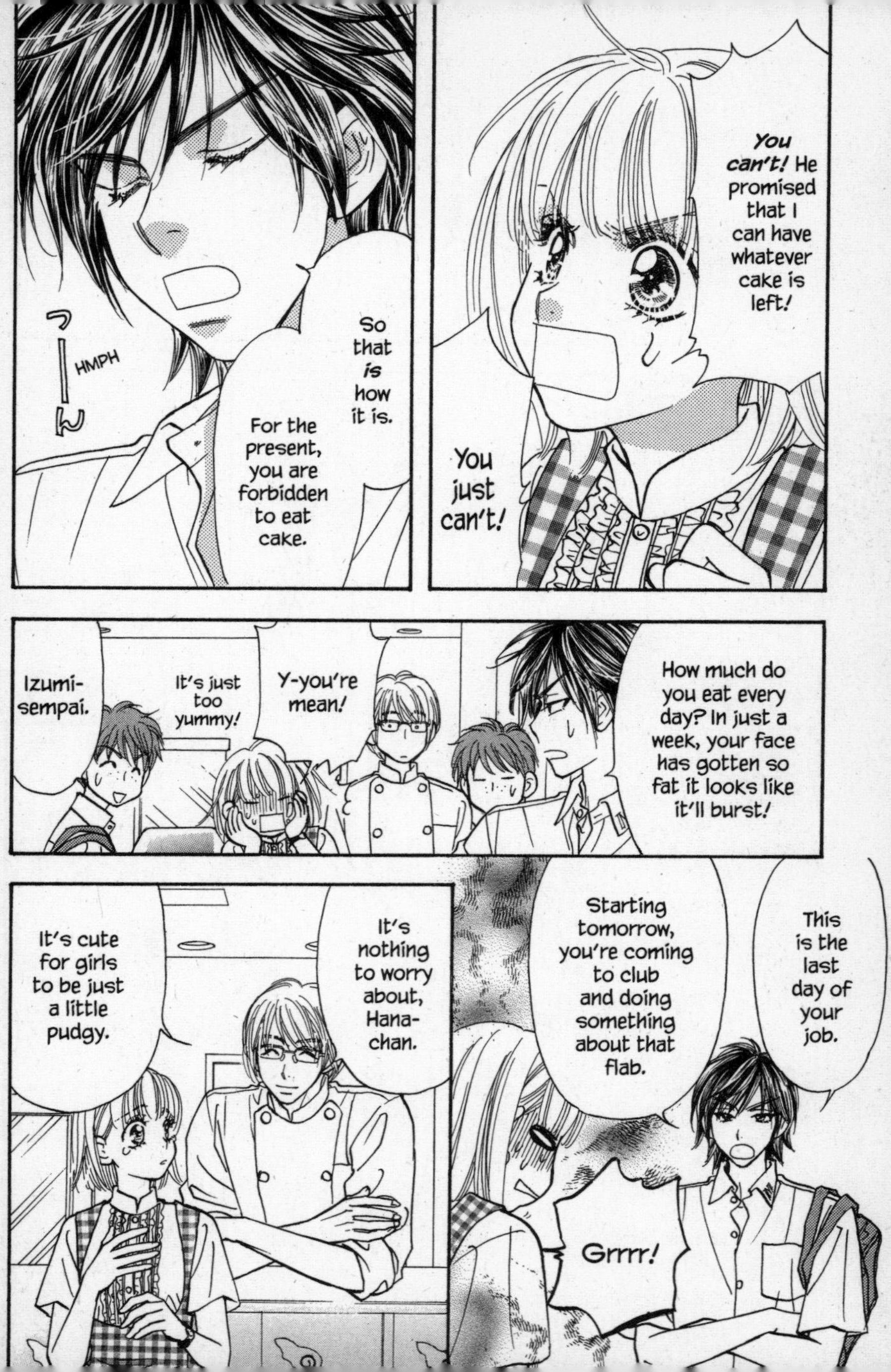
You can't! He promised that I can have whatever cake is left!
You just can't!
So that is how it is.
For the present, you are forbidden to eat cake.
つーん
HMPH
How much do you eat every day? In just a week, your face has gotten so fat it looks like it'll burst!
Y-you're mean!
It's just too yummy!
Izumi-sempai.
This is the last day of your job.
Starting tomorrow, you're coming to club and doing something about that flab.
Grrrr!
It's nothing to worry about, Hana-chan.
It's cute for girls to be just a little pudgy.

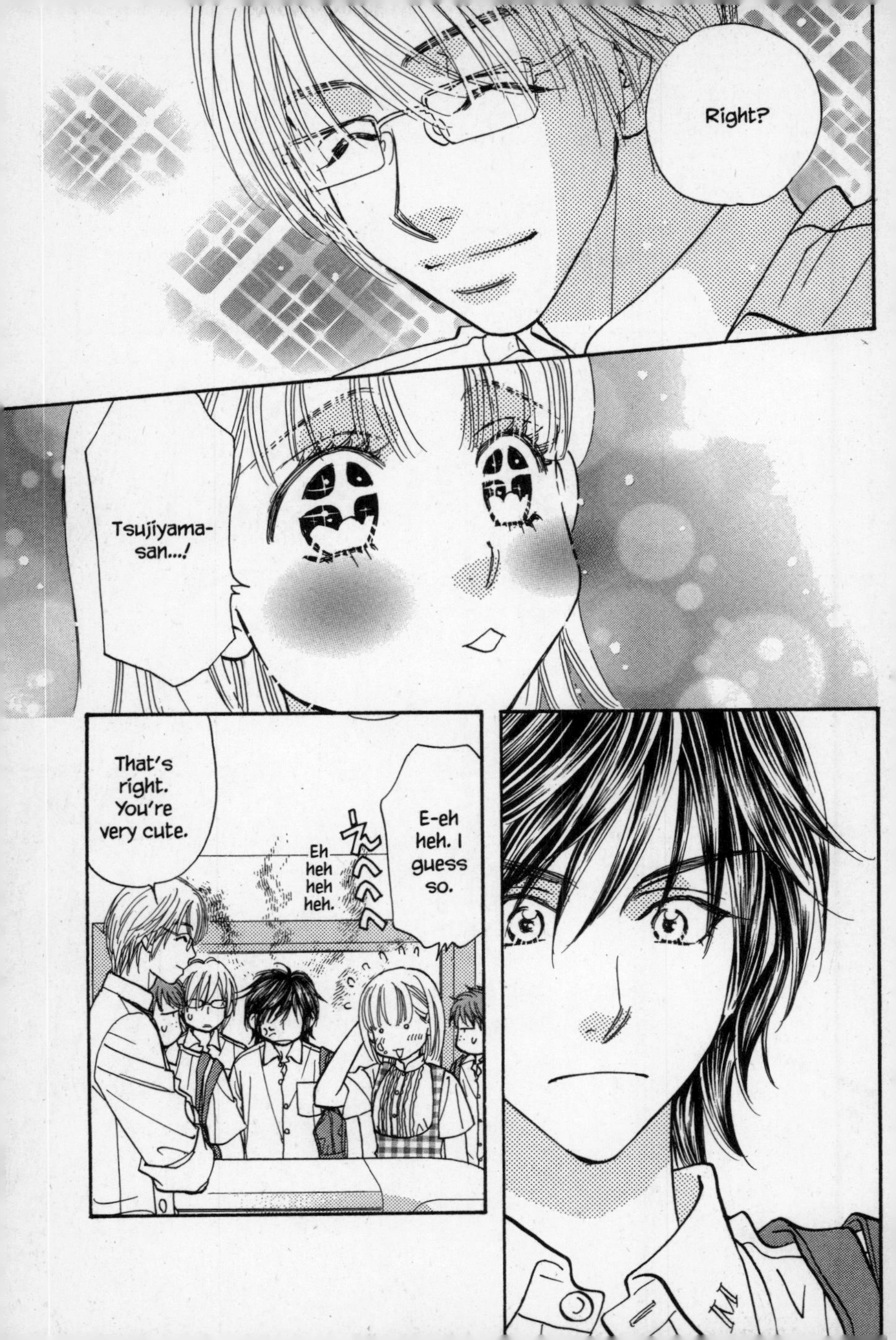
Right?
Tsujiyama-san...!
E-eh heh. I guess so.
Eh heh heh heh.
That's right. You're very cute.

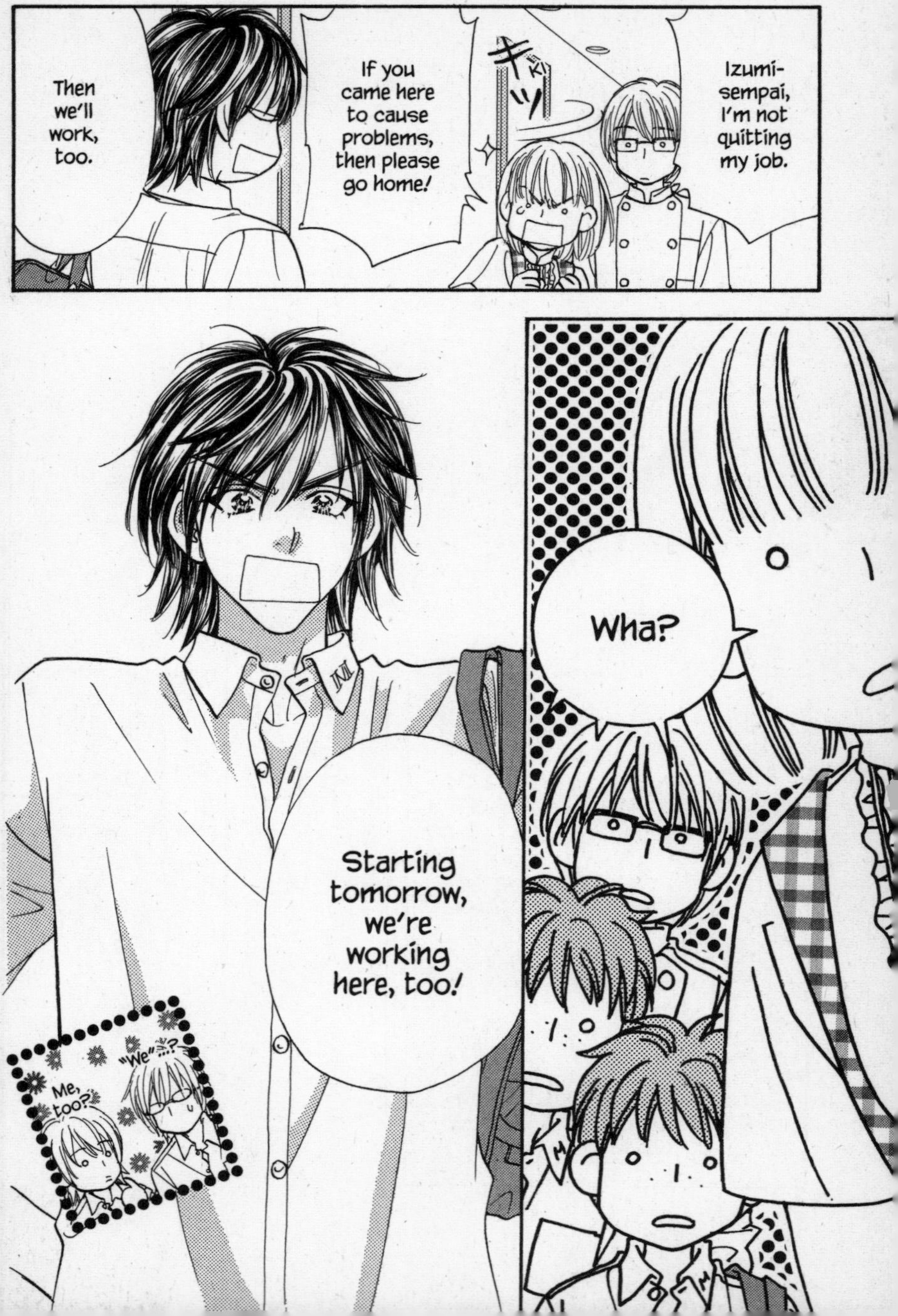
Izumi-sempai, I'm not quitting my job.
KI
If you came here to cause problems, then please go home!
Then we'll work, too.
Wha?
Starting tomorrow, we're working here, too!
"We"...?
Me, too?

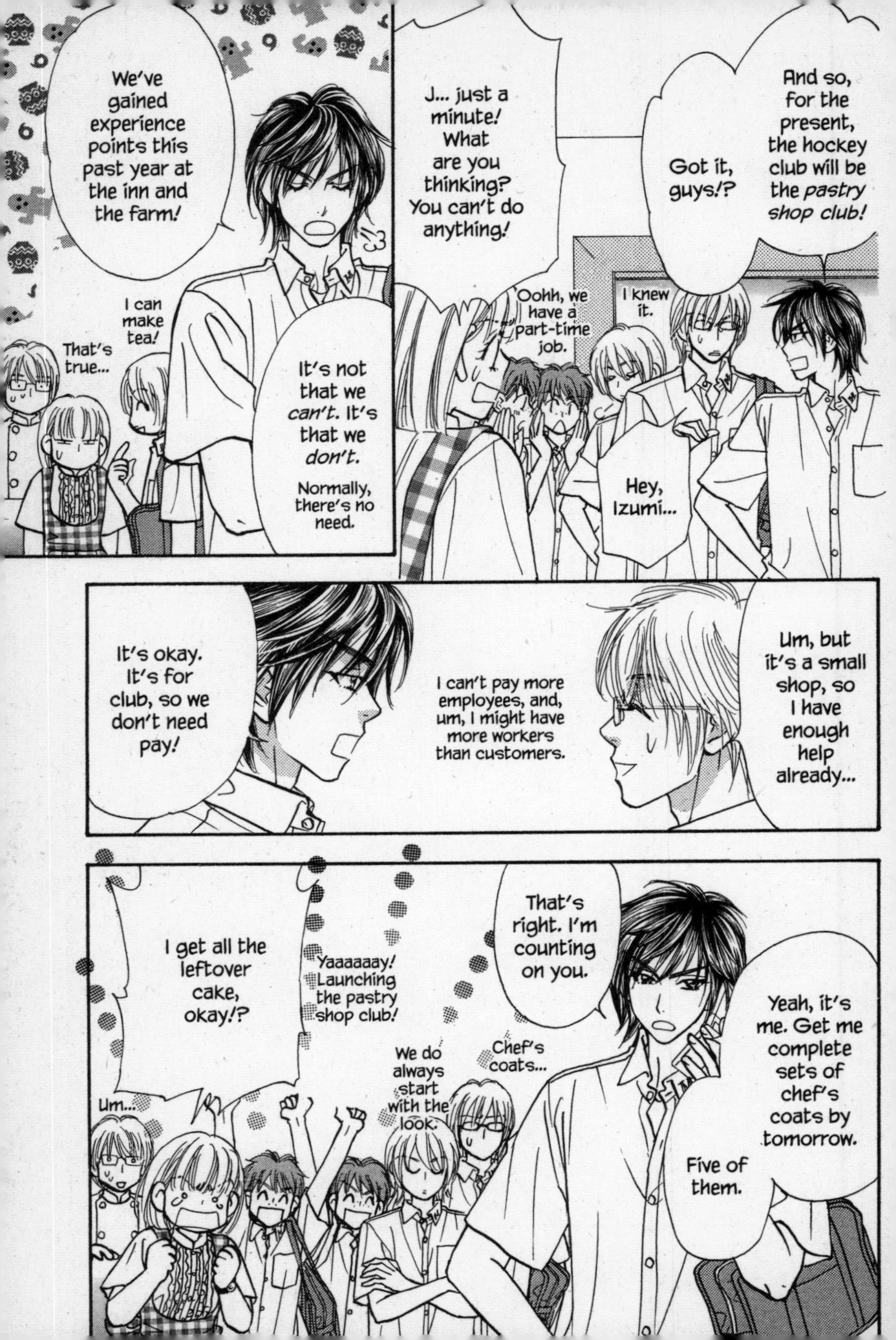
And so, for the present, the hockey club will be the *pastry shop club!*
Got it, guys!?
J... just a minute! What are you thinking? You can't do anything!
I knew it.
Oohh, we have a part-time job.
Hey, Izumi...
We've gained experience points this past year at the inn and the farm!
It's not that we *can't*. It's that we *don't*.
Normally, there's no need.
I can make tea!
That's true...
Um, but it's a small shop, so I have enough help already...
I can't pay more employees, and, um, I might have more workers than customers.
It's okay. It's for club, so we don't need pay!
Yeah, it's me. Get me complete sets of chef's coats by tomorrow.
Five of them.
That's right. I'm counting on you.
Chef's coats...
We do always start with the look.
Yaaaaaay! Launching the pastry shop club!
I get all the leftover cake, okay!?
Um...

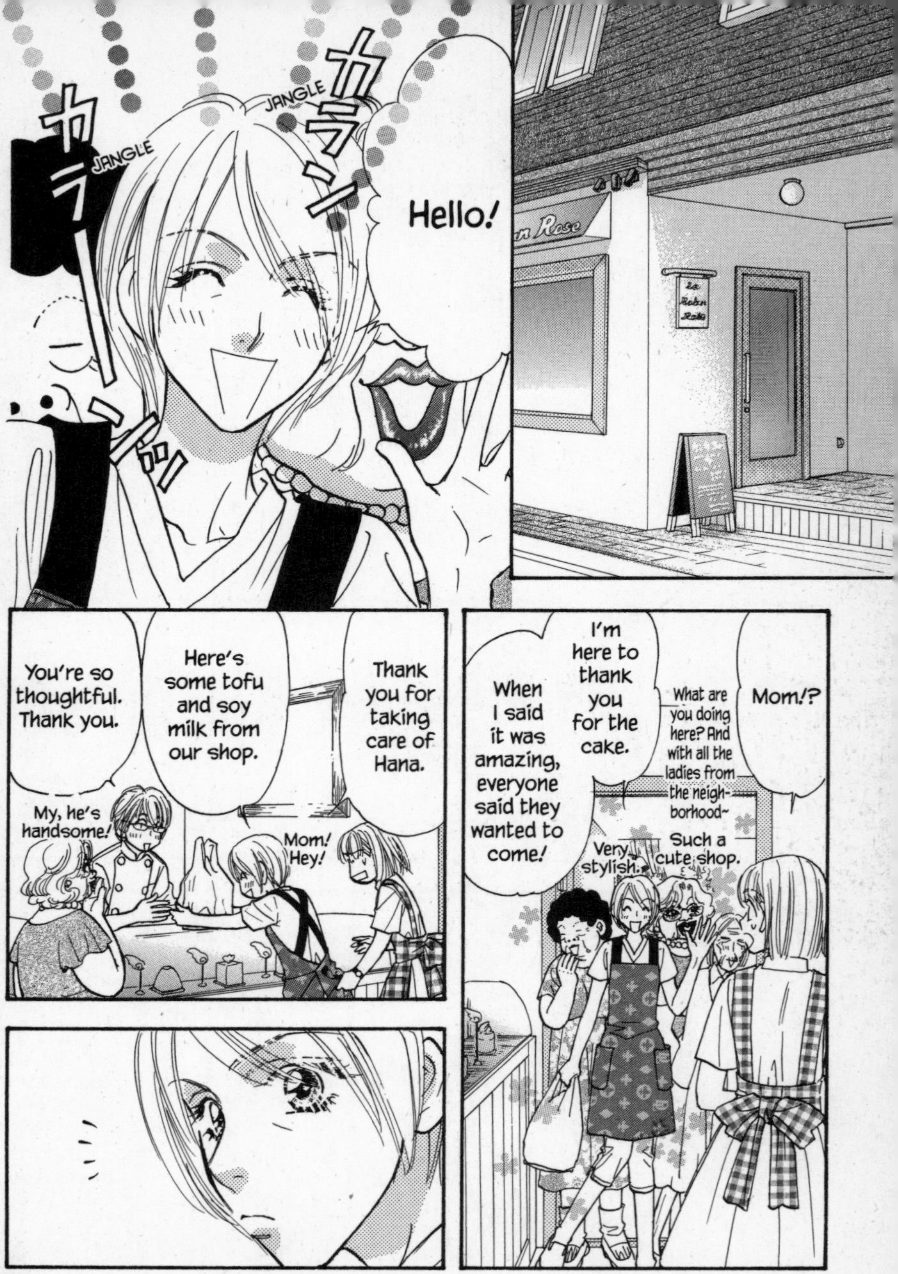
カラン
JANGLE
カラーン
JANGLE
Hello!
Mom!?
What are you doing here? And with all the ladies from the neighborhood~
I'm here to thank you for the cake.
When I said it was amazing, everyone said they wanted to come!
Very stylish.
Such a cute shop.
Thank you for taking care of Hana.
Mom! Hey!
Here's some tofu and soy milk from our shop.
You're so thoughtful. Thank you.
My, he's handsome!

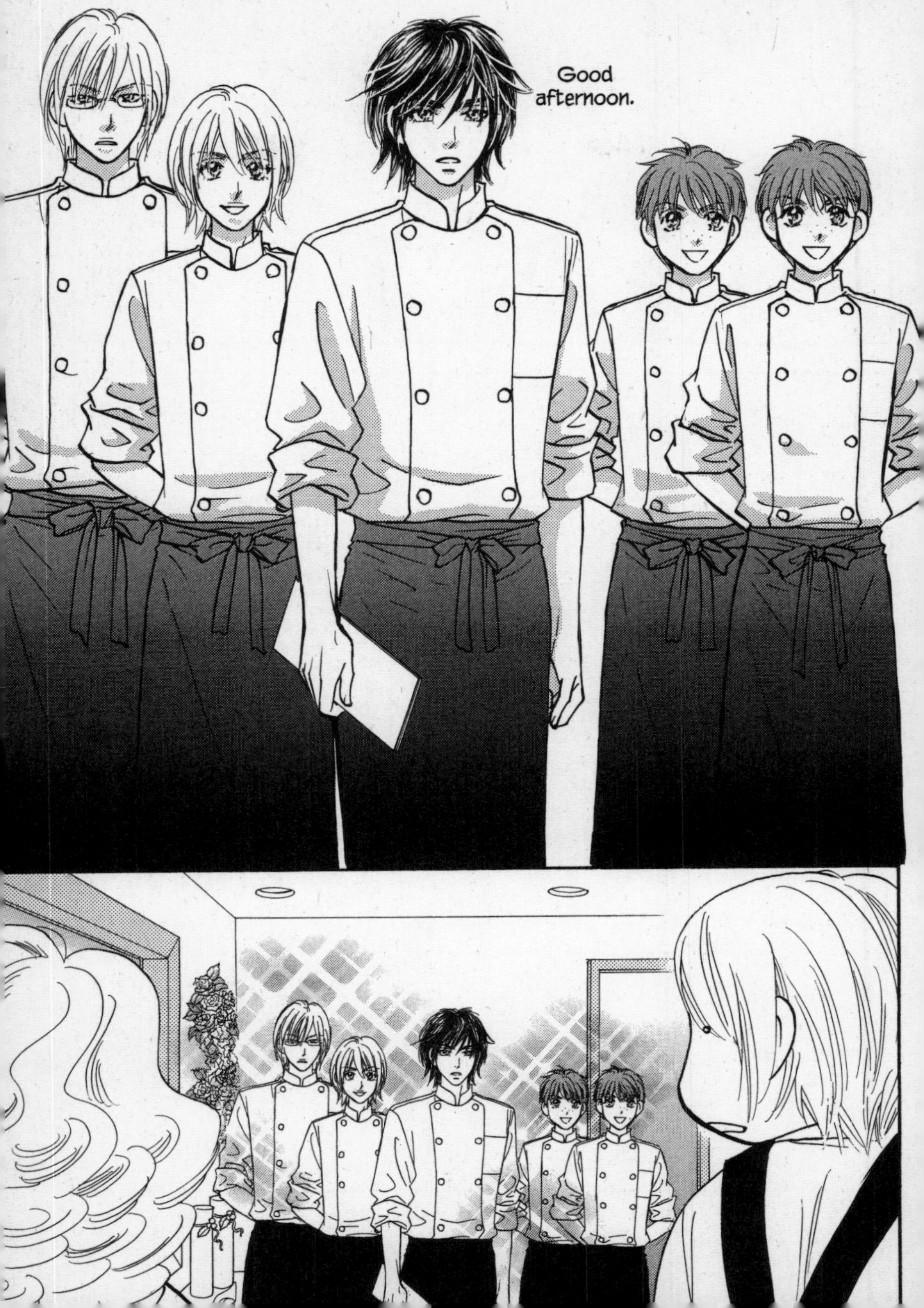
Good afternoon.

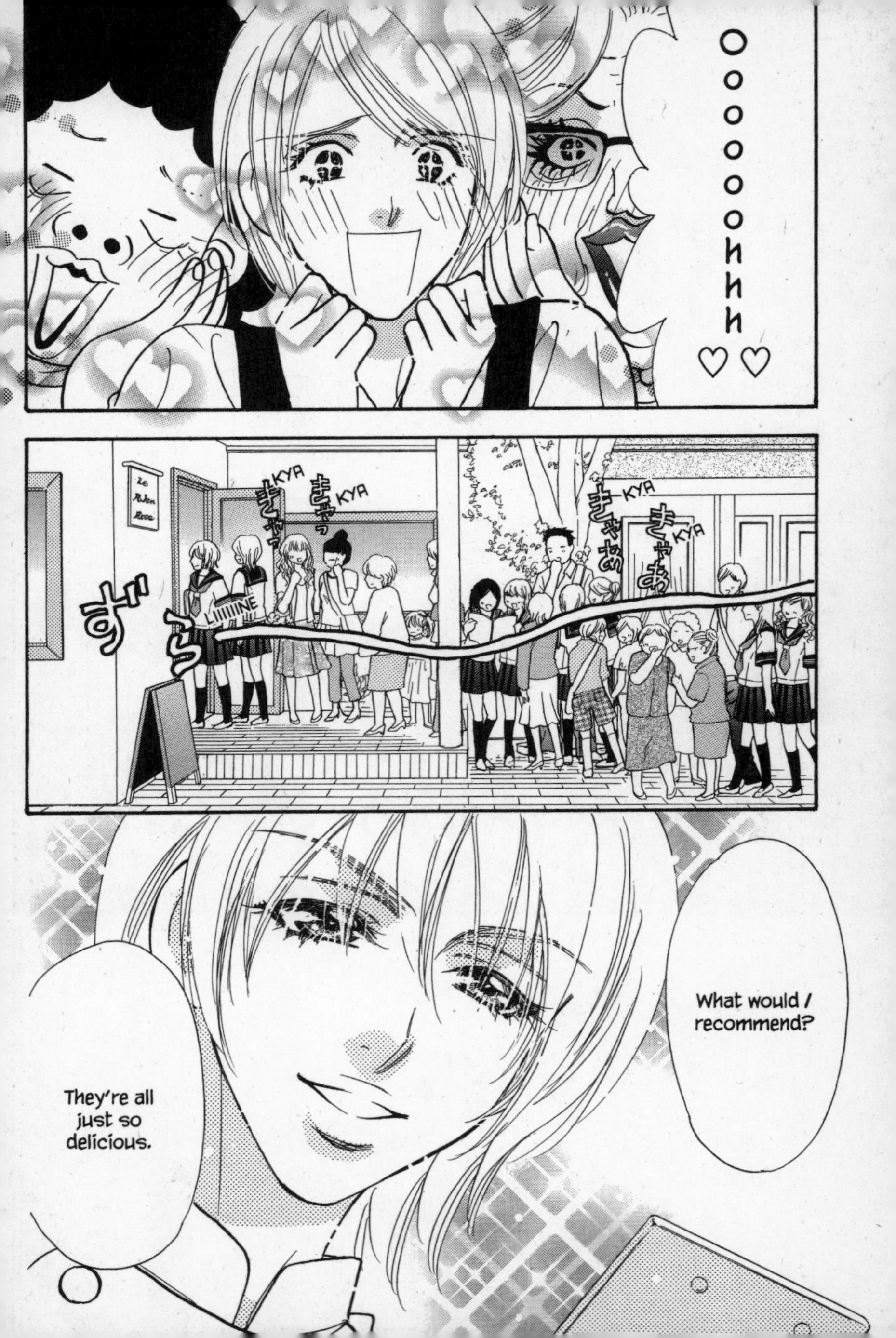
Ooooooohhh ♡♡
きゃあ KYA
きゃあ KYA
きゃっ KYA
きゃっ KYA
LIIIIINE
ずらっ
What would I recommend?
They're all just so delicious.

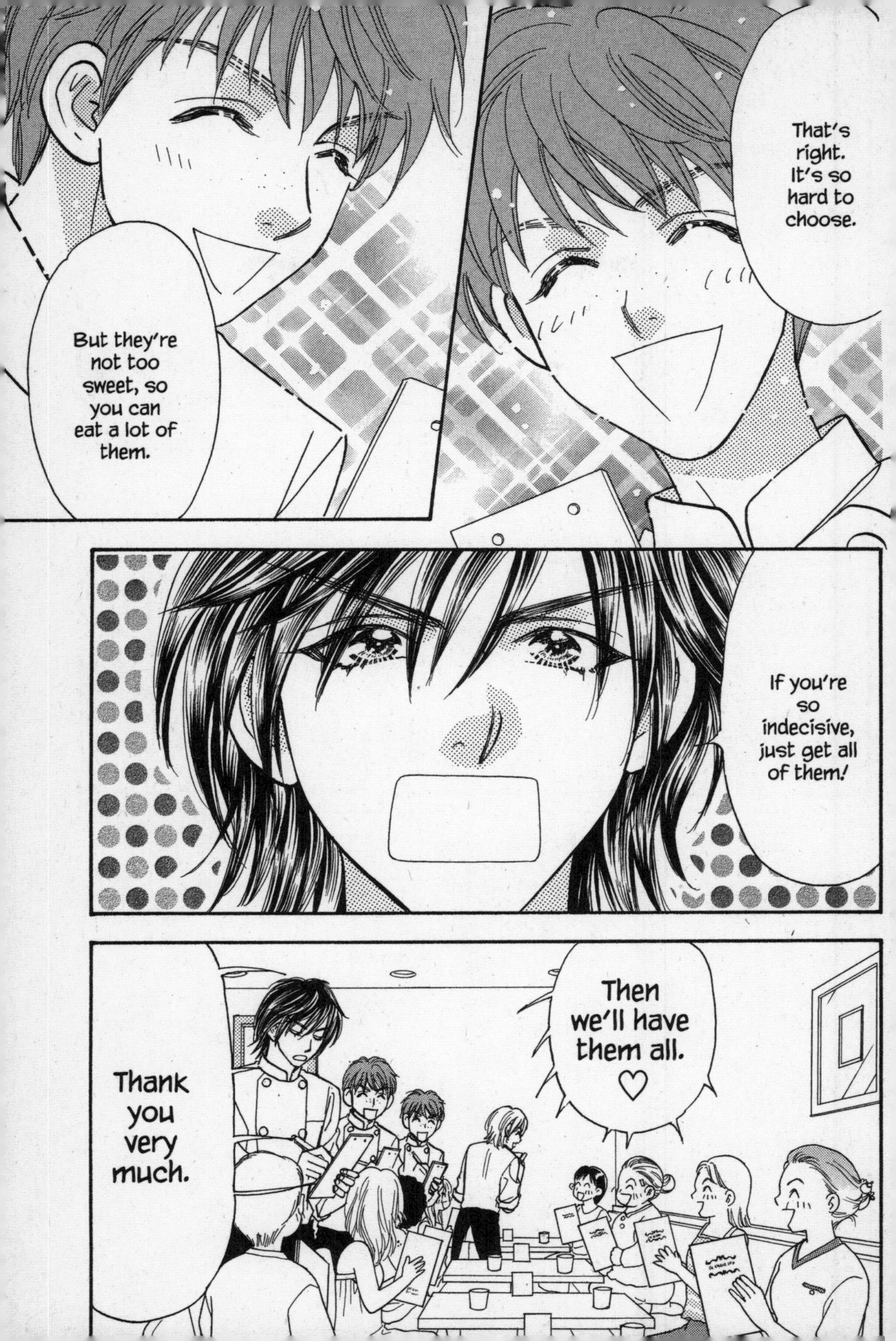
That's right. It's so hard to choose.
But they're not too sweet, so you can eat a lot of them.
If you're so indecisive, just get all of them!
Then we'll have them all. ♡
Thank you very much.

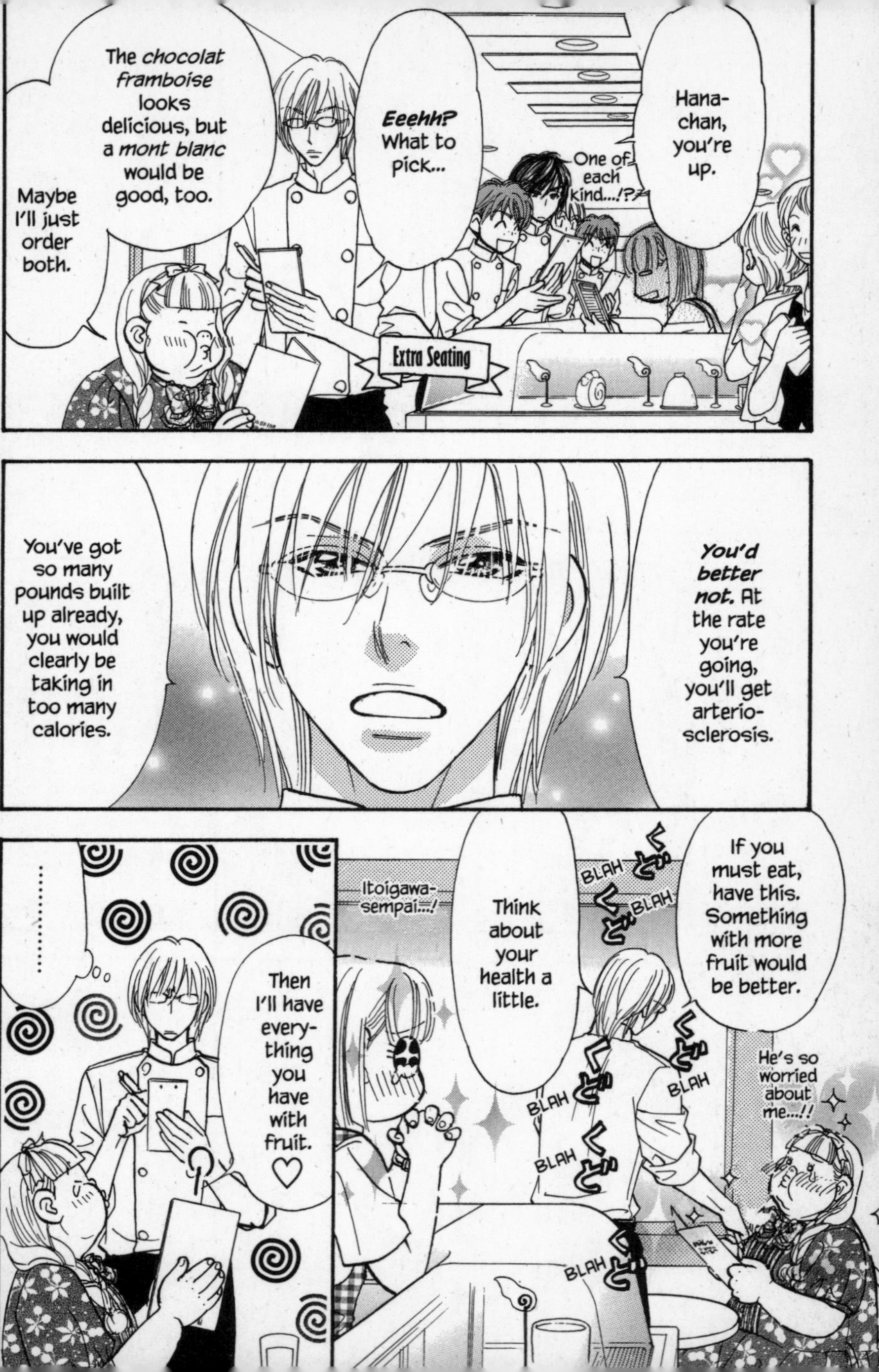

Hana-chan, you're up.
One of each kind...!?
Eeehh? What to pick...
The chocolat framboise looks delicious, but a mont blanc would be good, too.
Maybe I'll just order both.
Extra Seating
You'd better not. At the rate you're going, you'll get arterio-sclerosis.
You've got so many pounds built up already, you would clearly be taking in too many calories.
If you must eat, have this. Something with more fruit would be better.
BLAH BLAH
He's so worried about me...!!
Think about your health a little.
BLAH BLAH BLAH BLAH
Itoigawa-sempai...!
Then I'll have everything you have with fruit. ♡
....

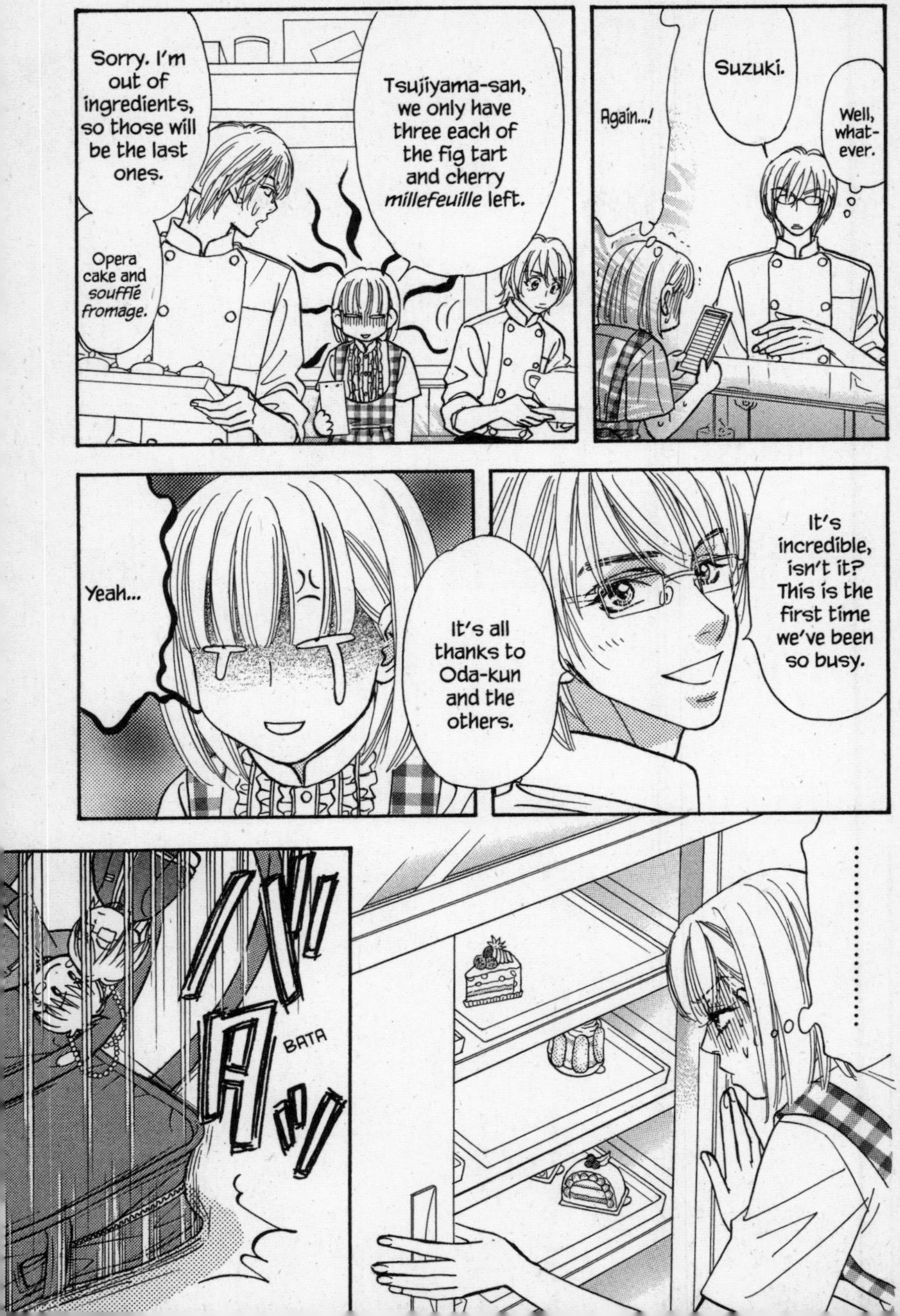

Suzuki.
Well, whatever.
Again...!
Tsujiyama-san, we only have three each of the fig tart and cherry *millefeuille* left.
Sorry. I'm out of ingredients, so those will be the last ones.
Opera cake and *soufflé fromage*.
It's incredible, isn't it? This is the first time we've been so busy.
It's all thanks to Oda-kun and the others.
Yeah...
BATA

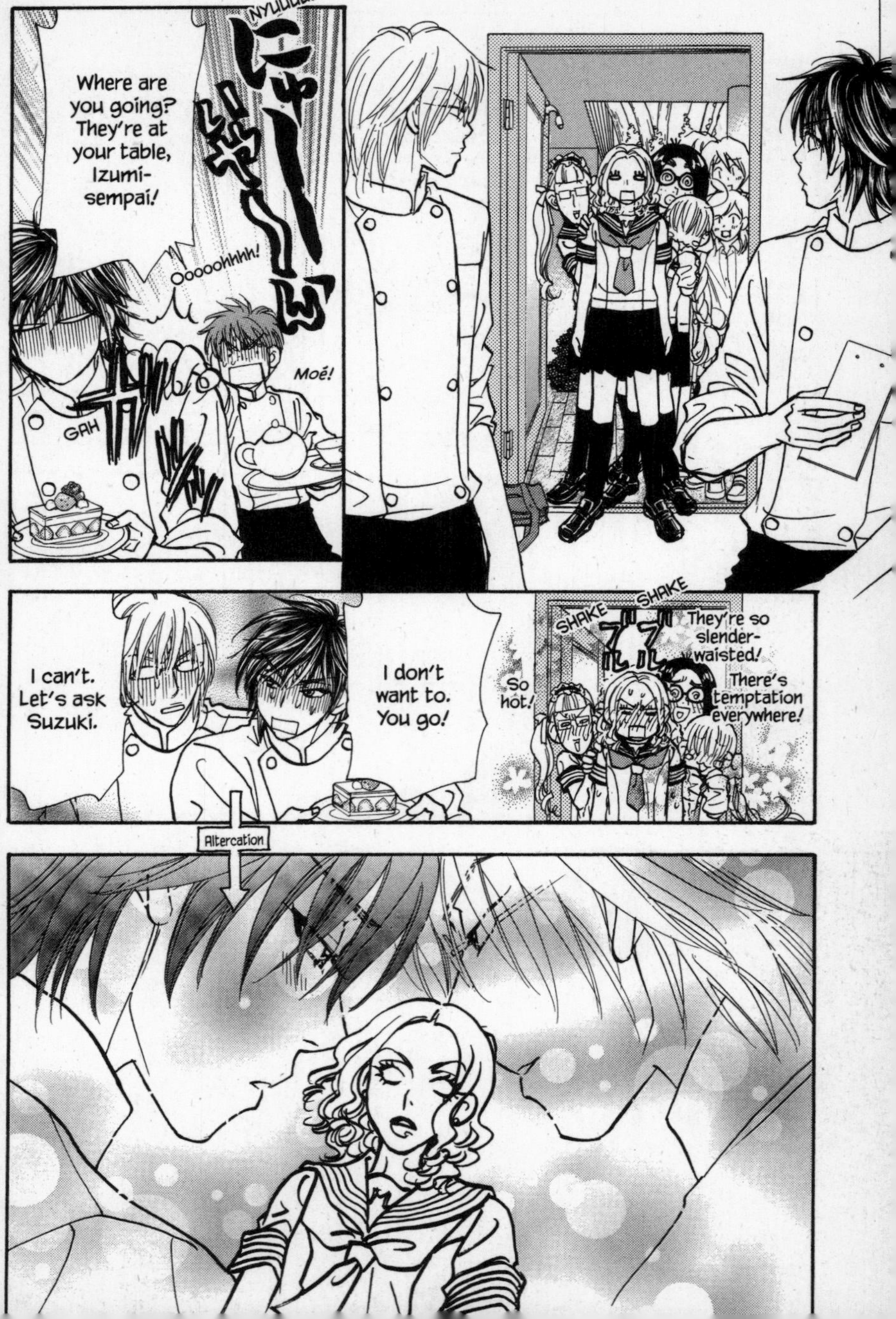
NYUUUUU!
Where are you going? They're at your table, Izumi-sempai!
Ooooohhhh!
Moé!
GAH
SHAKE SHAKE
They're so slender-waisted!
There's temptation everywhere!
So hot!
I don't want to. You go!
I can't. Let's ask Suzuki.
Altercation

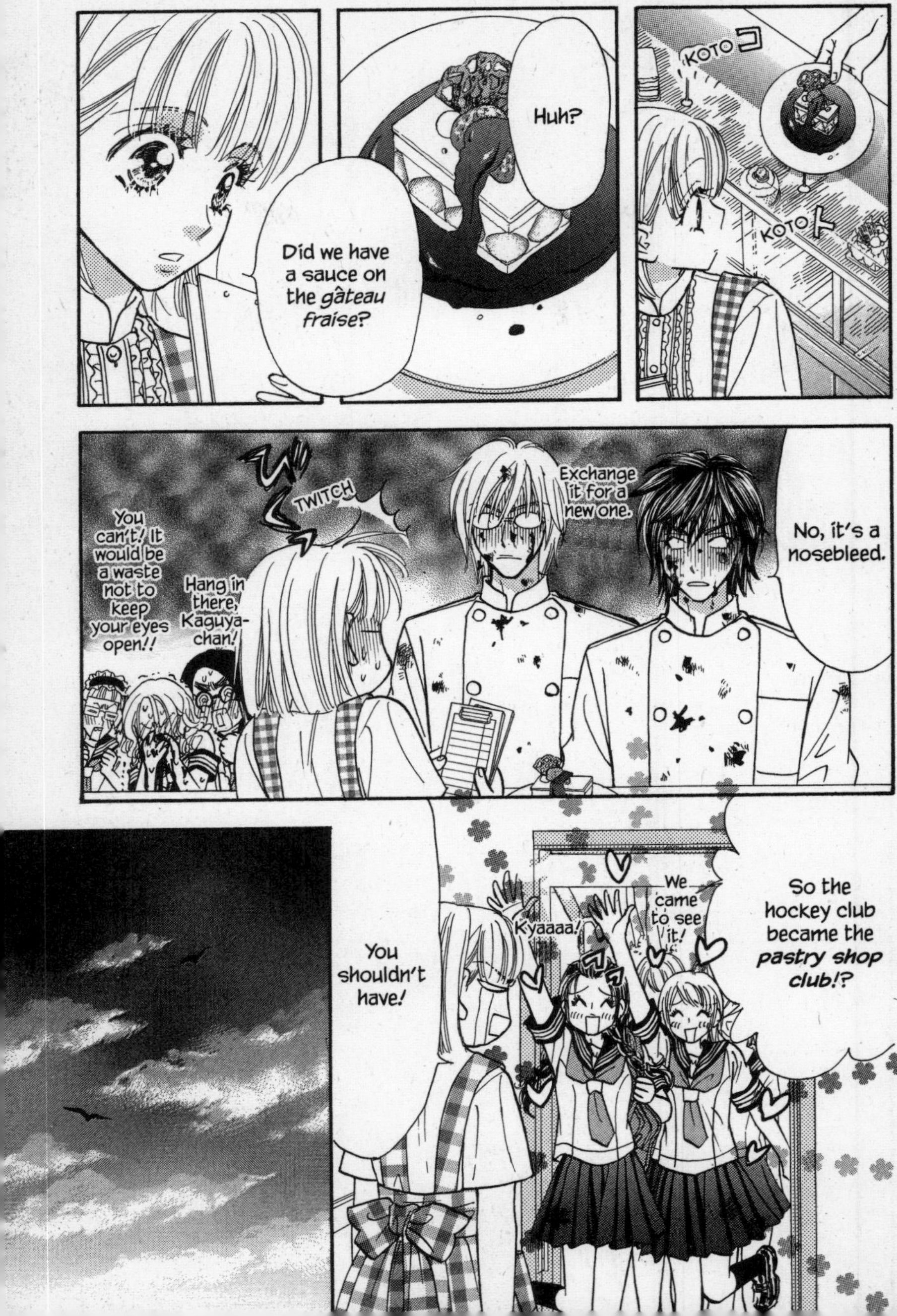
KOTO
KOTO
Huh?
Did we have a sauce on the *gâteau fraise*?
No, it's a nosebleed.
Exchange it for a new one.
TWITCH
Hang in there, Kaguya-chan!
You can't! It would be a waste not to keep your eyes open!!
So the hockey club became the *pastry shop club!?*
We came to see it!
Kyaaaa!
You shouldn't have!

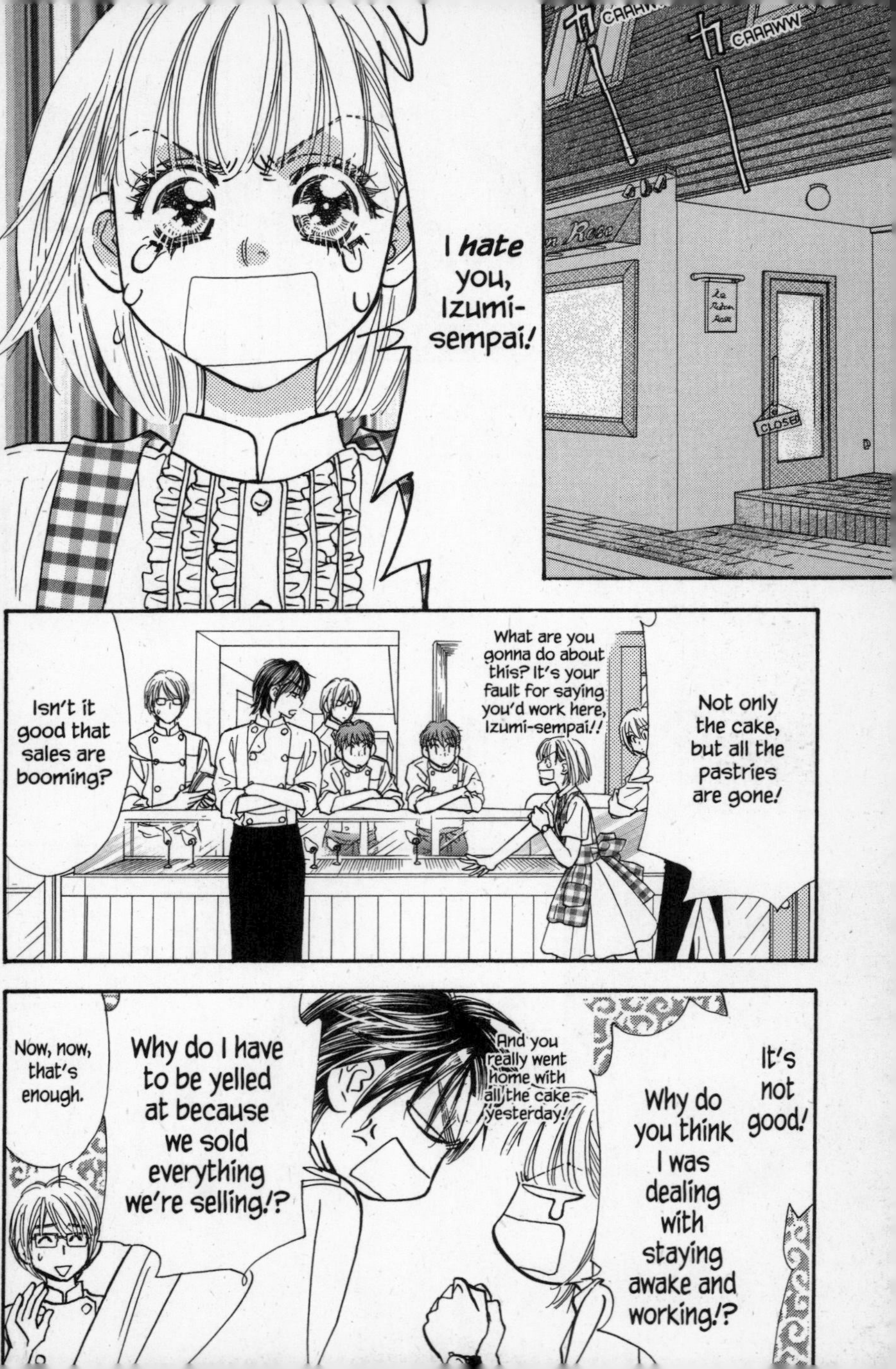
CAAAWW
CAAAWW
CLOSED
I hate you, Izumi-sempai!
Not only the cake, but all the pastries are gone!
What are you gonna do about this? It's your fault for saying you'd work here, Izumi-sempai!!
Isn't it good that sales are booming?
It's not good!
Why do you think I was dealing with staying awake and working!?
And you really went home with all the cake yesterday!
Why do I have to be yelled at because we sold everything we're selling!?
Now, now, that's enough.

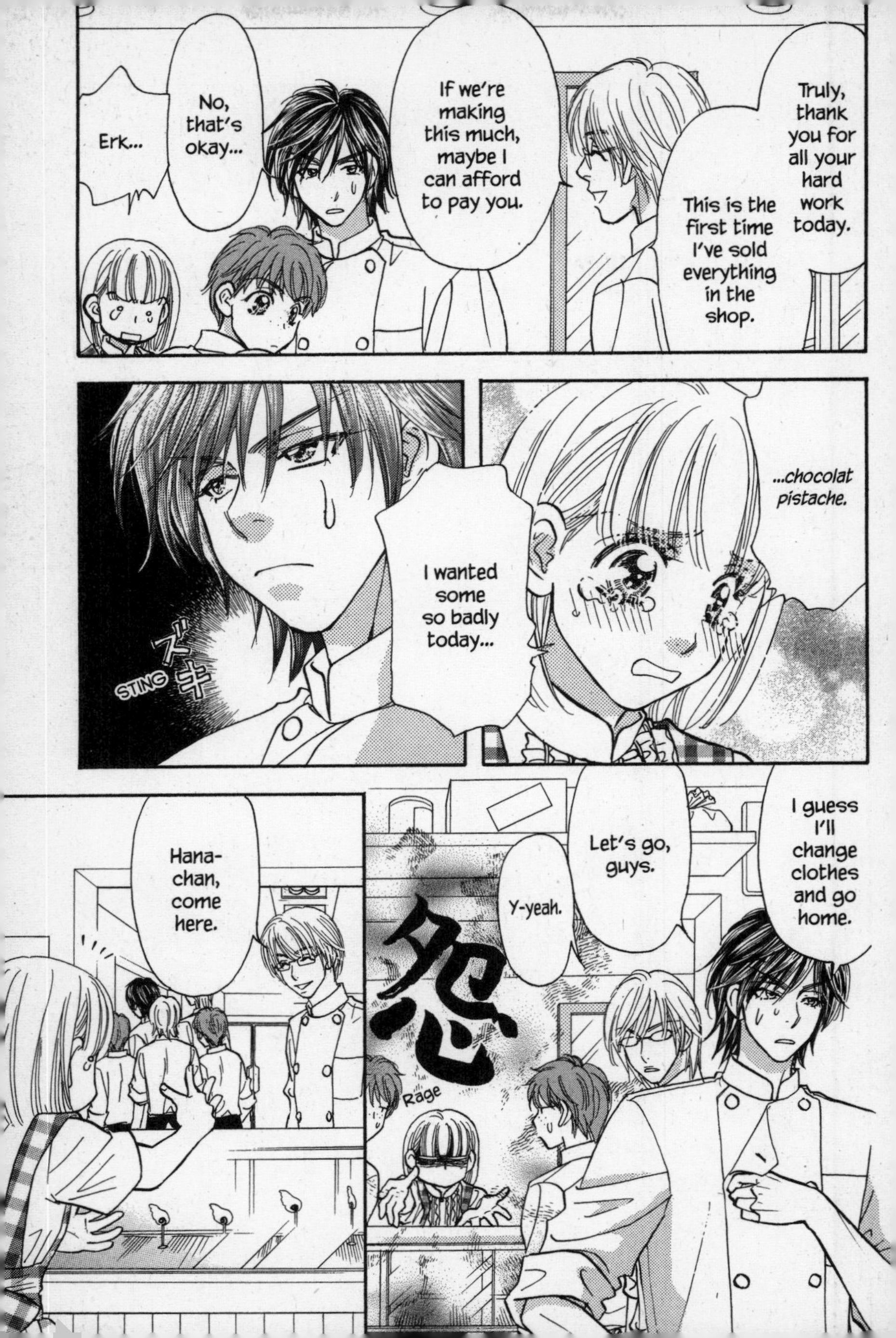
Truly, thank you for all your hard work today.
This is the first time I've sold everything in the shop.
If we're making this much, maybe I can afford to pay you.
No, that's okay...
Erk...
...chocolat pistache.
I wanted some so badly today...
ズキ
STING
I guess I'll change clothes and go home.
Let's go, guys.
Y-yeah.
怨
Rage
Hana-chan, come here.

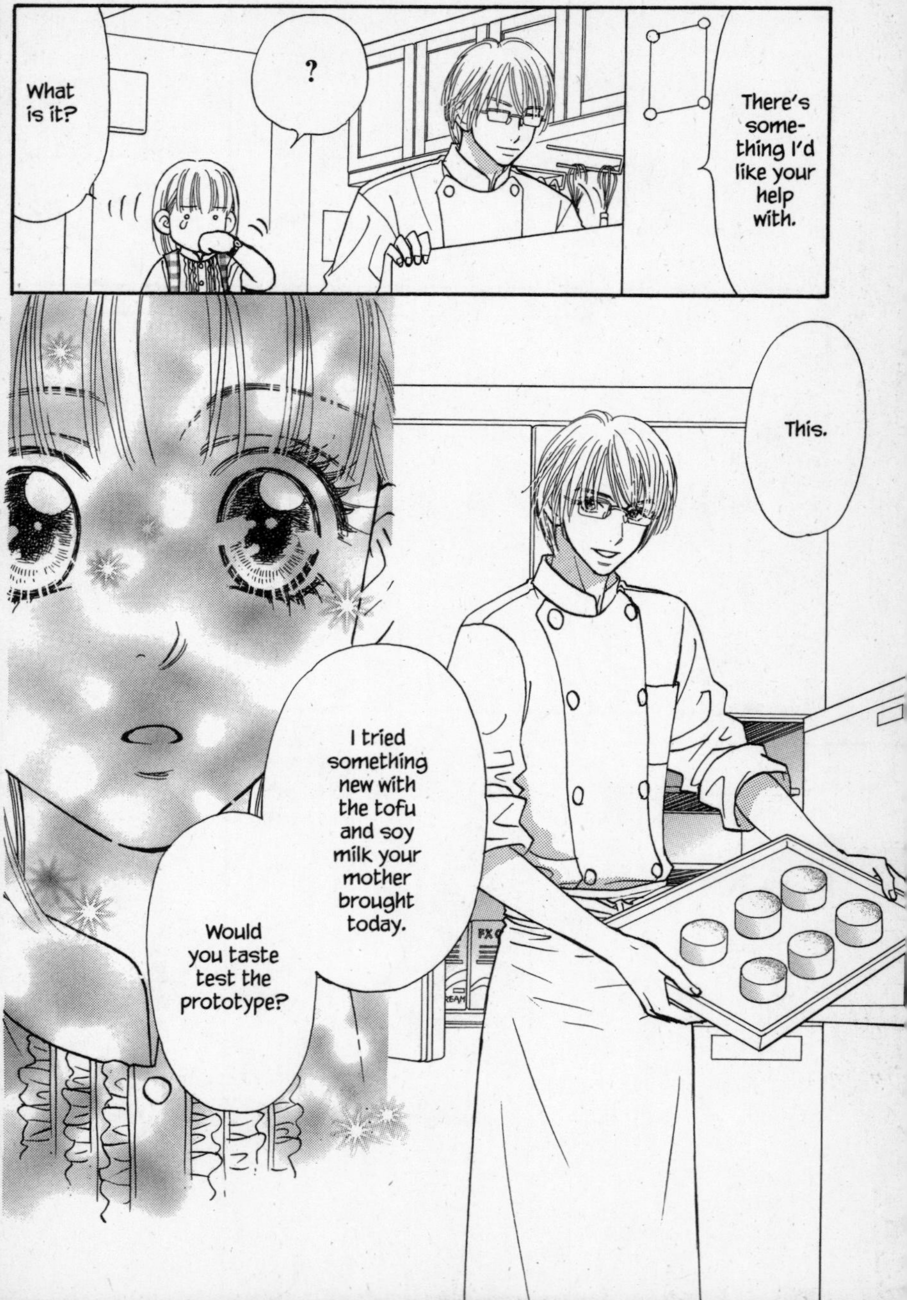
There's some-thing I'd like your help with.
?
What is it?
This.
I tried something new with the tofu and soy milk your mother brought today.
Would you taste test the prototype?

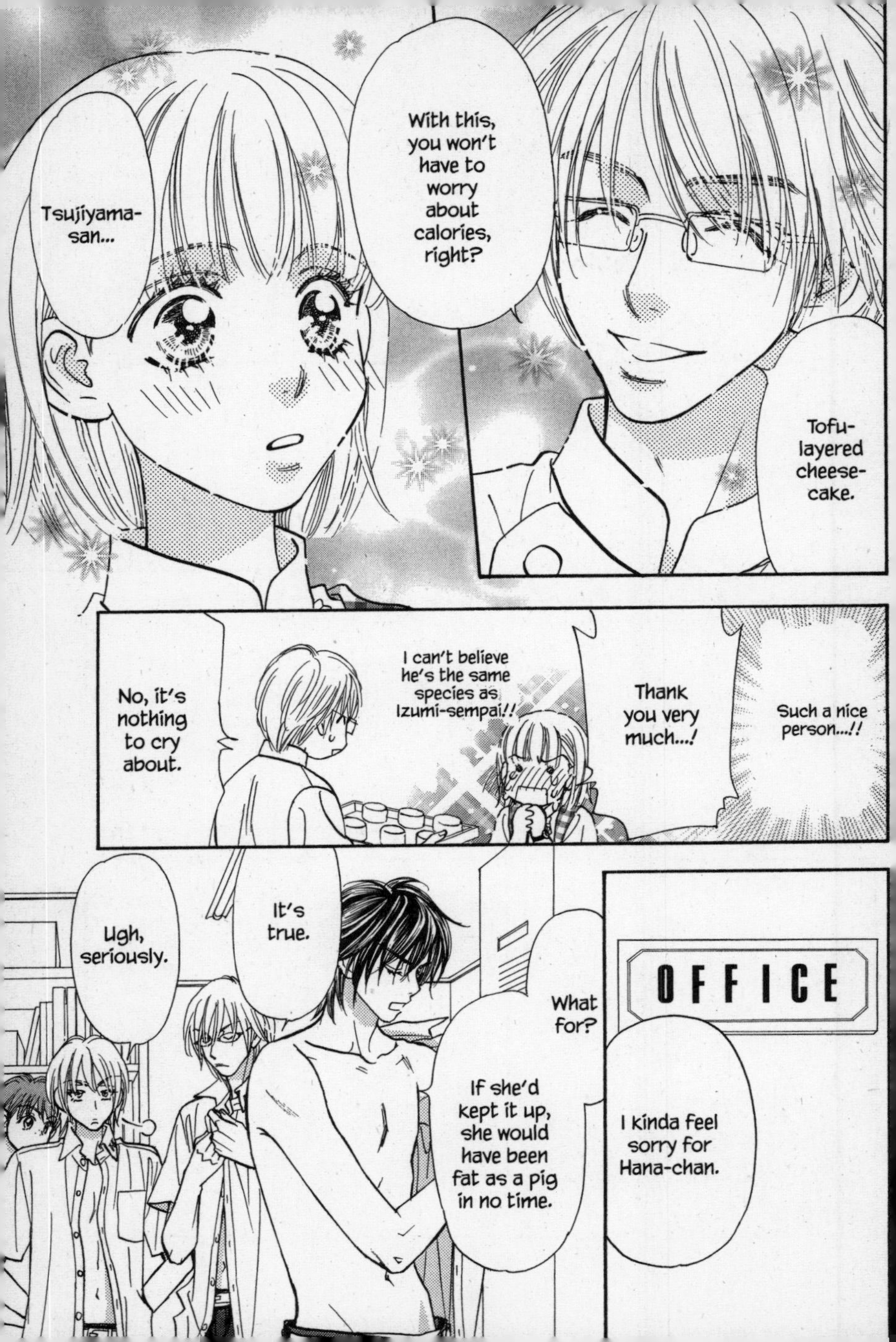
Tofu-layered cheese-cake.
With this, you won't have to worry about calories, right?
Tsujiyama-san...
Such a nice person...!!
Thank you very much...!
I can't believe he's the same species as Izumi-sempai!!
No, it's nothing to cry about.
OFFICE
I kinda feel sorry for Hana-chan.
What for?
If she'd kept it up, she would have been fat as a pig in no time.
It's true.
Ugh, seriously.

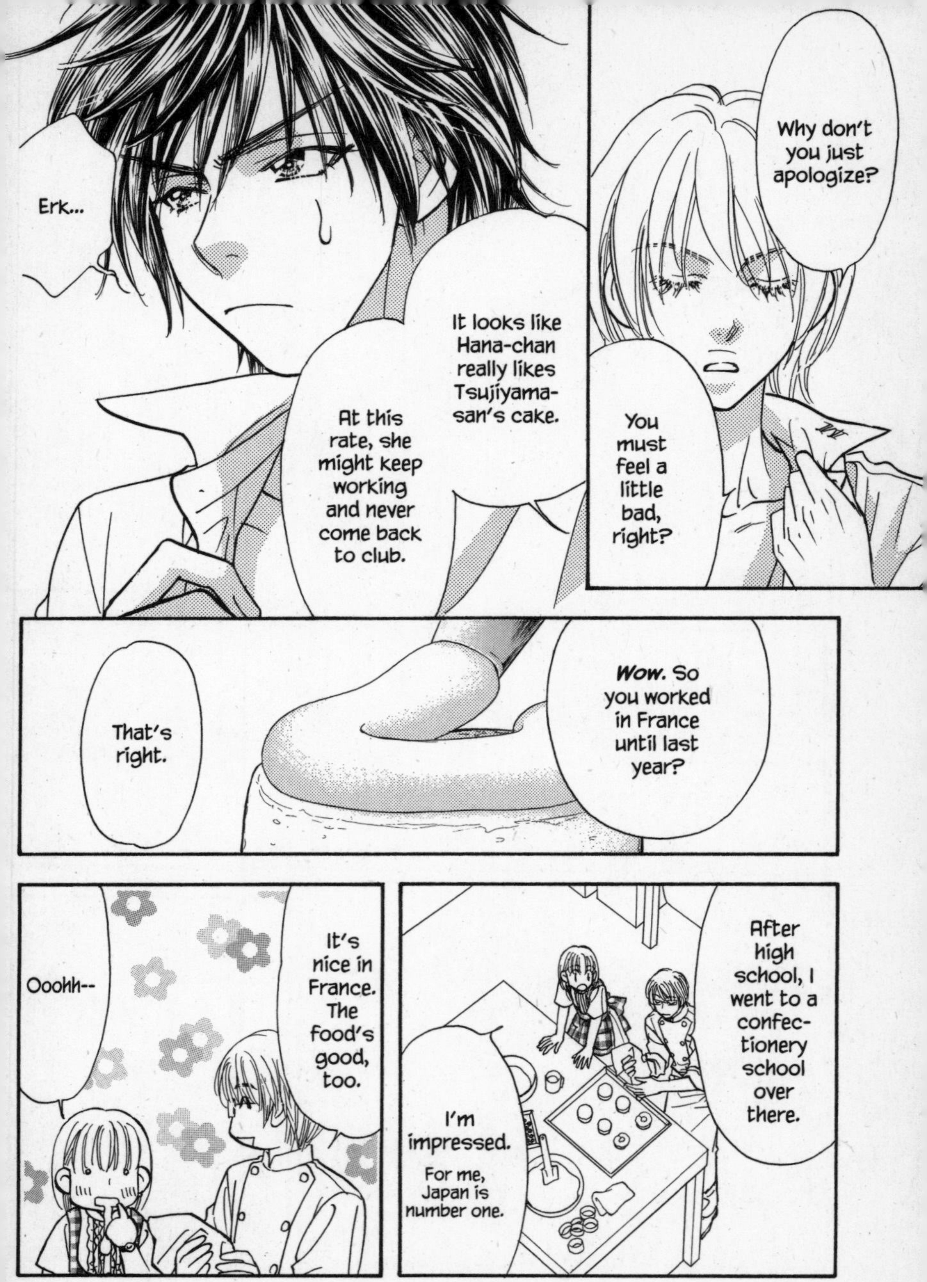
Why don't you just apologize?
You must feel a little bad, right?
It looks like Hana-chan really likes Tsujiyama-san's cake.
At this rate, she might keep working and never come back to club.
Erk...
Wow. So you worked in France until last year?
That's right.
After high school, I went to a confectionery school over there.
I'm impressed.
For me, Japan is number one.
It's nice in France. The food's good, too.
Ooohh--

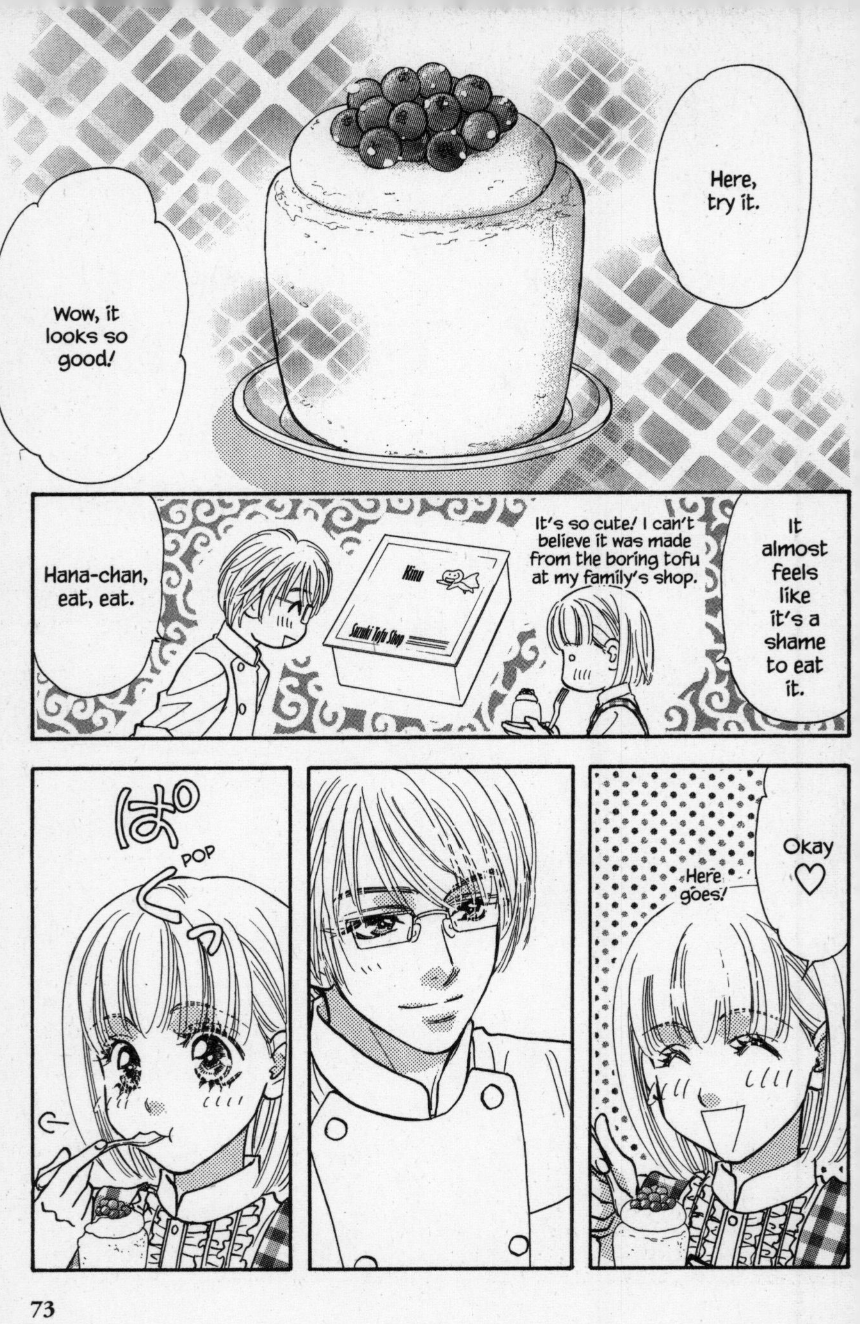
Here, try it.
Wow, it looks so good!
It almost feels like it's a shame to eat it.
It's so cute! I can't believe it was made from the boring tofu at my family's shop.
Kinu
Suzuki Tofu Shop
Hana-chan, eat, eat.
Okay ♡
Here goes!
ぱくっ
POP

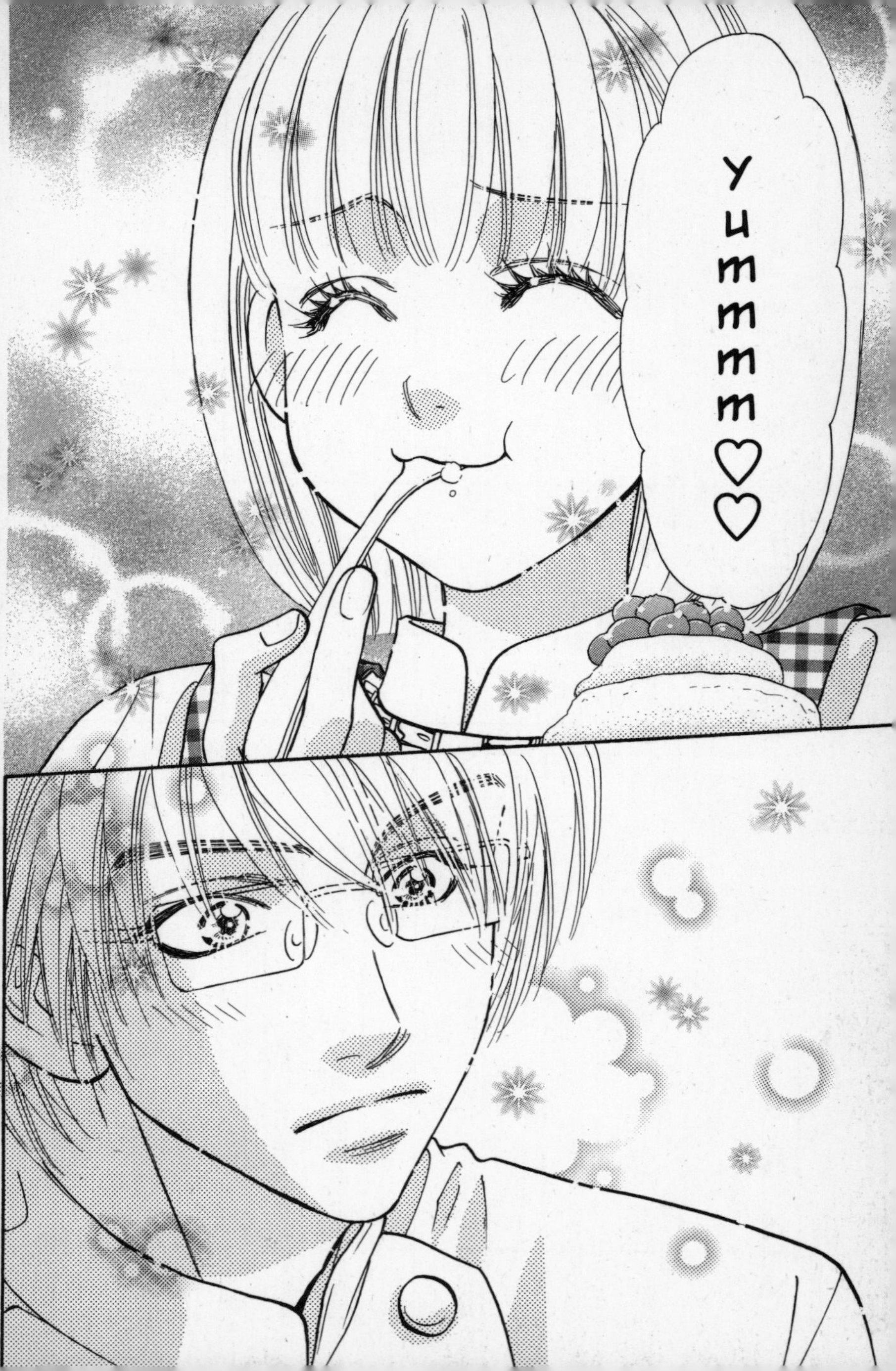
Yummmm♡♡

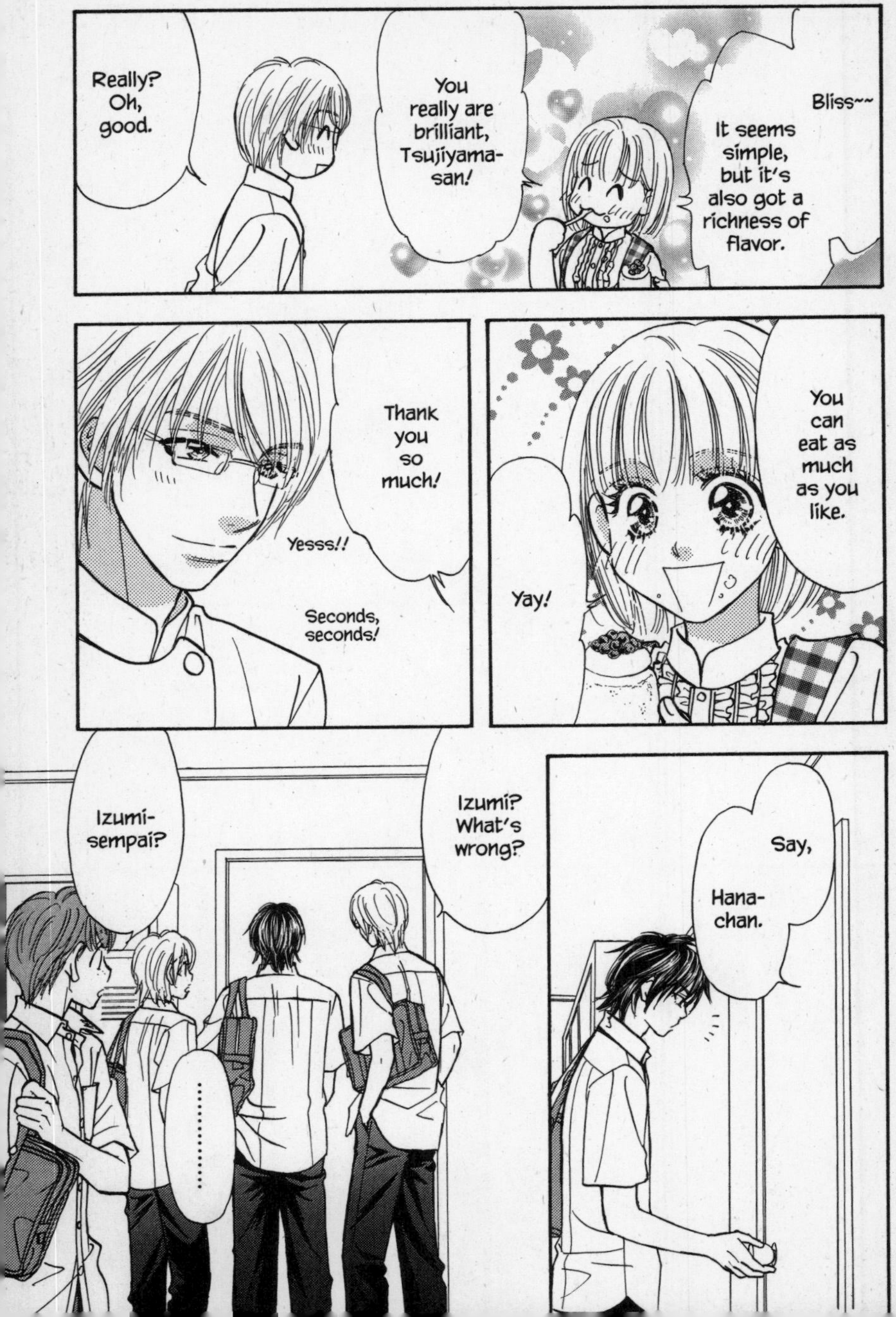
Bliss~~
It seems simple, but it's also got a richness of flavor.
You really are brilliant, Tsujiyama-san!
Really? Oh, good.
You can eat as much as you like.
Yay!
Thank you so much!
Yesss!!
Seconds, seconds!
Say, Hana-chan.
Izumi? What's wrong?
Izumi-sempai?
......

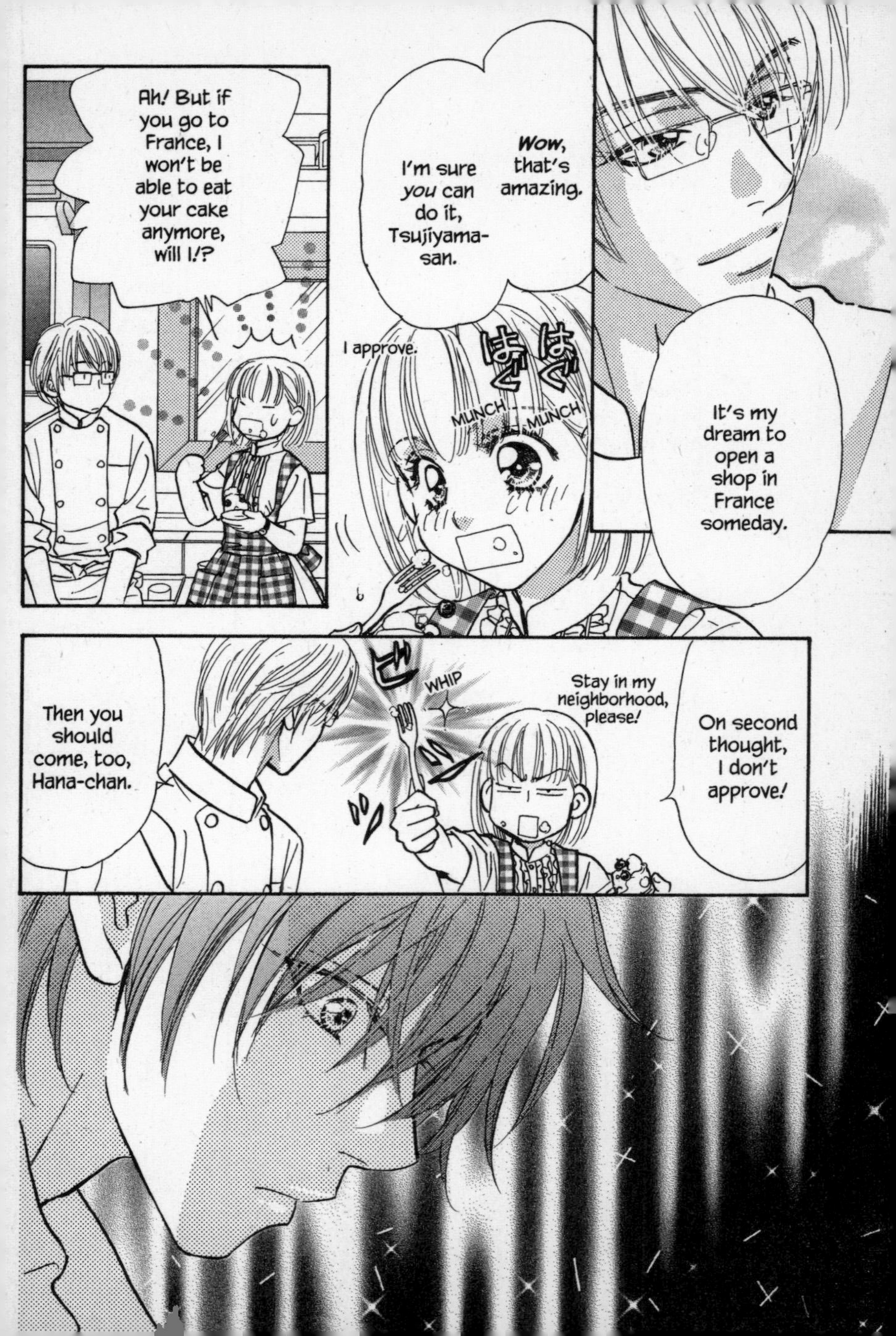
It's my dream to open a shop in France someday.
Wow, that's amazing.
I'm sure you can do it, Tsujiyama-san.
はぐはぐ
MUNCH MUNCH
I approve.
Ah! But if you go to France, I won't be able to eat your cake anymore, will I!?
On second thought, I don't approve!
Stay in my neighborhood, please!
WHIP
Then you should come, too, Hana-chan.

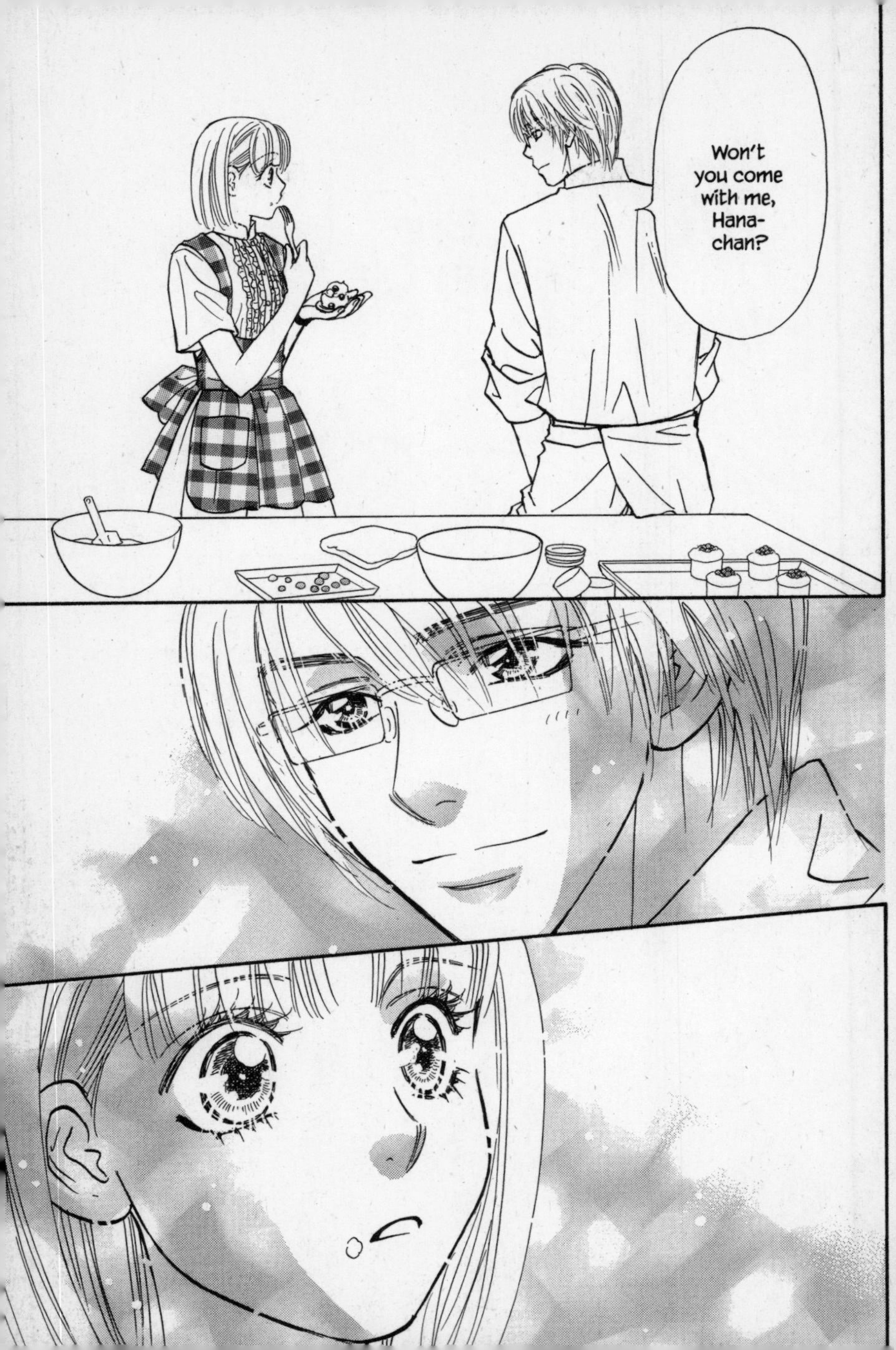
Won't you come with me, Hana-chan?

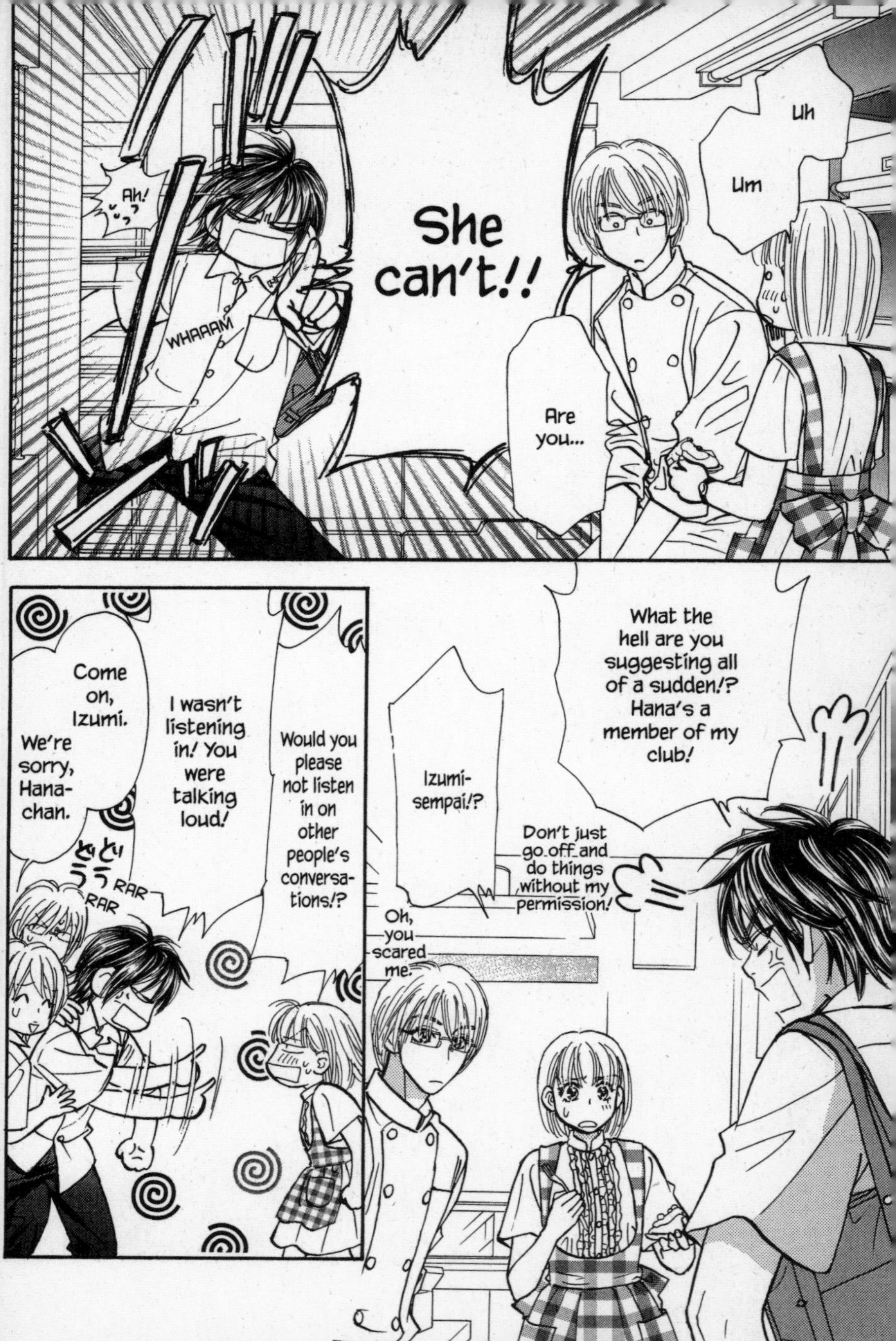
Uh
Um
She can't!!
Are you...
Ah!
WHAAAM
What the hell are you suggesting all of a sudden!? Hana's a member of my club!
Izumi-sempai!?
Don't just go off and do things without my permission!
Oh, you scared me.
Would you please not listen in on other people's conversations!?
I wasn't listening in! You were talking loud!
Come on, Izumi.
We're sorry, Hana-chan.
RAR RAR

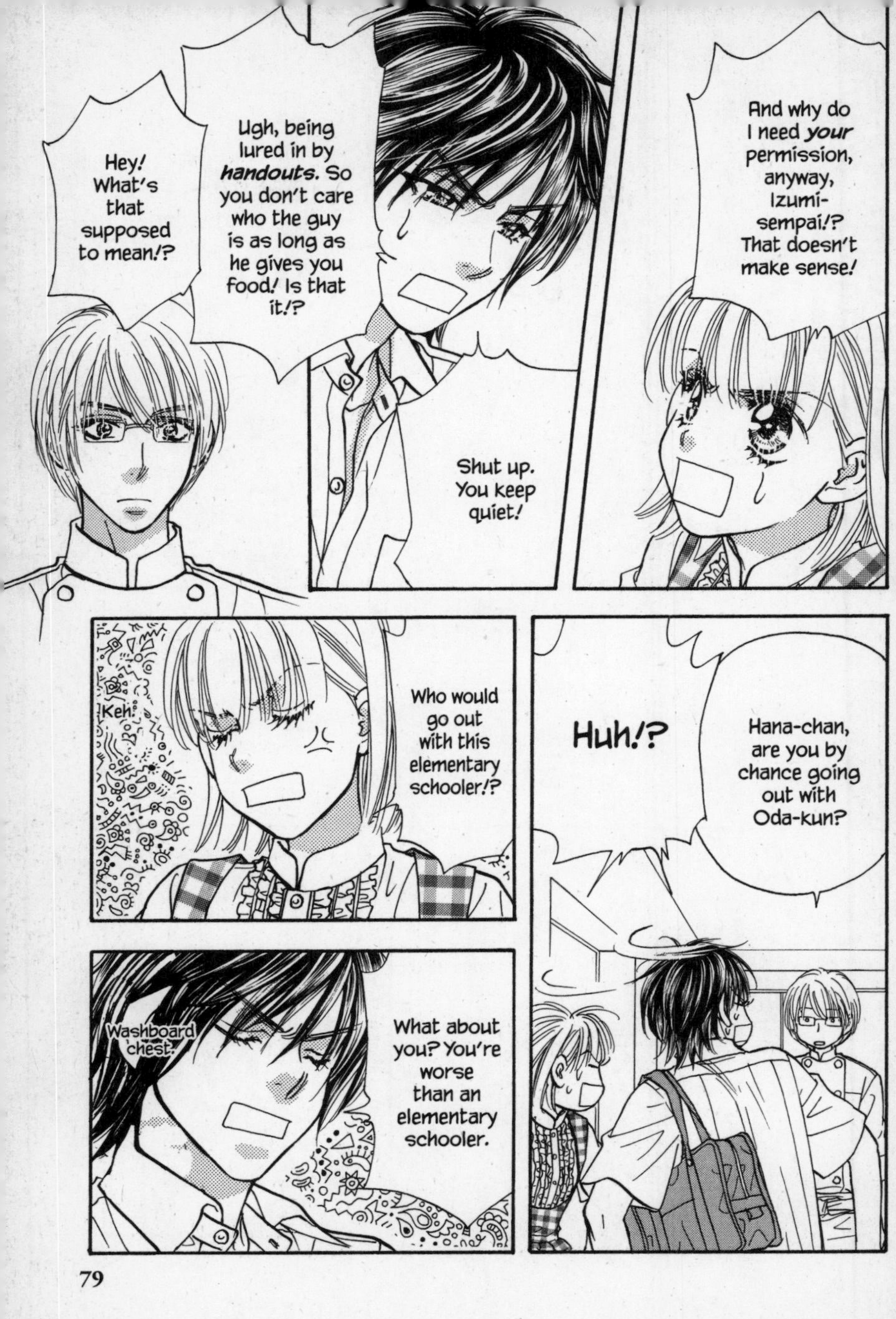
And why do I need *your* permission, anyway, Izumi-sempai!? That doesn't make sense!
Ugh, being lured in by **handouts.** So you don't care who the guy is as long as he gives you food! Is that it!?
Hey! What's that supposed to mean!?
Shut up. You keep quiet!
Hana-chan, are you by chance going out with Oda-kun?
Huh!?
Who would go out with this elementary schooler!?
Keh.
What about you? You're worse than an elementary schooler.
Washboard chest.

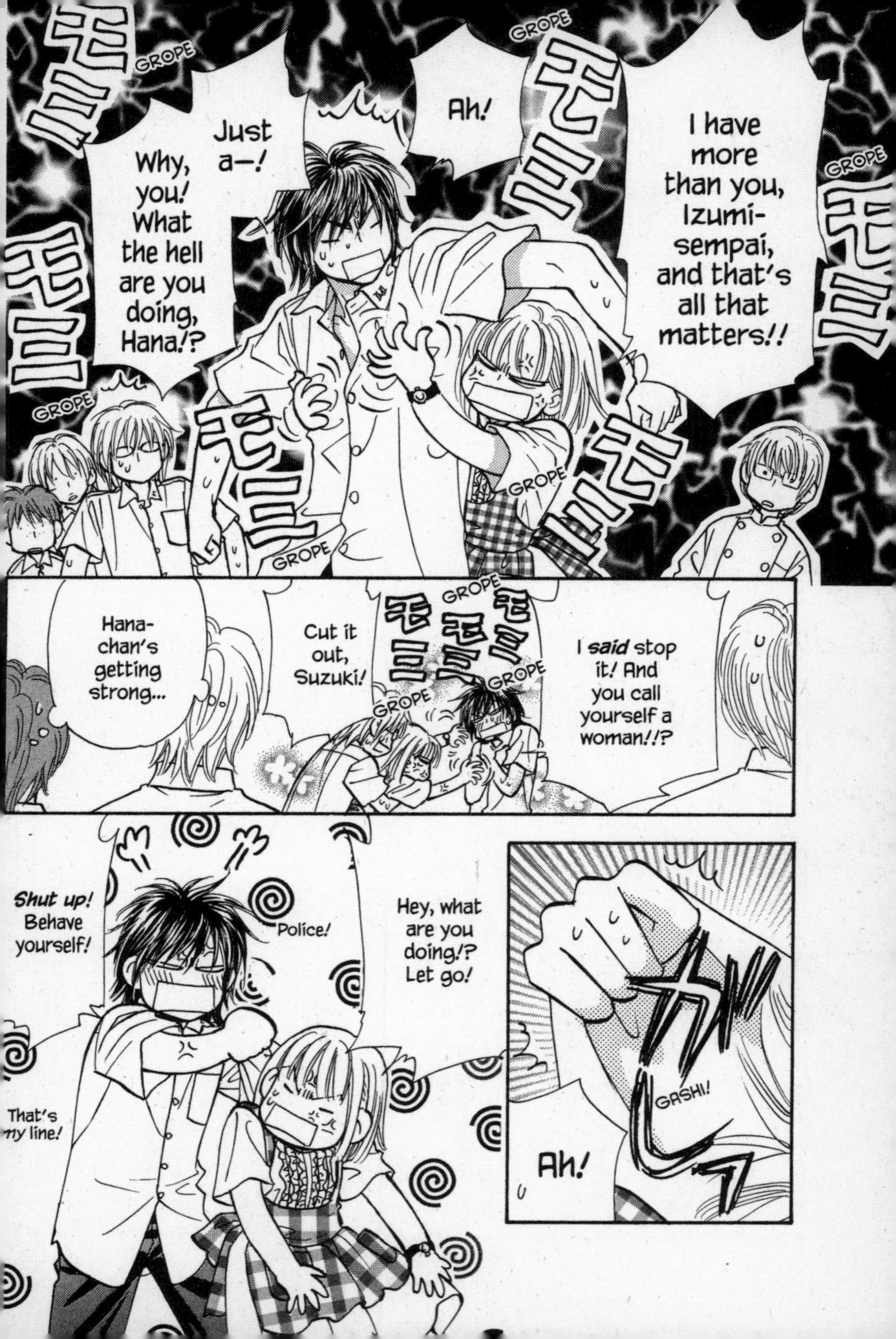
GROPE
モミ
I have more than you, Izumi-sempai, and that's all that matters!!
GROPE
モミ
Ah!
Just a—!
GROPE
モミ
Why, you! What the hell are you doing, Hana!?
モミ
GROPE
GROPE
モミ
GROPE
モミ
GROPE
I *said* stop it! And you call yourself a woman!!?
GROPE
モミモミ
GROPE
GROPE
Cut it out, Suzuki!
Hana-chan's getting strong...
GASHI!
Ah!
Hey, what are you doing!? Let go!
Police!
Shut up! Behave yourself!
That's my line!

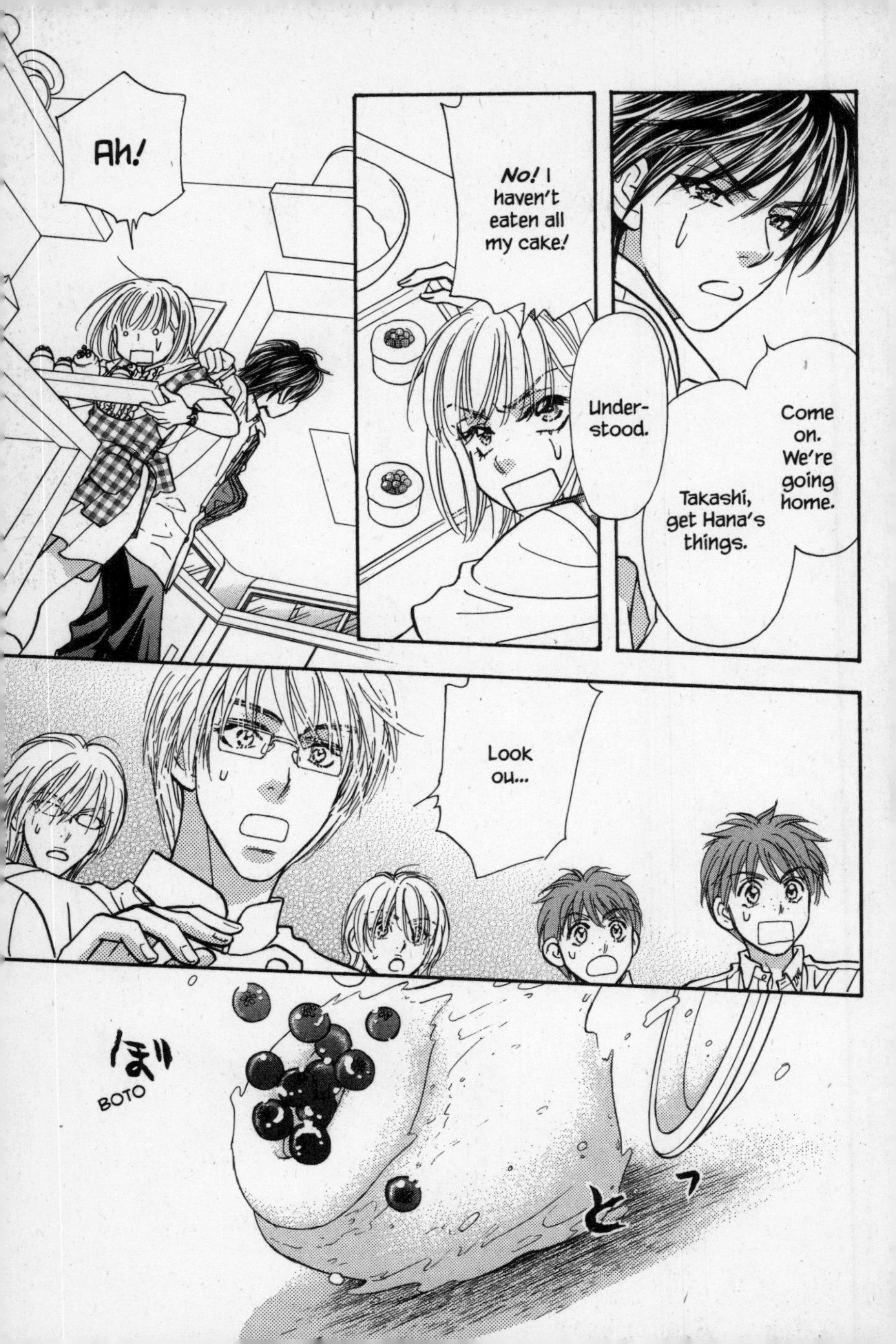

Come on. We're going home.
Takashi, get Hana's things.
Understood.
No! I haven't eaten all my cake!
Ah!
Look ou...
BOTO

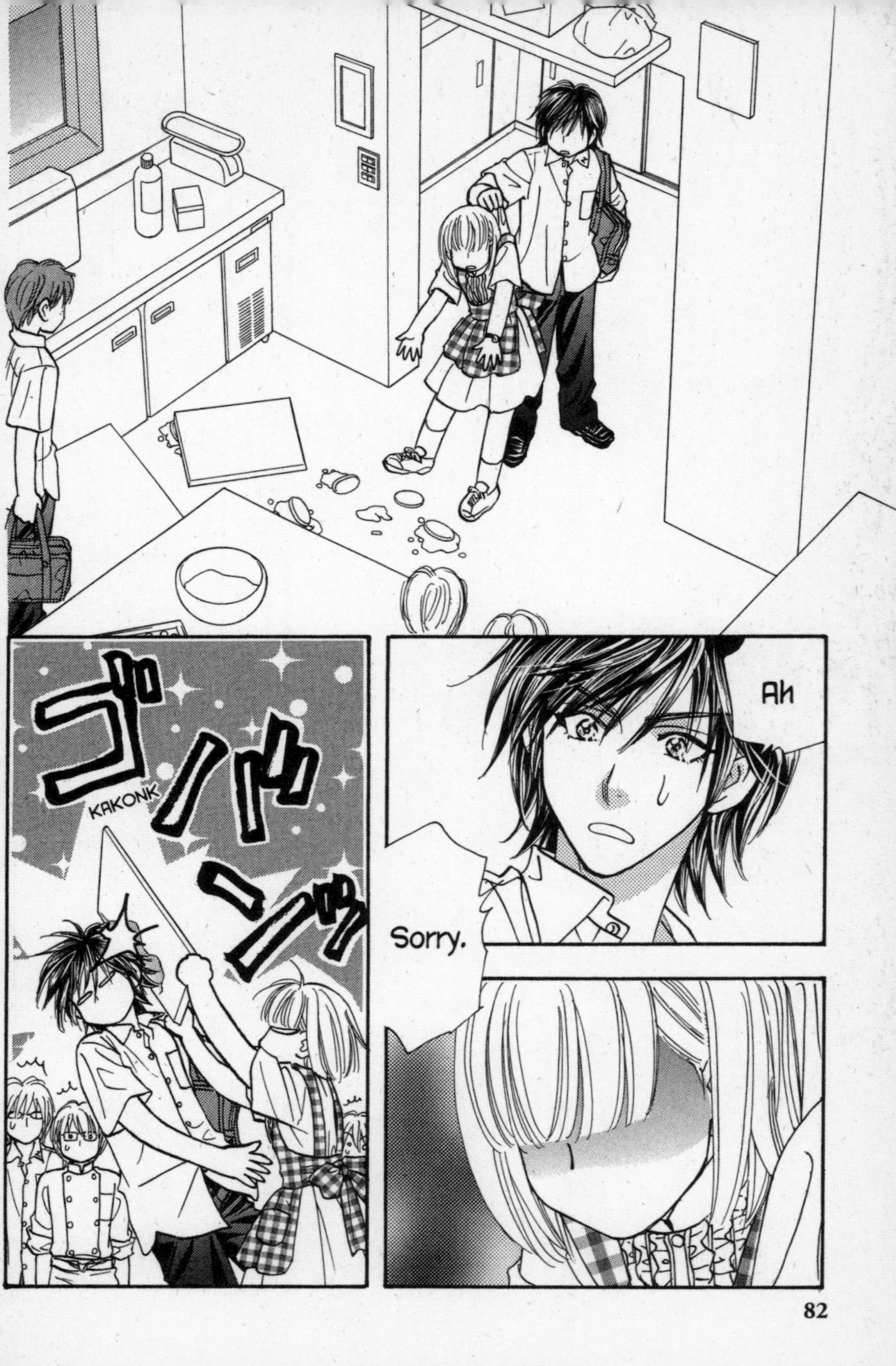
Ah
Sorry.
KAKONK

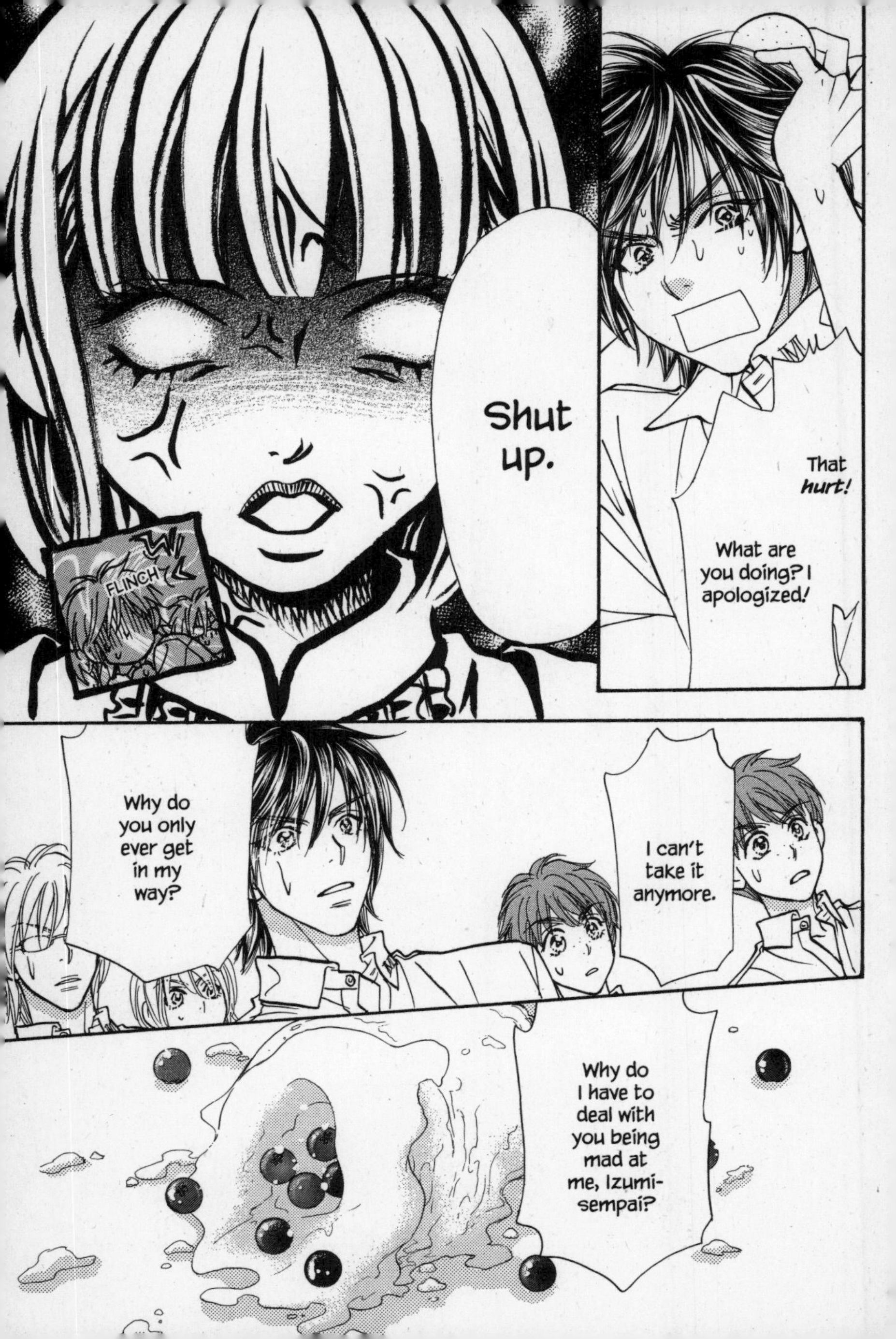
That *hurt!*
What are you doing? I apologized!
Shut up.
FLINCH
I can't take it anymore.
Why do you only ever get in my way?
Why do I have to deal with you being mad at me, Izumi-sempai?

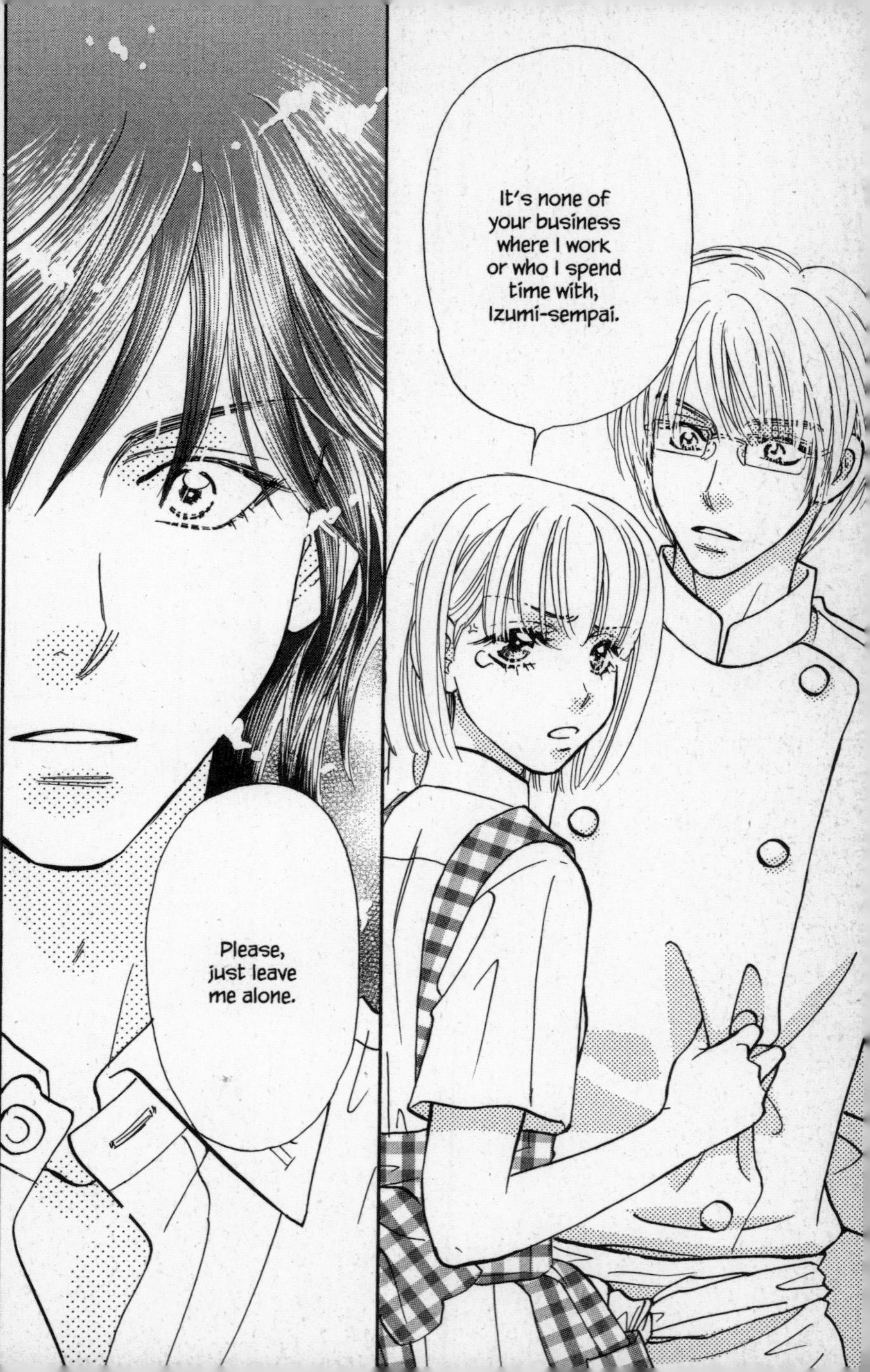
It's none of your business where I work or who I spend time with, Izumi-sempai.
Please, just leave me alone.

My Heavenly
Hockey Club

My Heavenly Hockey Club

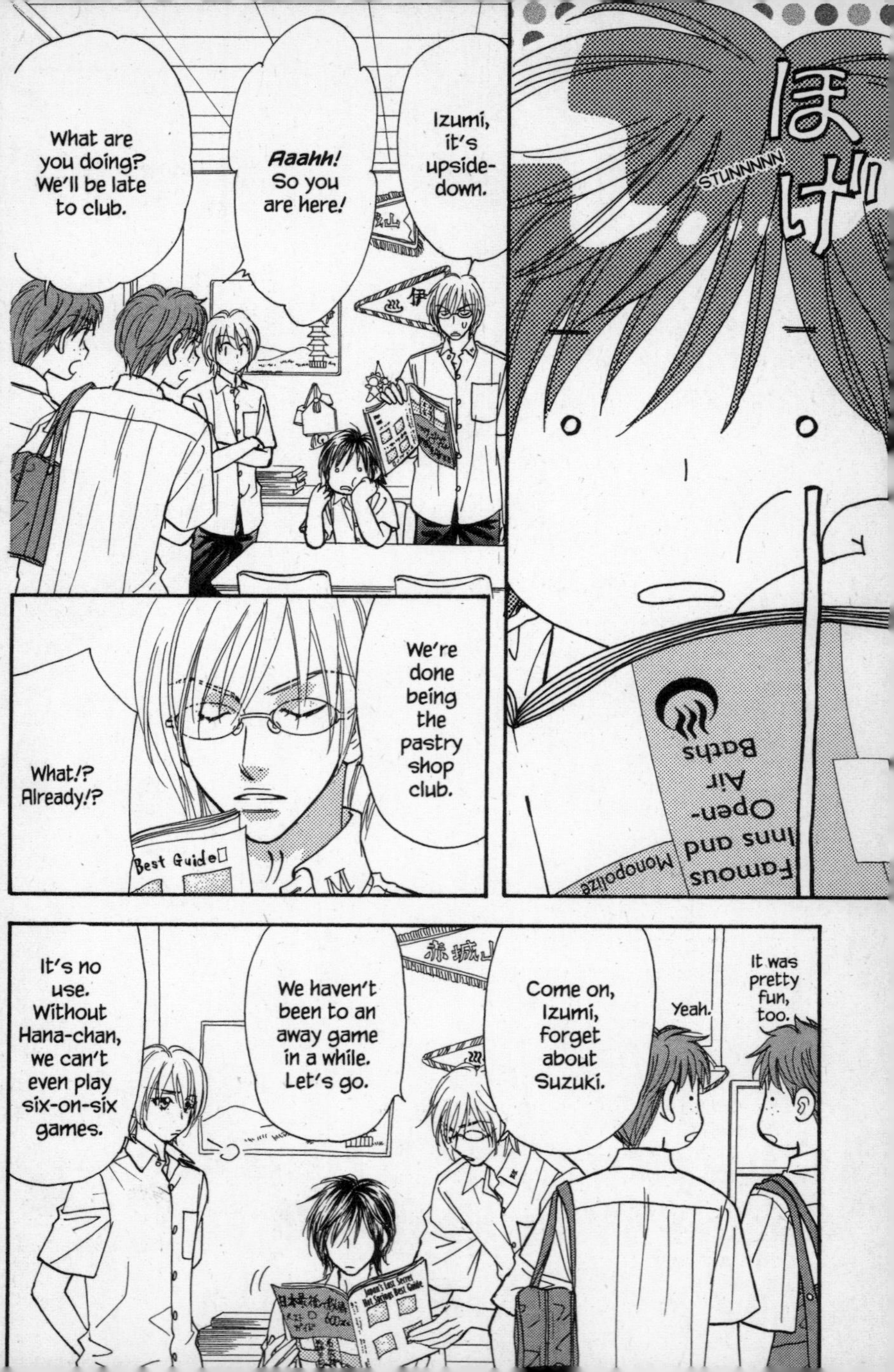
ほげ
STUNNNNN
Famous Inns and Open-Air Baths
Monopolize
Izumi, it's upside-down.
Aaahh! So you are here!
What are you doing? We'll be late to club.
We're done being the pastry shop club.
What!? Already!?
Best Guide
It was pretty fun, too.
Yeah.
Come on, Izumi, forget about Suzuki.
We haven't been to an away game in a while. Let's go.
It's no use. Without Hana-chan, we can't even play six-on-six games.
Japan's Last Secret Hot Springs Best Guide

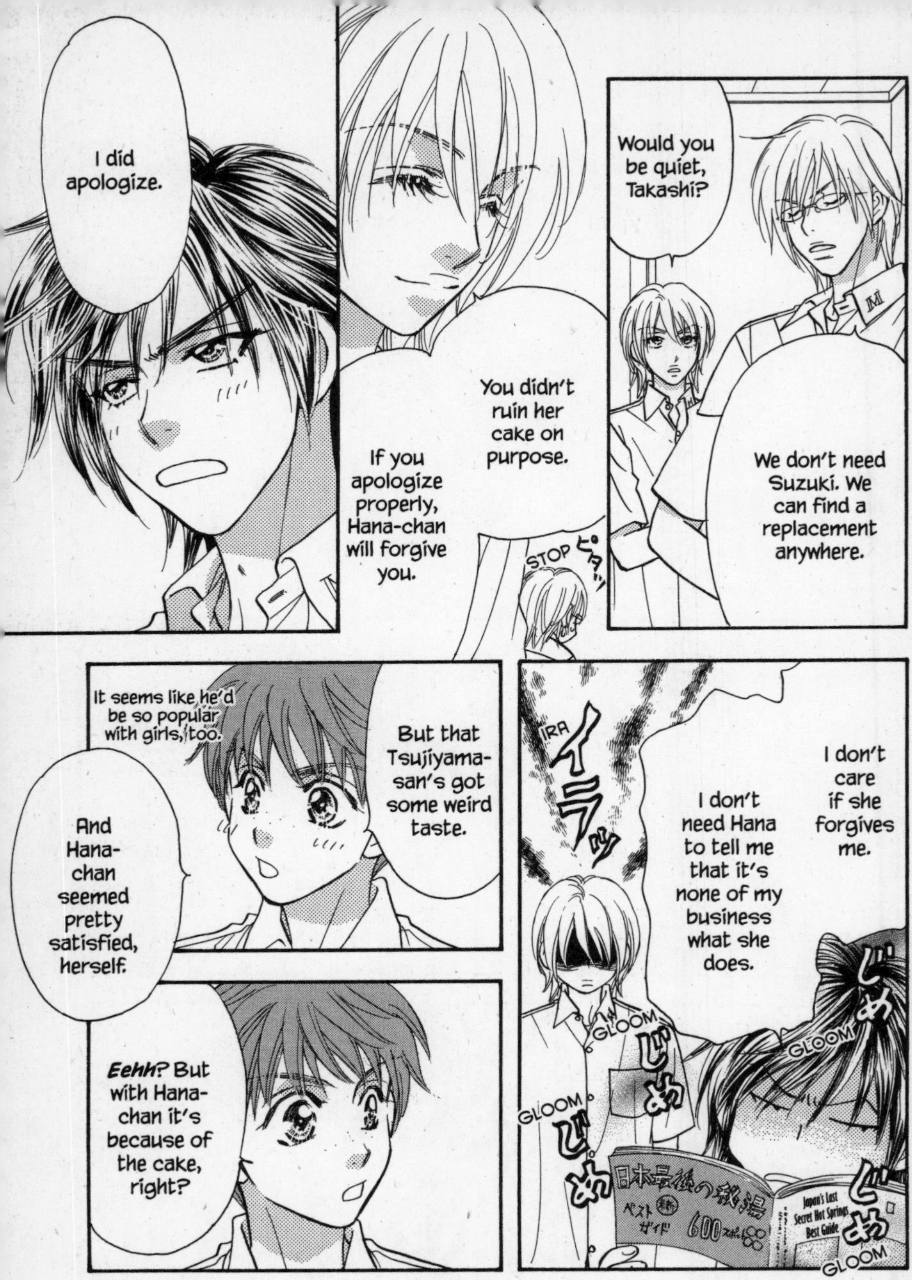
Would you be quiet, Takashi?
We don't need Suzuki. We can find a replacement anywhere.
STOP
You didn't ruin her cake on purpose.
If you apologize properly, Hana-chan will forgive you.
I did apologize.
IRA
I don't care if she forgives me.
I don't need Hana to tell me that it's none of my business what she does.
GLOOM
GLOOM
GLOOM
GLOOM
Japan's Last Secret Hot Springs Best Guide
But that Tsujiyama-san's got some weird taste.
It seems like he'd be so popular with girls, too.
And Hana-chan seemed pretty satisfied, herself.
Eehh? But with Hana-chan it's because of the cake, right?

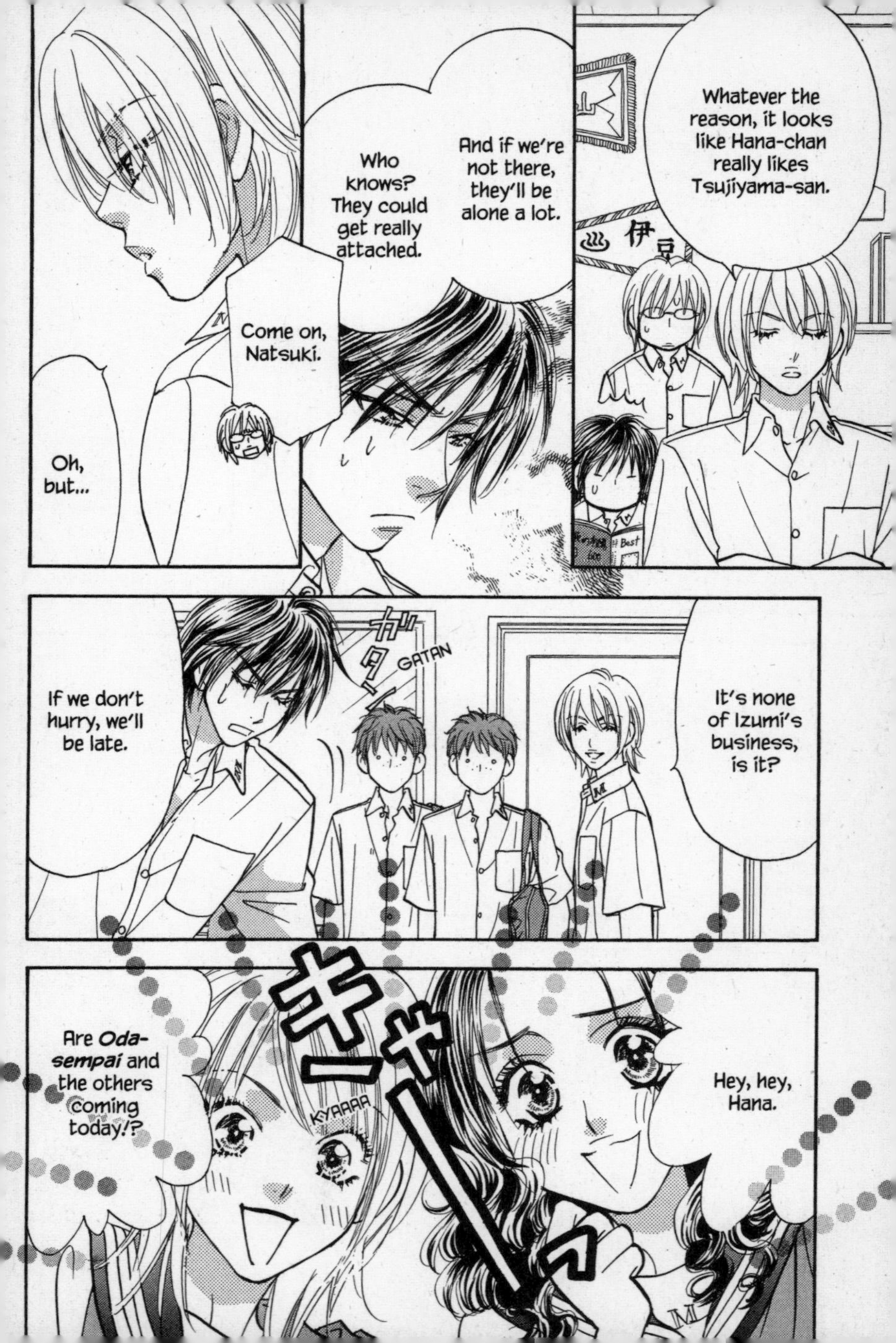
Whatever the reason, it looks like Hana-chan really likes Tsujiyama-san.
And if we're not there, they'll be alone a lot.
Who knows? They could get really attached.
Come on, Natsuki.
Oh, but...
It's none of Izumi's business, is it?
GATAN
If we don't hurry, we'll be late.
Hey, hey, Hana.
KYAAAA
Are *Oda-sempai* and the others coming today!?

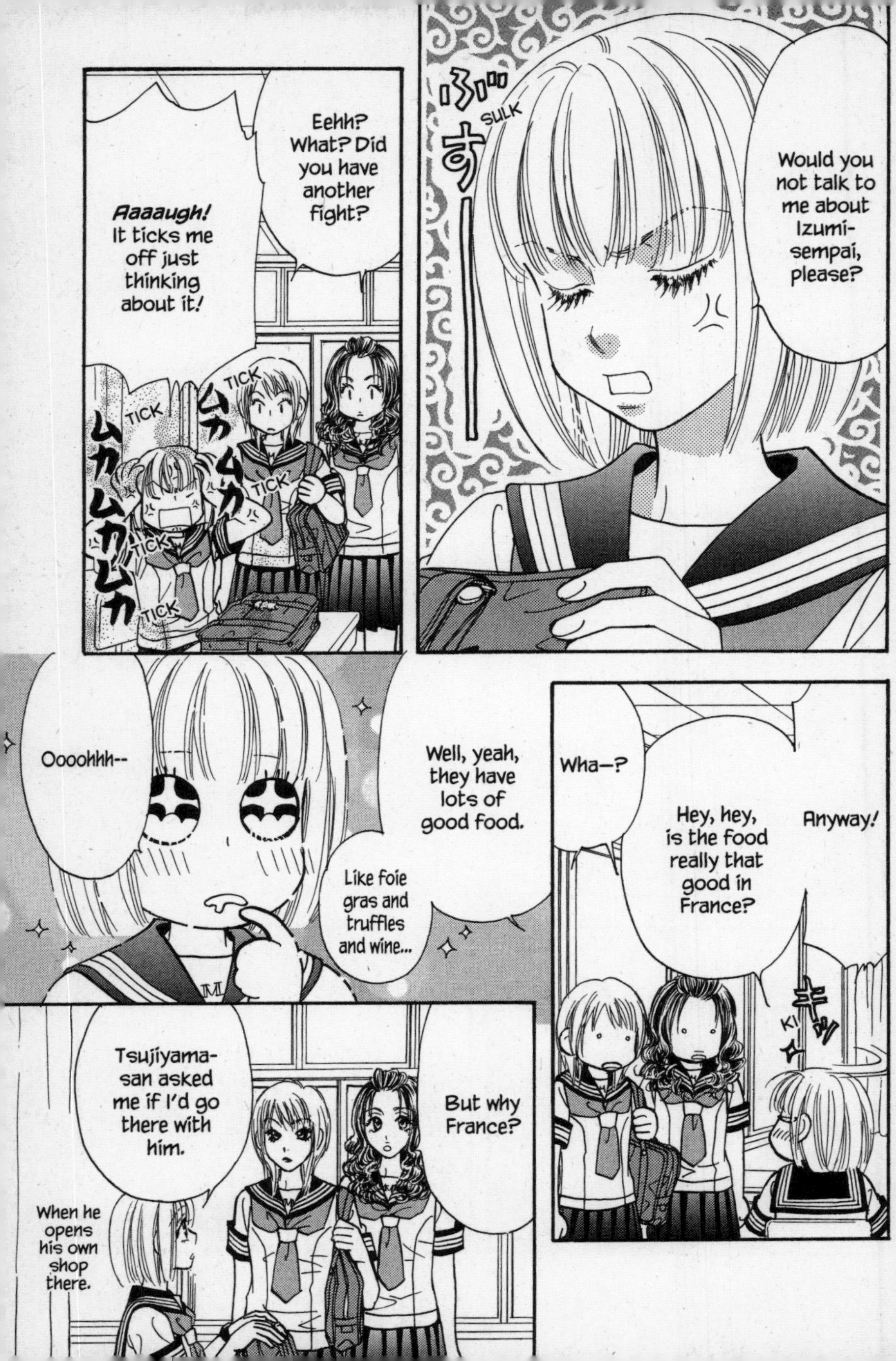
SULK
Would you not talk to me about Izumi-sempai, please?
Eehh? What? Did you have another fight?
Aaaaugh! It ticks me off just thinking about it!
TICK
TICK
TICK
TICK
TICK
Anyway!
Hey, hey, is the food really that good in France?
Wha—?
KI
Well, yeah, they have lots of good food.
Like foie gras and truffles and wine...
Oooohhh--
But why France?
Tsujiyama-san asked me if I'd go there with him.
When he opens his own shop there.

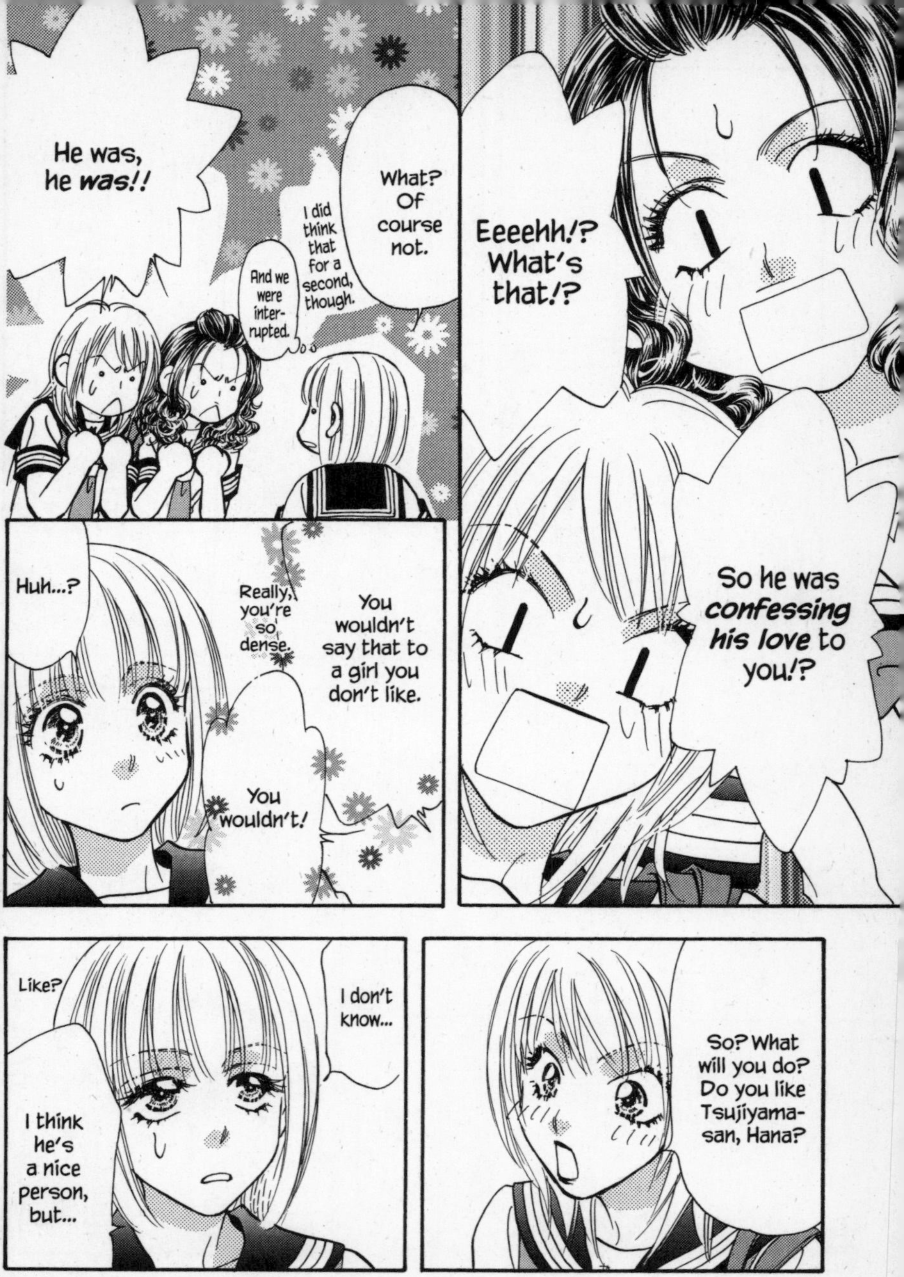
Eeeehh!? What's that!?
So he was *confessing his love* to you!?
What? Of course not.
I did think that for a second, though.
And we were inter-rupted.
He was, he *was*!!
You wouldn't say that to a girl you don't like.
Really, you're so dense.
Huh...?
You wouldn't!
So? What will you do? Do you like Tsujiyama-san, Hana?
I don't know...
Like?
I think he's a nice person, but...

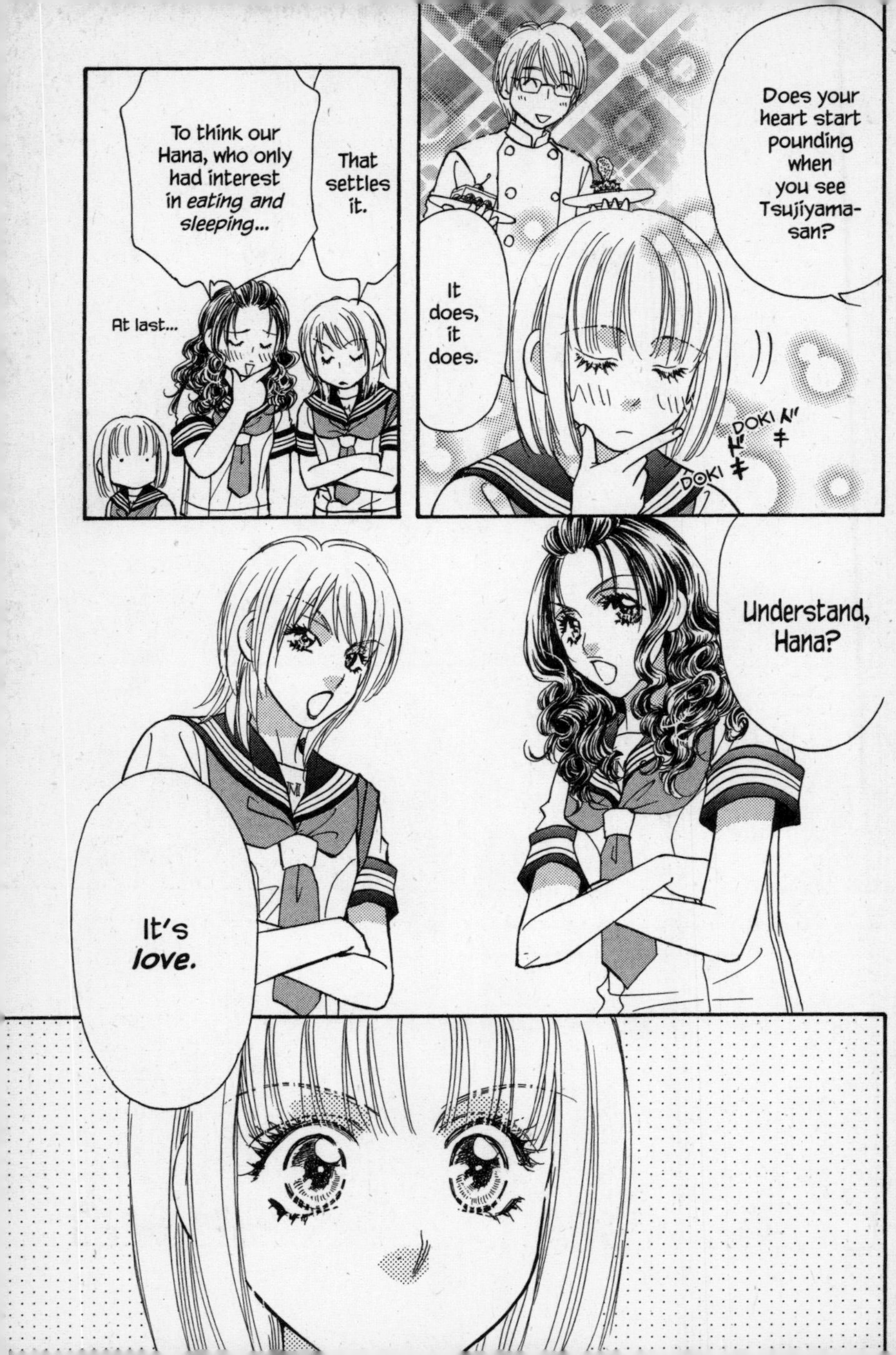
Does your heart start pounding when you see Tsujiyama-san?
It does, it does.
DOKI
DOKI
That settles it.
To think our Hana, who only had interest in eating and sleeping...
At last...
Understand, Hana?
It's love.

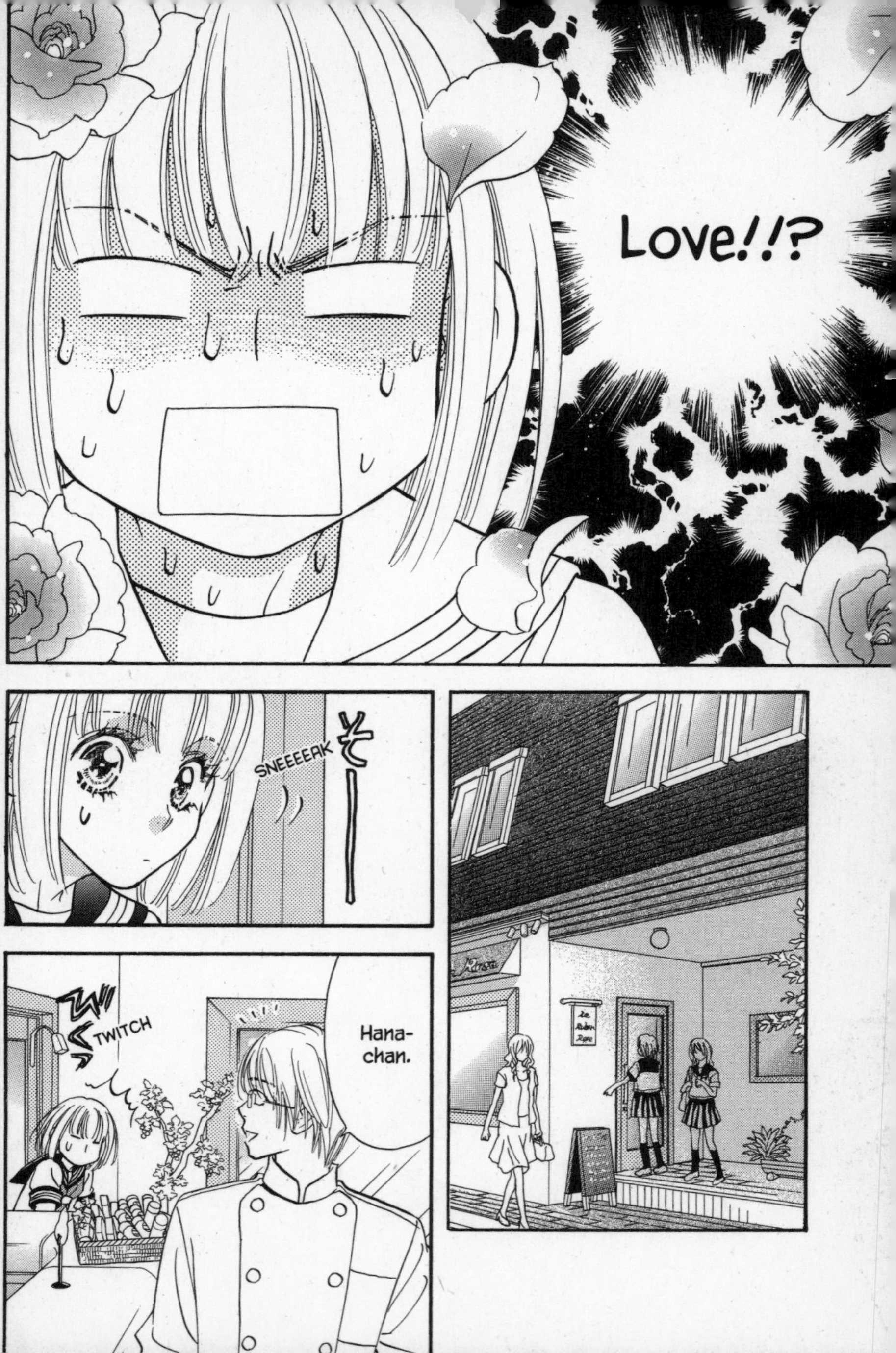
Love!!?
そー
SNEEEEAK
Hana-chan.
TWITCH

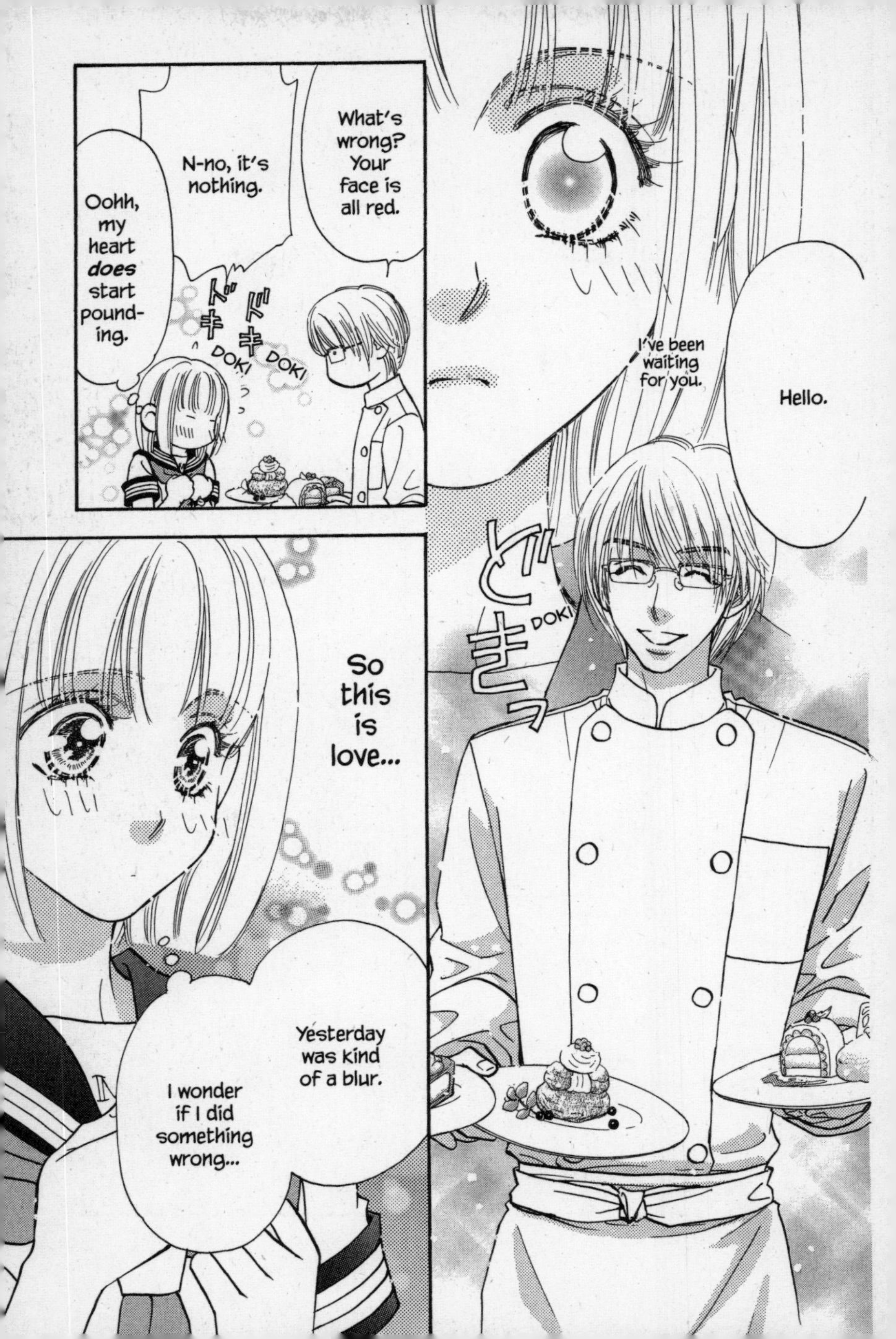
Hello.
I've been waiting for you.
どきっ
DOKI
What's wrong? Your face is all red.
N-no, it's nothing.
Oohh, my heart **does** start pounding.
ドキドキ
DOKI DOKI
So this is love...
Yesterday was kind of a blur.
I wonder if I did something wrong...

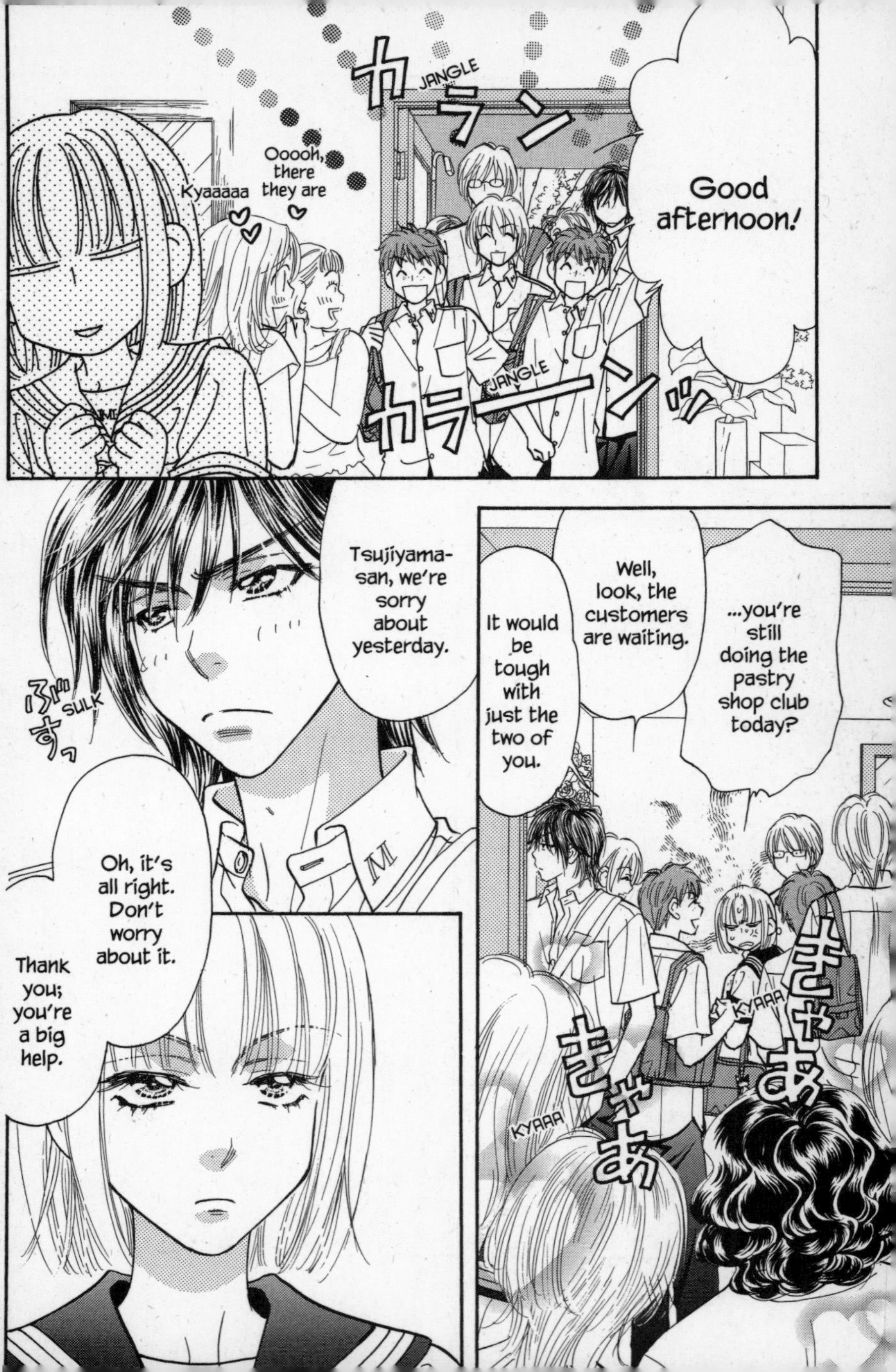
Good afternoon!
カラン
JANGLE
Ooooh, there they are
Kyaaaaa
カラーン
JANGLE
...you're still doing the pastry shop club today?
Well, look, the customers are waiting.
It would be tough with just the two of you.
きゃあ
KYAAA
きゃあ
KYAAA
Tsujiyama-san, we're sorry about yesterday.
ぶすっ
SULK
Oh, it's all right. Don't worry about it.
Thank you; you're a big help.

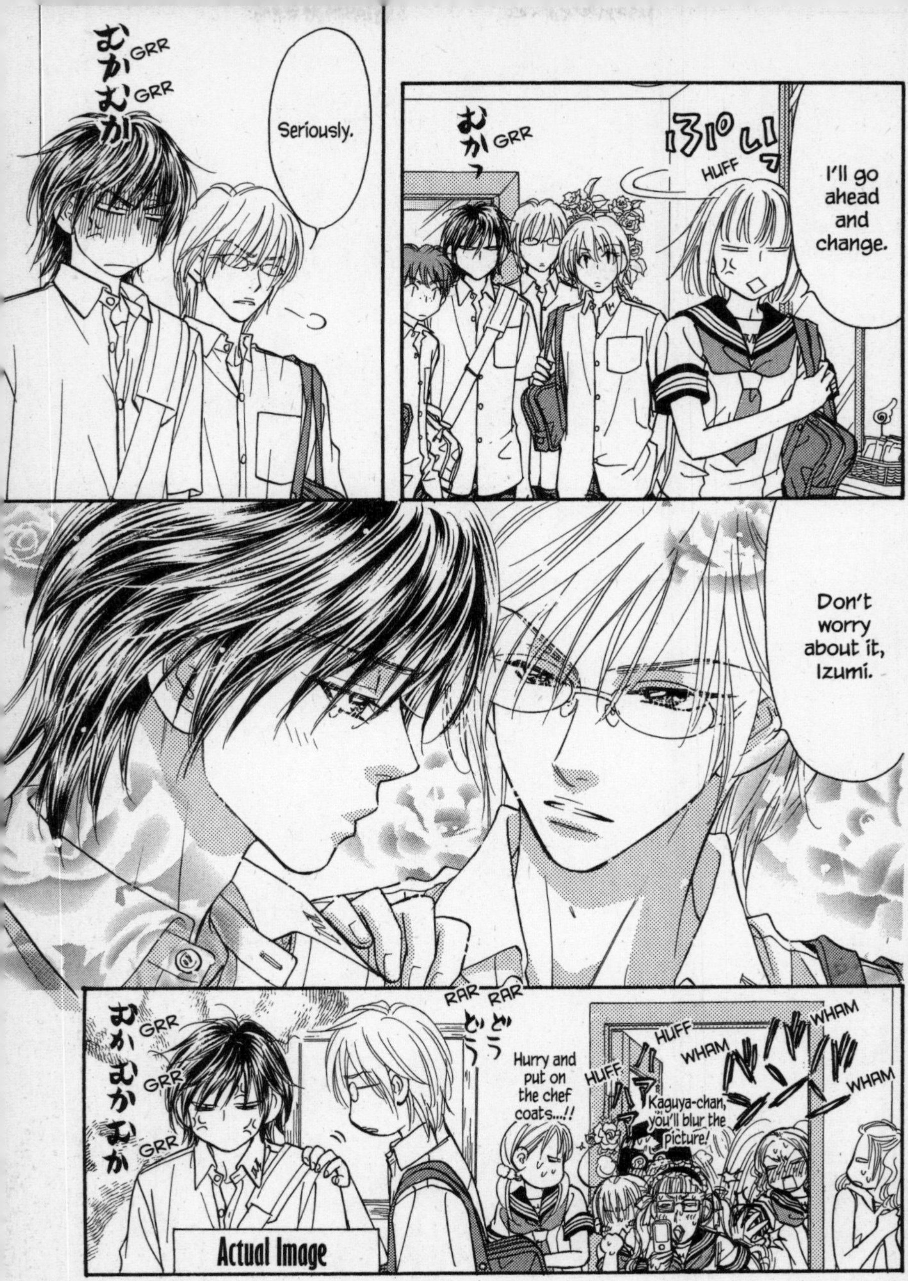
I'll go ahead and change.
HUFF
むかっ GRR
Seriously.
むかむか GRR GRR
Don't worry about it, Izumi.
WHAM
WHAM
WHAM
Kaguya-chan, you'll blur the picture!
HUFF HUFF
Hurry and put on the chef coats...!!
どうどう RAR RAR
むかむかむか GRR GRR GRR
Actual Image

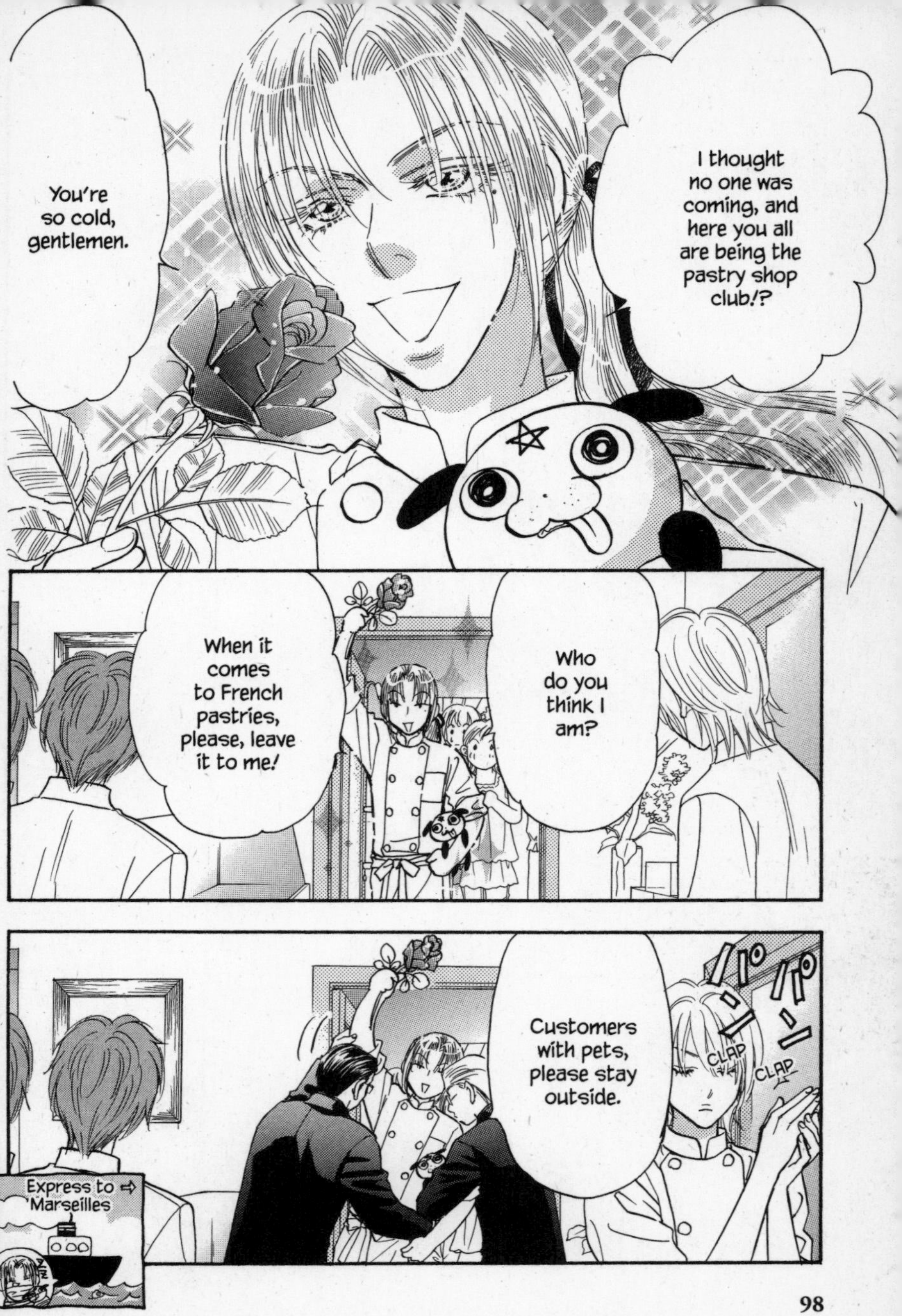
I thought no one was coming, and here you all are being the pastry shop club!?
You're so cold, gentlemen.
Who do you think I am?
When it comes to French pastries, please, leave it to me!
CLAP
CLAP
Customers with pets, please stay outside.
Express to Marseilles

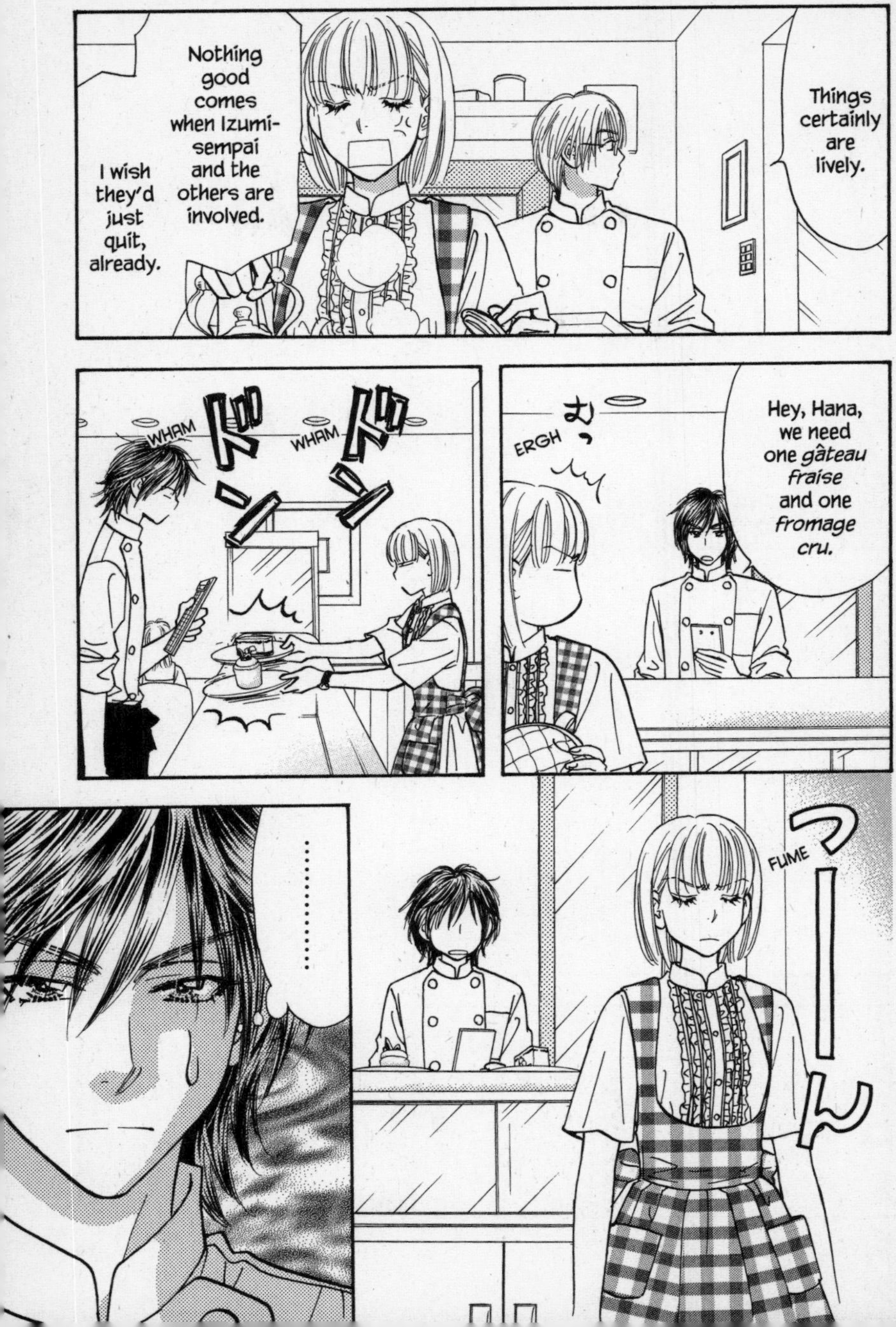
Things certainly are lively.
Nothing good comes when Izumi-sempai and the others are involved.
I wish they'd just quit, already.
Hey, Hana, we need one *gâteau fraise* and one *fromage cru.*
ERGH
WHAM
WHAM
FUME
......

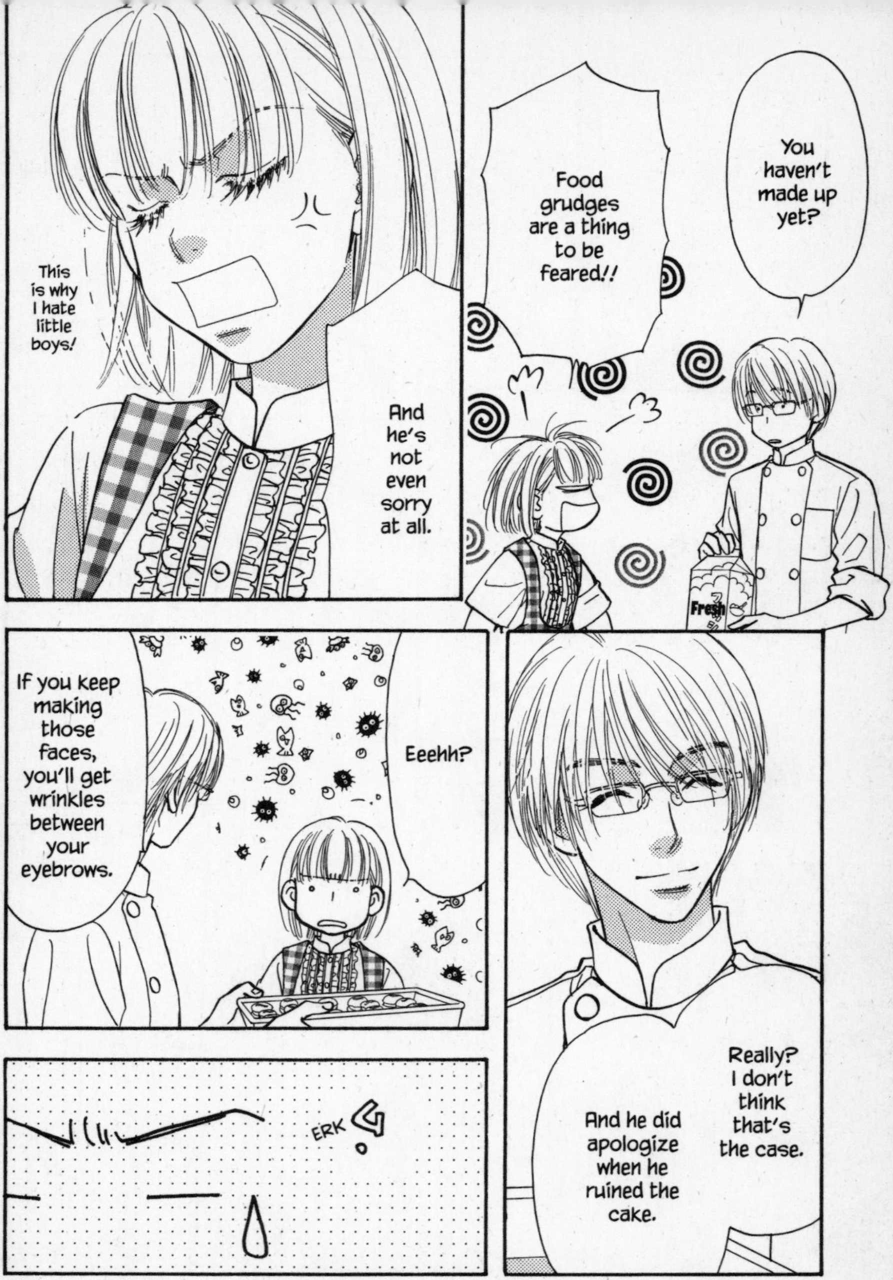
You haven't made up yet?
Food grudges are a thing to be feared!!
And he's not even sorry at all.
This is why I hate little boys!
Really? I don't think that's the case.
And he did apologize when he ruined the cake.
Eeehh?
If you keep making those faces, you'll get wrinkles between your eyebrows.
ERK

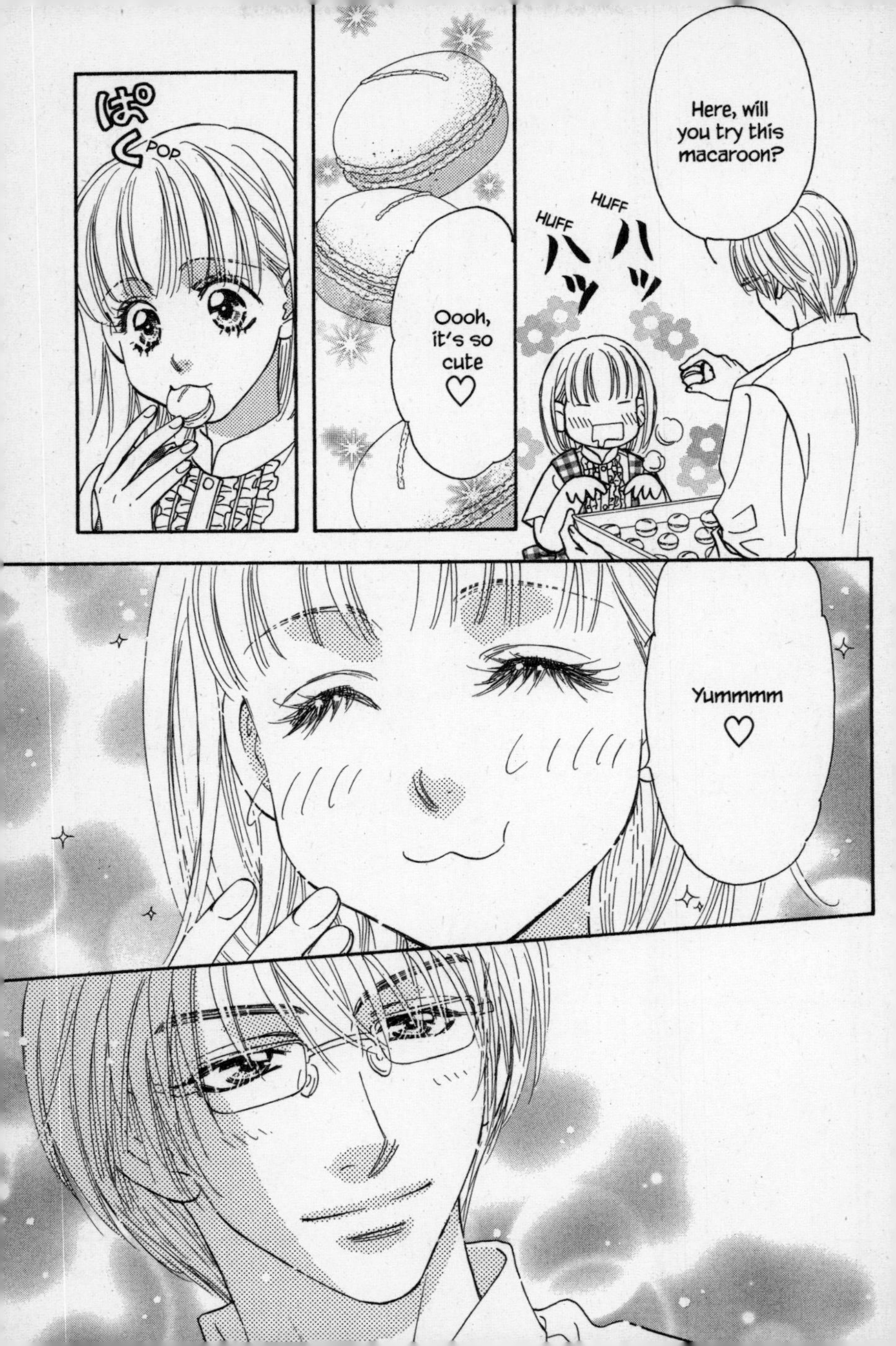
Here, will you try this macaroon?
HUFF HUFF
ハッ ハッ
Oooh, it's so cute ♡
ぱく
POP
Yummmm ♡

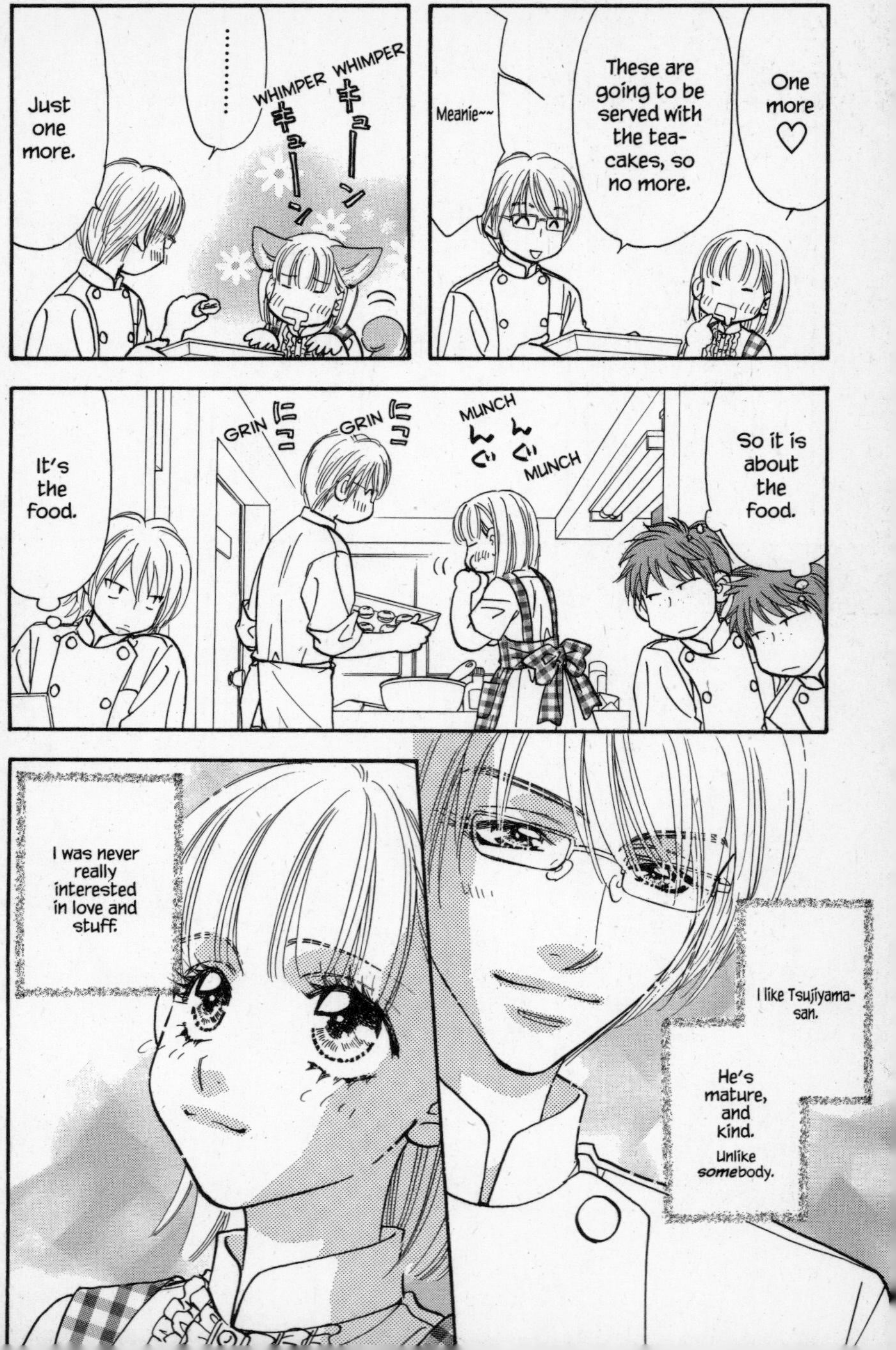
One more ♡
These are going to be served with the tea-cakes, so no more.
Meanie~~
WHIMPER キューン
WHIMPER キューン
……
Just one more.
So it is about the food.
MUNCH んぐ
MUNCH んぐ
GRIN ニコ
GRIN ニコ
It's the food.
I was never really interested in love and stuff.
I like Tsujiyama-san.
He's mature, and kind.
Unlike *some*body.

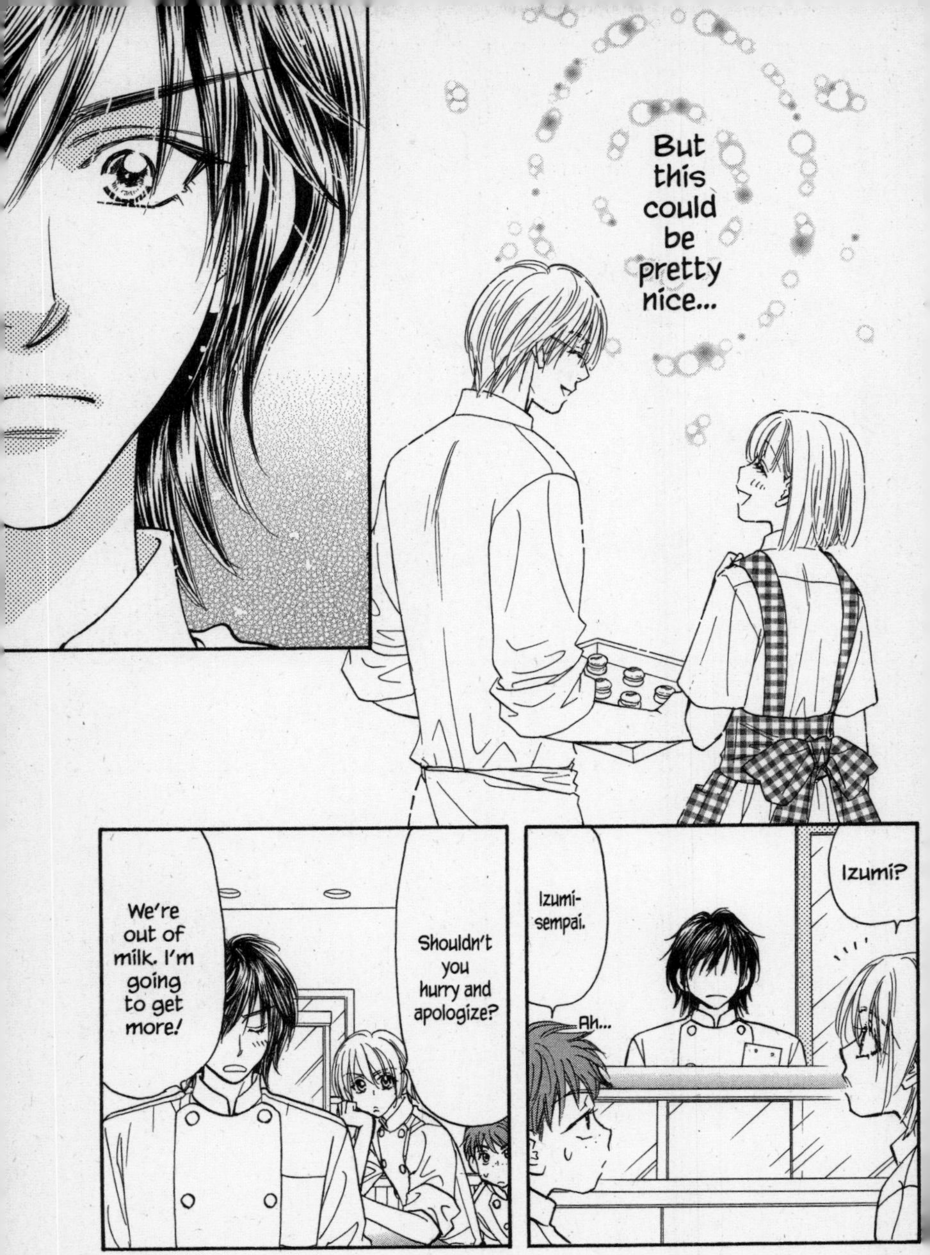
But this could be pretty nice...
Izumi?
Izumi-sempai.
Ah...
Shouldn't you hurry and apologize?
We're out of milk. I'm going to get more!

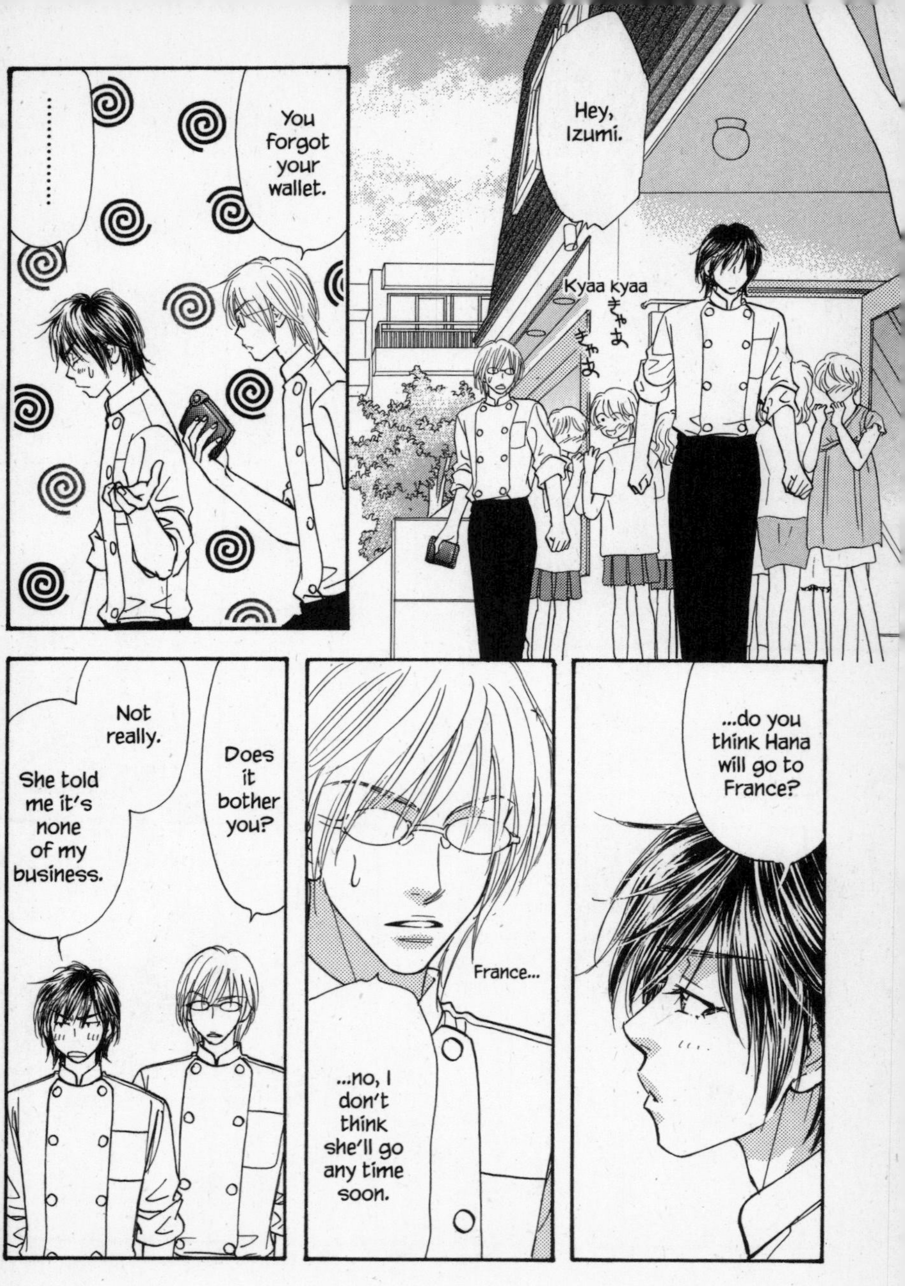
Hey, Izumi.
Kyaa kyaa
きゃあ
きゃあ
You forgot your wallet.
……
...do you think Hana will go to France?
France...
...no, I don't think she'll go any time soon.
Does it bother you?
Not really.
She told me it's none of my business.

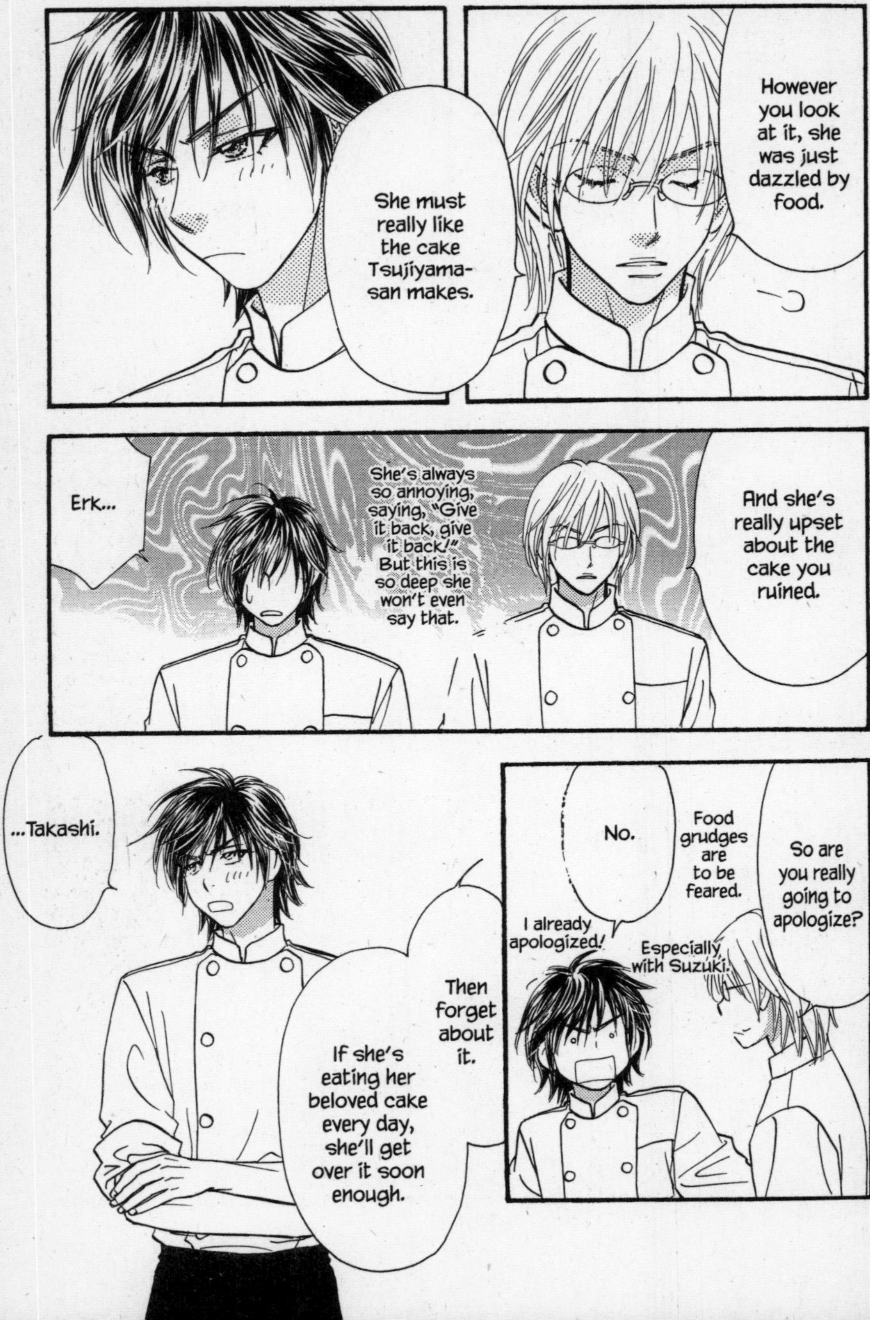

However you look at it, she was just dazzled by food.
She must really like the cake Tsujiyama-san makes.
And she's really upset about the cake you ruined.
She's always so annoying, saying, "Give it back, give it back!" But this is so deep she won't even say that.
Erk...
So are you really going to apologize?
Food grudges are to be feared.
No.
Especially with Suzuki.
I already apologized!
...Takashi.
Then forget about it.
If she's eating her beloved cake every day, she'll get over it soon enough.

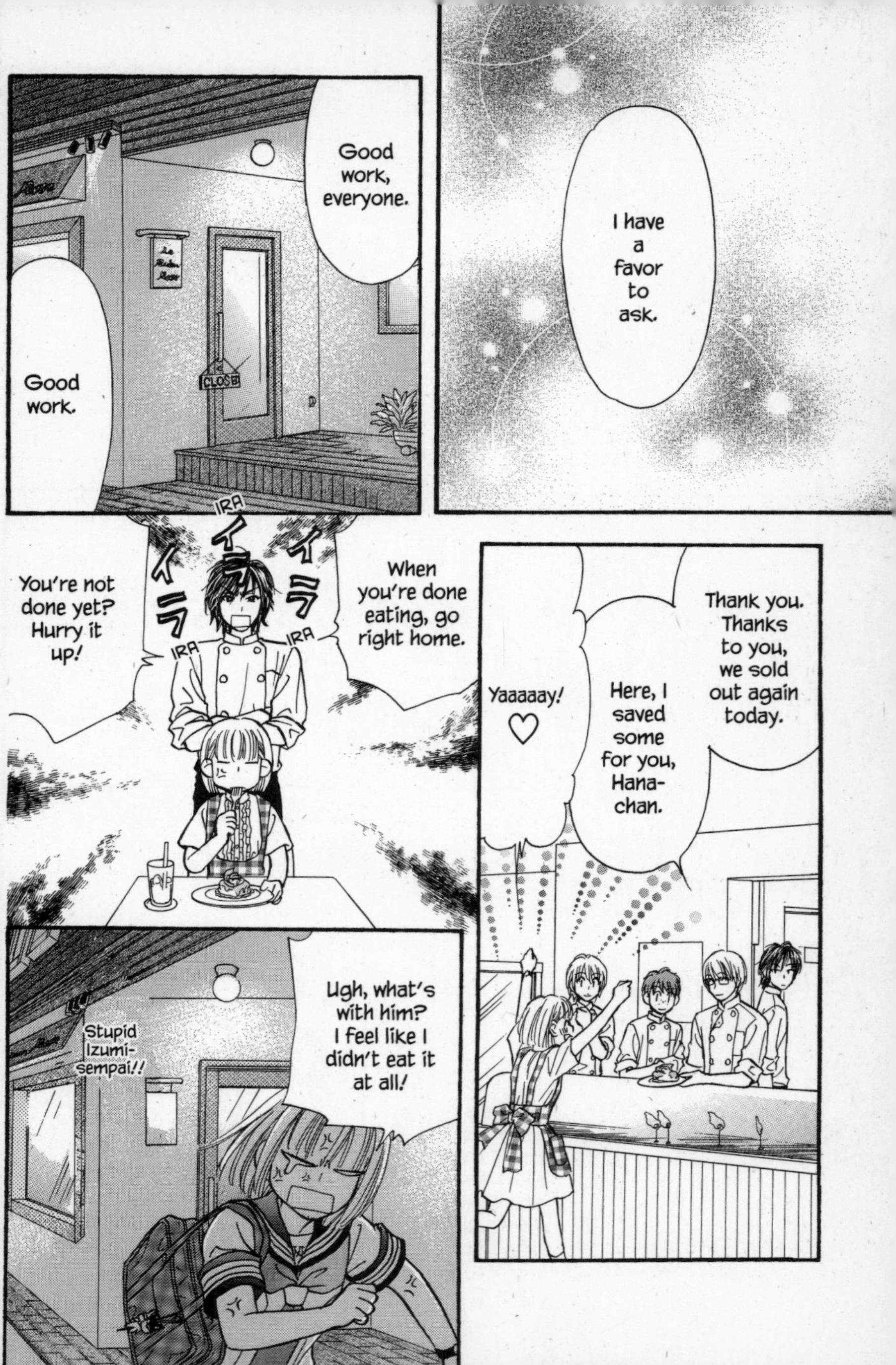
I have a favor to ask.
Good work, everyone.
Good work.
Thank you. Thanks to you, we sold out again today.
Here, I saved some for you, Hana-chan.
Yaaaaay! ♡
When you're done eating, go right home.
IRA IRA IRA IRA
You're not done yet? Hurry it up!
Ugh, what's with him? I feel like I didn't eat it at all!
Stupid Izumi-sempai!!

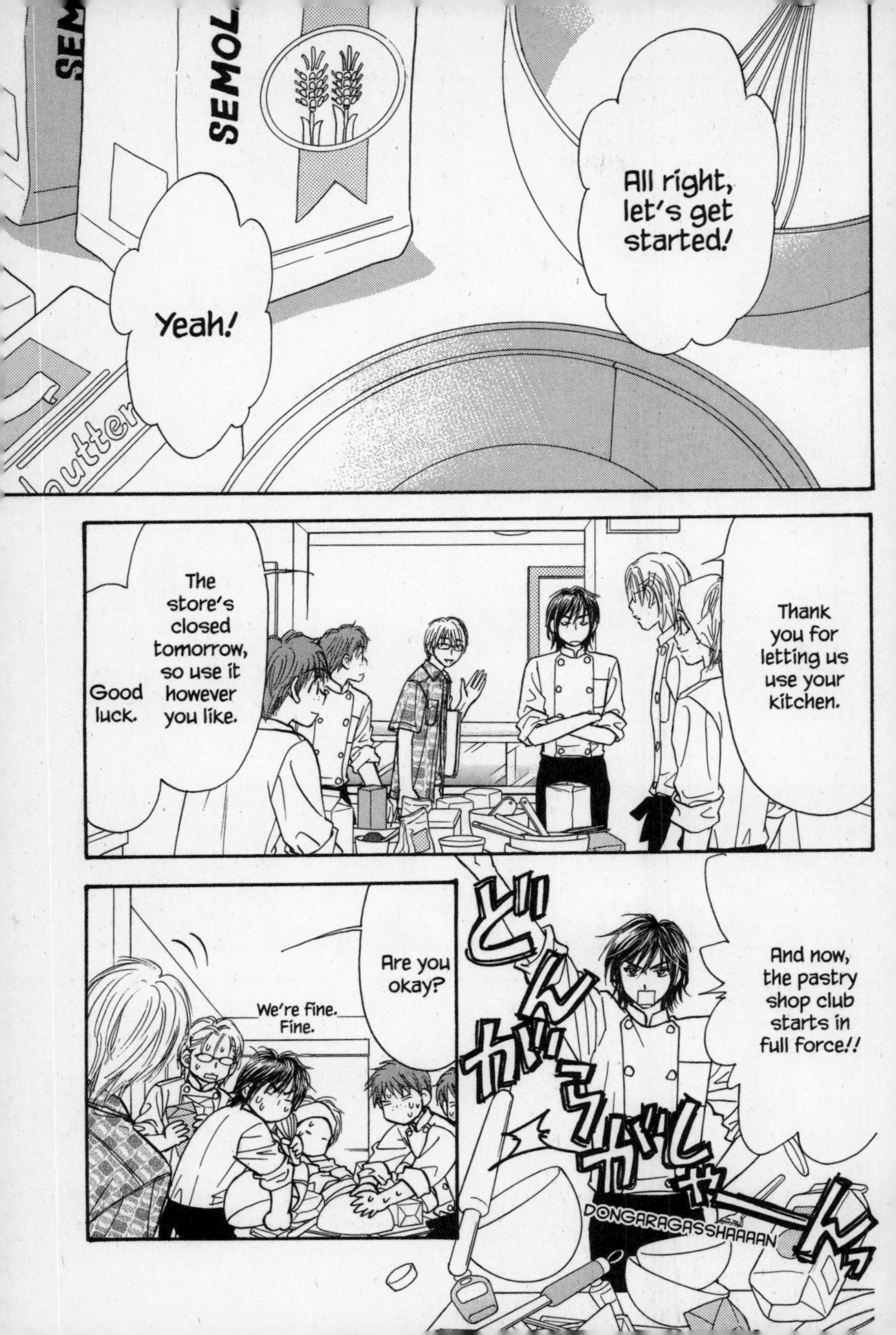
All right, let's get started!
Yeah!
SEMOL
SEM
butter
Thank you for letting us use your kitchen.
The store's closed tomorrow, so use it however you like.
Good luck.
And now, the pastry shop club starts in full force!!
どんがらがしゃーん
DONGARAGASSHAAAAN
Are you okay?
We're fine. Fine.

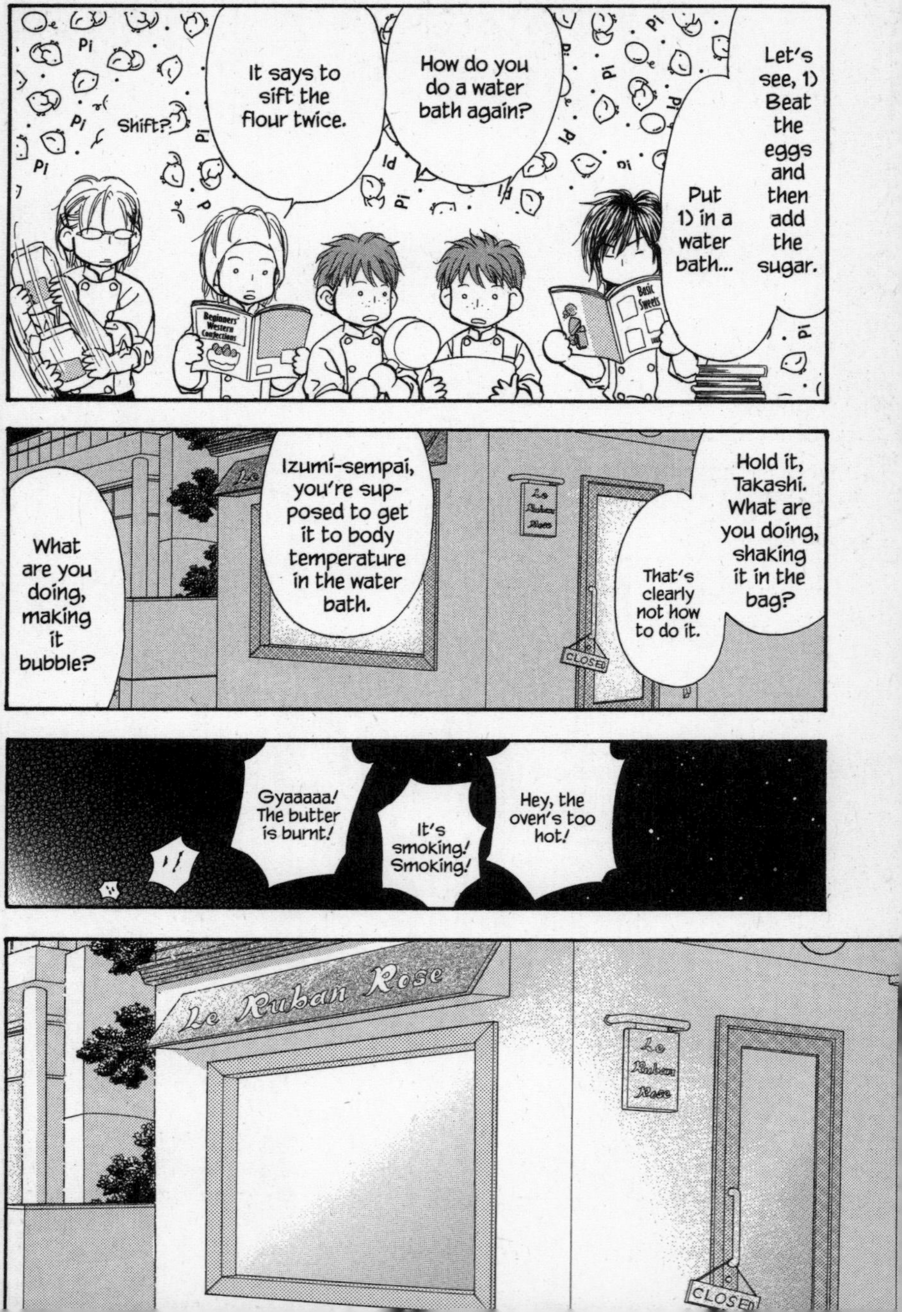
Let's see, 1) Beat the eggs and then add the sugar.
Put 1) in a water bath...
Basic Sweets
How do you do a water bath again?
It says to sift the flour twice.
Beginners' Western Confections
Shift?
Pi
Hold it, Takashi. What are you doing, shaking it in the bag?
That's clearly not how to do it.
CLOSE
Izumi-sempai, you're supposed to get it to body temperature in the water bath.
What are you doing, making it bubble?
Hey, the oven's too hot!
It's smoking! Smoking!
Gyaaaaa! The butter is burnt!
Le Ruban Rose
Le Ruban Rose
CLOSE

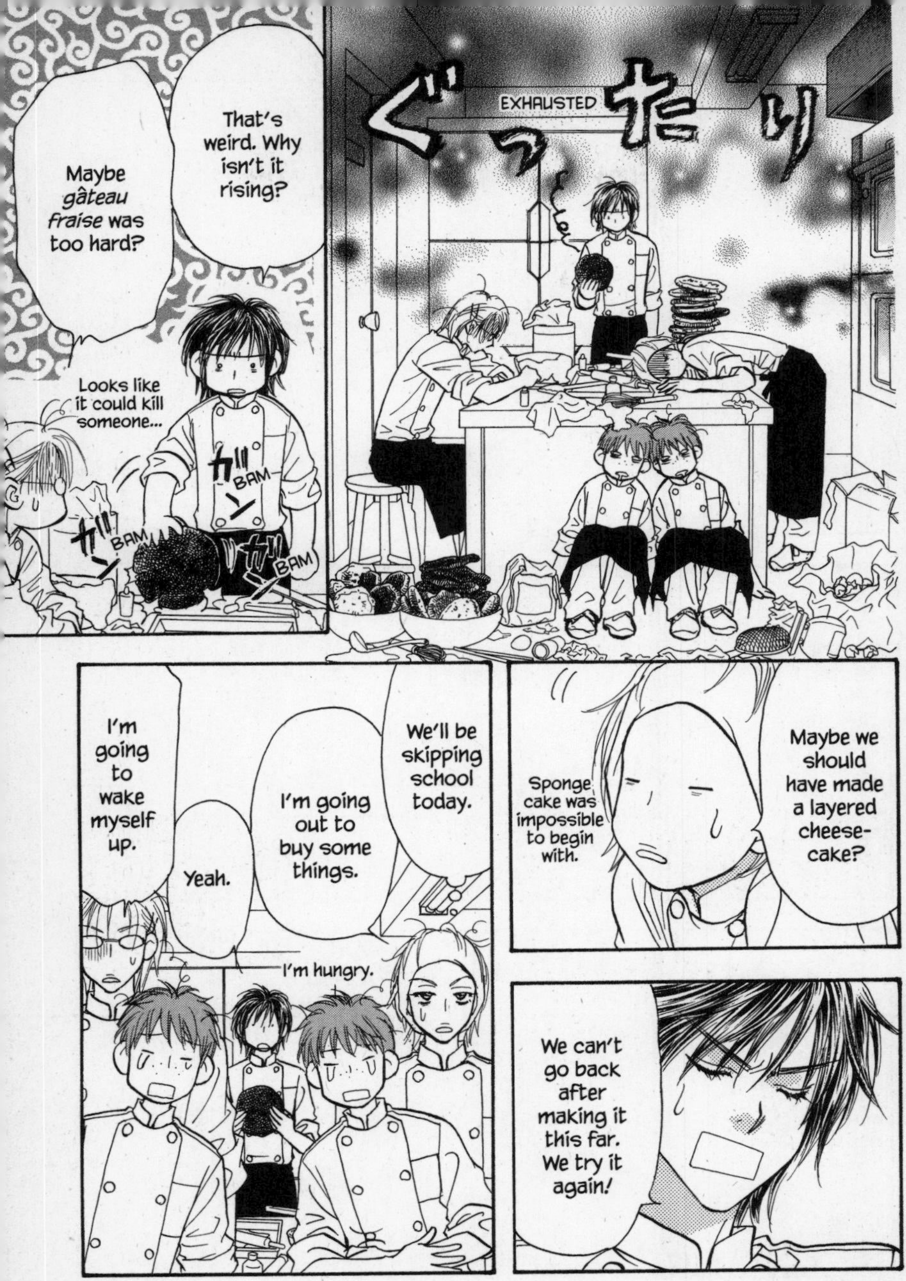
ぐったり
EXHAUSTED
That's weird. Why isn't it rising?
Maybe gâteau fraise was too hard?
Looks like it could kill someone...
BAM
BAM
BAM
Maybe we should have made a layered cheese-cake?
Sponge cake was impossible to begin with.
We can't go back after making it this far. We try it again!
We'll be skipping school today.
I'm going out to buy some things.
Yeah.
I'm going to wake myself up.
I'm hungry.

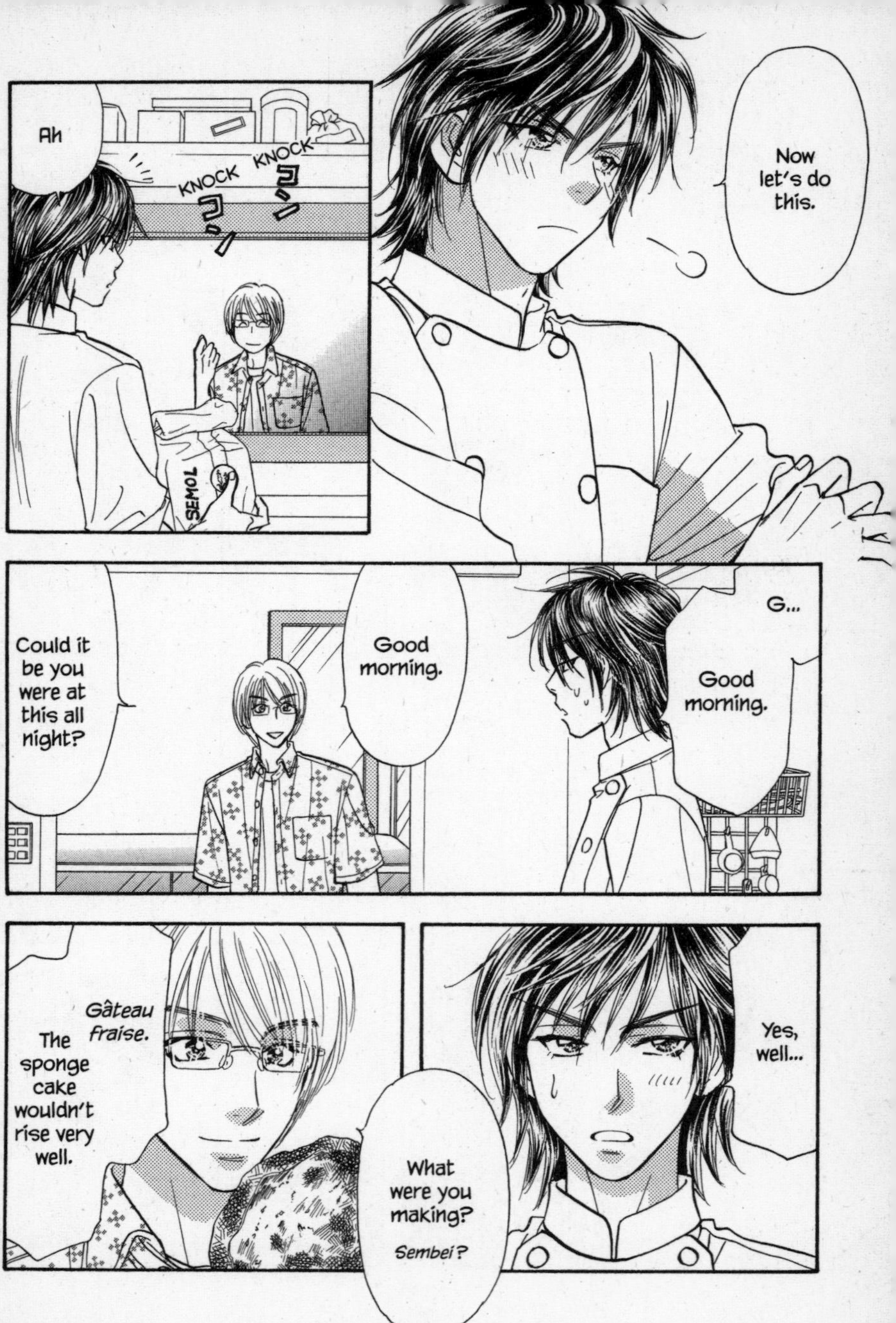
Now let's do this.
Ah
KNOCK
KNOCK
SEMOL
G...
Good morning.
Good morning.
Could it be you were at this all night?
Yes, well...
What were you making?
Sembei?
Gâteau fraise.
The sponge cake wouldn't rise very well.

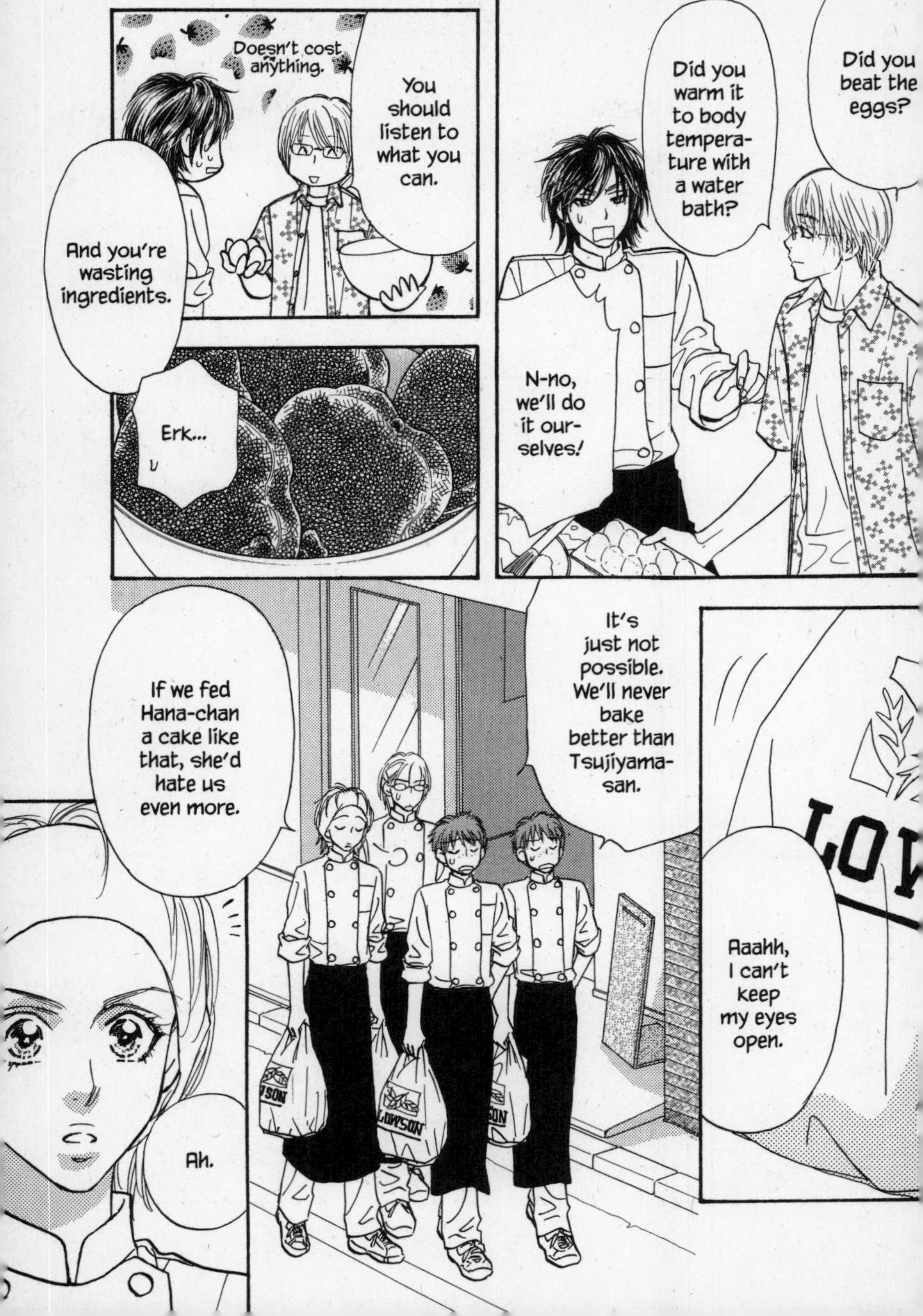
Did you beat the eggs?
Did you warm it to body temperature with a water bath?
N-no, we'll do it ourselves!
You should listen to what you can.
Doesn't cost anything.
And you're wasting ingredients.
Erk...
Aaahh, I can't keep my eyes open.
It's just not possible. We'll never bake better than Tsujiyama-san.
If we fed Hana-chan a cake like that, she'd hate us even more.
Ah.

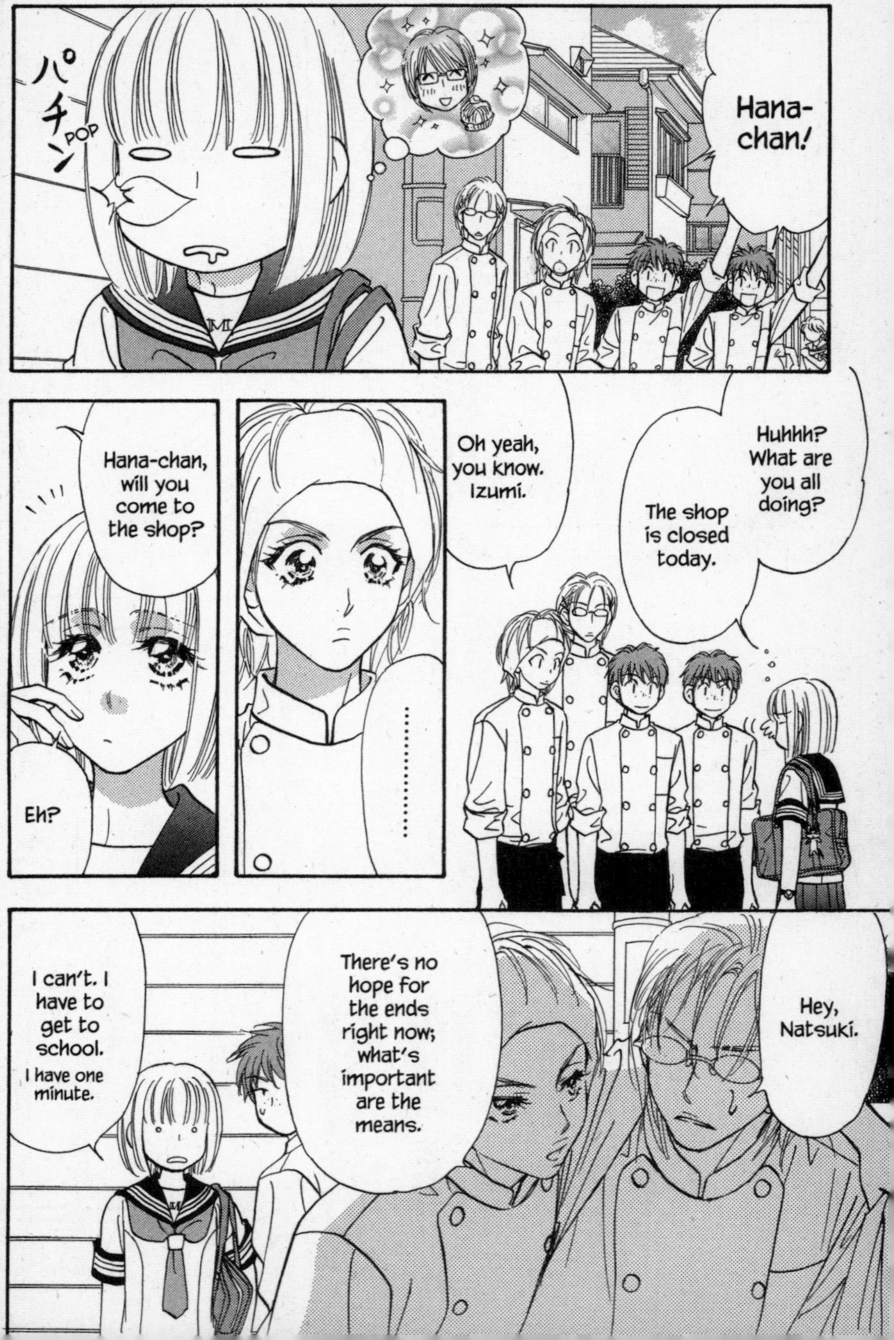
Hana-chan!
パチン
POP
Huhhh? What are you all doing?
The shop is closed today.
Oh yeah, you know. Izumi.
....
Hana-chan, will you come to the shop?
Eh?
Hey, Natsuki.
There's no hope for the ends right now; what's important are the means.
I can't. I have to get to school.
I have one minute.

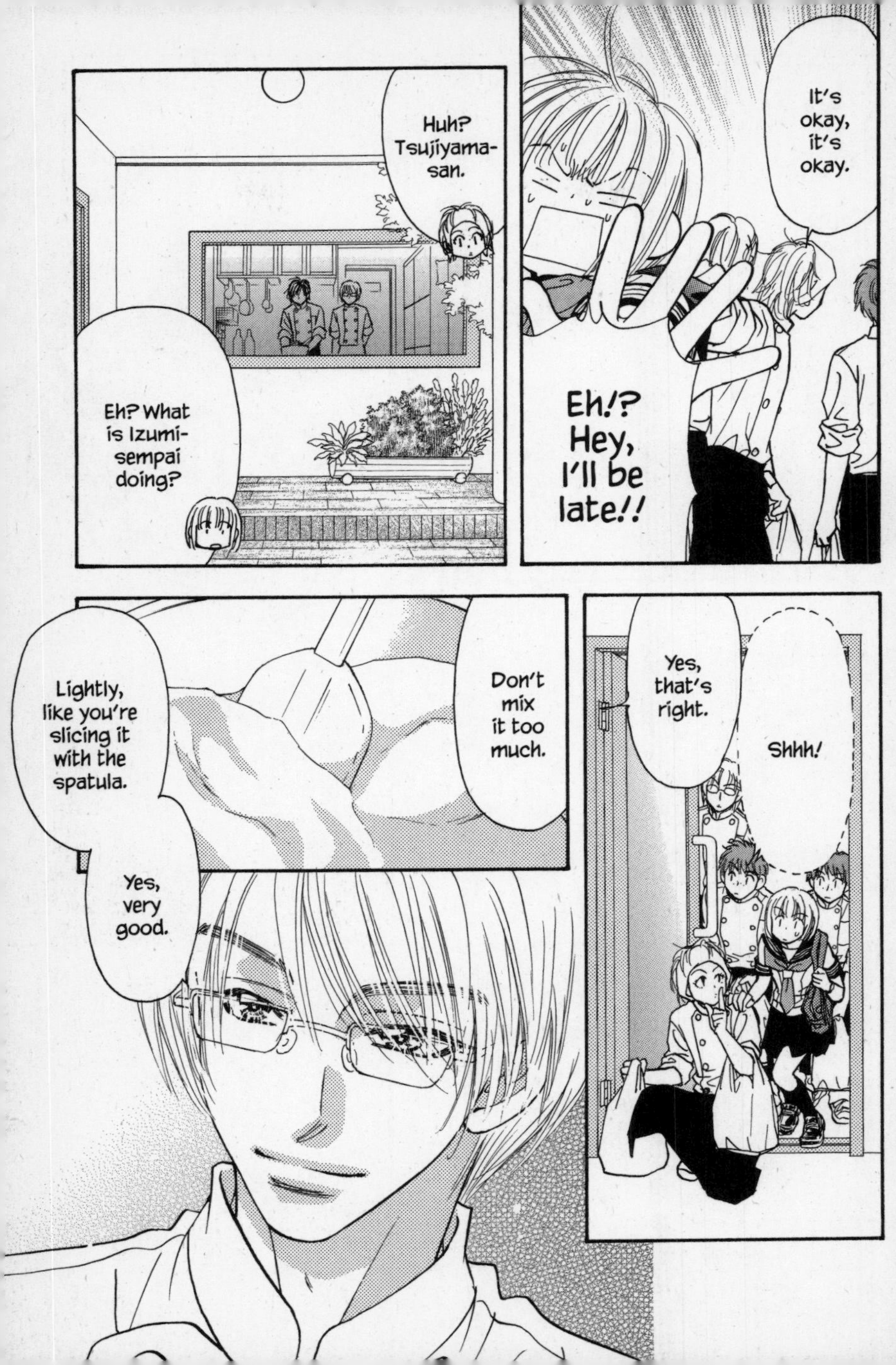
It's okay, it's okay.
Eh!? Hey, I'll be late!!
Huh? Tsujiyama-san.
Eh? What is Izumi-sempai doing?
Yes, that's right.
Shhh!
Don't mix it too much.
Lightly, like you're slicing it with the spatula.
Yes, very good.

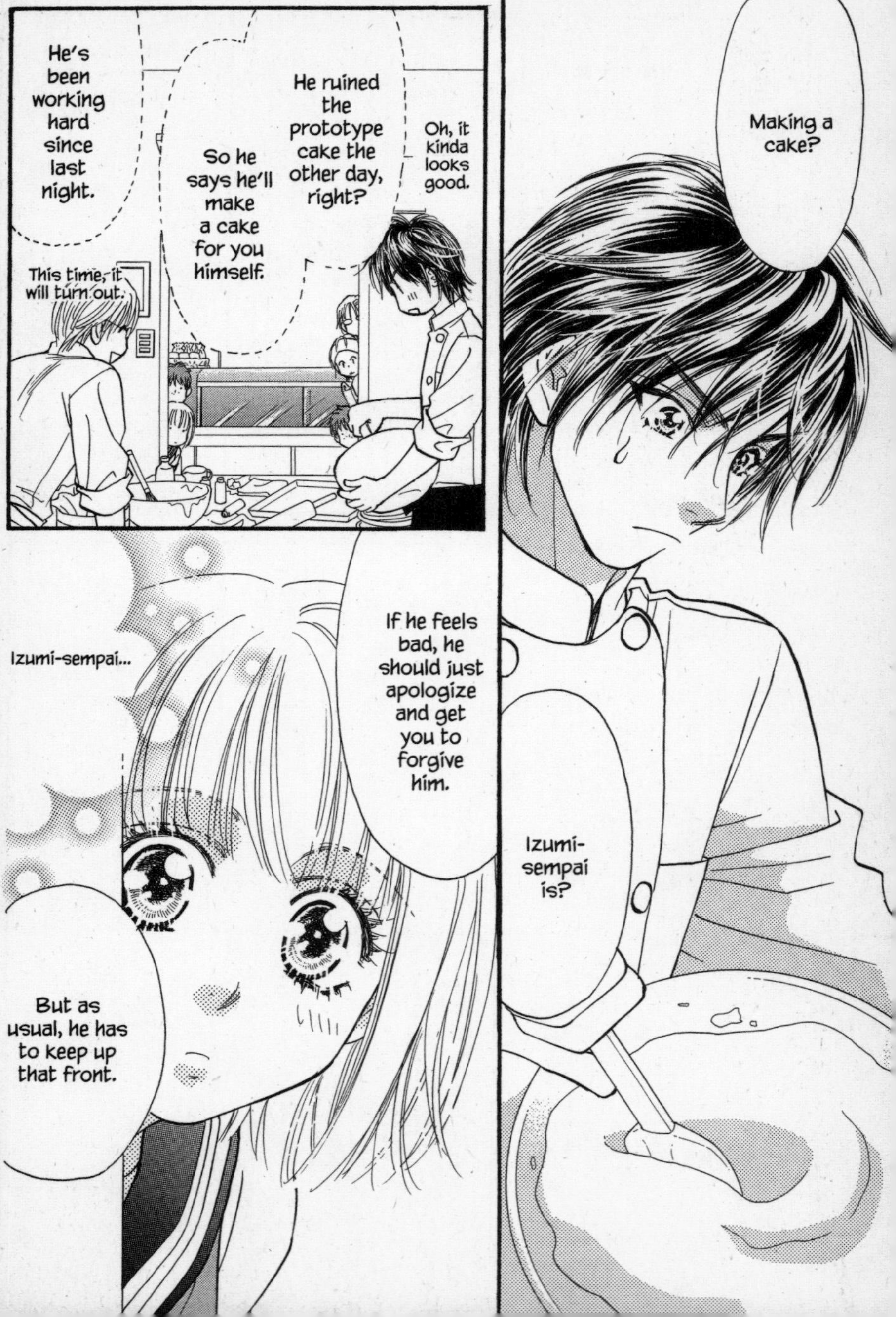
Making a cake?
Izumi-sempai is?
Oh, it kinda looks good.
He ruined the prototype cake the other day, right?
So he says he'll make a cake for you himself.
He's been working hard since last night.
This time, it will turn out.
If he feels bad, he should just apologize and get you to forgive him.
Izumi-sempai...
But as usual, he has to keep up that front.

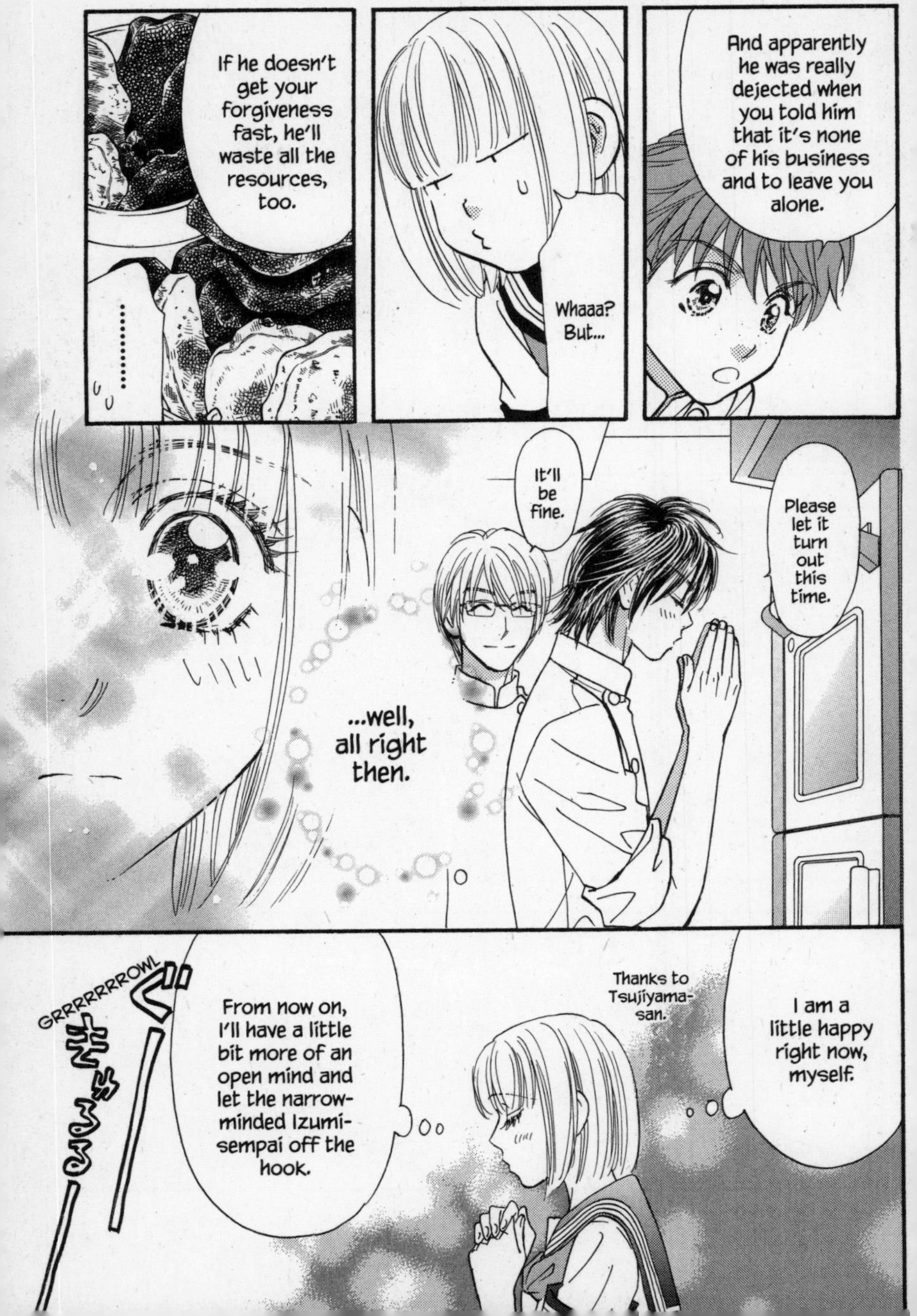

And apparently he was really dejected when you told him that it's none of his business and to leave you alone.
Whaaa? But...
If he doesn't get your forgiveness fast, he'll waste all the resources, too.
....
Please let it turn out this time.
It'll be fine.
...well, all right then.
I am a little happy right now, myself.
Thanks to Tsujiyama-san.
From now on, I'll have a little bit more of an open mind and let the narrow-minded Izumi-sempai off the hook.
GRRRRRRROWL

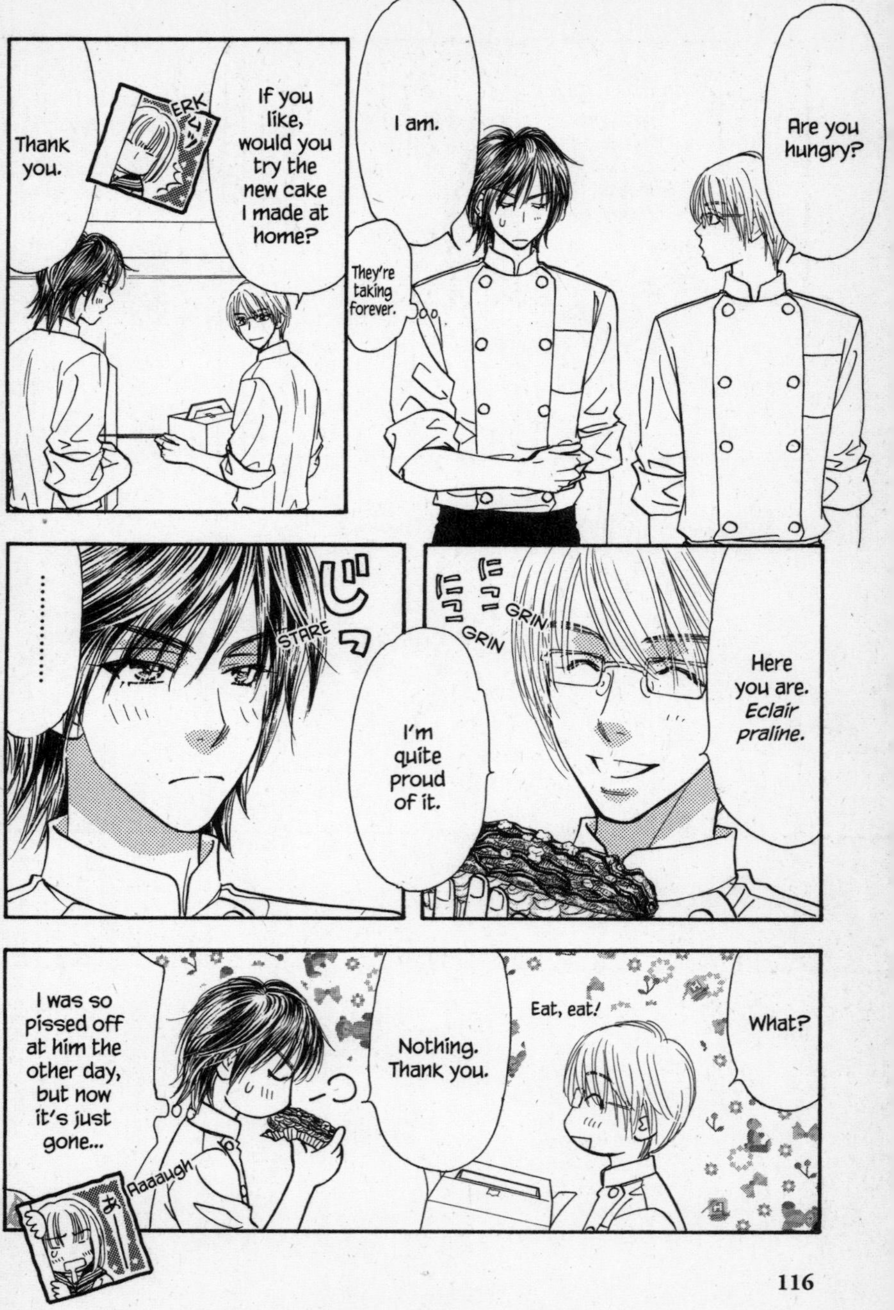

Are you hungry?
I am.
They're taking forever.
If you like, would you try the new cake I made at home?
ERK
ムッ
Thank you.
Here you are. *Eclair praline.*
GRIN
ニコ
GRIN
ニコ
I'm quite proud of it.
STARE
じっ
....
What?
Eat, eat!
Nothing. Thank you.
I was so pissed off at him the other day, but now it's just gone...
Raaaugh
あー

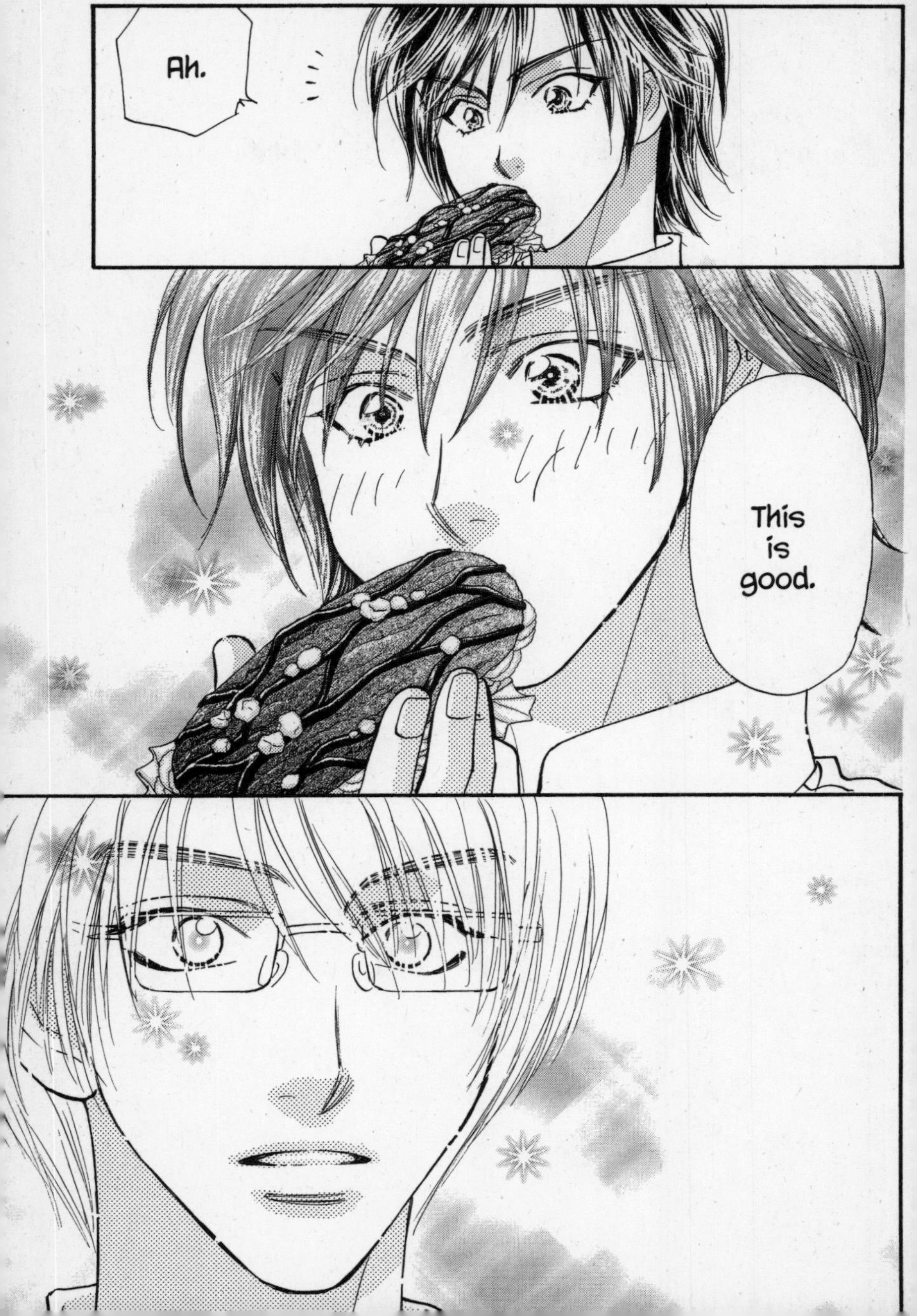
Ah.
This is good.

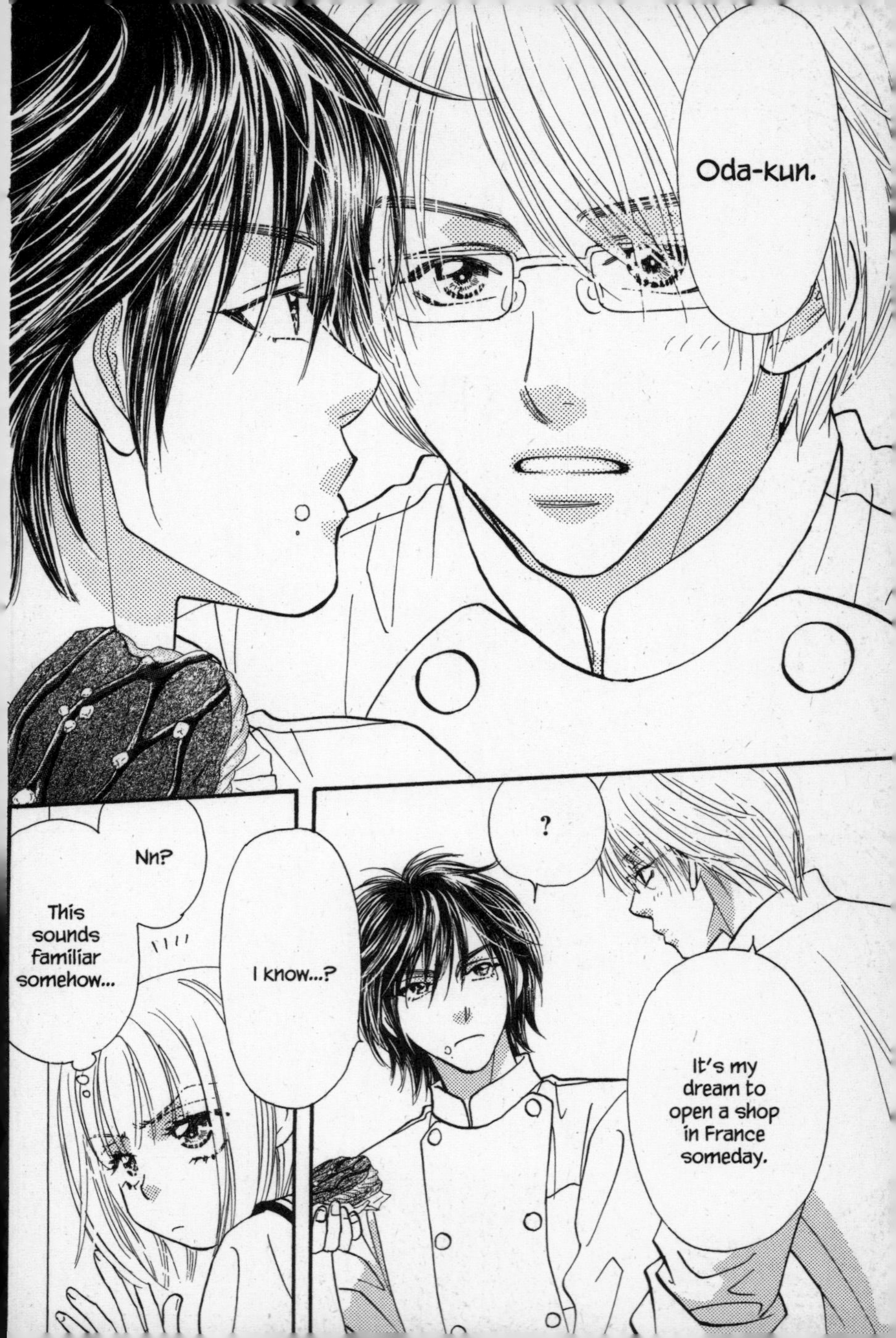
Oda-kun.
It's my dream to open a shop in France someday.
?
Nn?
This sounds familiar somehow...
I know...?

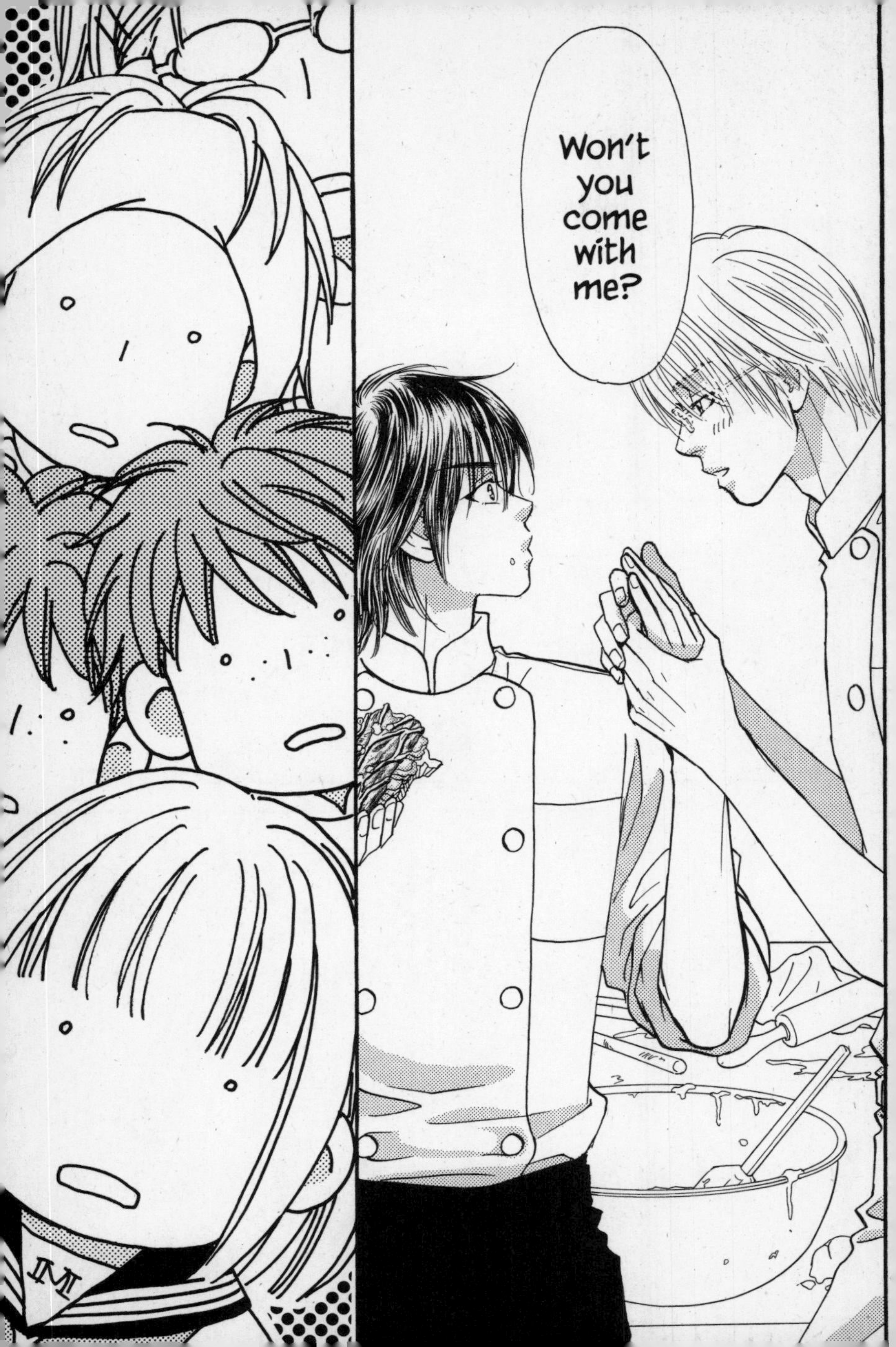
Won't you come with me?

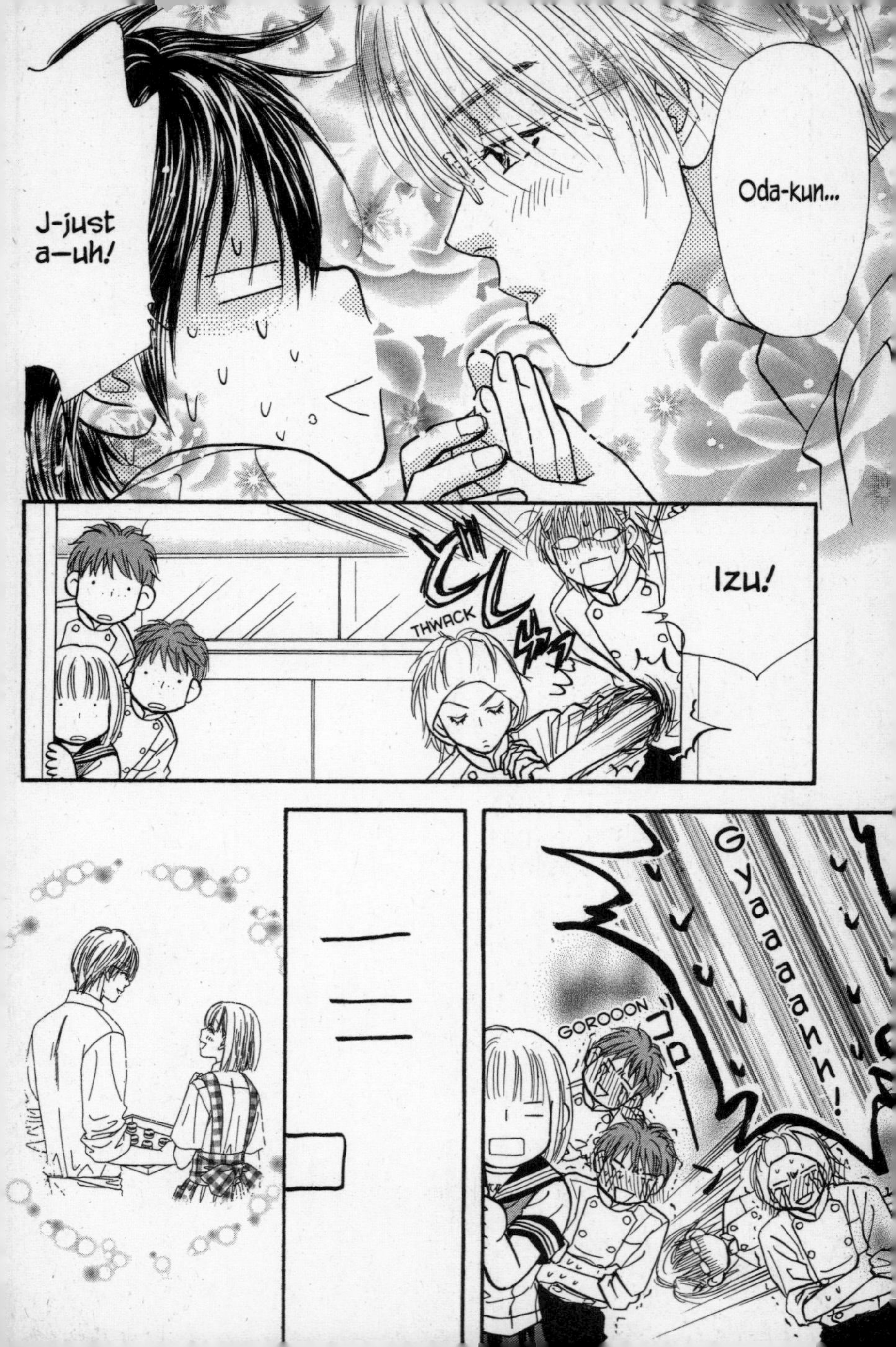
Oda-kun...
J-just a—uh!
Izu!
THWACK
Gyaaaaahh!
GOROOON

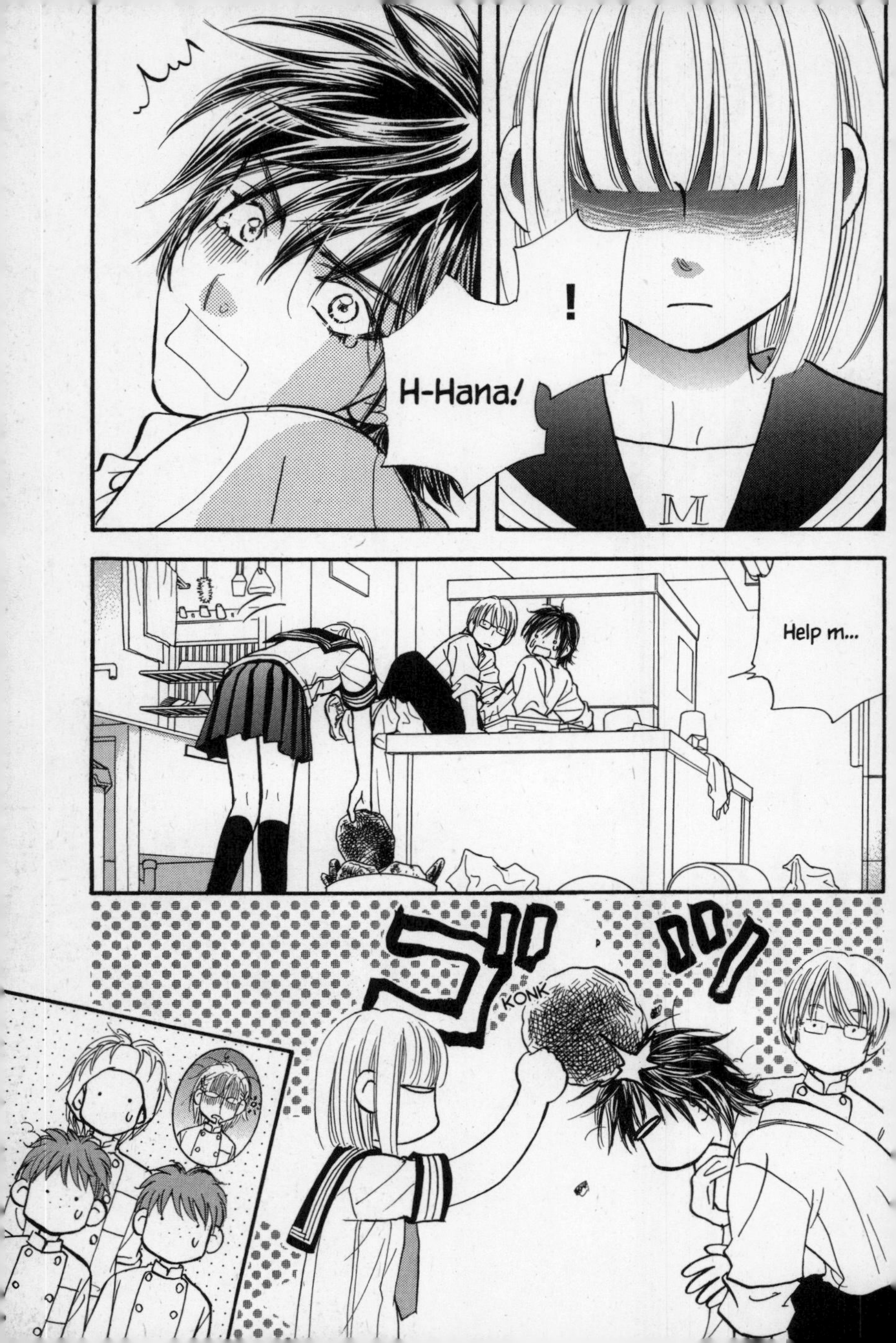
!
H-Hana!
Help m...
KONK

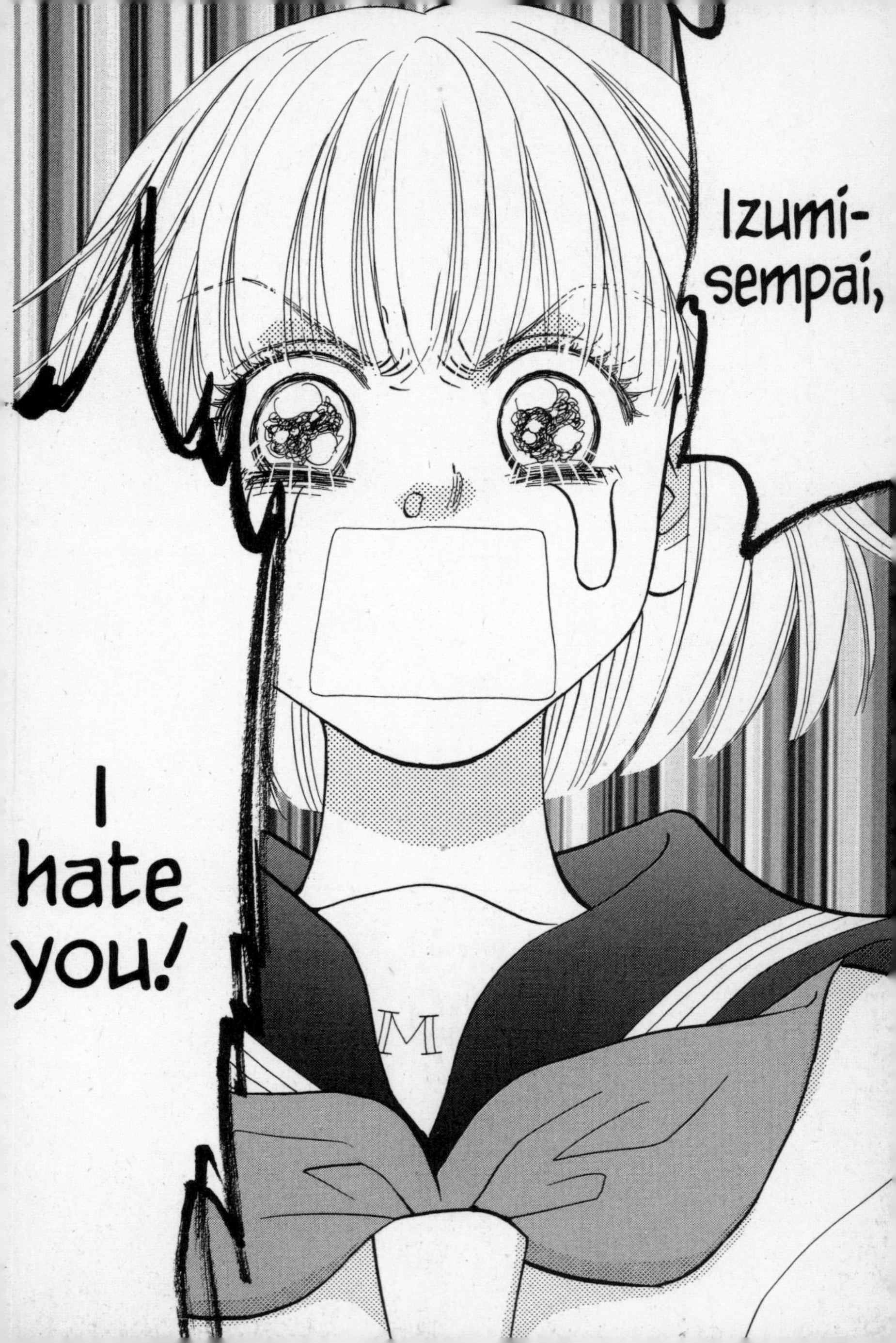
Izumi-sempai,
I hate you!

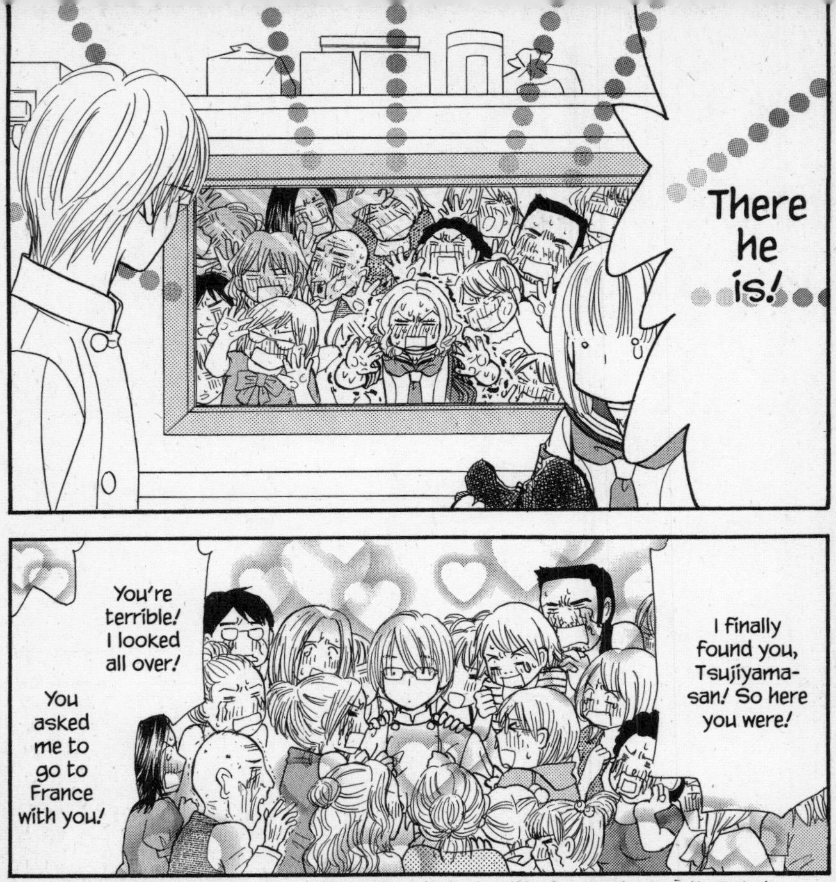
There he is!
I finally found you, Tsujiyama-san! So here you were!
You're terrible! I looked all over!
You asked me to go to France with you!

Question: Now, how many people are on this page? You don't get anything for answering correctly. Too bad.

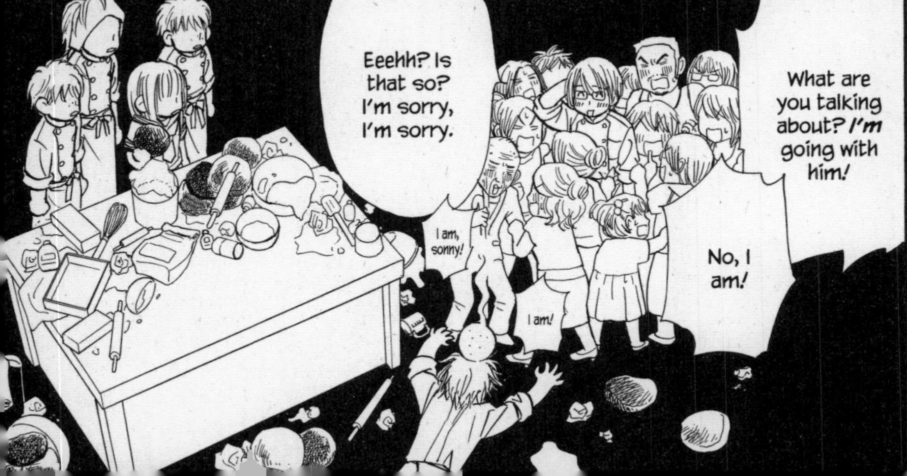
What are you talking about? *I'm* going with him!
Eeehh? Is that so? I'm sorry, I'm sorry.
No, I am!
I am, sonny!
I am!

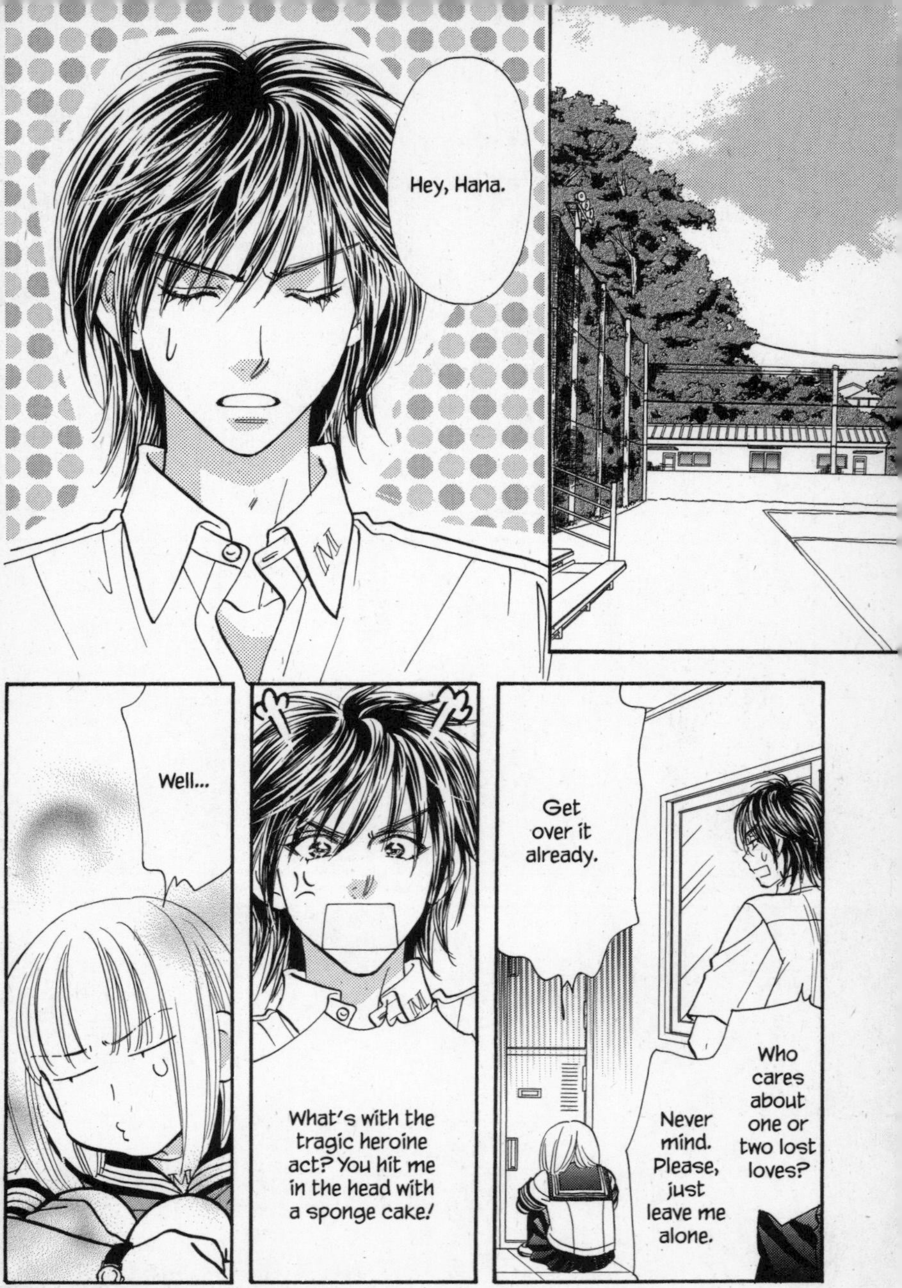
Hey, Hana.
Get over it already.
Who cares about one or two lost loves?
Never mind. Please, just leave me alone.
What's with the tragic heroine act? You hit me in the head with a sponge cake!
Well...

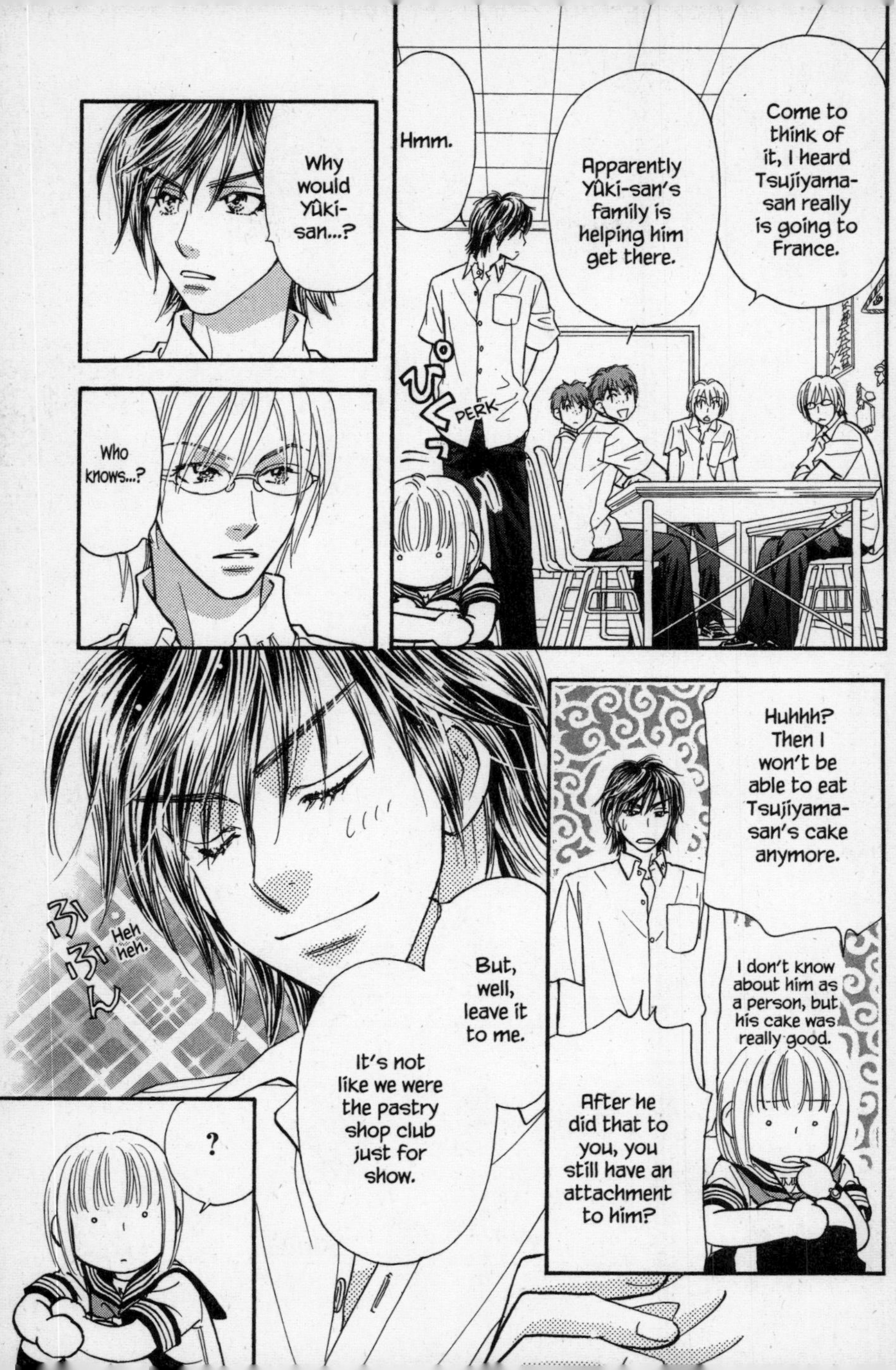

Come to think of it, I heard Tsujiyama-san really is going to France.
Apparently Yûki-san's family is helping him get there.
Hmm.
PERK
Why would Yûki-san...?
Who knows...?
Huhhh? Then I won't be able to eat Tsujiyama-san's cake anymore.
I don't know about him as a person, but his cake was really good.
After he did that to you, you still have an attachment to him?
Heh heh.
But, well, leave it to me.
It's not like we were the pastry shop club just for show.
?

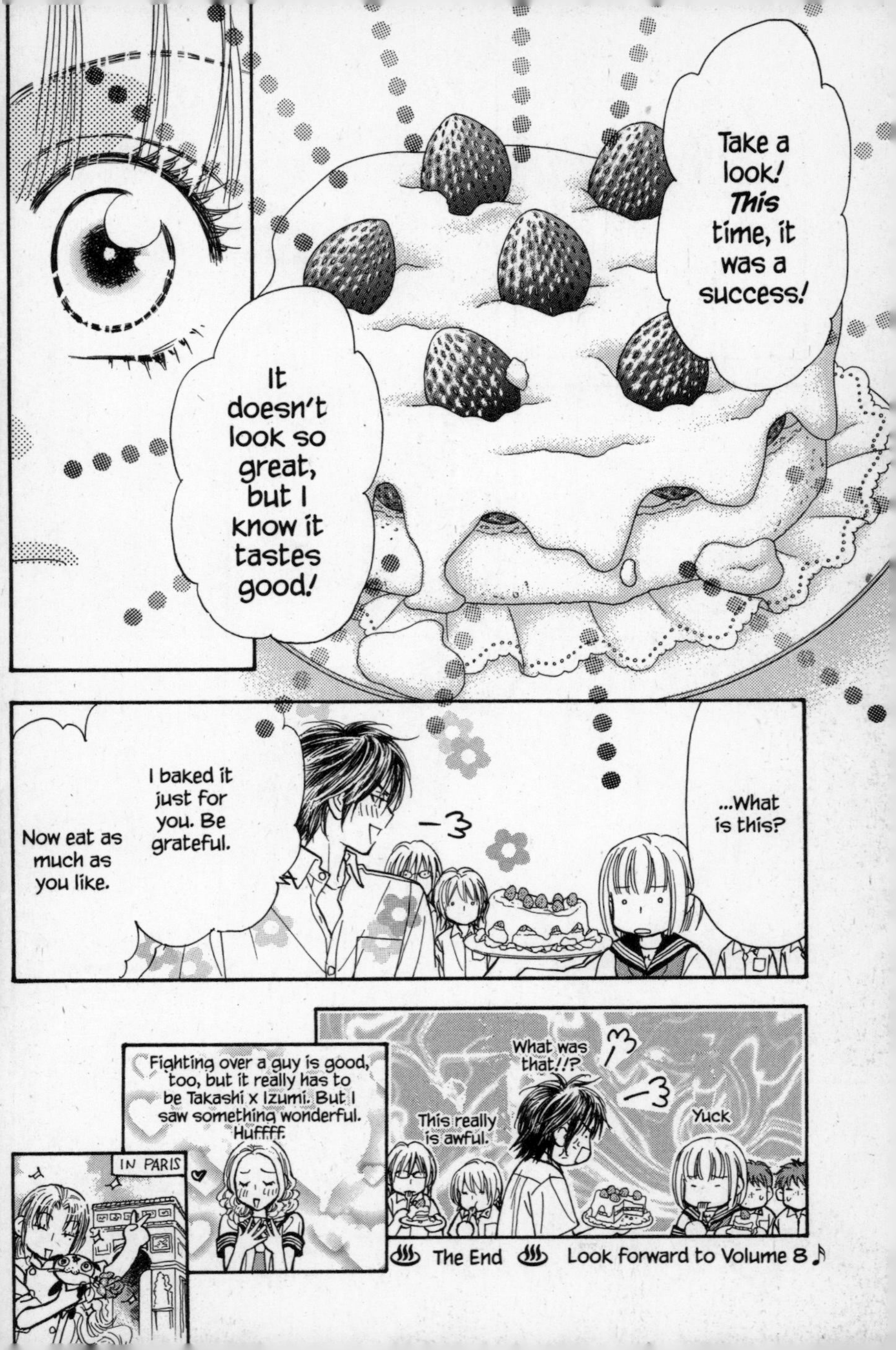

Take a look! *This* time, it was a success!
It doesn't look so great, but I know it tastes good!
...What is this?
I baked it just for you. Be grateful.
Now eat as much as you like.
What was that!!?
Yuck
This really is awful.
Fighting over a guy is good, too, but it really has to be Takashi x Izumi. But I saw something wonderful. Hufffff.
IN PARIS
The End
Look forward to Volume 8♪

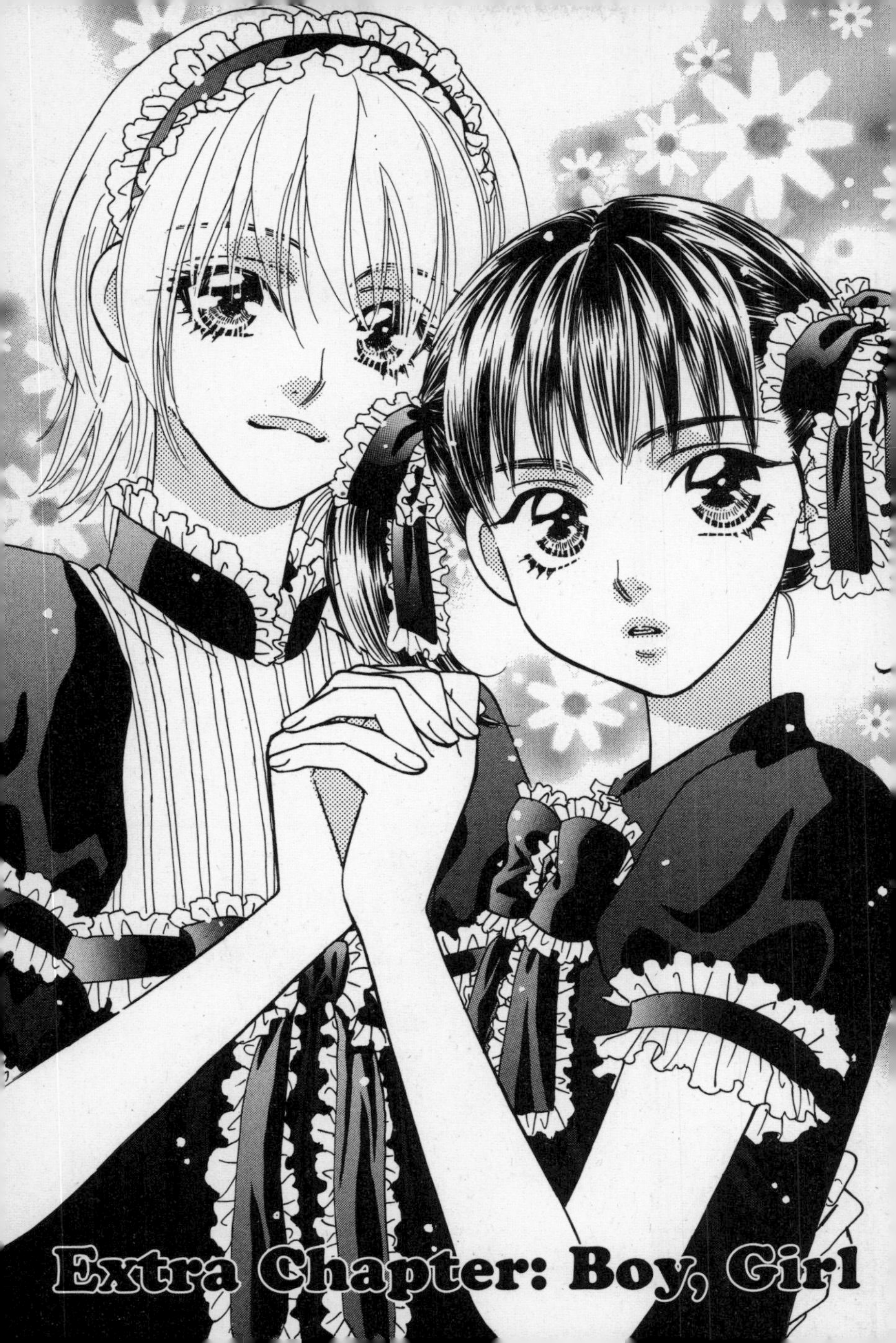

Extra Chapter: Boy, Girl

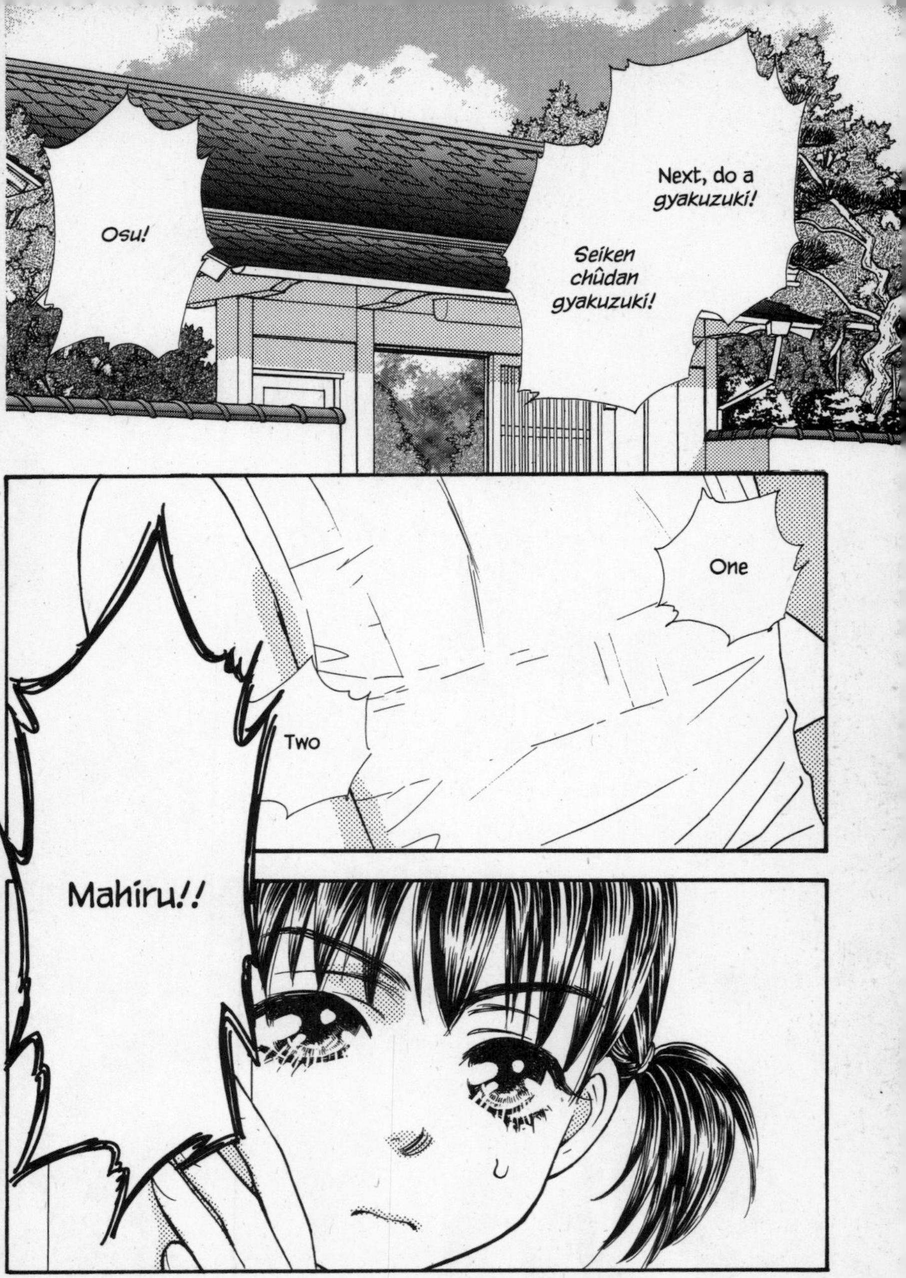
Next, do a gyakuzuki!
Seiken chûdan gyakuzuki!
Osu!
One
Two
Mahiru!!

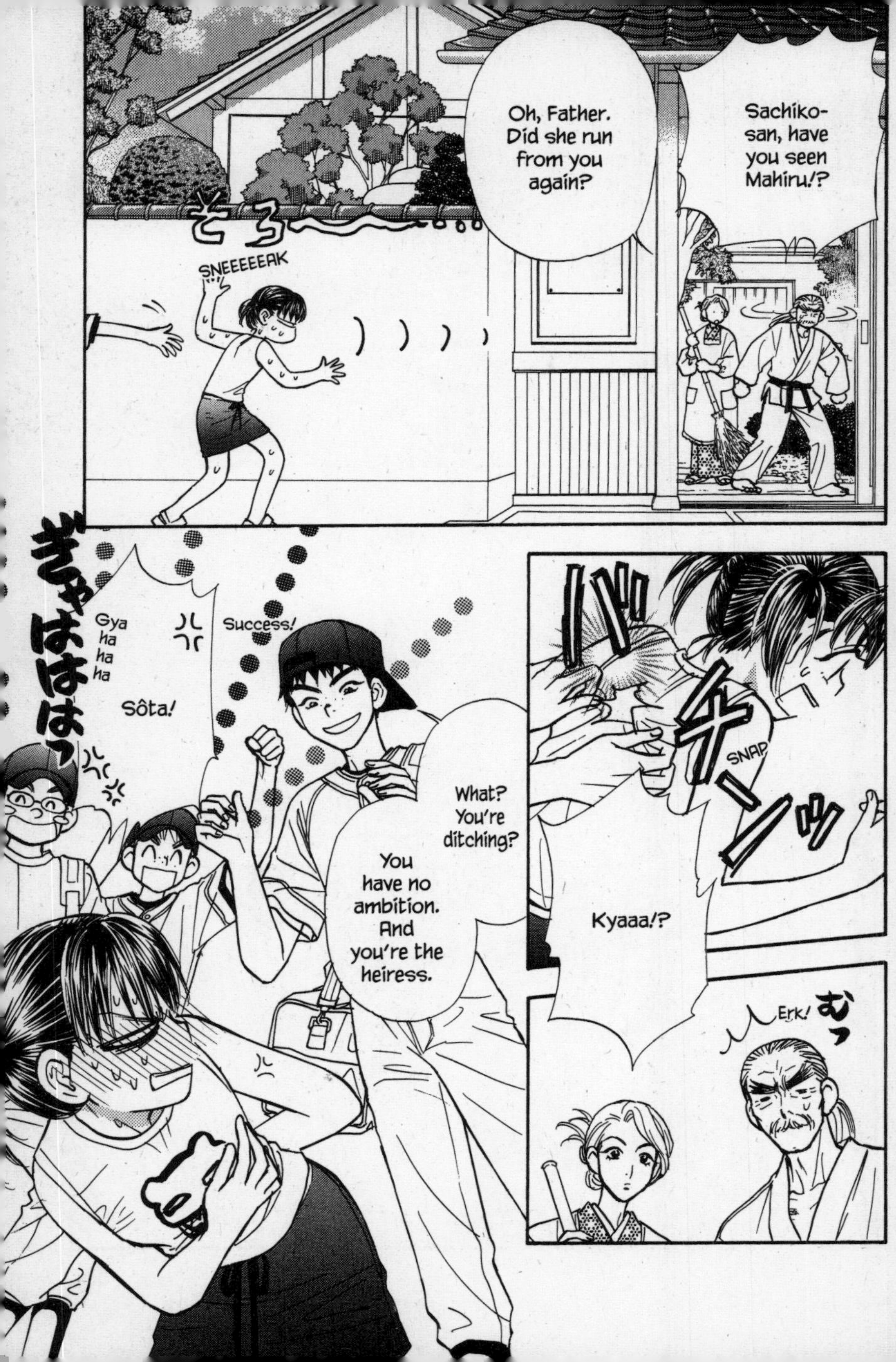

Sachiko-san, have you seen Mahiru!?
Oh, Father. Did she run from you again?
そろ〜〜〜
SNEEEEEAK
バチーンッ
SNAP
Kyaaa!?
むっ
Erk!
ぎゃはははっ
Gya ha ha ha
Success!
Sôta!
What? You're ditching?
You have no ambition. And you're the heiress.

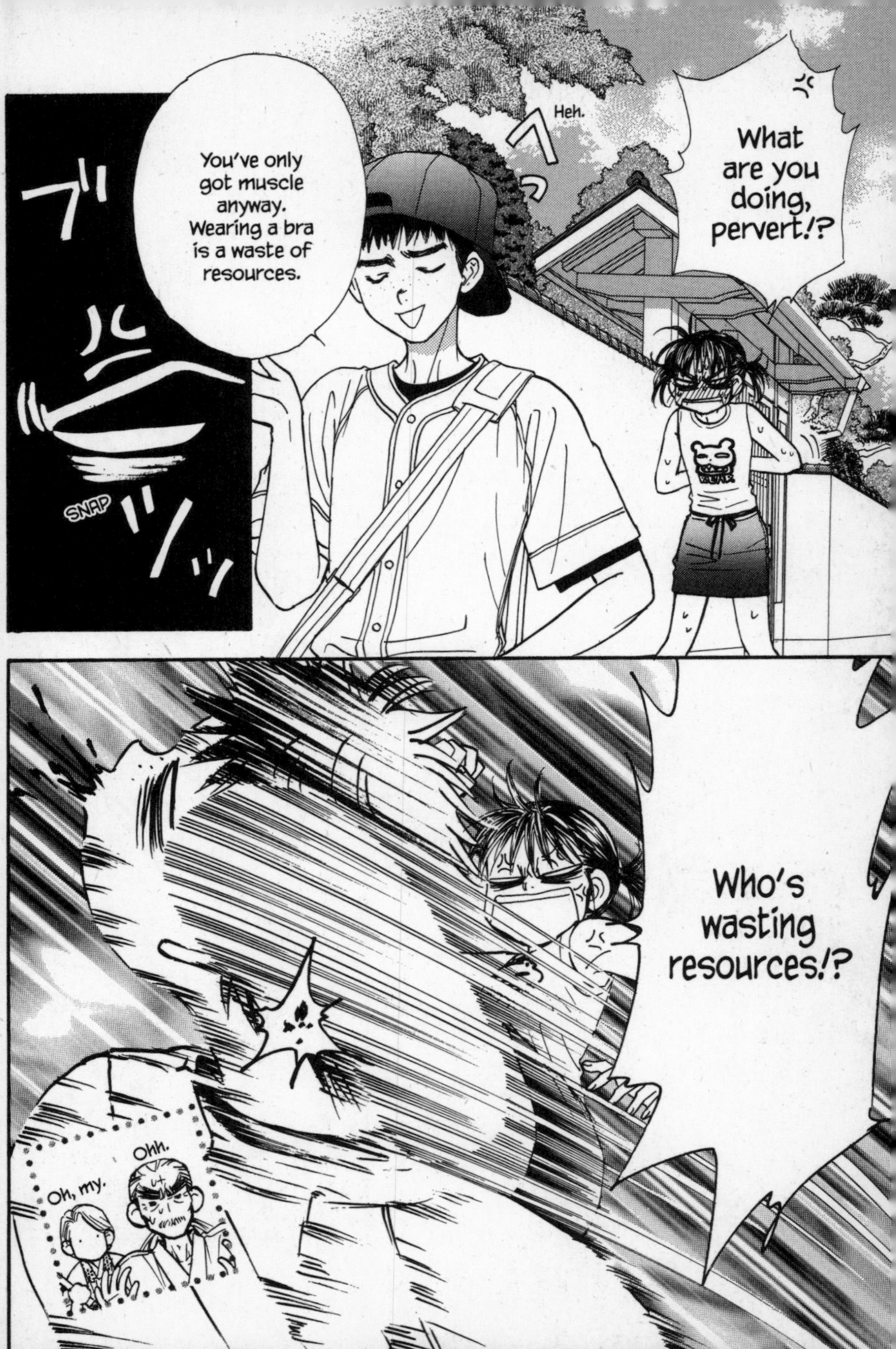
What are you doing, pervert!?
Heh.
You've only got muscle anyway. Wearing a bra is a waste of resources.
SNAP
Who's wasting resources!?
Ohh.
Oh, my.

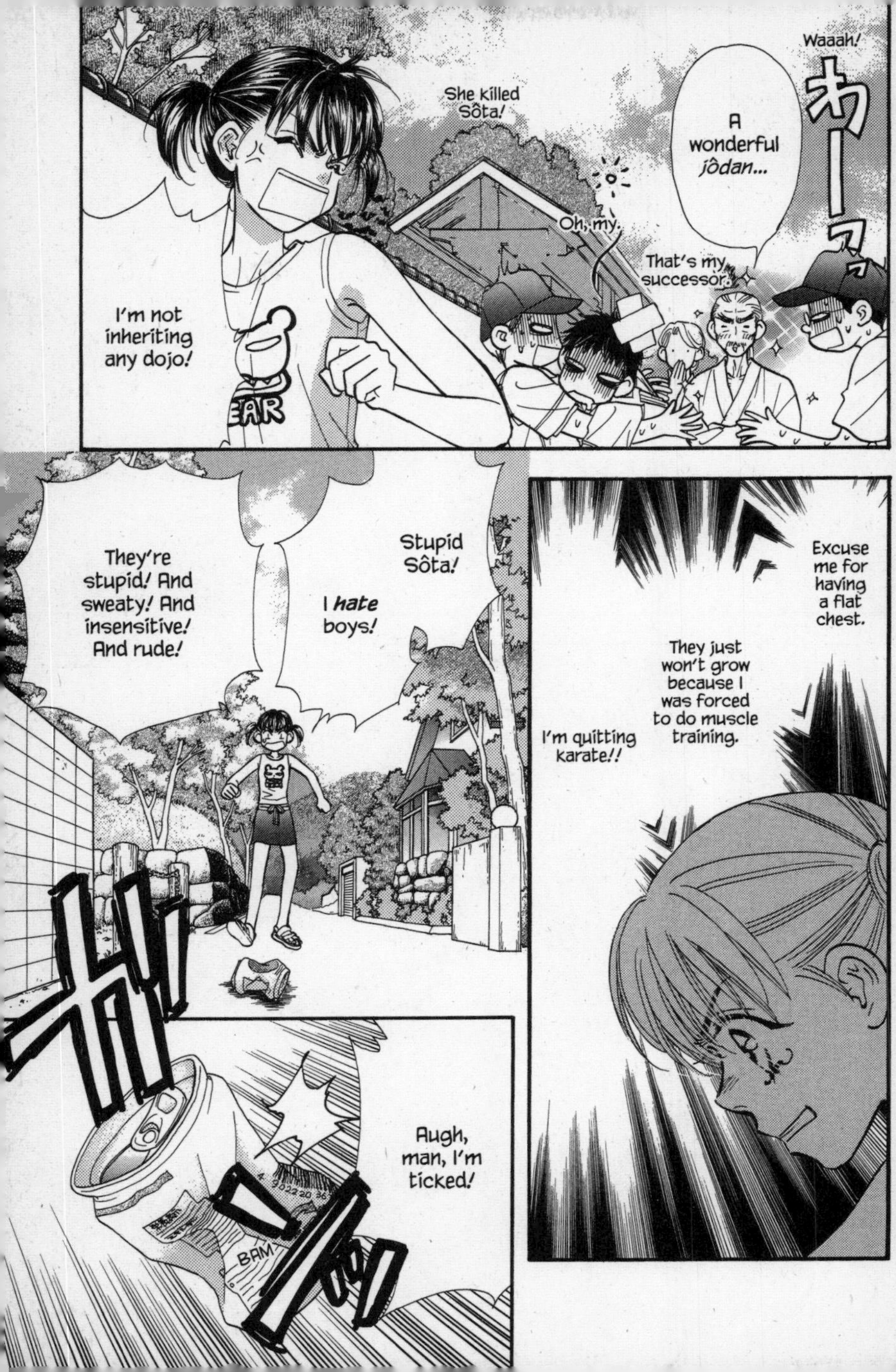
Waaah!
A wonderful *jôdan*...
That's my successor.
Oh, my.
She killed Sôta!
I'm not inheriting any dojo!
Excuse me for having a flat chest.
They just won't grow because I was forced to do muscle training.
I'm quitting karate!!
Stupid Sôta!
I ***hate*** boys!
They're stupid! And sweaty! And insensitive! And rude!
Augh, man, I'm ticked!
BAM

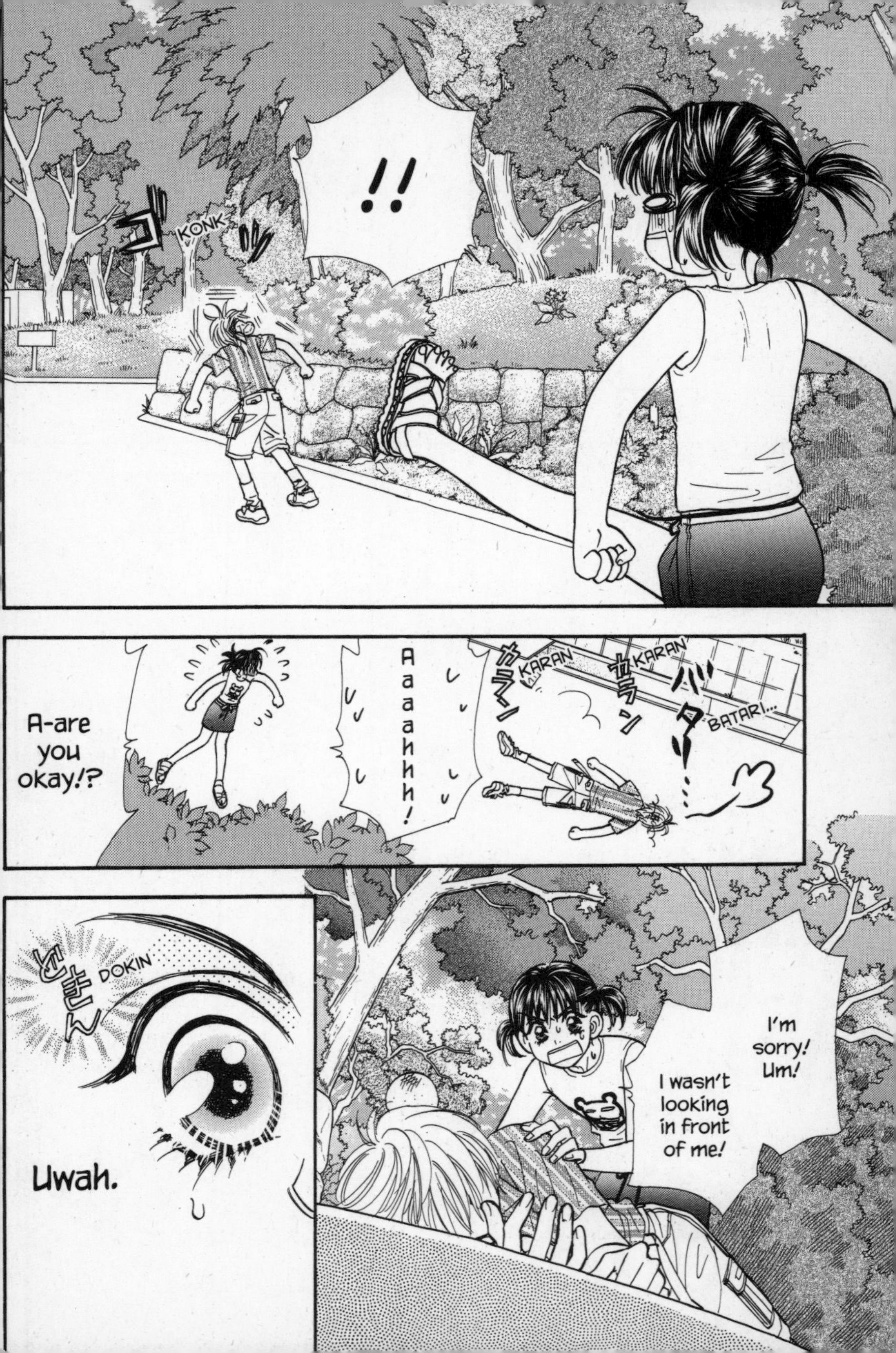
!!
KONK
KARAN
KARAN
BATARI...
Aaaahhh!
A-are you okay!?
I'm sorry! Um!
I wasn't looking in front of me!
DOKIN
Uwah.

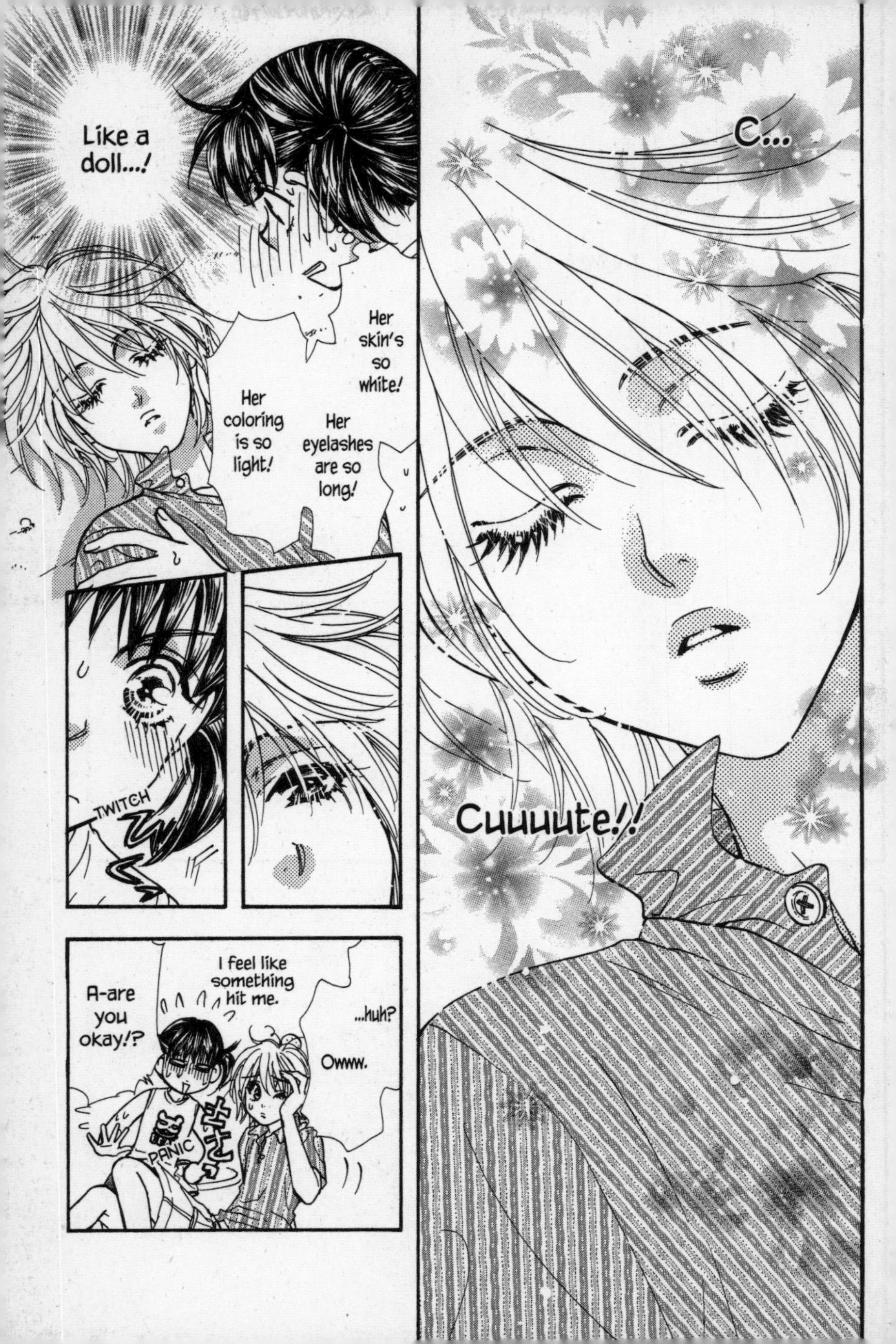
C...
Cuuuute!!
Like a doll...!
Her skin's so white!
Her eyelashes are so long!
Her coloring is so light!
TWITCH
...huh?
Owww.
I feel like something hit me.
A-are you okay!?
PANIC

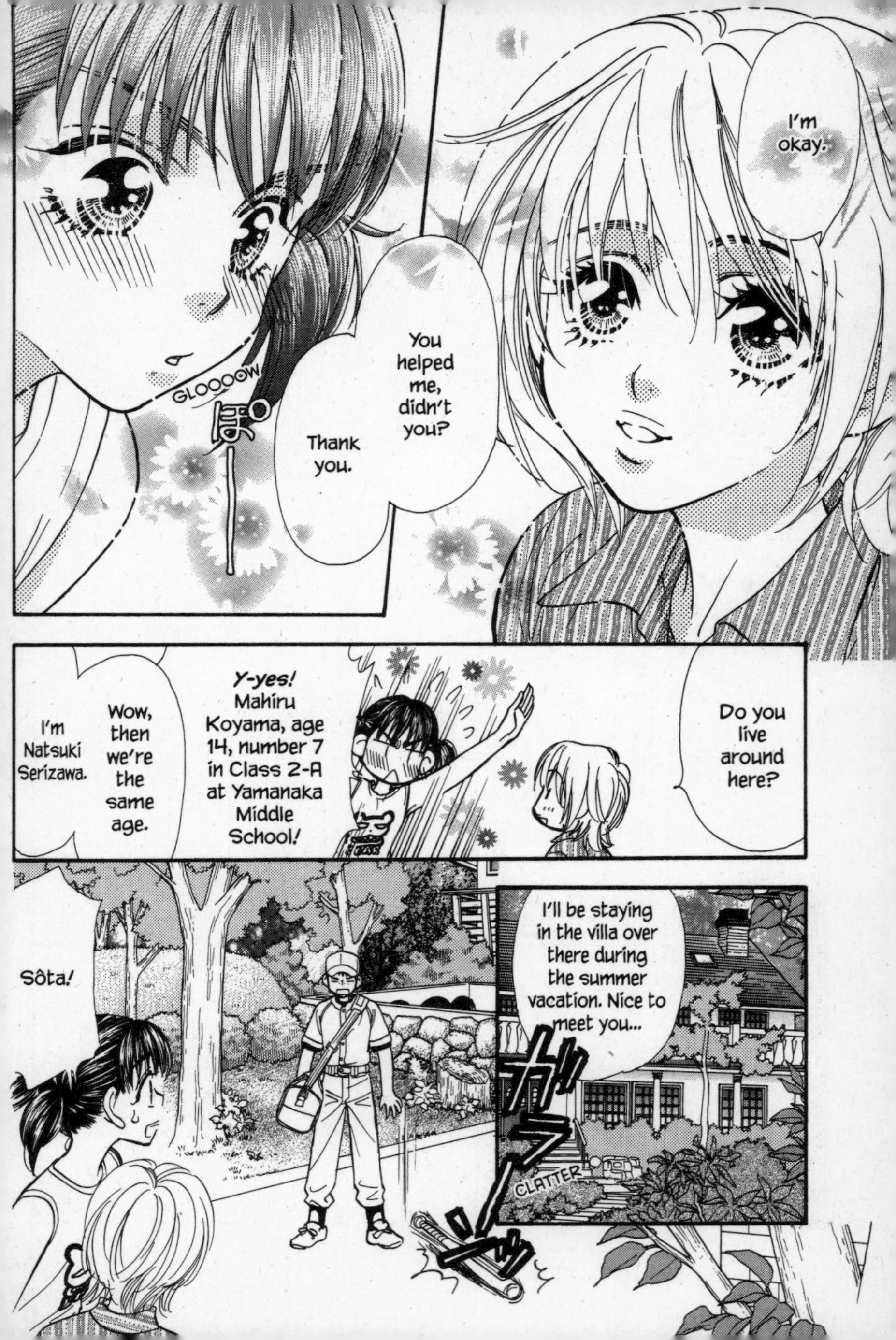

I'm okay.
You helped me, didn't you?
Thank you.
GLOOOOW
Do you live around here?
Y-yes! Mahiru Koyama, age 14, number 7 in Class 2-A at Yamanaka Middle School!
Wow, then we're the same age.
I'm Natsuki Serizawa.
I'll be staying in the villa over there during the summer vacation. Nice to meet you...
CLATTER
Sôta!

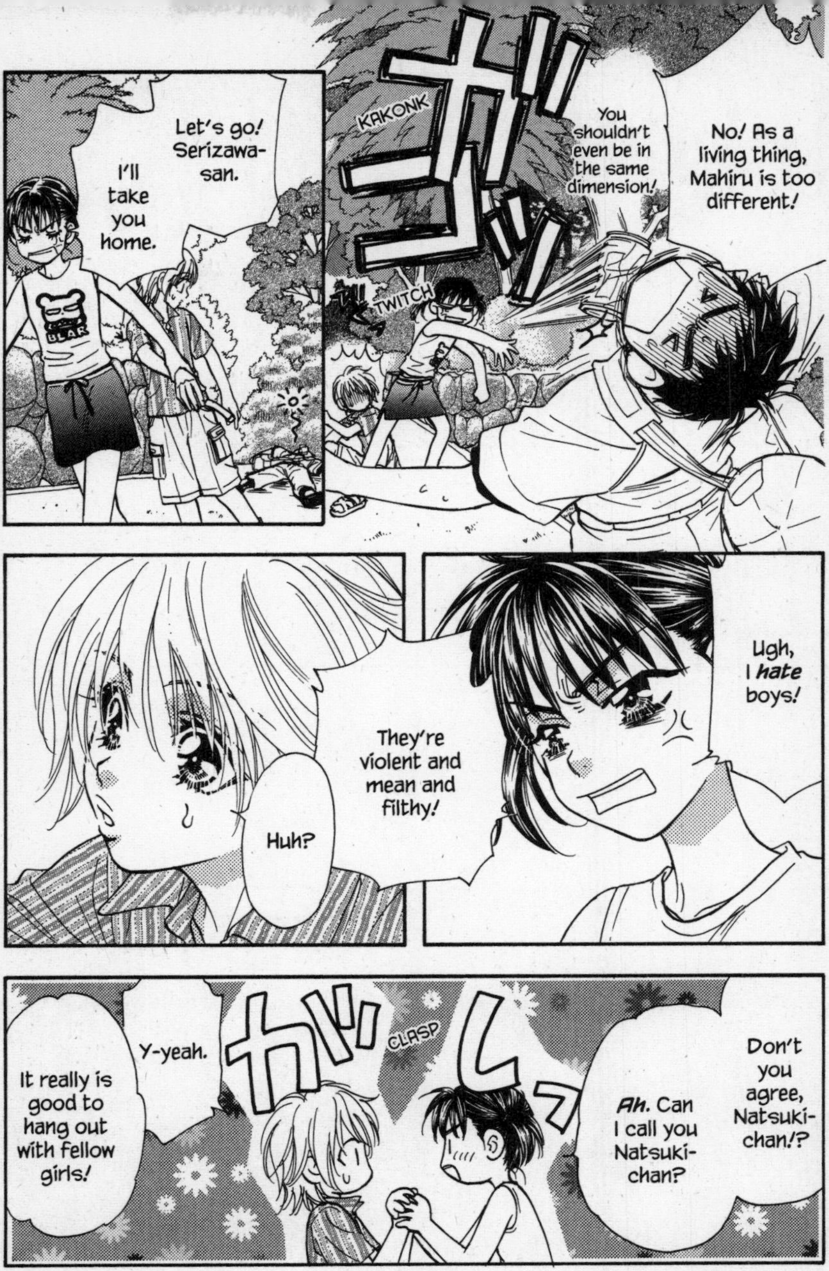
No! As a living thing, Mahiru is too different!
You shouldn't even be in the same dimension!
KAKONK
TWITCH
Let's go! Serizawa-san.
I'll take you home.
Ugh, I *hate* boys!
They're violent and mean and filthy!
Huh?
Don't you agree, Natsuki-chan!?
Ah. Can I call you Natsuki-chan?
CLASP
Y-yeah.
It really is good to hang out with fellow girls!

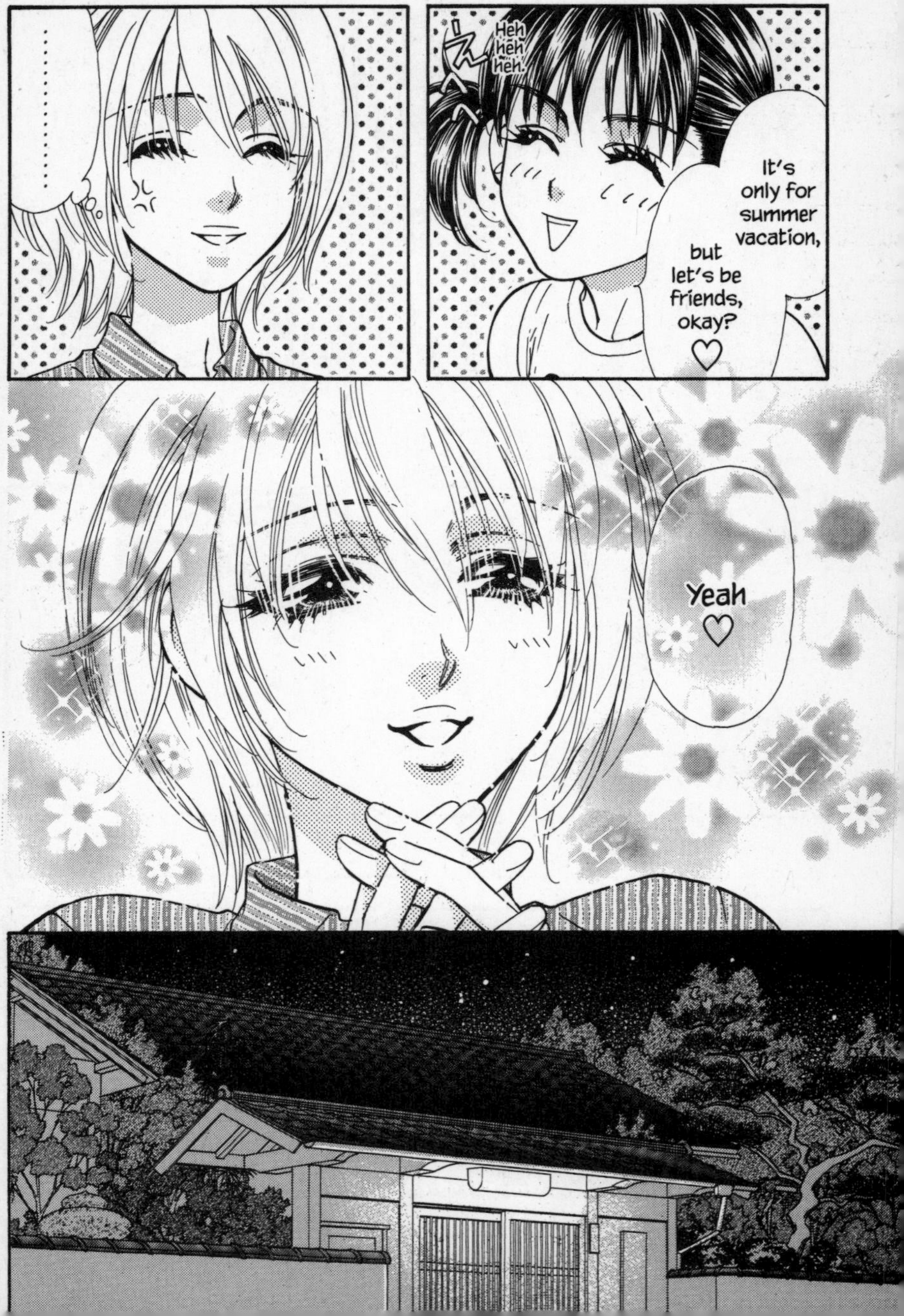
Heh heh heh.
It's only for summer vacation, but let's be friends, okay? ♡
......
Yeah ♡

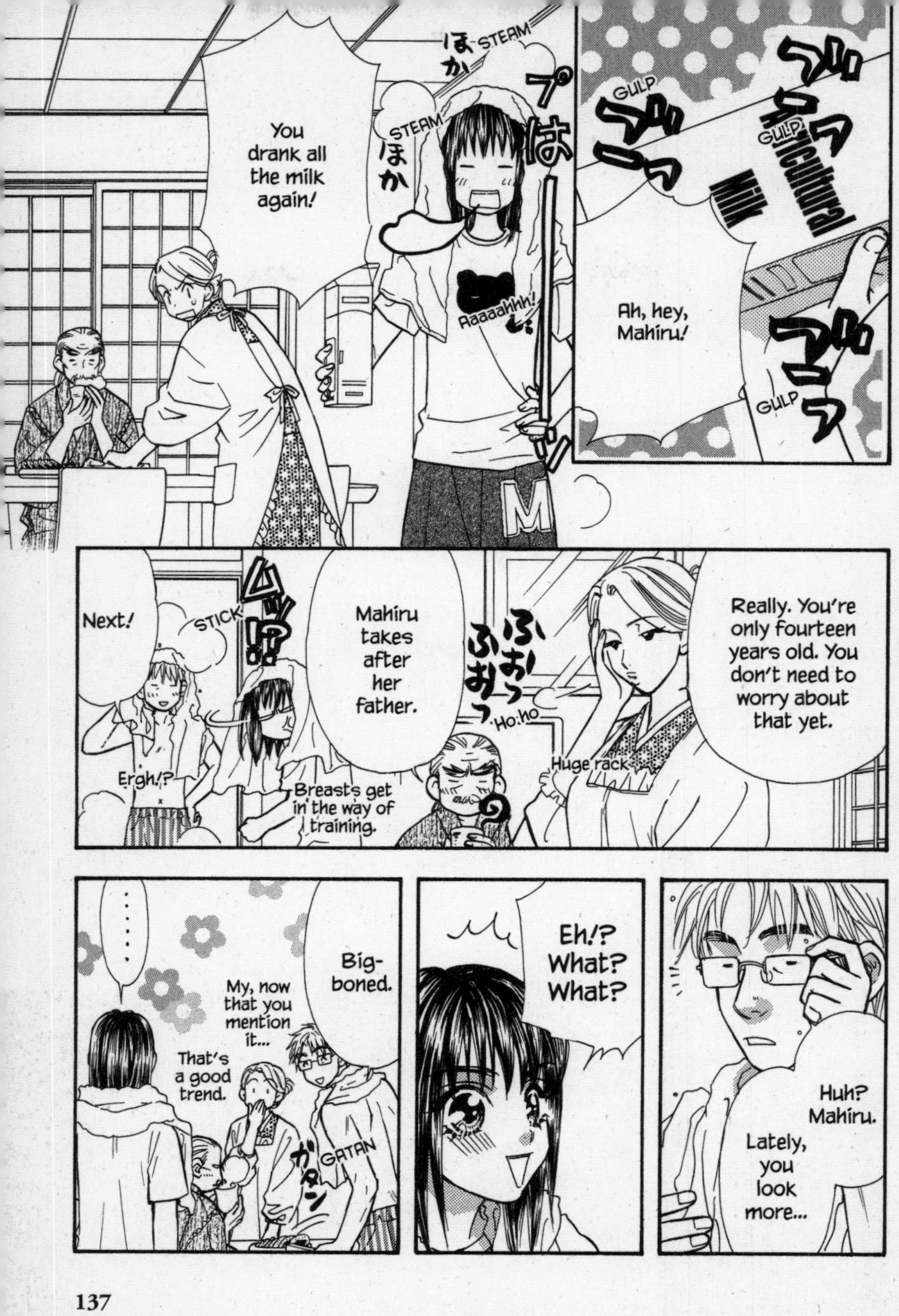
GULP
Agricultural Milk
GULP
Ah, hey, Mahiru!
GULP
ほか STEAM
ほか STEAM
ぷは
Aaaaaahh!
You drank all the milk again!
Really. You're only fourteen years old. You don't need to worry about that yet.
Huge rack
ふぉっふぉっ Ho ho
Mahiru takes after her father.
Breasts get in the way of training.
STICK
Next!
Ergh!?
Huh? Mahiru.
Lately, you look more...
Eh!? What? What?
Big-boned.
My, now that you mention it...
That's a good trend.
ガタン GATAN
......

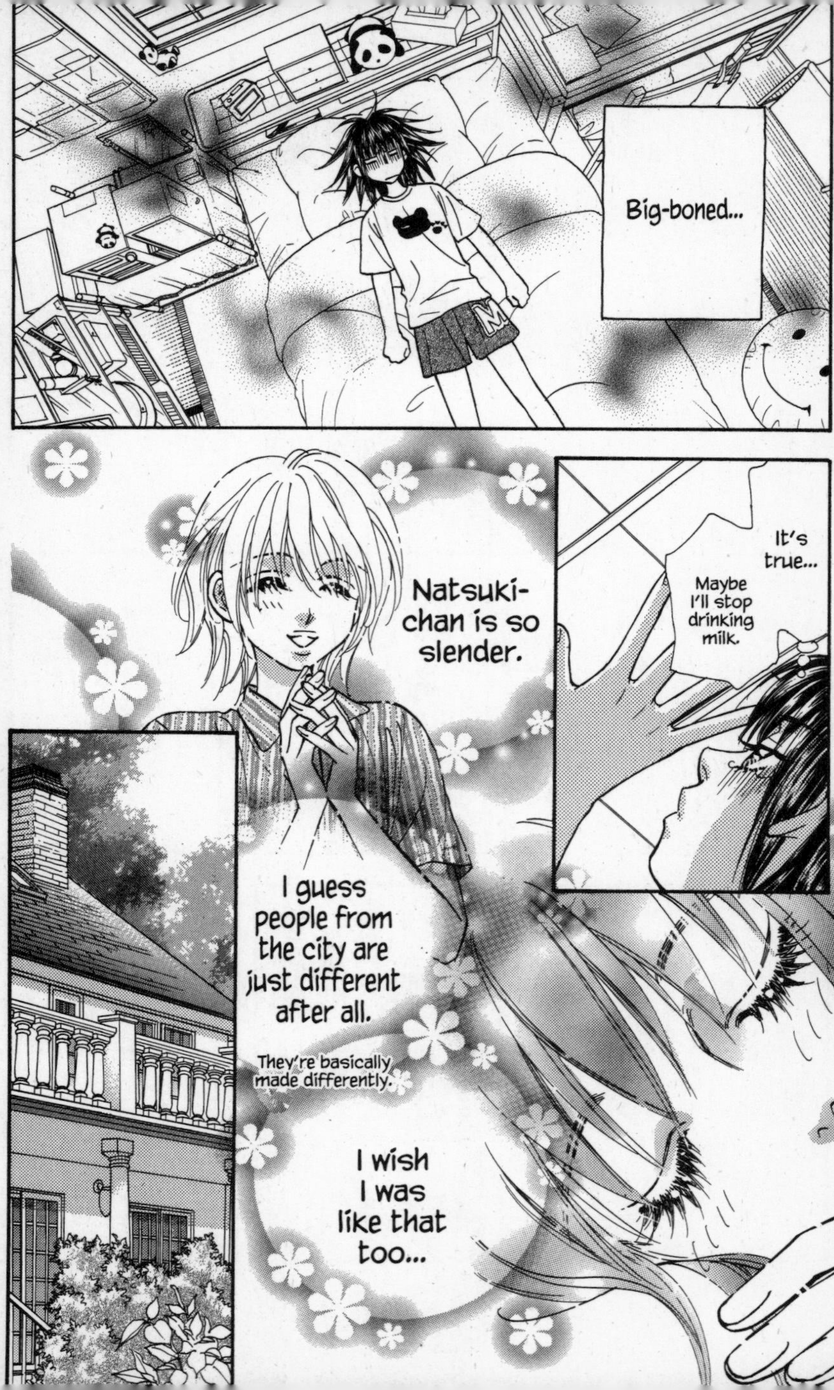
Big-boned...
It's true...
Maybe I'll stop drinking milk.
Natsuki-chan is so slender.
I guess people from the city are just different after all.
They're basically made differently.
I wish I was like that too...

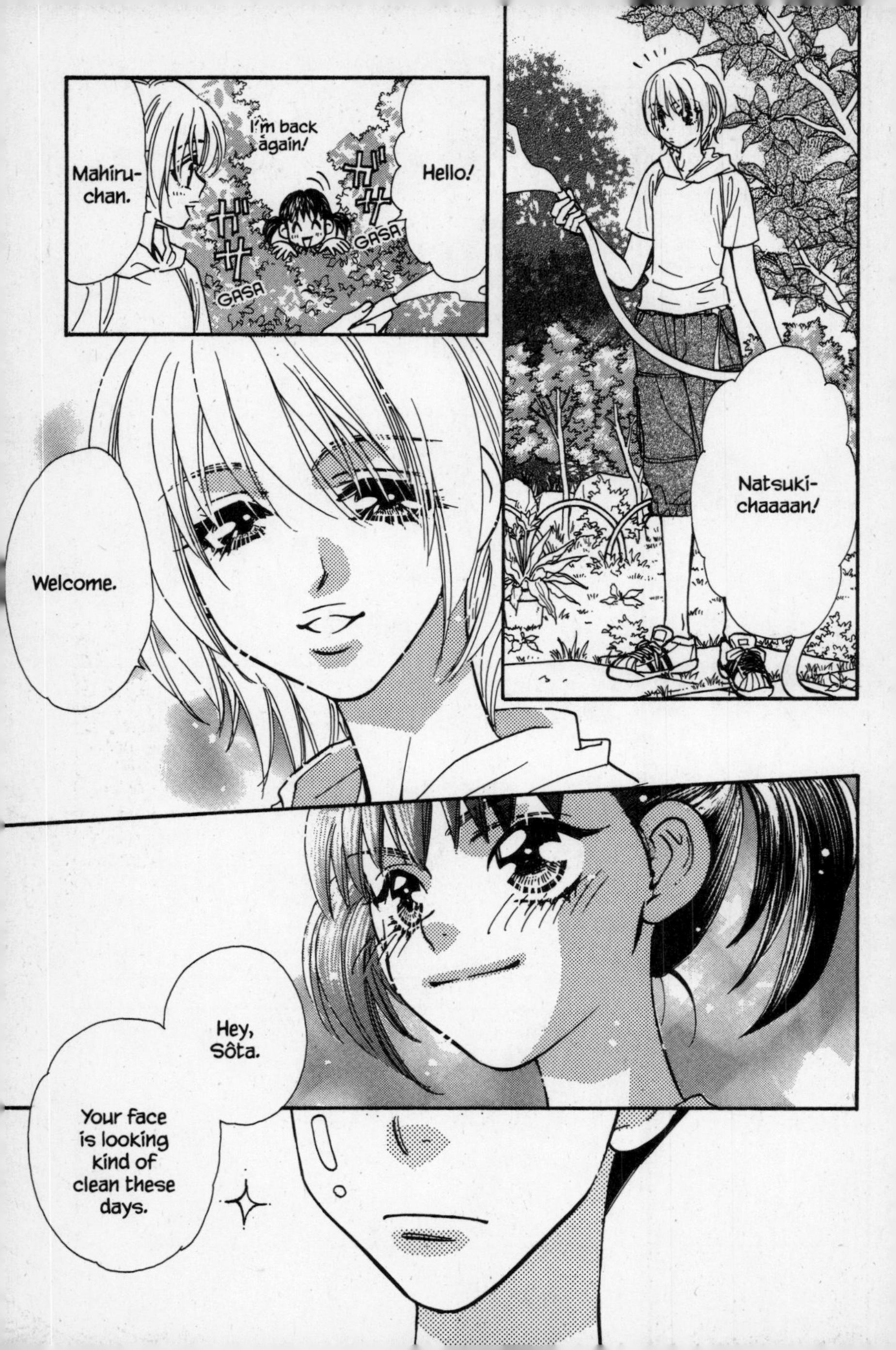
Natsuki-chaaaan!
Hello!
ガサ
GASA
I'm back again!
ガサ
GASA
Mahiru-chan.
Welcome.
Hey, Sôta.
Your face is looking kind of clean these days.

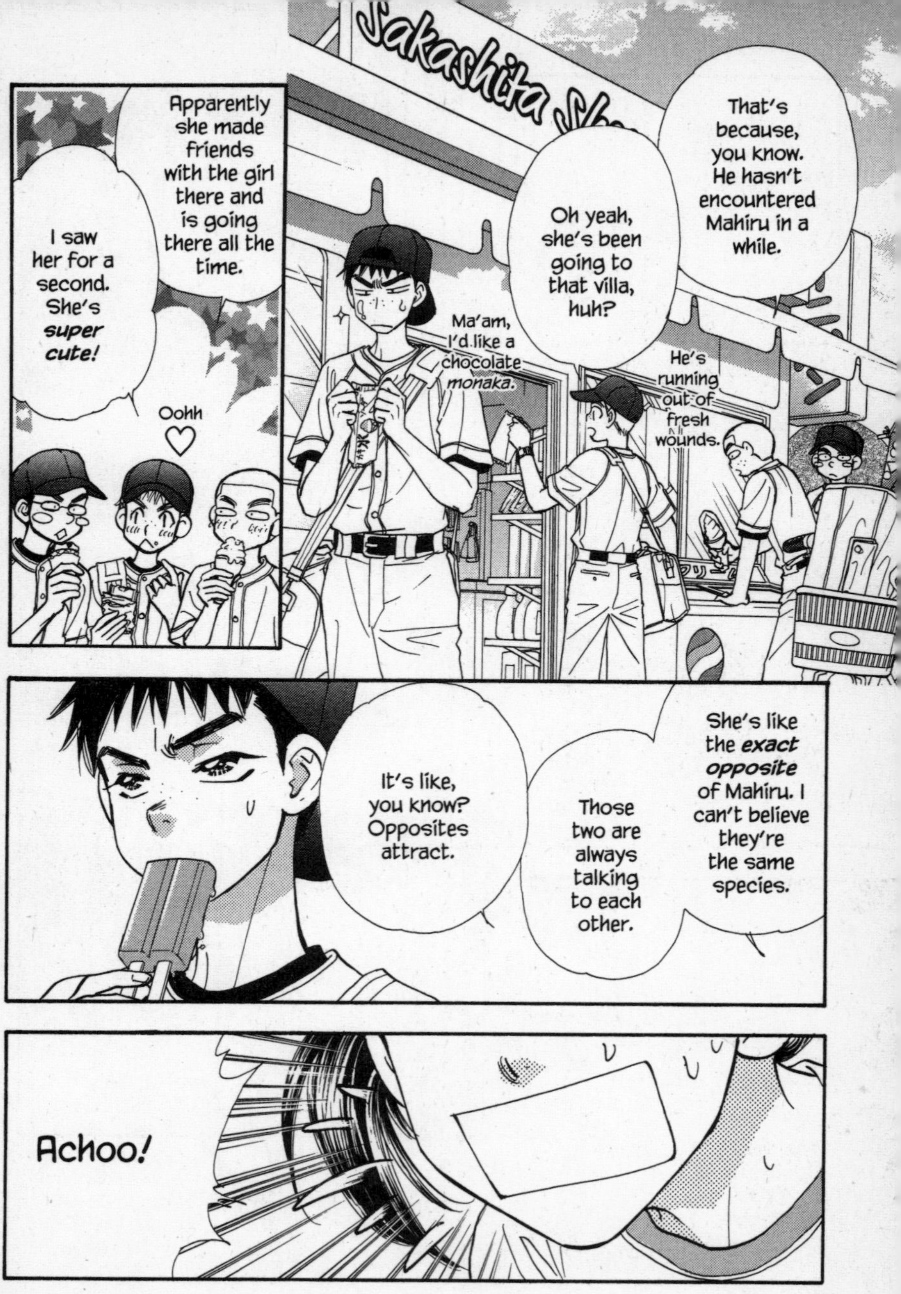
Sakashita
That's because, you know. He hasn't encountered Mahiru in a while.
Oh yeah, she's been going to that villa, huh?
He's running out of fresh wounds.
Ma'am, I'd like a chocolate *monaka.*
Apparently she made friends with the girl there and is going there all the time.
I saw her for a second. She's ***super cute!***
Oohh ♡
She's like the ***exact opposite*** of Mahiru. I can't believe they're the same species.
Those two are always talking to each other.
It's like, you know? Opposites attract.
Achoo!

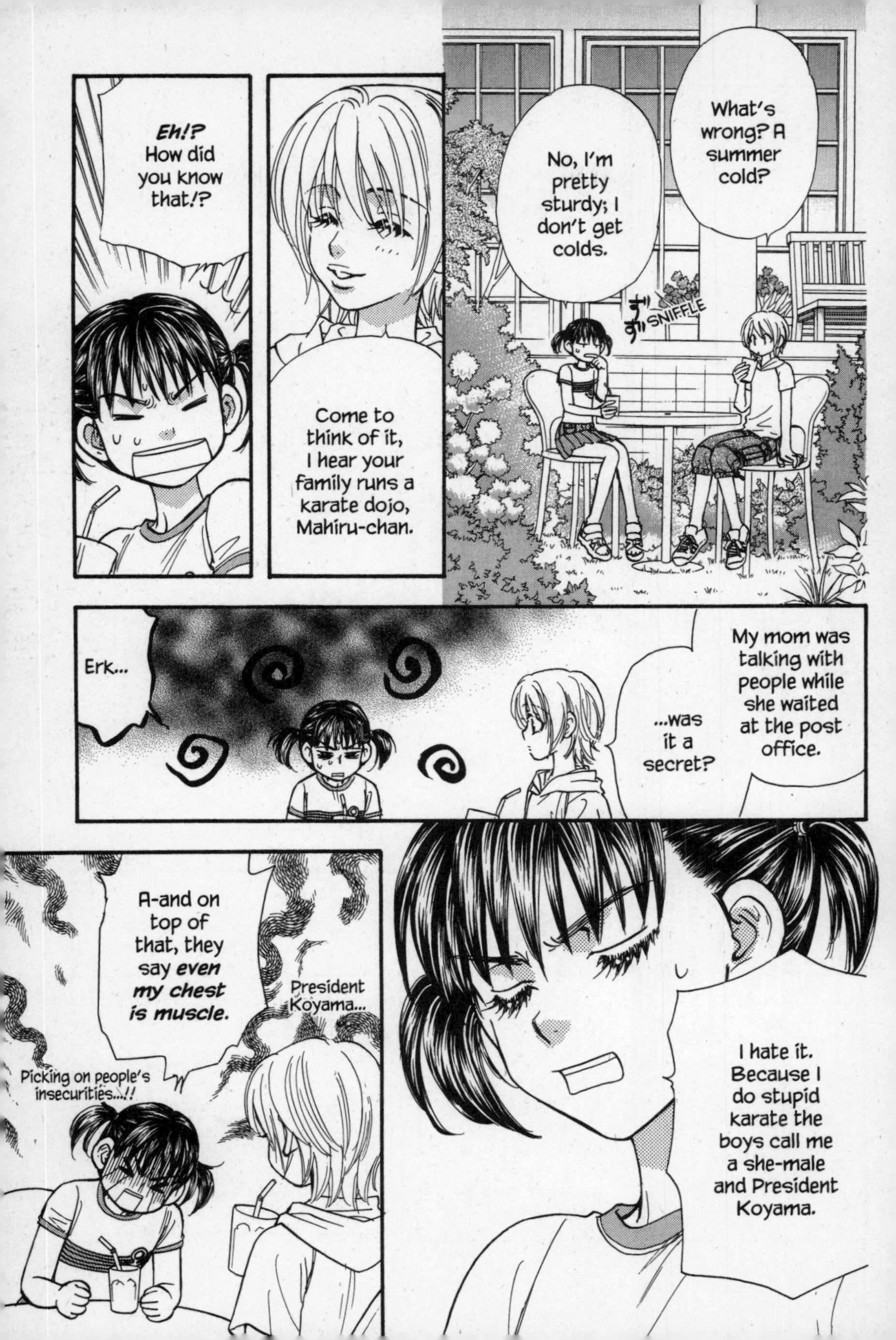

What's wrong? A summer cold?
No, I'm pretty sturdy; I don't get colds.
ずず SNIFFLE
Come to think of it, I hear your family runs a karate dojo, Mahiru-chan.
Eh!? How did you know that!?
My mom was talking with people while she waited at the post office.
...was it a secret?
Erk...
I hate it. Because I do stupid karate the boys call me a she-male and President Koyama.
A-and on top of that, they say even my chest is muscle.
President Koyama...
Picking on people's insecurities...!!

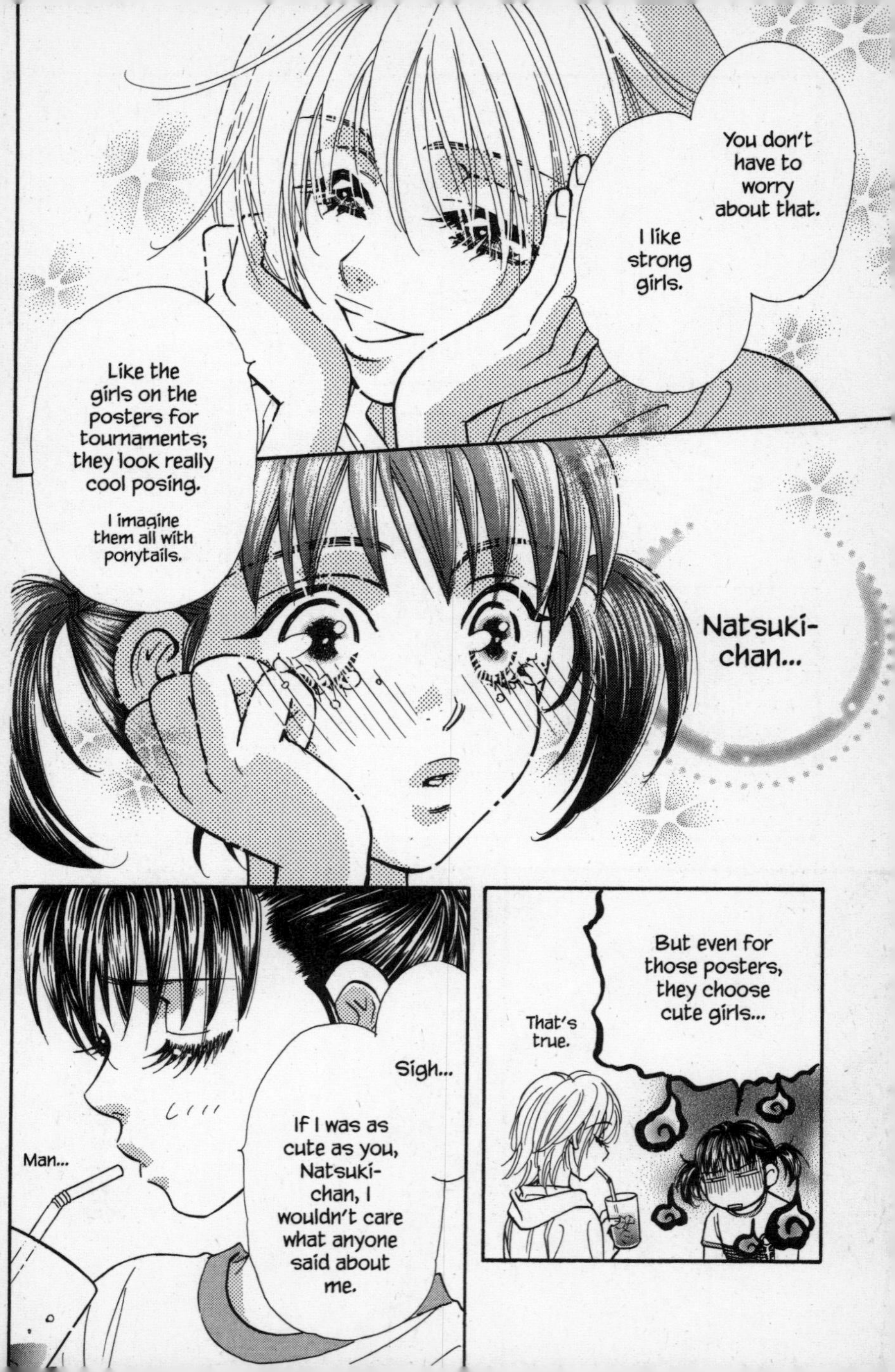
You don't have to worry about that.
I like strong girls.
Like the girls on the posters for tournaments; they look really cool posing.
I imagine them all with ponytails.
Natsuki-chan...
But even for those posters, they choose cute girls...
That's true.
Sigh...
If I was as cute as you, Natsuki-chan, I wouldn't care what anyone said about me.
Man...

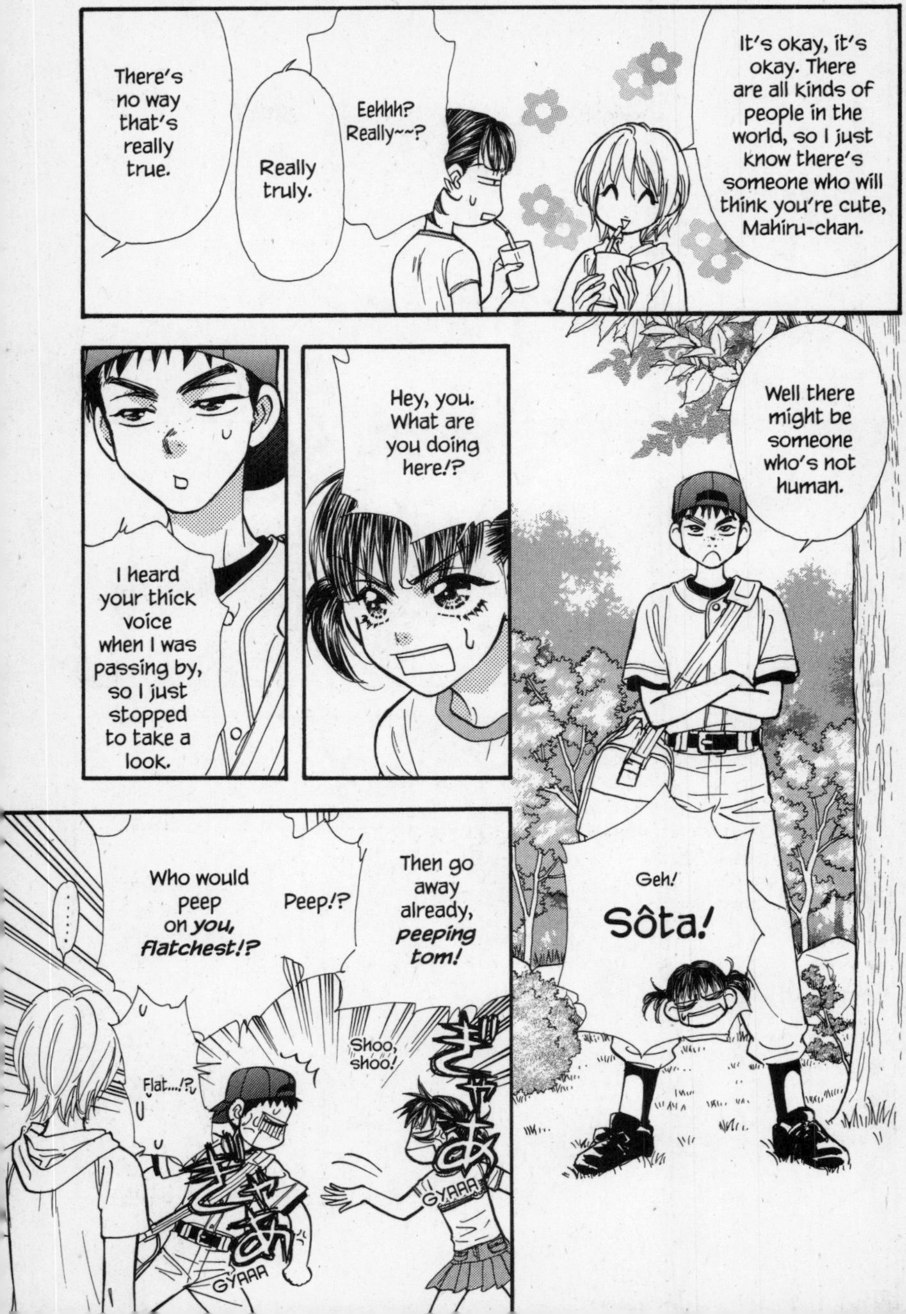
It's okay, it's okay. There are all kinds of people in the world, so I just know there's someone who will think you're cute, Mahiru-chan.
Eehhh? Really~~?
Really truly.
There's no way that's really true.
Well there might be someone who's not human.
Geh!
Sôta!
Hey, you. What are you doing here!?
I heard your thick voice when I was passing by, so I just stopped to take a look.
Then go away already, peeping tom!
Peep!?
Who would peep on you, flatchest!?
.....
Shoo, shoo!
GYAAA
Flat...!?
GYAAA

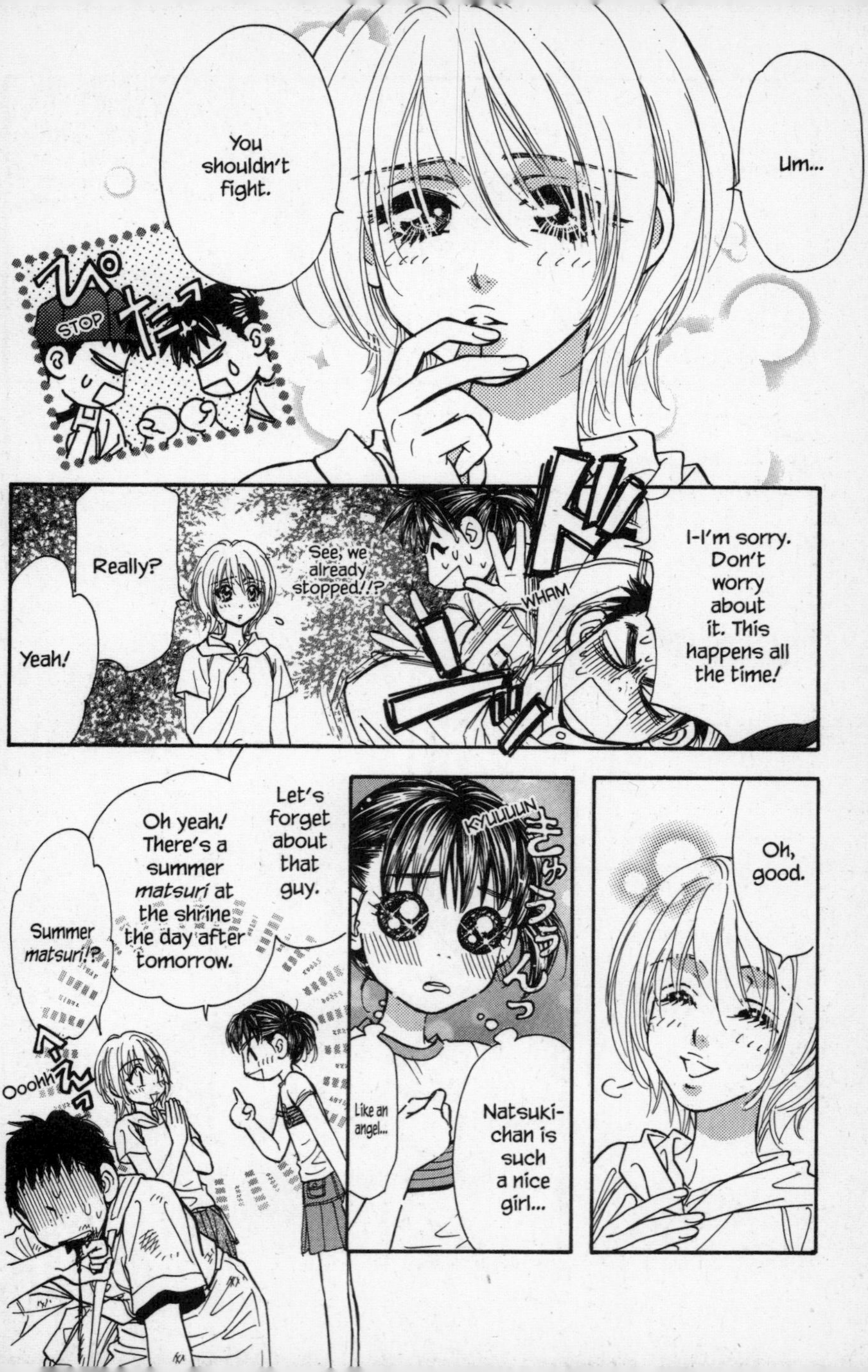
Um...
You shouldn't fight.
STOP
I-I'm sorry. Don't worry about it. This happens all the time!
WHAM
See, we already stopped!!?
Really?
Yeah!
Oh, good.
KYUUUUN
Natsuki-chan is such a nice girl...
Like an angel...
Let's forget about that guy.
Oh yeah! There's a summer *matsuri* at the shrine the day after tomorrow.
Summer *matsuri*!?
Ooohh

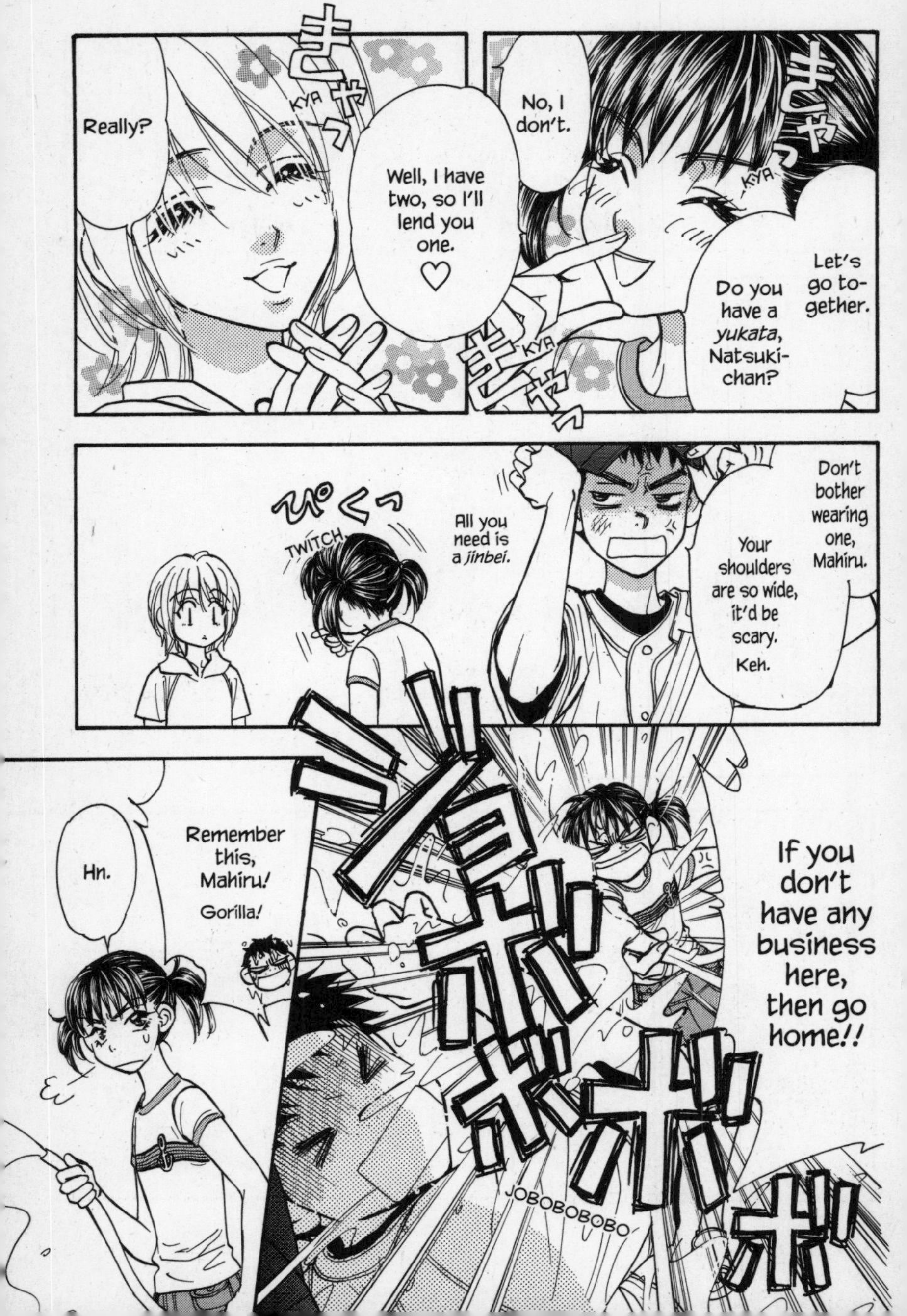
KYA
Let's go together.
Do you have a yukata, Natsuki-chan?
No, I don't.
KYA
Well, I have two, so I'll lend you one. ♡
Really?
KYA
Don't bother wearing one, Mahiru.
Your shoulders are so wide, it'd be scary.
Keh.
All you need is a jinbei.
TWITCH
If you don't have any business here, then go home!!
JOBOBOBOBO
Remember this, Mahiru!
Gorilla!
Hn.

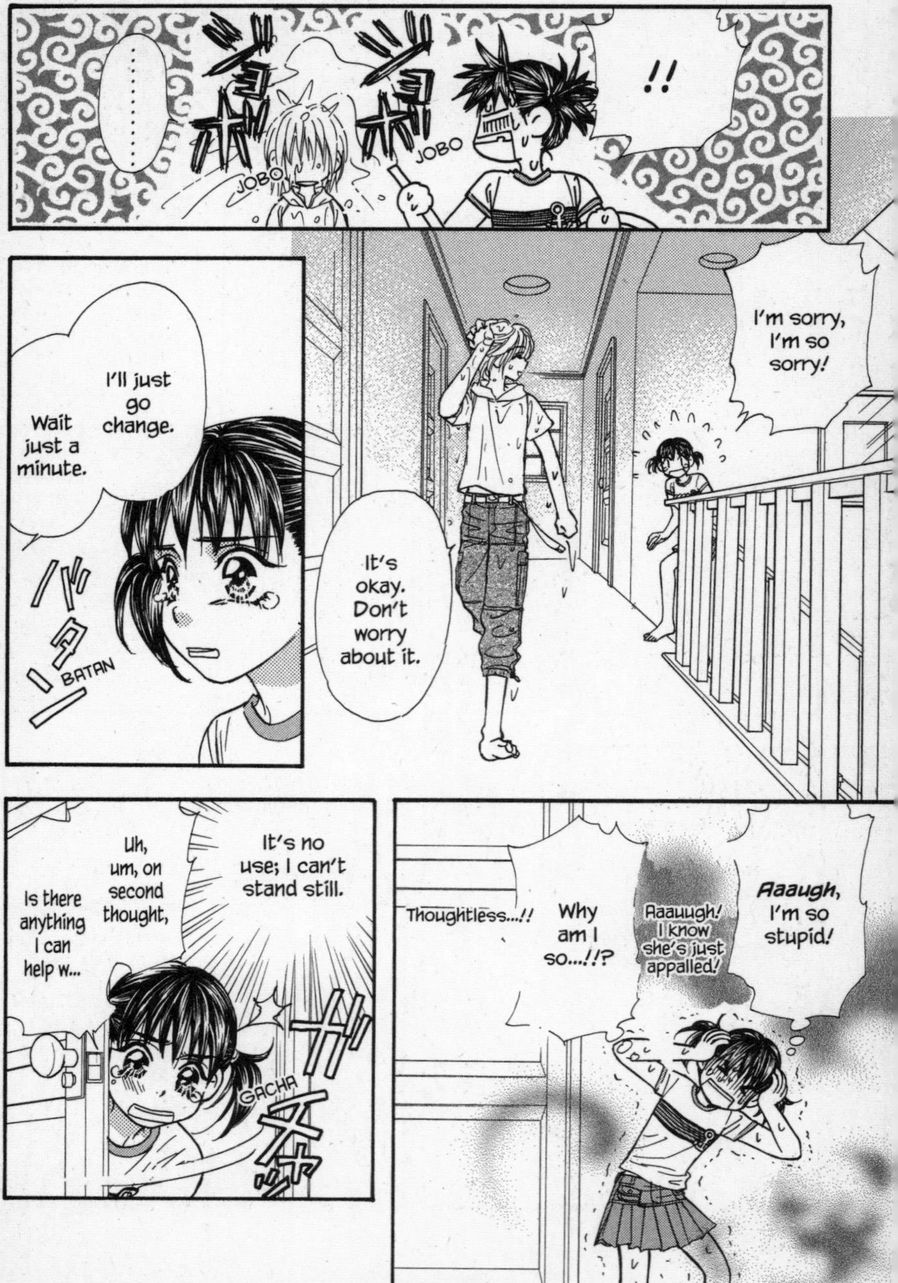
!!
JOBO
JOBO
......
I'm sorry, I'm so sorry!
It's okay. Don't worry about it.
I'll just go change.
Wait just a minute.
BATAN
Aaaugh, I'm so stupid!
Aaauugh! I know she's just appalled!
Why am I so...!!?
Thoughtless...!!
It's no use; I can't stand still.
Uh, um, on second thought,
Is there anything I can help w...
GACHA

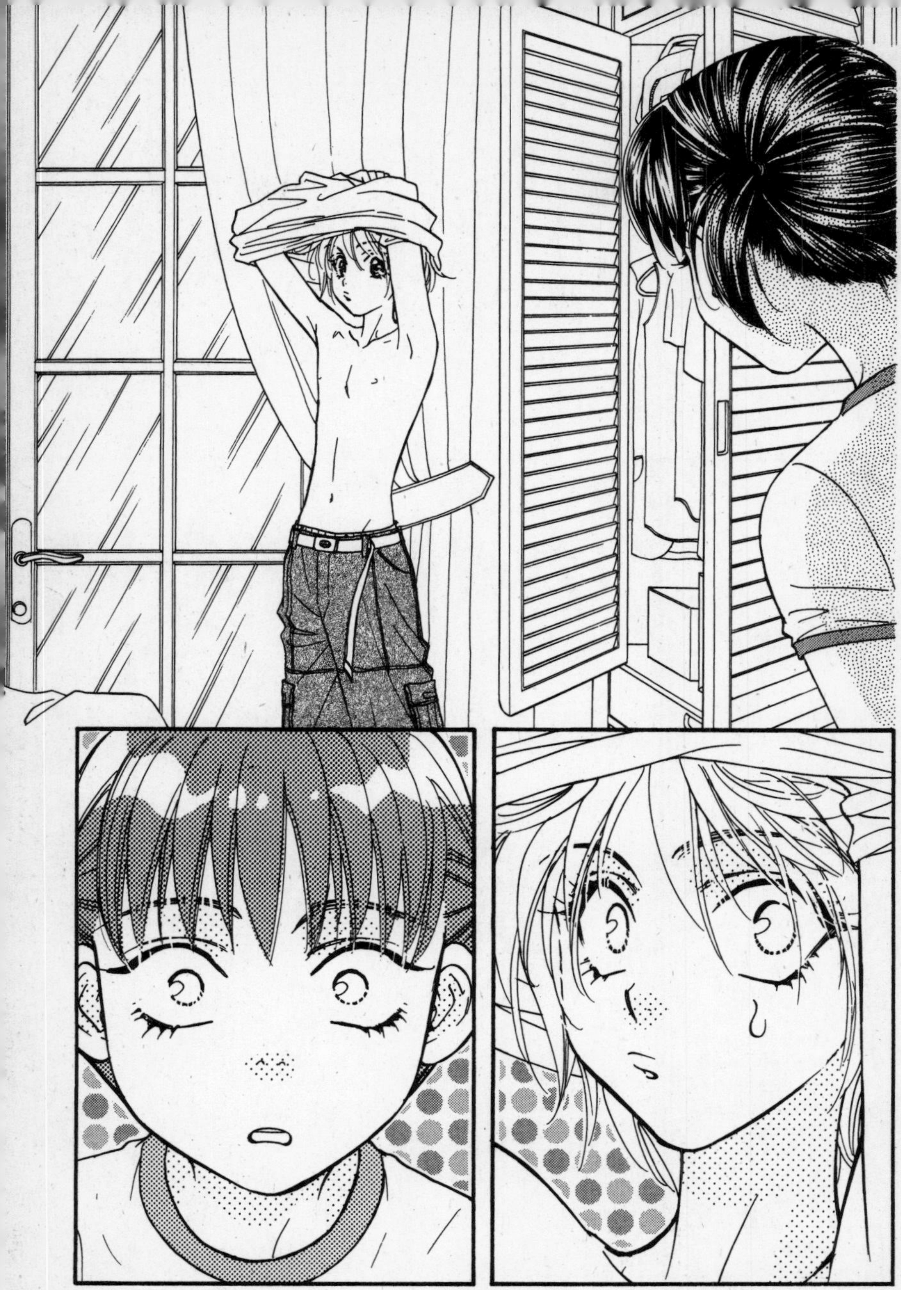

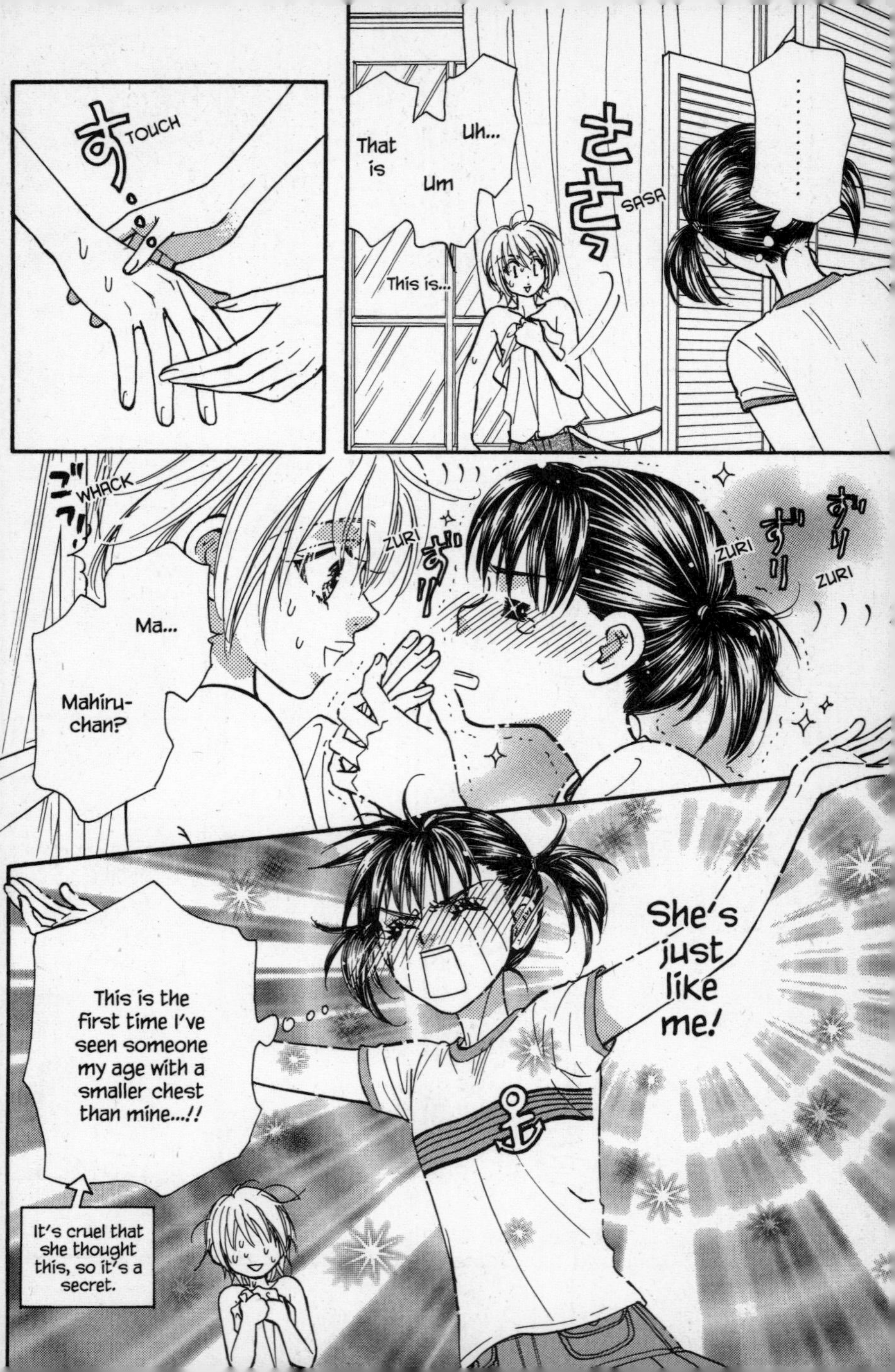

……
さっ SASA
Uh... That is Um
This is...
す。TOUCH
ずり ZURI ずり ZURI ずり ZURI
ゴッ!! WHACK
Ma...
Mahiru-chan?
She's just like me!
This is the first time I've seen someone my age with a smaller chest than mine...!!
It's cruel that she thought this, so it's a secret.

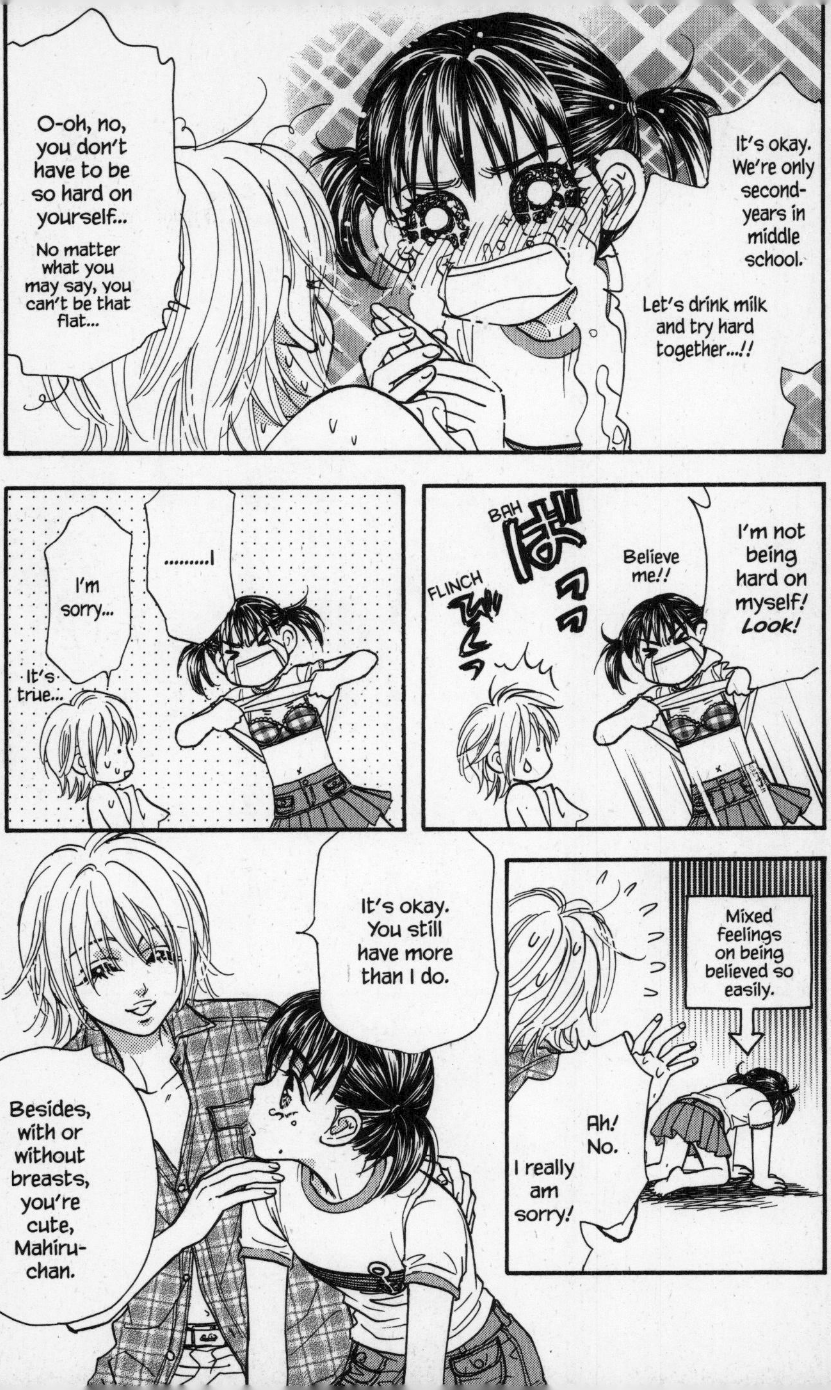
It's okay. We're only second-years in middle school.
Let's drink milk and try hard together...!!
O-oh, no, you don't have to be so hard on yourself...
No matter what you may say, you can't be that flat...
I'm not being hard on myself! *Look!*
Believe me!!
BAH
FLINCH
.........!
I'm sorry...
It's true...
Mixed feelings on being believed so easily.
Ah! No.
I really am sorry!
It's okay. You still have more than I do.
Besides, with or without breasts, you're cute, Mahiru-chan.

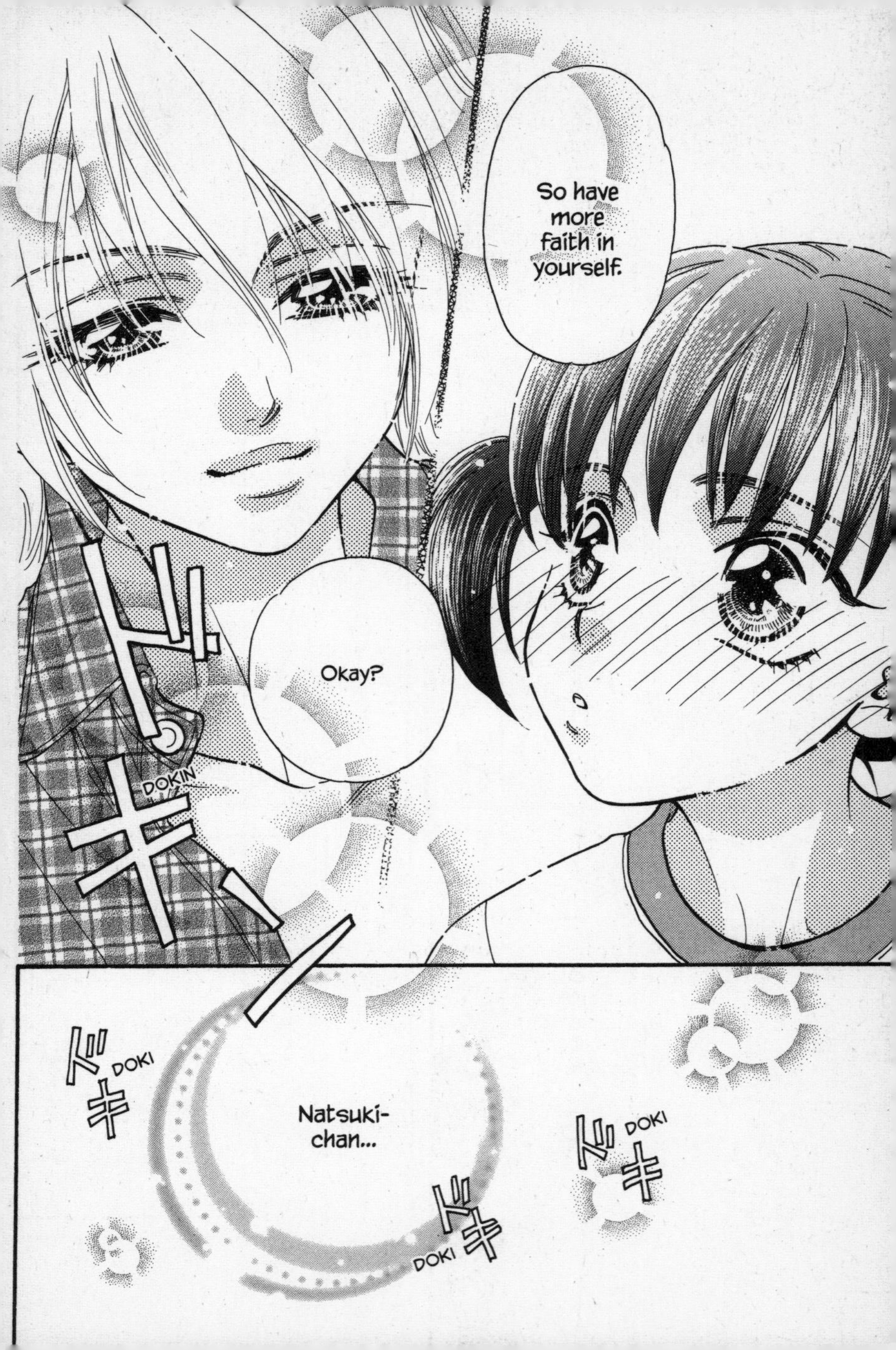
So have more faith in yourself.
Okay?
ドキン
DOKIN
ドキ
DOKI
ドキ
DOKI
Natsuki-chan...
ドキ
DOKI

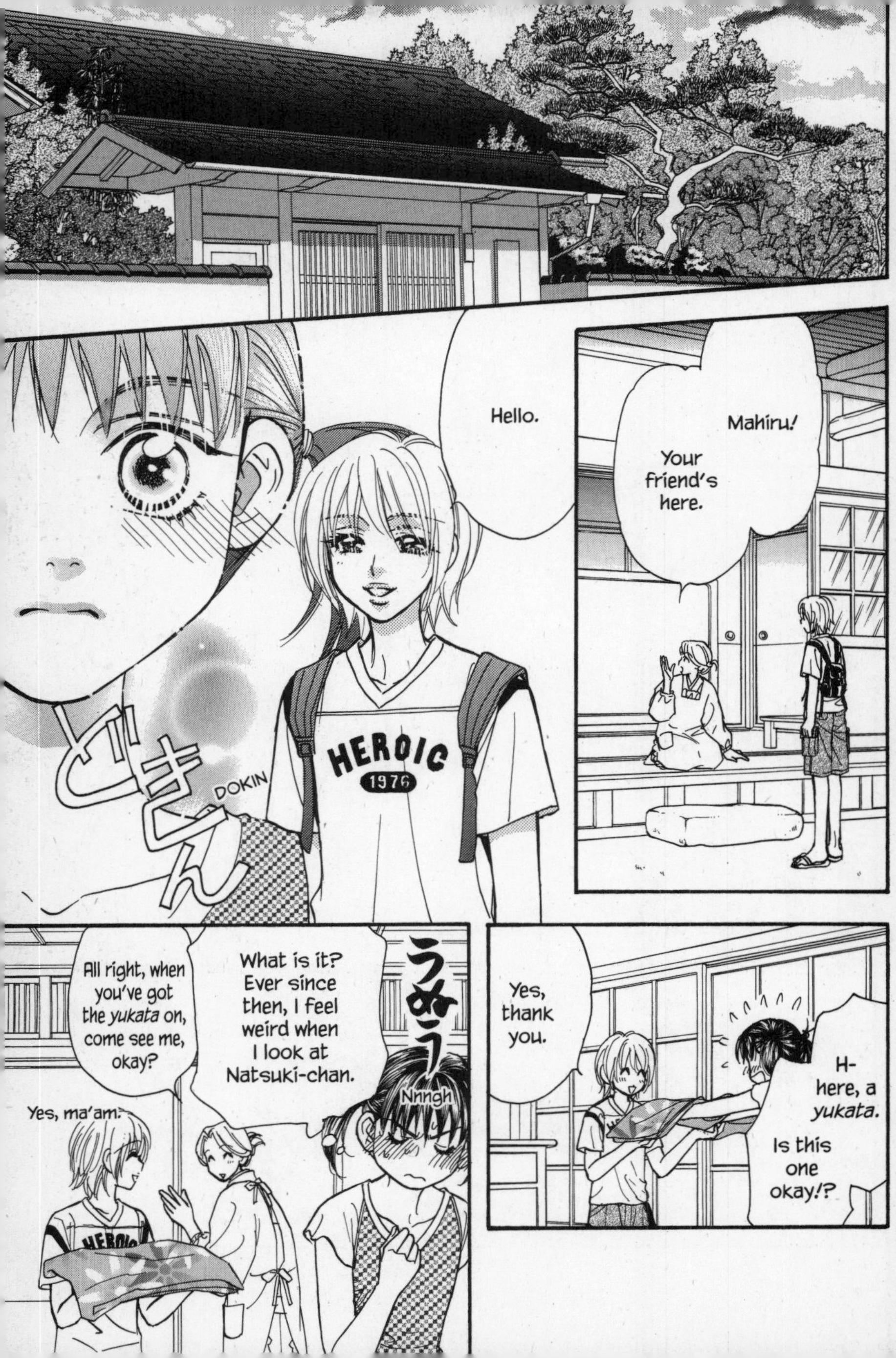
Mahiru!
Your friend's here.
Hello.
どきん
DOKIN
H-here, a *yukata*.
Is this one okay!?
Yes, thank you.
うぬう
Nnngh
What is it? Ever since then, I feel weird when I look at Natsuki-chan.
All right, when you've got the *yukata* on, come see me, okay?
Yes, ma'am.

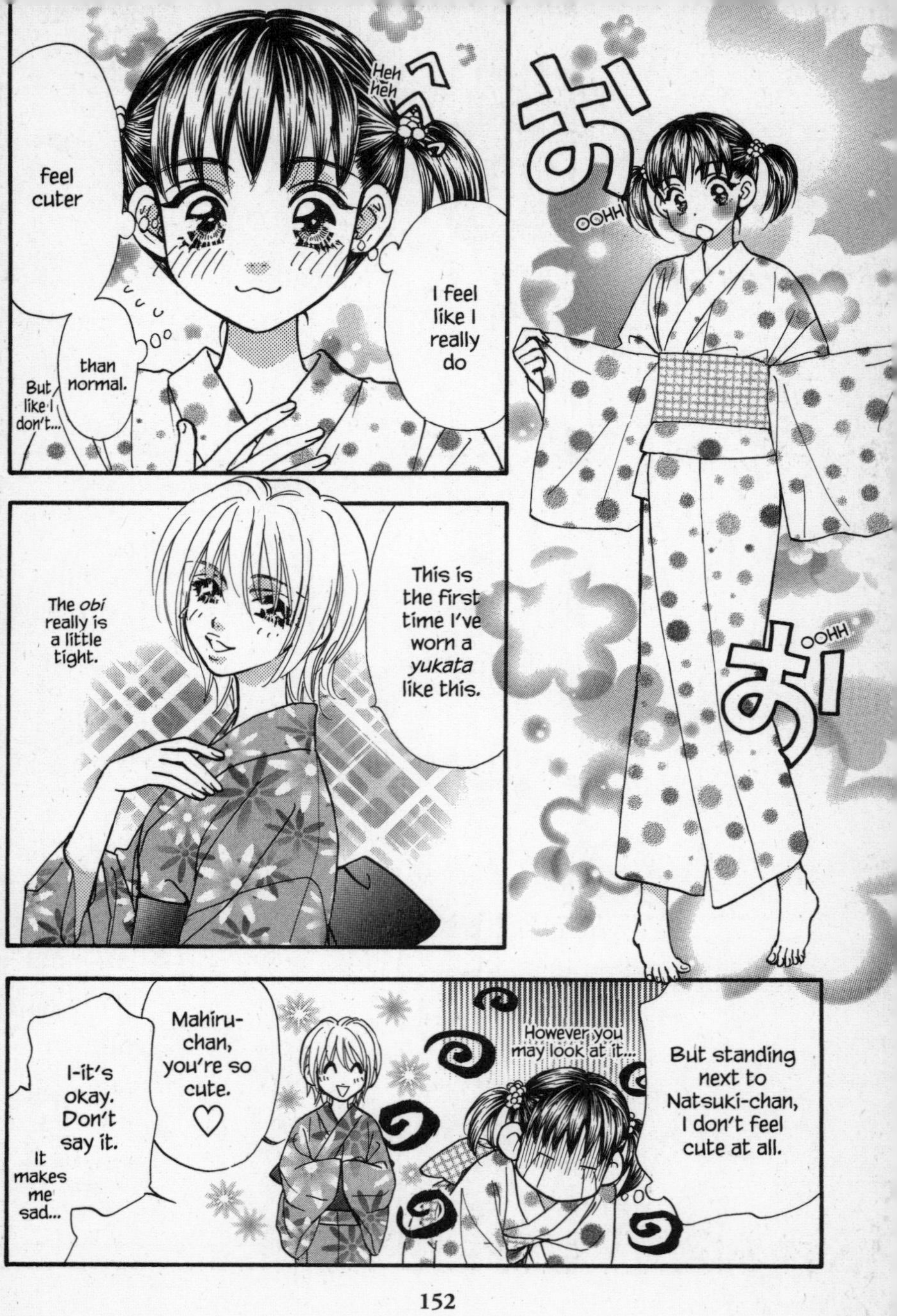
お OOHH
お OOHH
Heh heh
I feel like I really do
feel cuter
than normal.
But like I don't...
This is the first time I've worn a *yukata* like this.
The *obi* really is a little tight.
But standing next to Natsuki-chan, I don't feel cute at all.
However you may look at it...
Mahiru-chan, you're so cute. ♡
I-it's okay. Don't say it.
It makes me sad...

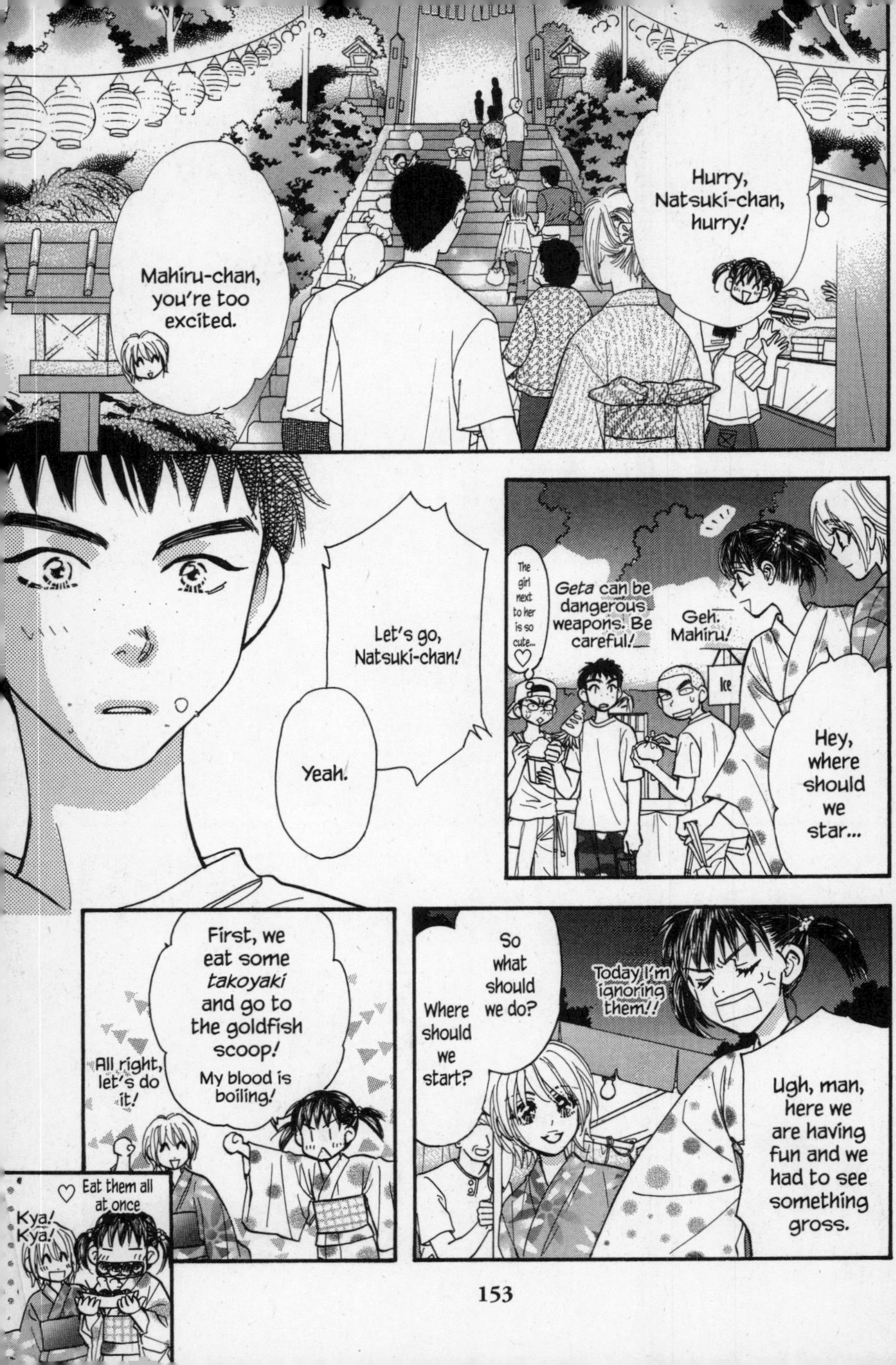
Hurry, Natsuki-chan, hurry!
Mahiru-chan, you're too excited.
Hey, where should we star...
Ice
Geh. Mahiru!
Geta can be dangerous weapons. Be careful!
The girl next to her is so cute... ♡
Let's go, Natsuki-chan!
Yeah.
Ugh, man, here we are having fun and we had to see something gross.
Today I'm ignoring them!!
So what should we do?
Where should we start?
First, we eat some *takoyaki* and go to the goldfish scoop!
My blood is boiling!
All right, let's do it!
♡ Eat them all at once
Kya! Kya!

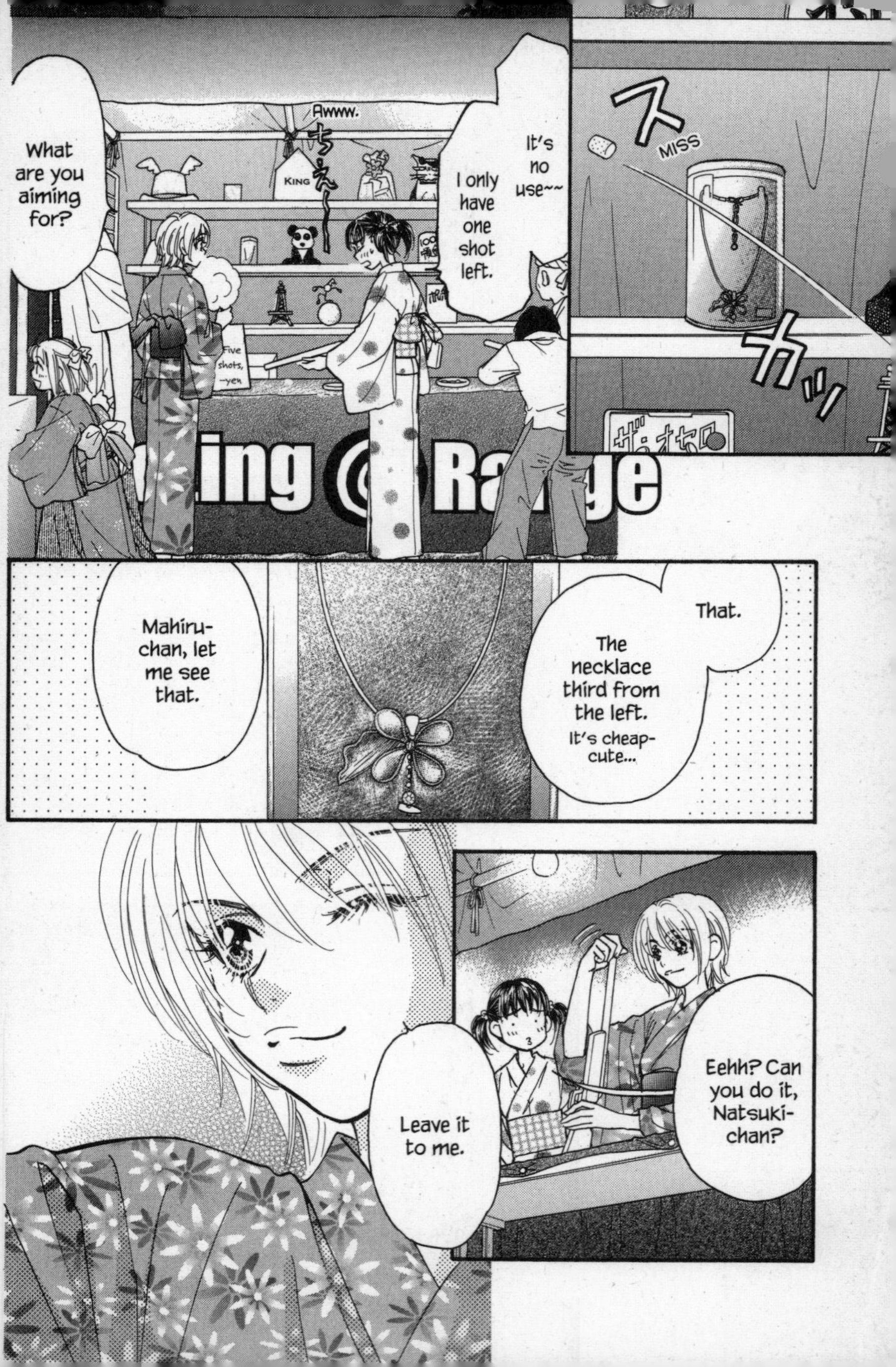

ス
MISS
カッ
It's no use~~
I only have one shot left.
Awww.
ちぇ〜
What are you aiming for?
KING
Five shots, —yen
That.
The necklace third from the left.
It's cheap-cute...
Mahiru-chan, let me see that.
Eehh? Can you do it, Natsuki-chan?
Leave it to me.

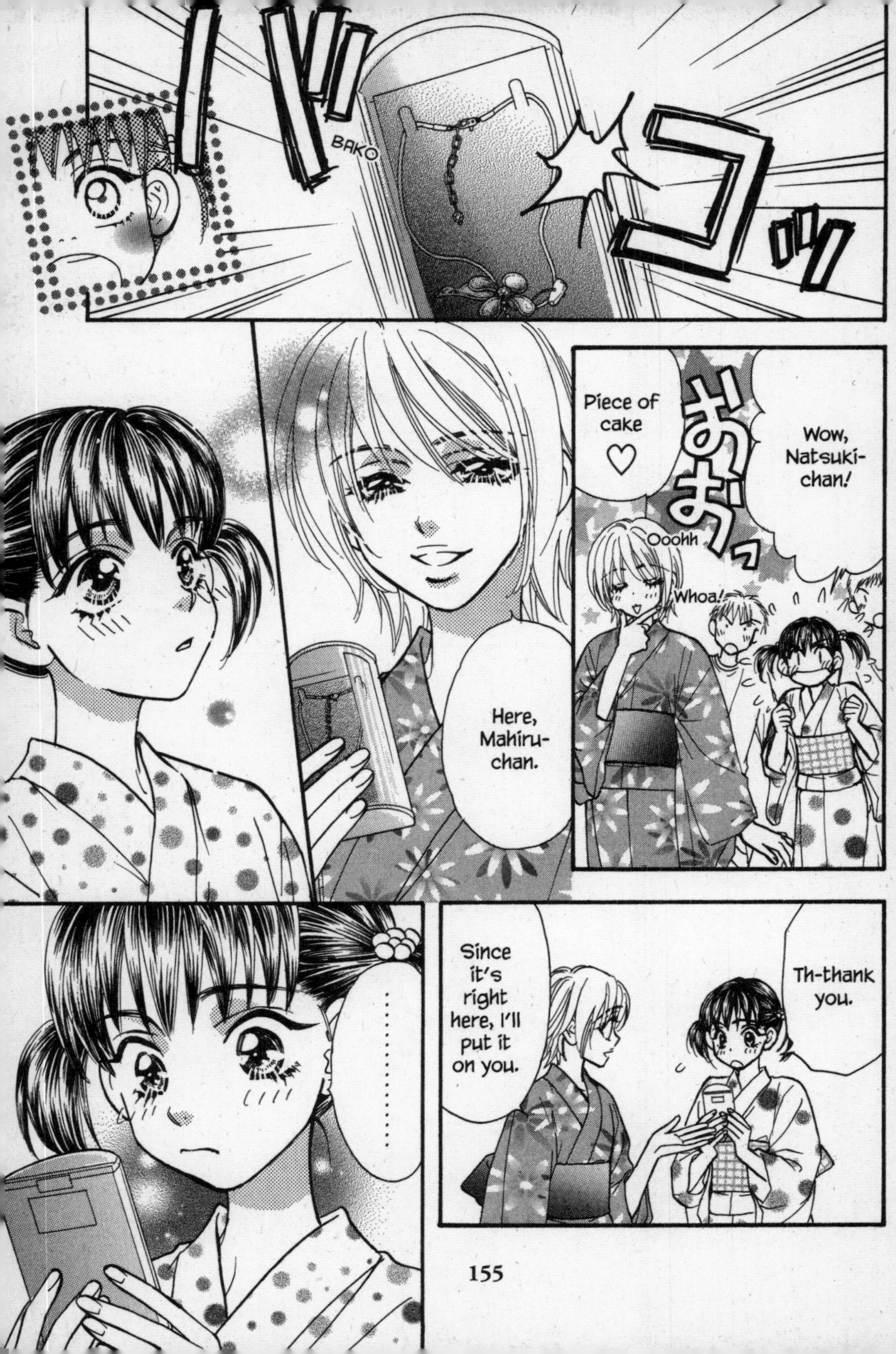

BAKO
Wow, Natsuki-chan!
おおっ
Ooohh
Whoa!
Piece of cake ♡
Here, Mahiru-chan.
Th-thank you.
Since it's right here, I'll put it on you.
....

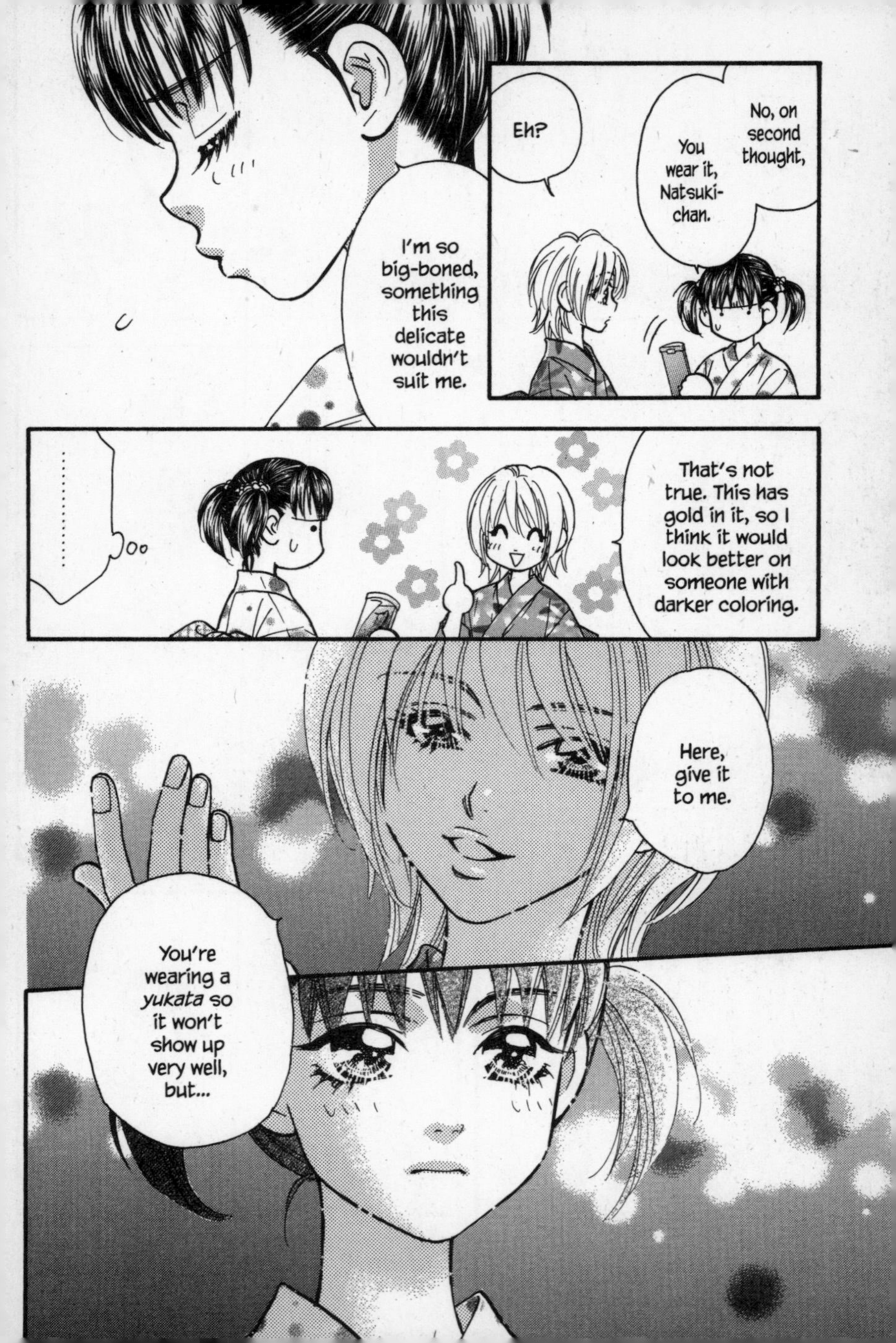
No, on second thought,
You wear it, Natsuki-chan.
Eh?
I'm so big-boned, something this delicate wouldn't suit me.
That's not true. This has gold in it, so I think it would look better on someone with darker coloring.
......
Here, give it to me.
You're wearing a *yukata* so it won't show up very well, but...

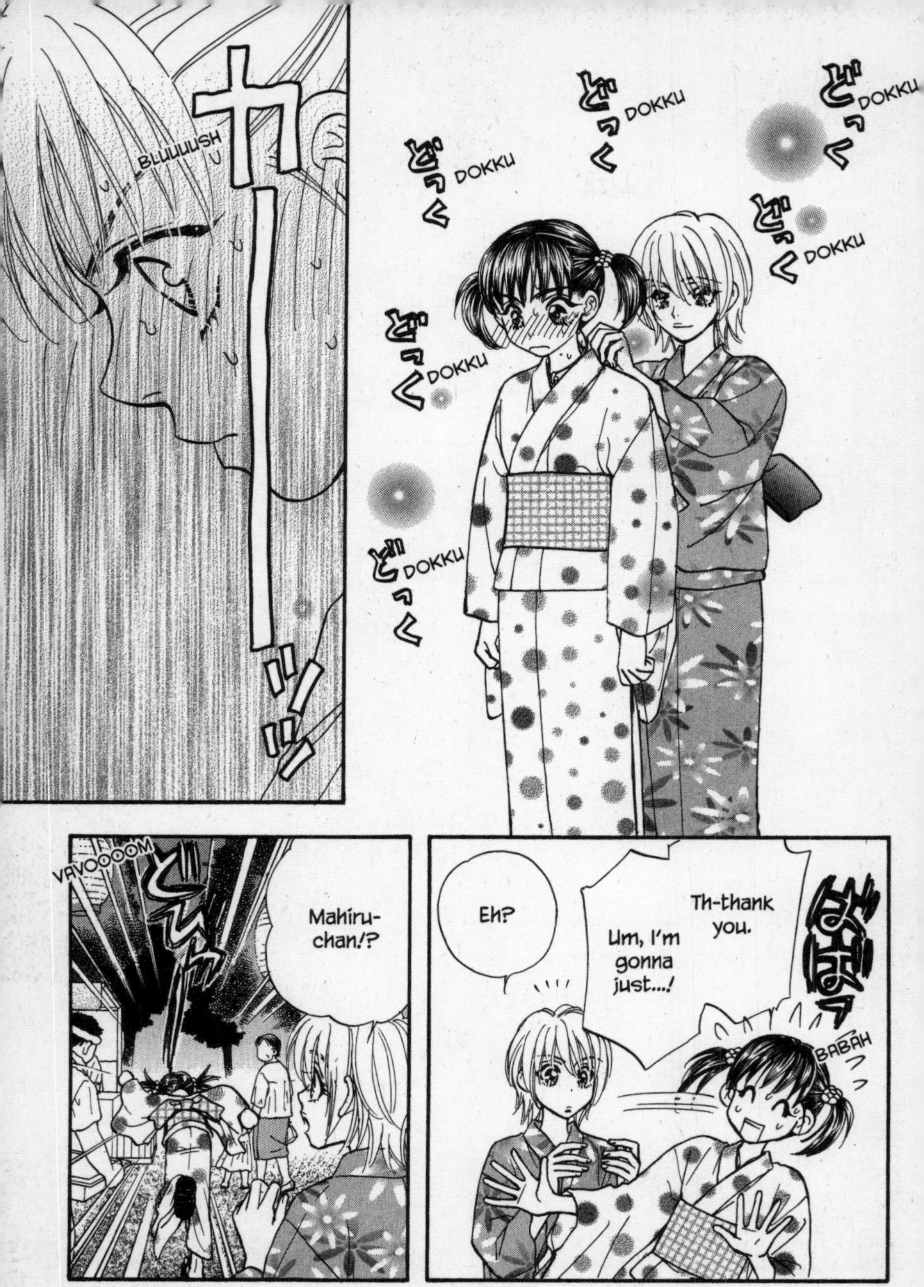
DOKKU
DOKKU
DOKKU
DOKKU
DOKKU
DOKKU
BLUUUUSH
Th-thank you.
Um, I'm gonna just...!
BABAH
Eh?
VAVOOOOM
Mahiru-chan!?

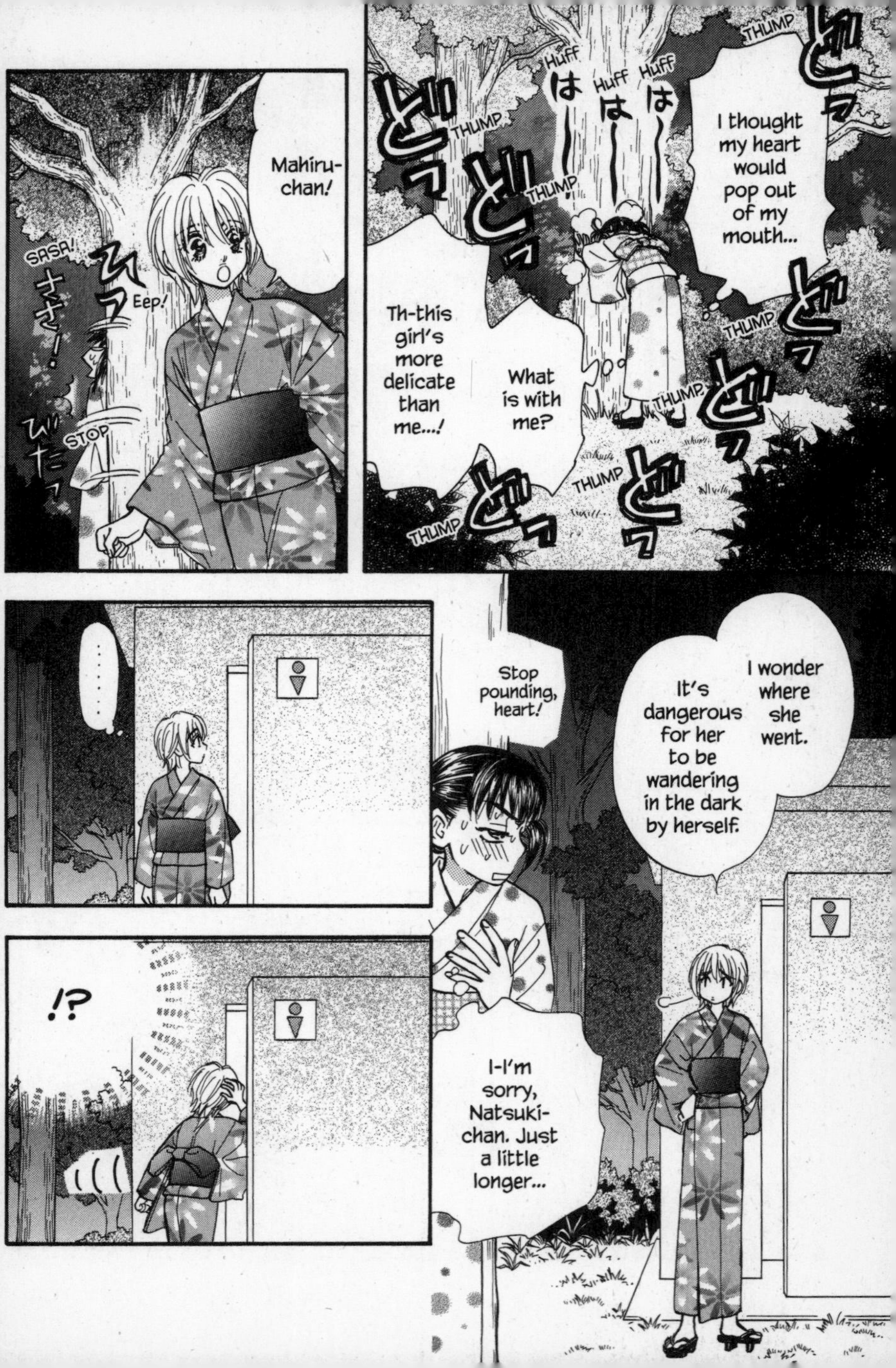
THUMP
どっ
Huff Huff Huff
はーー はーー はーー
I thought my heart would pop out of my mouth...
THUMP どっ
THUMP どっ
THUMP どっ
THUMP どっ
THUMP どっ
THUMP どっ
THUMP どっ
What is with me?
Th-this girl's more delicate than me...!
Mahiru-chan!
SASA! ささ!
Eep! ひっ
STOP ぴた
I wonder where she went.
It's dangerous for her to be wandering in the dark by herself.
Stop pounding, heart!
I-I'm sorry, Natsuki-chan. Just a little longer...
......
!?

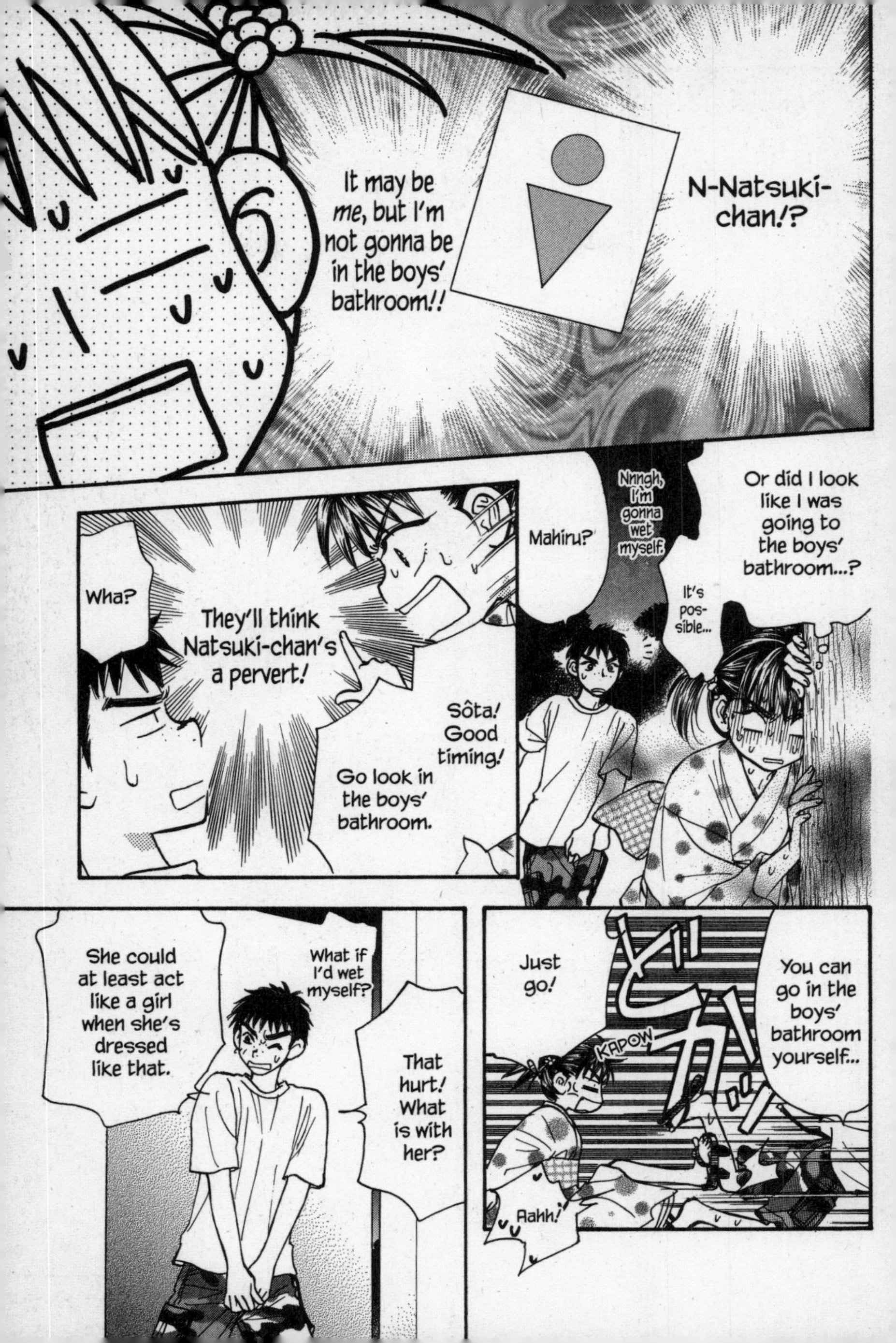

N-Natsuki-chan!?
It may be *me*, but I'm not gonna be in the boys' bathroom!!
Or did I look like I was going to the boys' bathroom...?
Nnngh, I'm gonna wet myself.
It's pos-sible...
Mahiru?
Sôta! Good timing!
Go look in the boys' bathroom.
They'll think Natsuki-chan's a pervert!
Wha?
You can go in the boys' bathroom yourself...
Just go!
KAPOW
Aahh!
What if I'd wet myself?
That hurt! What is with her?
She could at least act like a girl when she's dressed like that.

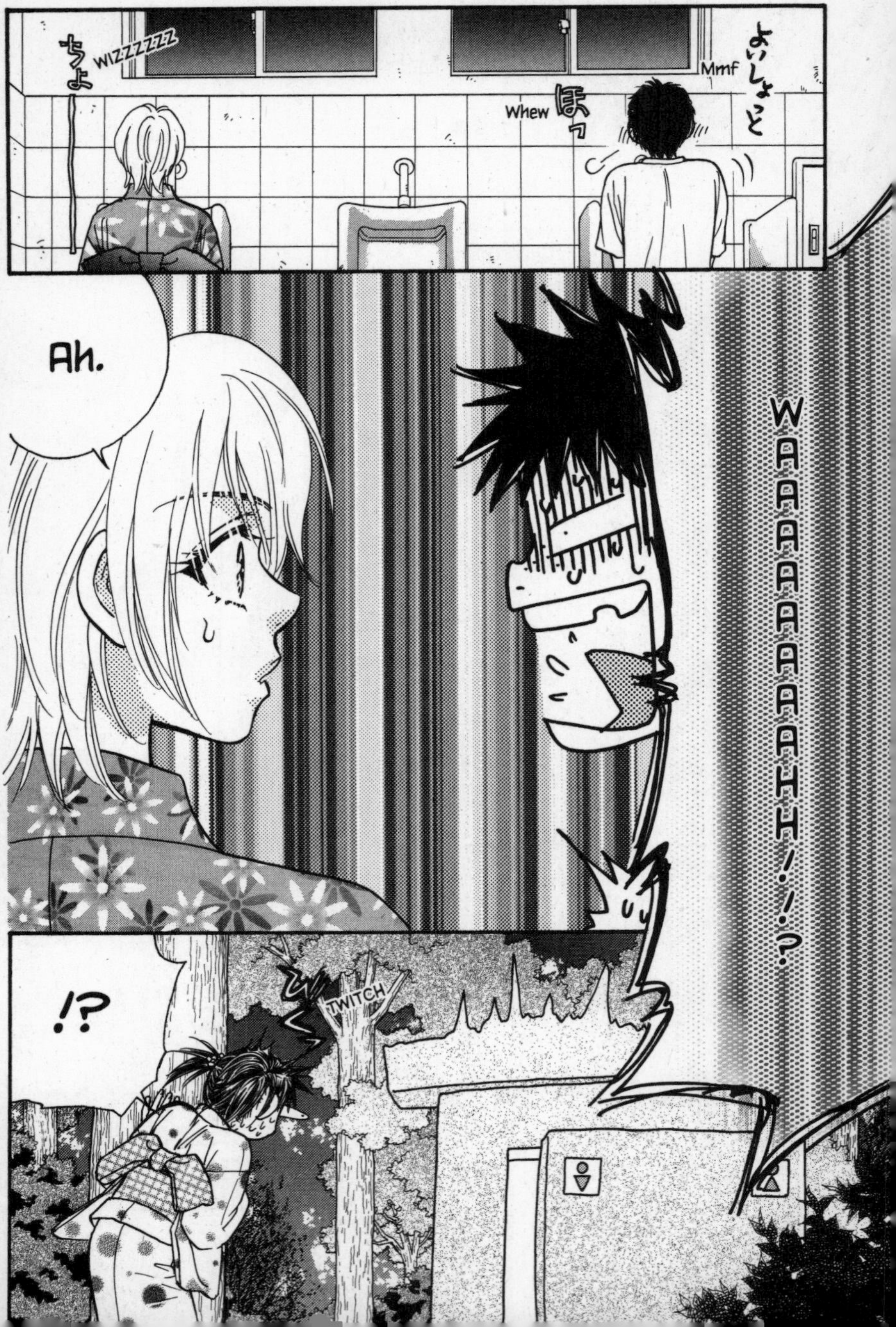

よいしょっと
Mmf
ほっ
Whew
ちょ
WIZZZZZZZ
WAAAAAAAAAAH!!?
Ah.
TWITCH
!?

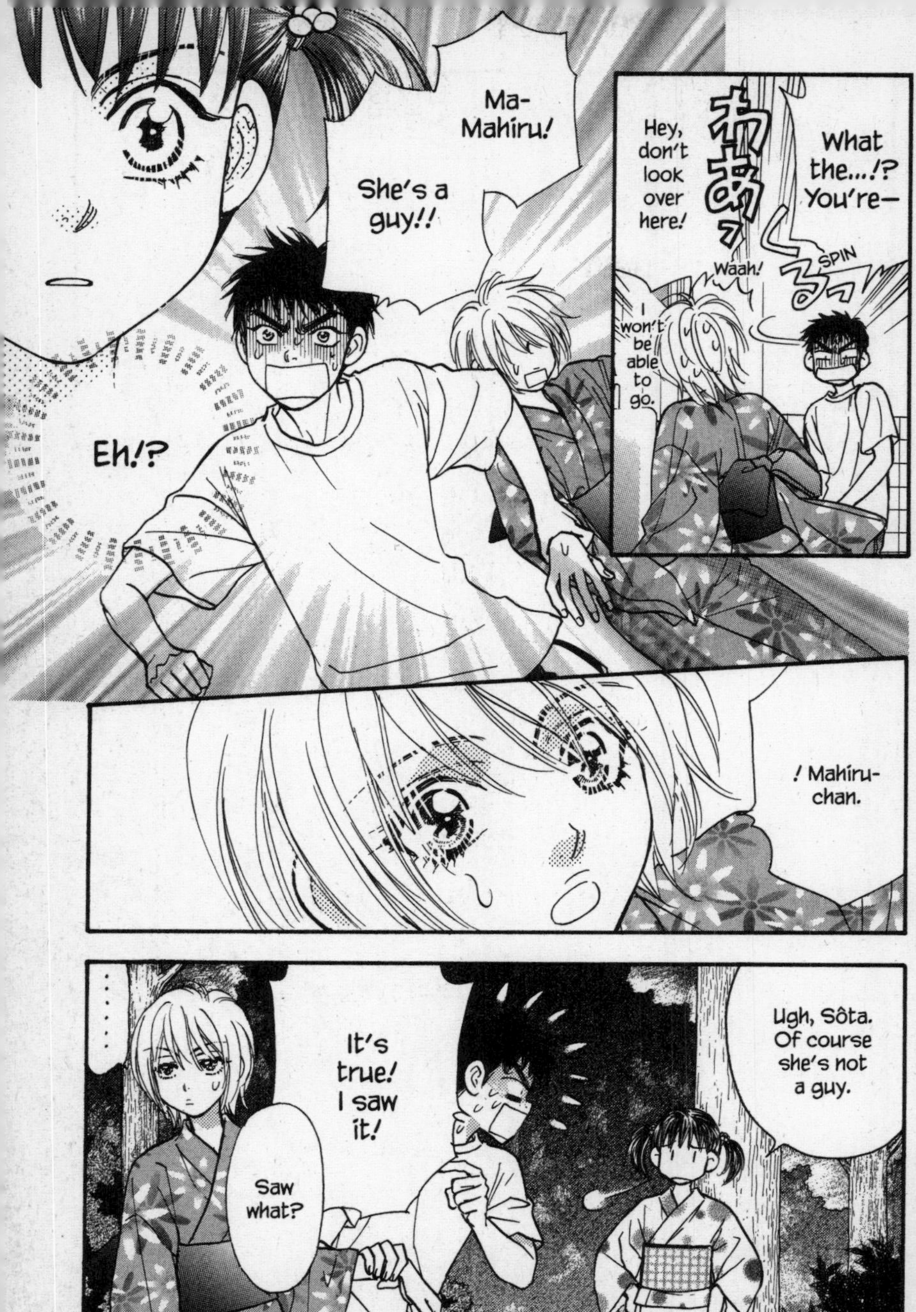
What the...!? You're—
くるっ
SPIN
わあっ
Waah!
Hey, don't look over here!
I won't be able to go.
Ma-Mahiru!
She's a guy!!
Eh!?
! Mahiru-chan.
Ugh, Sôta. Of course she's not a guy.
It's true! I saw it!
Saw what?
......

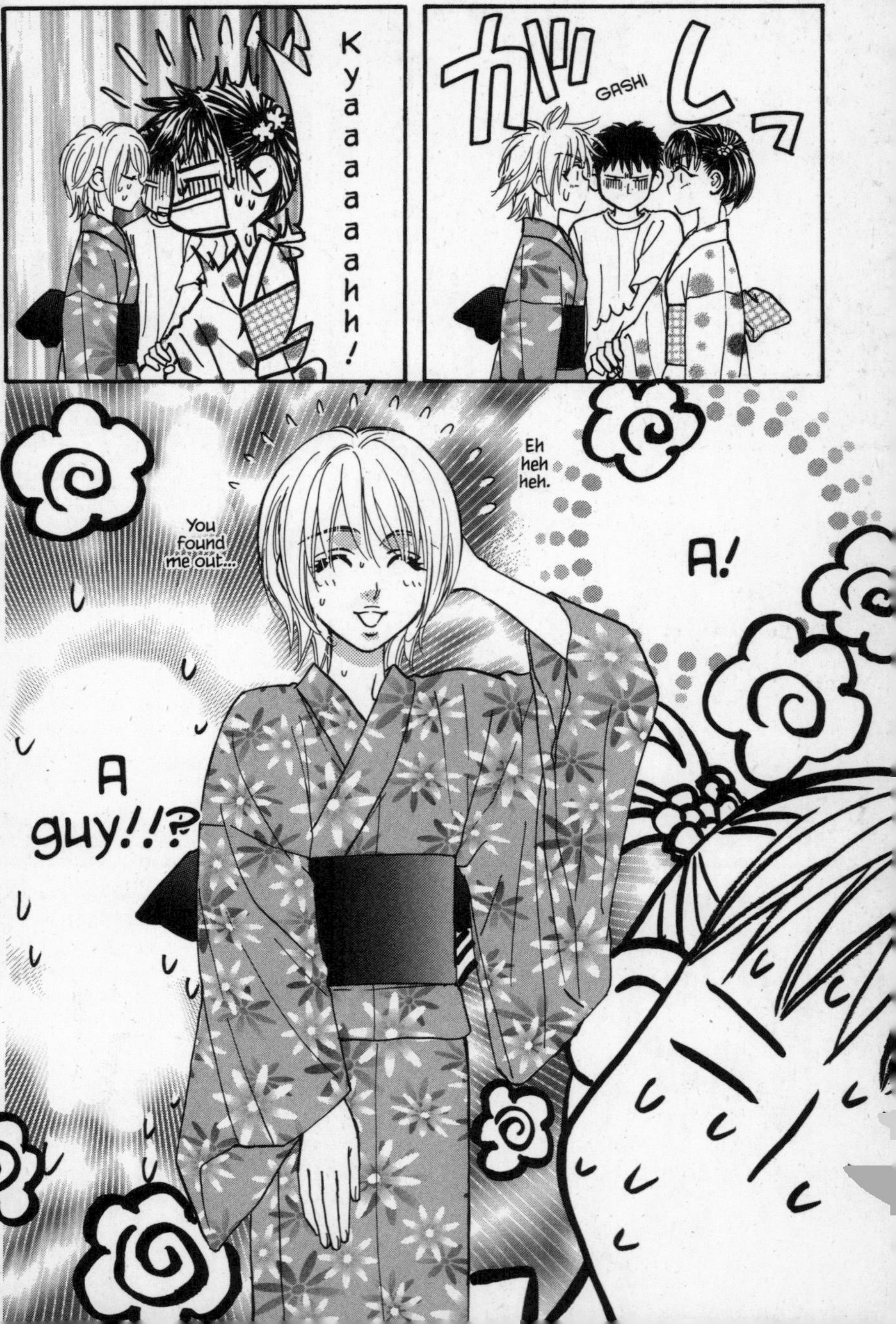
GASHI
Kyaaaaaahh!
Eh heh heh.
A!
You found me out...
A guy!!!?

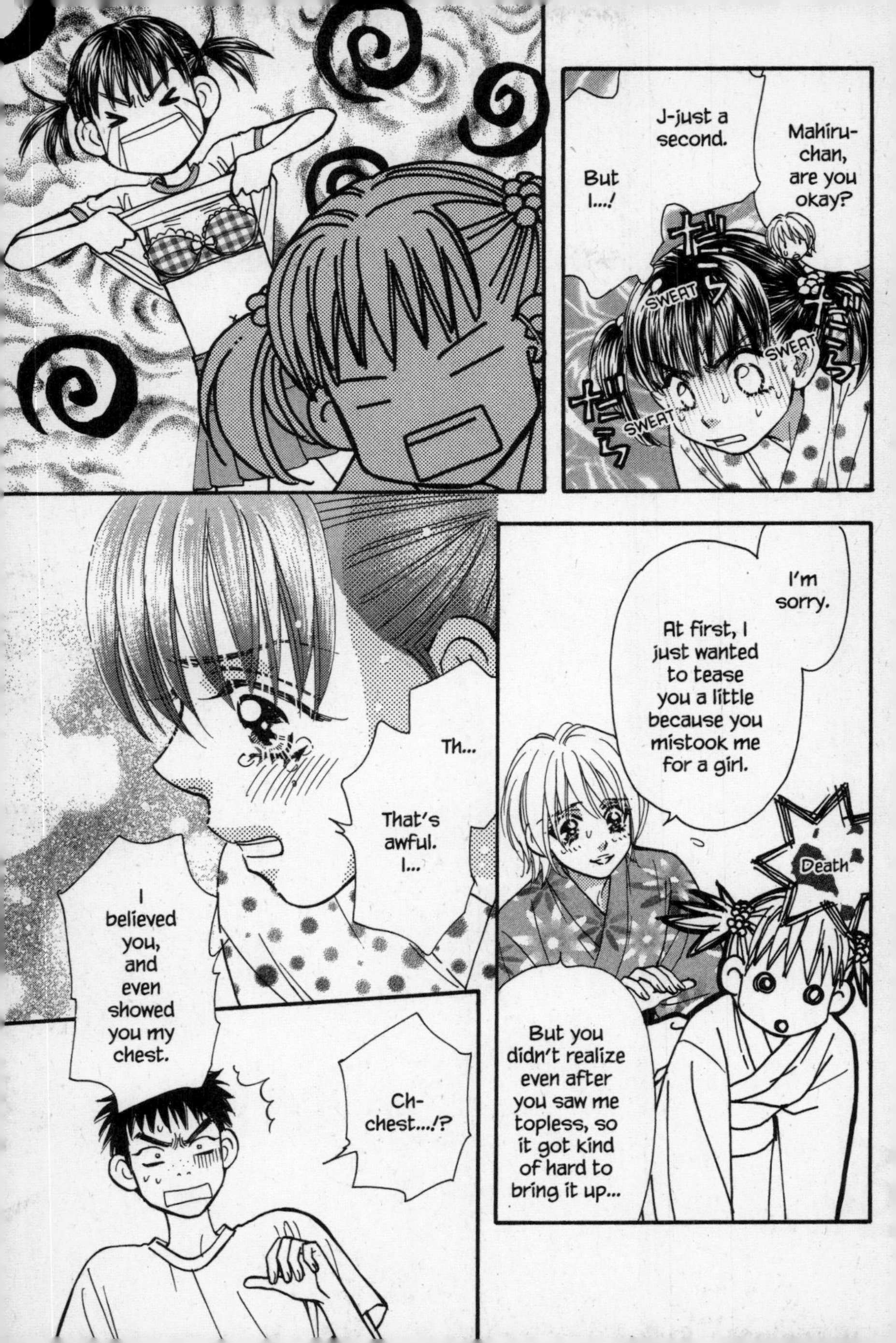
Mahiru-chan, are you okay?
J-just a second.
But I...!
SWEAT
SWEAT
SWEAT
I'm sorry.
At first, I just wanted to tease you a little because you mistook me for a girl.
Death
But you didn't realize even after you saw me topless, so it got kind of hard to bring it up...
Th...
That's awful. I...
I believed you, and even showed you my chest.
Ch-chest...!?

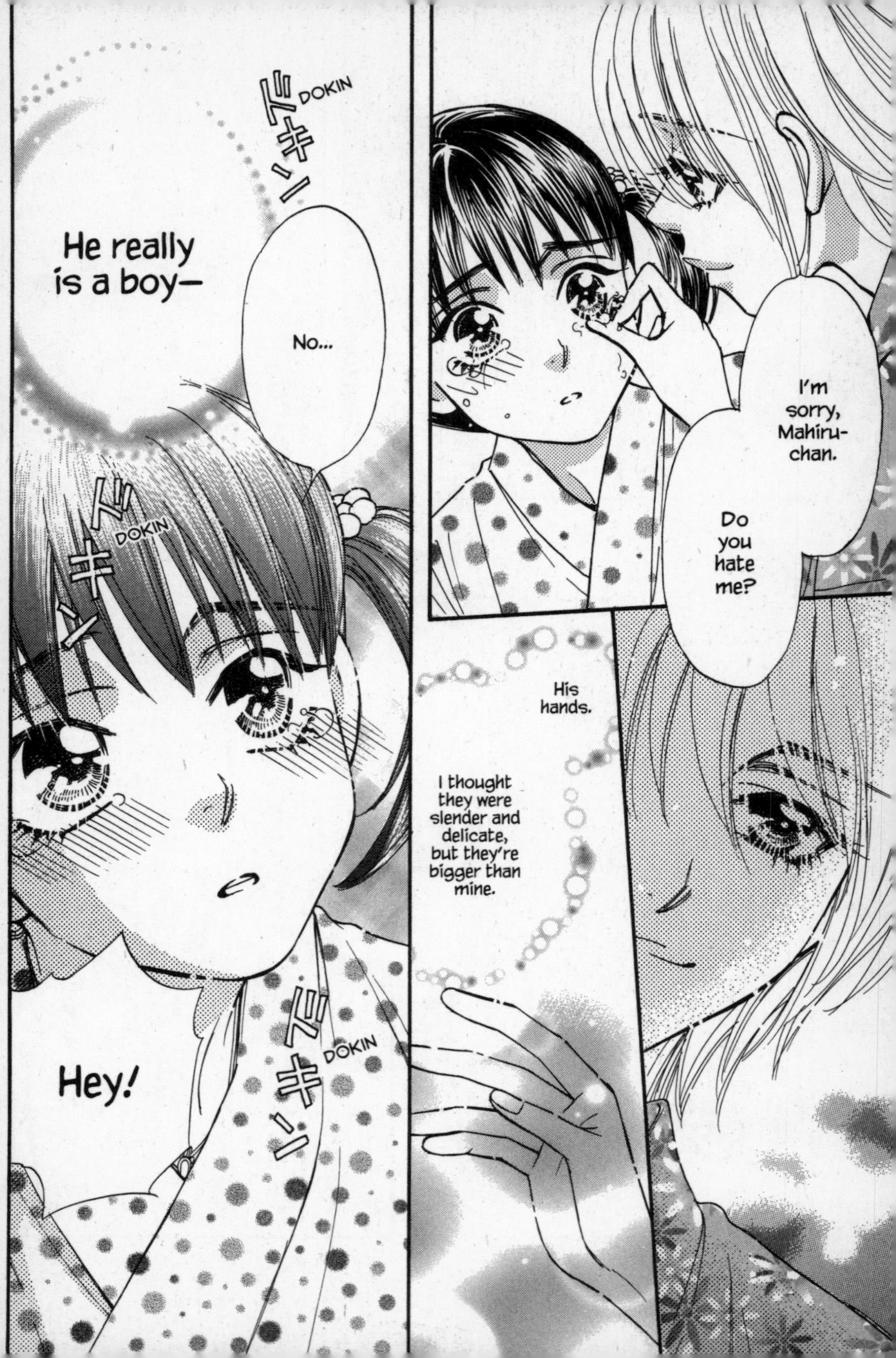
I'm sorry, Mahiru-chan.
Do you hate me?
His hands.
I thought they were slender and delicate, but they're bigger than mine.
DOKIN
No...
He really is a boy—
DOKIN
DOKIN
Hey!

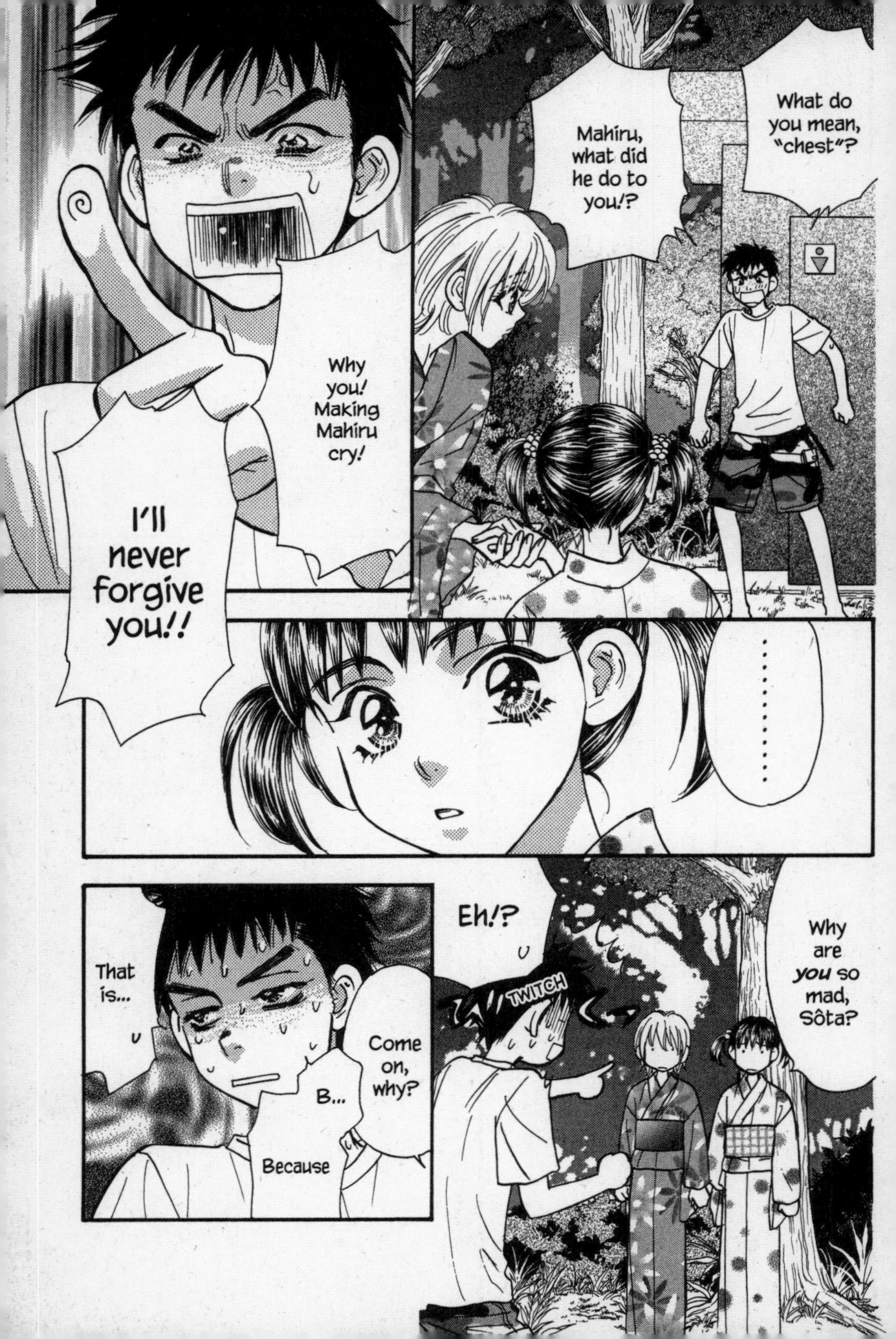
What do you mean, "chest"?
Mahiru, what did he do to you!?
Why you! Making Mahiru cry!
I'll never forgive you!!
......
Why are you so mad, Sôta?
Eh!?
TWITCH
Come on, why?
That is...
B...
Because

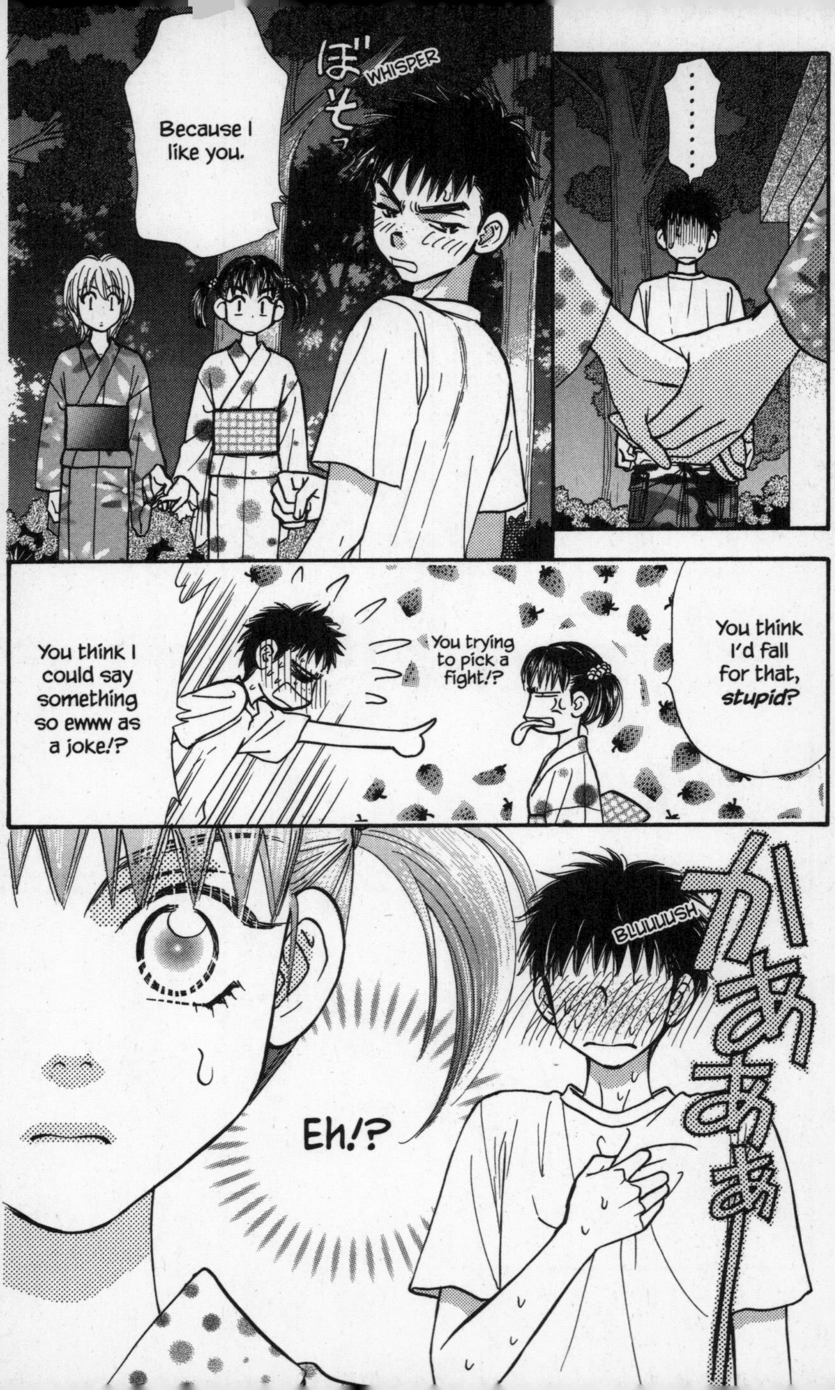
……
ぼそっ
WHISPER
Because I like you.
You think I'd fall for that, *stupid?*
You trying to pick a fight!?
You think I could say something so ewww as a joke!?
かあああ
BLUUUUSH
Eh!?

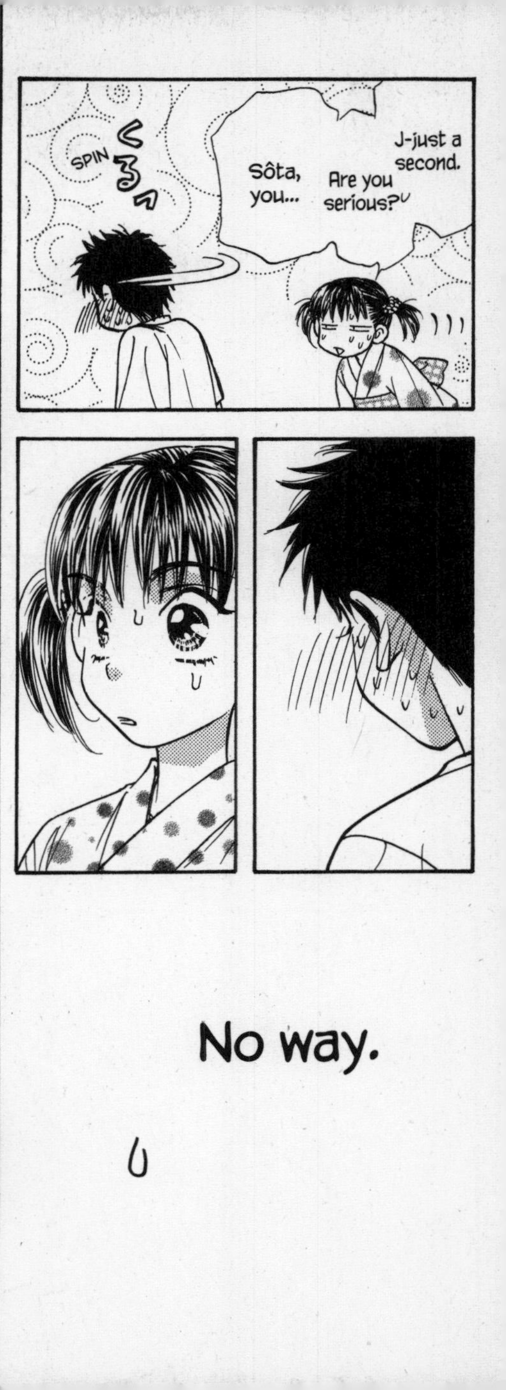
SPIN
J-just a second.
Are you serious?
Sôta, you...
No way.
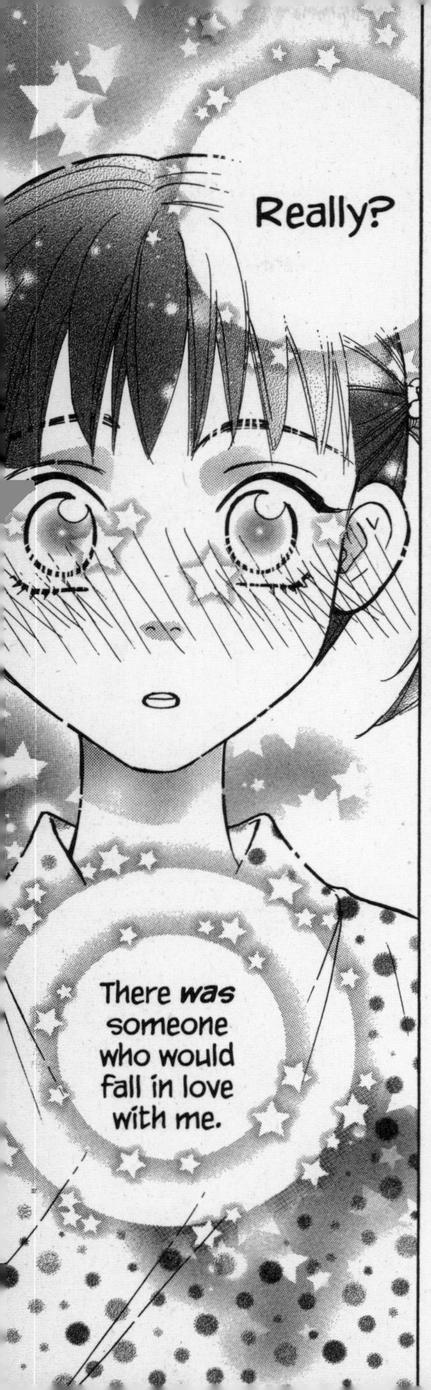
Really?
There *was* someone who would fall in love with me.

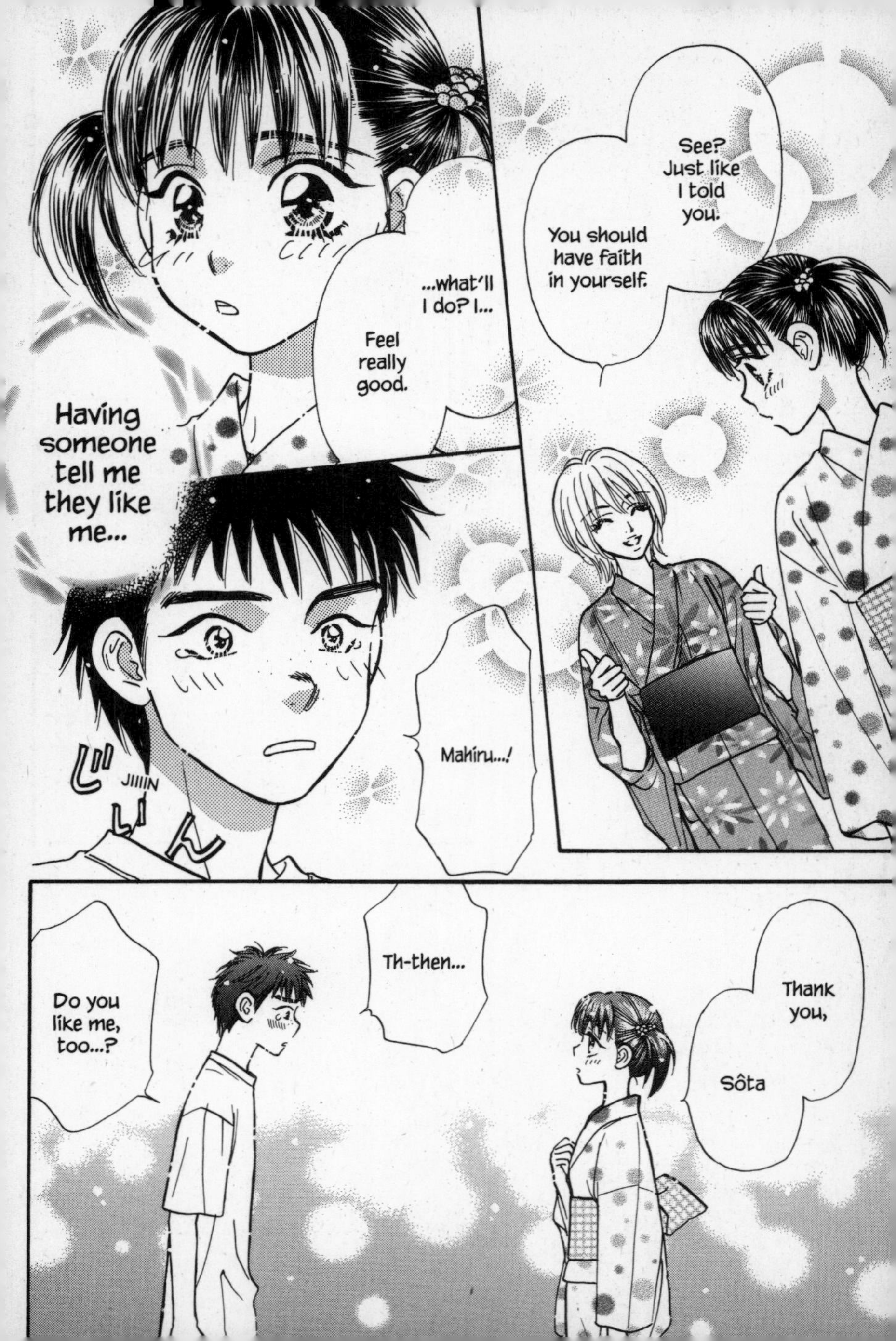
See? Just like I told you.
You should have faith in yourself.
...what'll I do? I...
Feel really good.
Having someone tell me they like me...
Mahiru...!
JIIIIN
Thank you,
Sôta
Th-then...
Do you like me, too...?

Huh?

Thanks to you, I have faith in myself!

I'll at least accept your feelings!

GAH

Well, I have always thought that I might be a little cute~~

CHUCKLE

CHUCKLE

Like that?

So what is this~~? Maybe I'm not so bad after all?

Ideals really do have to be high.

It's okay.

But I have a goal now.

I'm sorry, Sôta.

I'm sorry I thought you were a girl, Natsuki-chan.

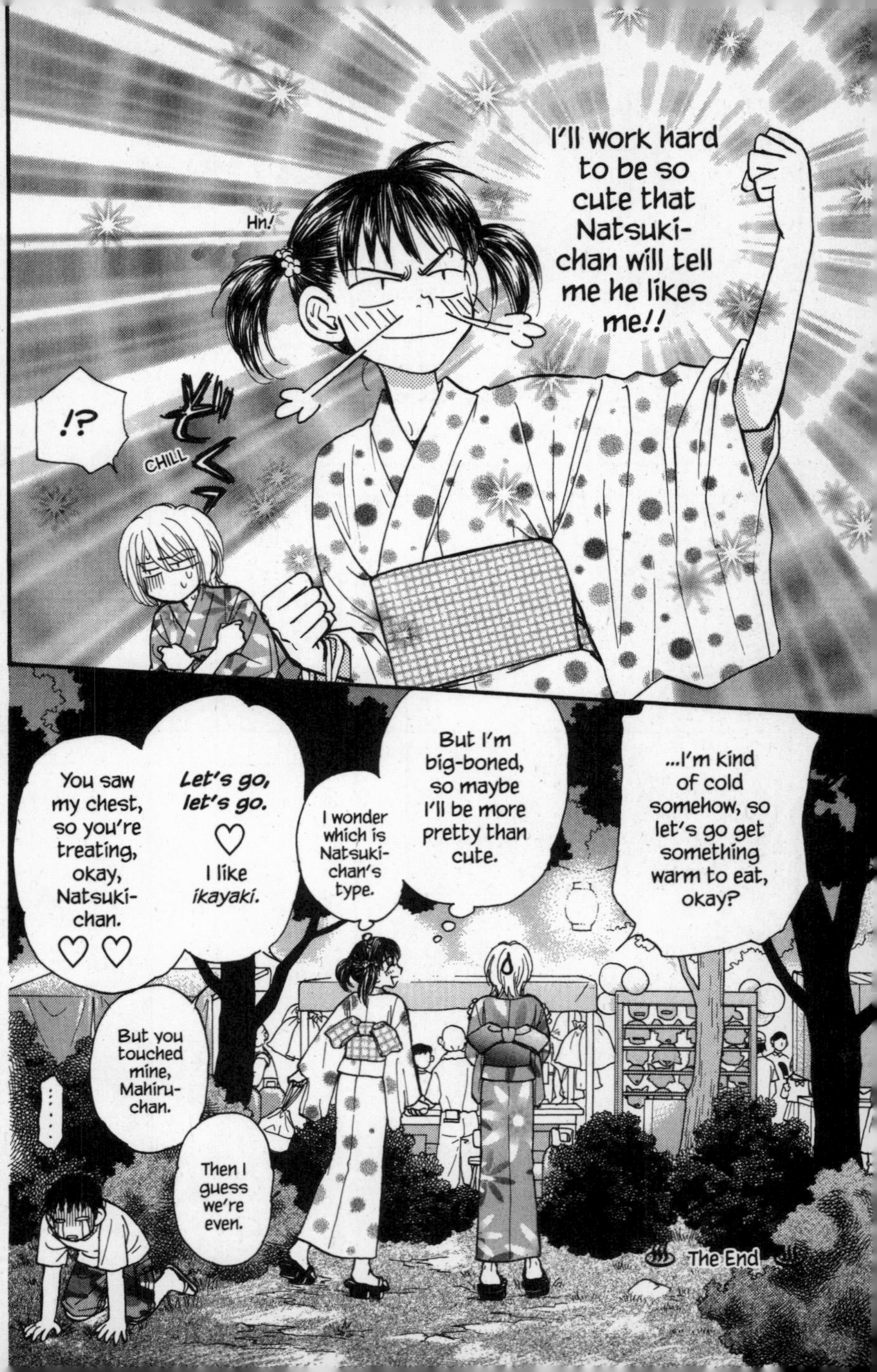
I'll work hard to be so cute that Natsuki-chan will tell me he likes me!!
Hn!
!?
CHILL
...I'm kind of cold somehow, so let's go get something warm to eat, okay?
But I'm big-boned, so maybe I'll be more pretty than cute.
I wonder which is Natsuki-chan's type.
Let's go, let's go. ♡ I like *ikayaki.*
You saw my chest, so you're treating, okay, Natsuki-chan. ♡ ♡
But you touched mine, Mahiru-chan.
Then I guess we're even.
......
The End

Translation Notes

Japanese is a tricky language for most Westerners, and translation is often more art than science. For your edification and reading pleasure, here are notes on some of the places where we could have gone in a different direction with our translation of the work, or where a Japanese cultural reference is used.

Shizuoka, page 5

Shizuoka is the capital of Shizuoka Prefecture, a prefecture in central Japan, not far from Tokyo.

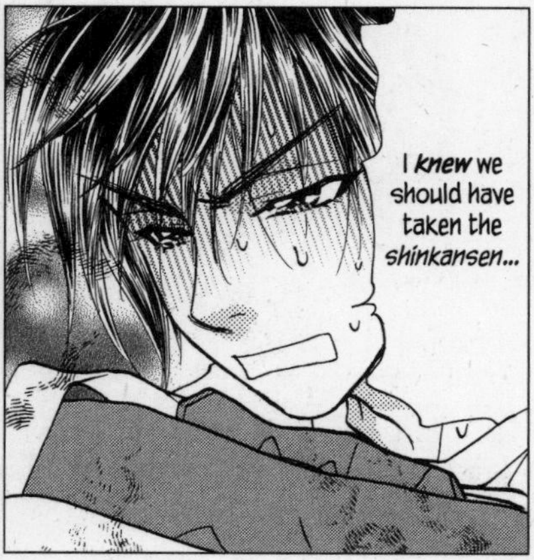
I *knew* we should have taken the *shinkansen*...

Shinkansen, page 6

The *shinkansen* is the bullet train.

Aichi Prefecture, page 10

Another prefecture in Japan, on the other side of Shizuoka from Tokyo.

Misokatsu, unagi, tenmusu, and *ebi-fry* page 11

All of these are local dishes of Nagoya, the capital city of Aichi Prefecture. *Misokatsu*, or miso cutlets, consists of pork cutlets with a red miso sauce. *Unagi*, or eel, is big in Aichi, and has been cooked into a wide variety of dishes. *Tenmusu*, short for *tempura musubi*, is a rice ball with shrimp tempura, and *ebi-fry* is fried shrimp.

Nagoya Cochin, page 12
A special breed of chicken found in Nagoya, and used in making Nagoya's many famous chicken dishes.

***Kishimen*, page 19**
The noodle specialty of Nagoya, *kishimen* is a flat, brown noodle often served with miso.

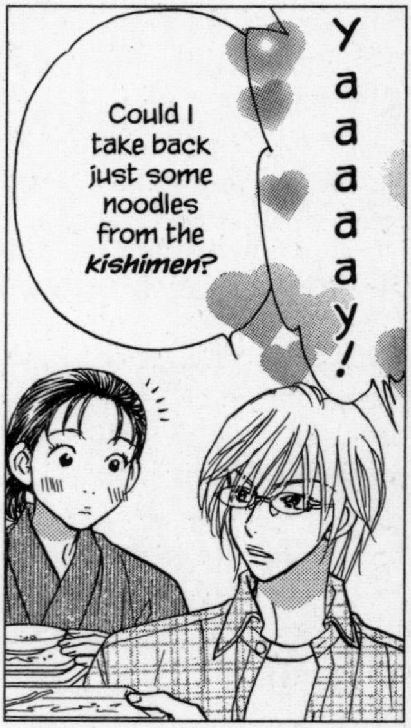
Could I take back just some noodles from the *kishimen*?
Yaaaaay!

***Kaeru manjû*, page 37**
Kaeru means frog, so a *kaeru manjû* is a steamed yeast bun shaped like a frog. It's a type of sweet you can buy in Nagoya.

Happiness fat, page 41
In Japan, this is what they call it when a man gains weight after getting married. The idea is that the man is happily eating his new wife's delicious food so much that he gets fat.

***Moé*, page 66**
Moé is a phrase used by fanboys and fangirls to describe the type of character from an anime or video game that they have a particular attraction to, and the strong feelings that those characters inspire.

Water bath, page 108

A water bath, or *yusen* in Japanese, is a way to cook something by putting a container holding the ingredients in warm or boiling water. Water baths are used to cook things that need careful temperature regulation, like chocolate and eggs, because the water serves as a buffer to prevent the ingredients from getting too hot too quickly.

Sembei, page 110

Sembei are Japanese rice crackers, known for being flat, quite the opposite of spongecake.

Takashi x Izumi, page 127

The line is said by a character from an earlier volume, who's obsessed with a genre of manga called *yaoi*. It's kind of like slash fiction in the U.S.—stories of homosexual relationships between male characters written for the enjoyment of a female readership. Just as writers of slash fiction denote the characters that are the subject of the relationship using a "slash" between their names— Kirk/Spock, Frodo/Sam—yaoi fans sometimes use an "x" for the same purpose, as in "Takashi x Izumi." This character is enjoying the idea of Izumi and the baker or Izumi and Takashi having a relationship.

Seiken chûdan gyakuzuki and *osu*, page 128

Seiken means "correct fist," and is a normal fist with the thumb outside the rest of the fingers. *Chûdan* means "middle level," and refers to a strike to the middle level, or the body/torso, and *gyakuzuki* is a "reverse strike." So the instructor is telling his students to do a reverse punch at body level using a *seiken* fist. *Osu*, in this case, means "yes, sir!"

Jôdan, page 131

Referencing Mahiru's attack on Sôta, Mahiru's grandfather is impressed with her *jôdan* kick. *Jôdan* means "higher level," and in karate refers to a strike to the head.

Chocolate *monaka*, page 140

A *monaka* is a wafer cake with filling. In this case, he's buying a chocolate *monaka*, which is kind of like an ice cream sandwich. In the center is a layer of chocolate, surrounded by ice cream, all contained in a waffle-like wafer.

Matsuri, page 144
A *matsuri* is a Japanese festival. There are food, games, and entertainment, like a fair, only without rides. Everyone dresses up in Japanese-style clothing.

Yukata, page 145
A *yukata* is a summer kimono, made of cotton and less formal than a normal kimono. Like a kimono, a *yukata* is tied with a belt called an *obi*, which, for girls, is wide and tied in a special, decorative way, and is a little more restrictive than the *obi* men wear. Girls like to show off how they look in *yukata* when they go to a *matsuri*.

Jinbei, page 145
Jinbei is informal summer clothing for men, consisting of a short coat and pants that go to the knees.

Geta, page 153
Geta is a type of Japanese shoe worn with *yukata*, kind of like flip-flops, only made of wood and standing on two wooden slats called "teeth." Since Mahiru is prone to kicking boys, they would certainly want to avoid her when she's wearing such potentially painful footwear.

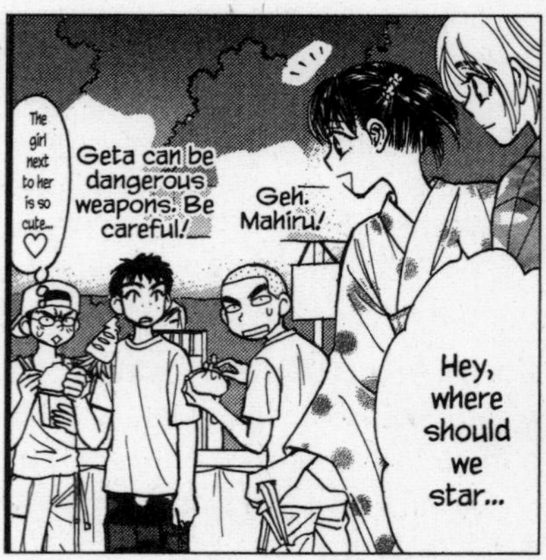

Hey, where should we star...
Geh. Mahiru!
Geta can be dangerous weapons. Be careful!
The girl next to her is so cute... ♡

Takoyaki and goldfish scoop, page 153
Both are musts for summer *matsuri*. *Takoyaki* is fried octopus, formed in balls and put on a skewer. The goldfish scoop is a game where you catch goldfish with paper nets.

Ikayaki, page 170
Fried squid.

Princess Tenko, author's note
Princess Tenko is a famous Japanese magician and illusionist, and even she would be shocked and amazed at Hogeo-kun's ability to look like just a head.

Preview of Volume 8

We're pleased to present you a preview from volume 8. Please check our website (www.delreymanga.com) to see when this volume will be available in English. For now you'll have to make do with Japanese!

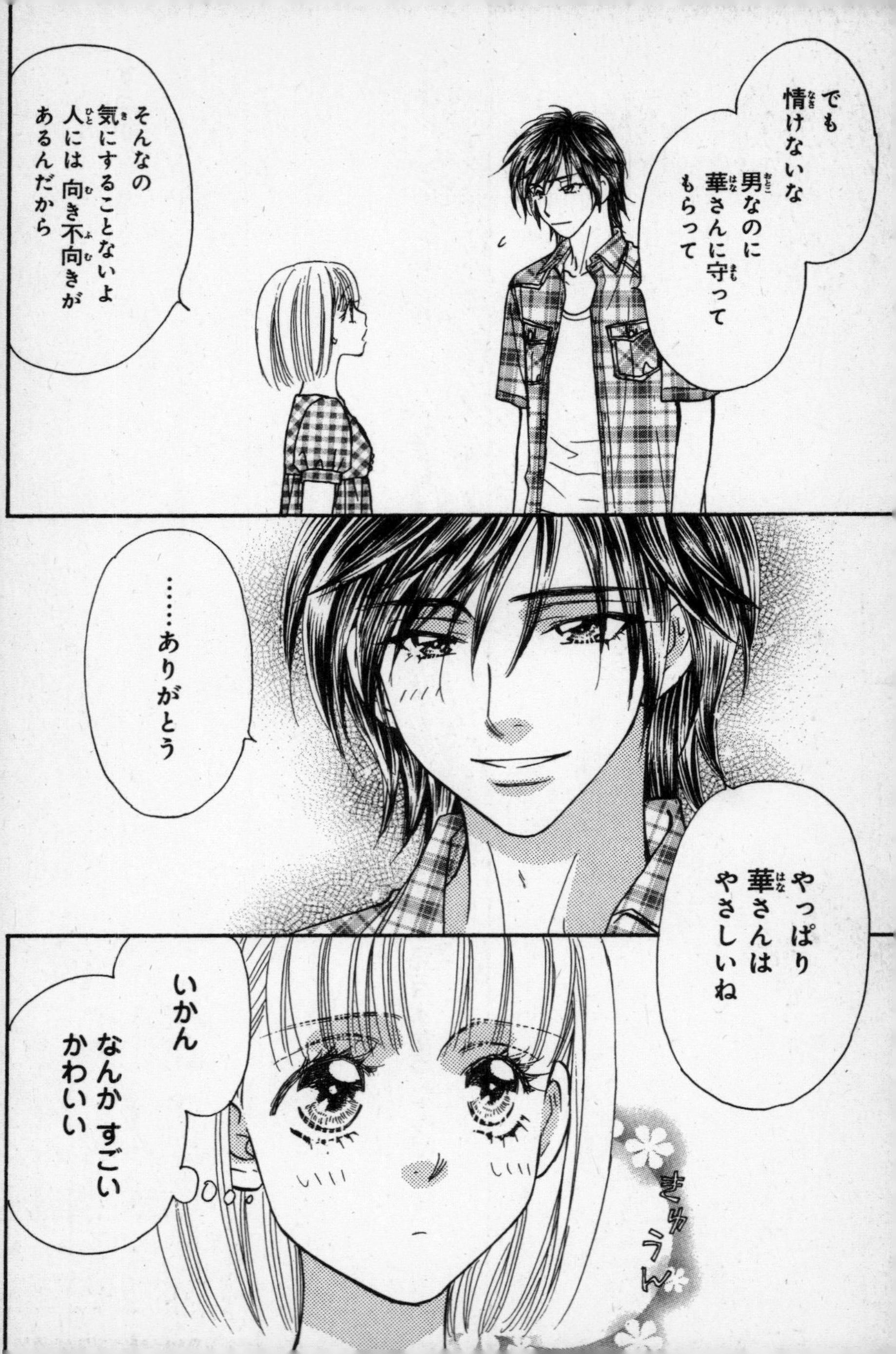
でも 情けないな 男なのに 華さんに守って もらって
そんなの 気にすることないよ 人には 向き不向きが あるんだから
……ありがとう
やっぱり 華さんは やさしいね
いかん なんか すごい かわいい
きゅうん

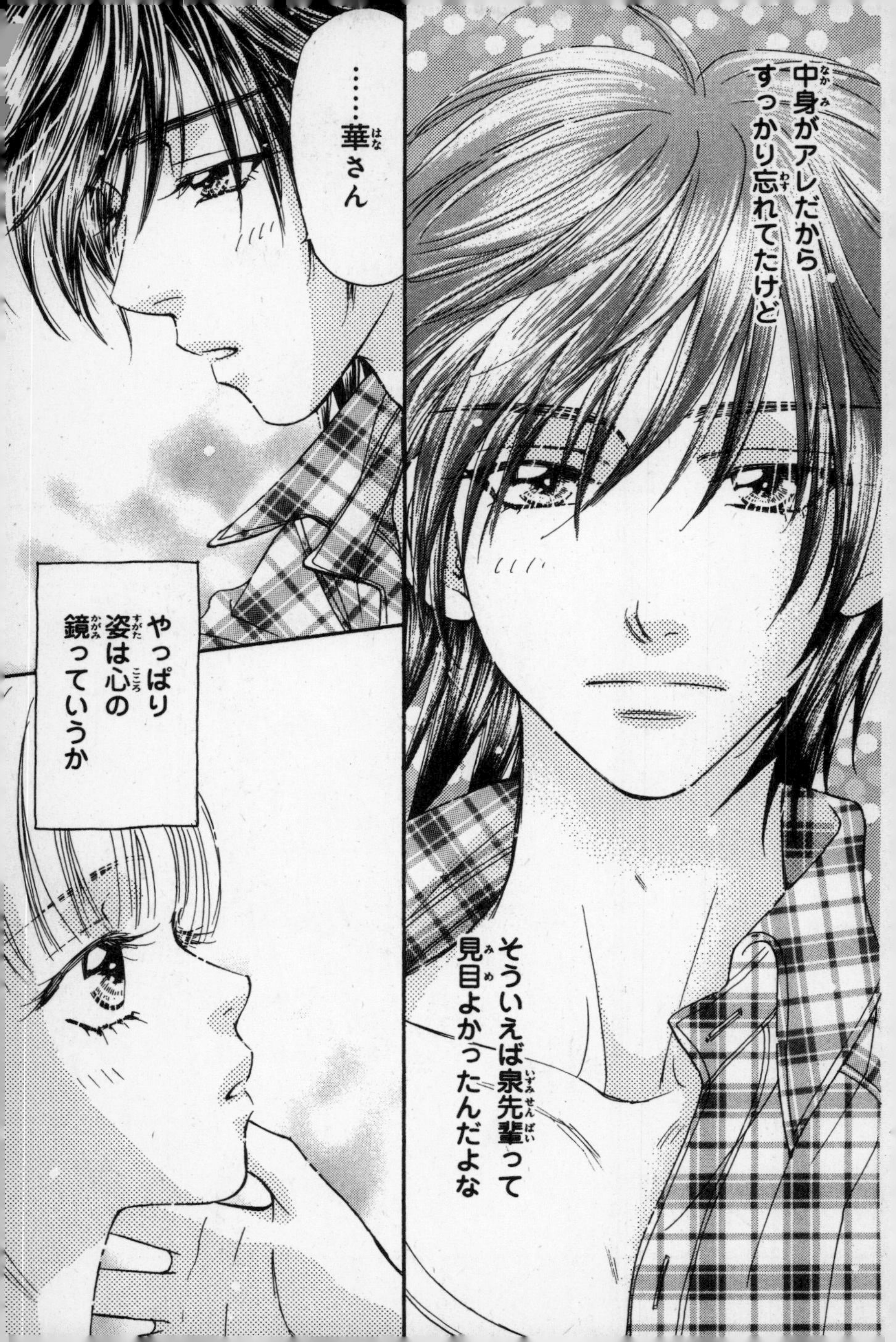
中身がアレだから すっかり忘れてたけど
そういえば泉先輩って 見目よかったんだよな
……華さん
やっぱり 姿は心の 鏡っていうか

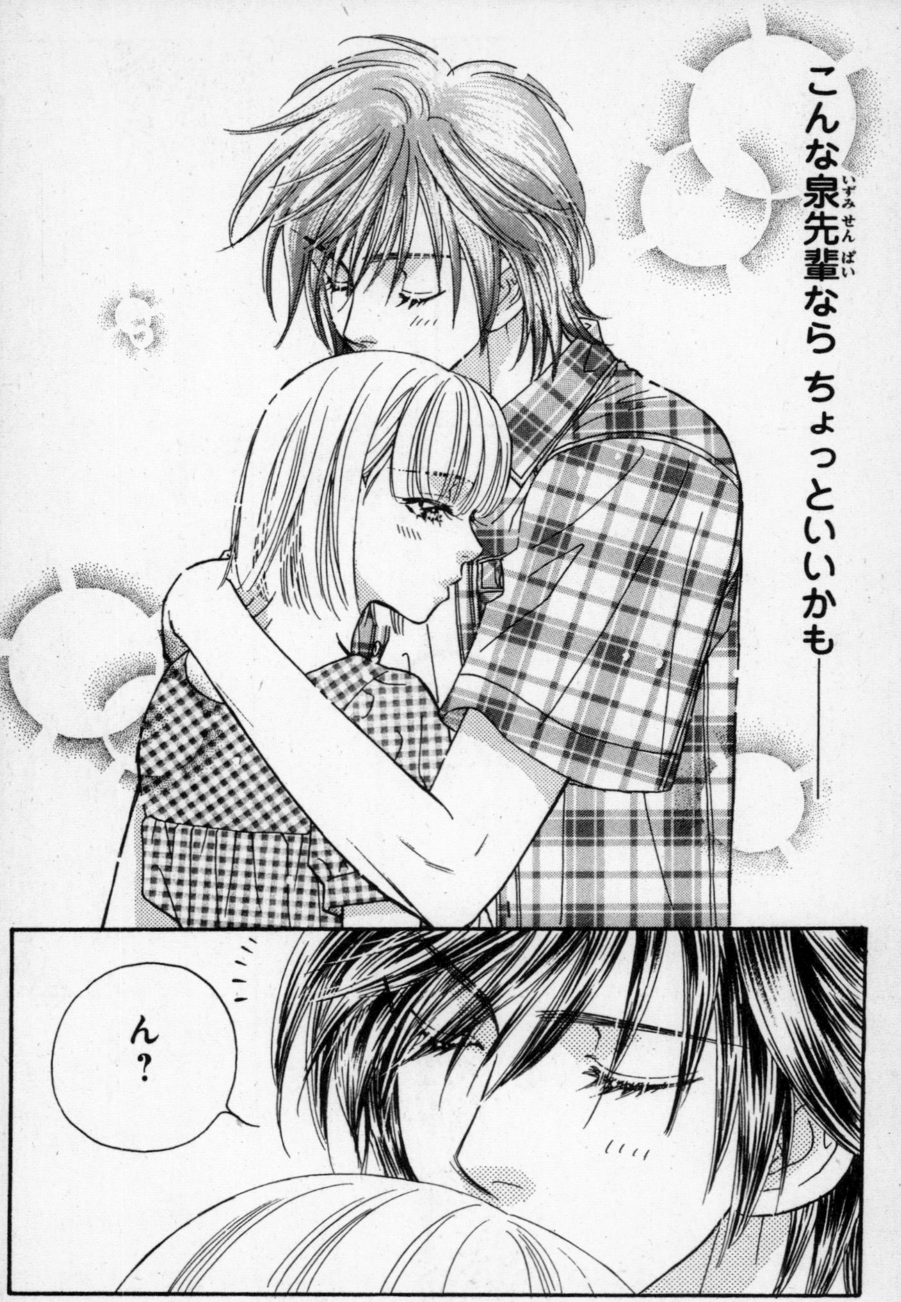
こんな泉先輩なら ちょっといいかも——
ん？

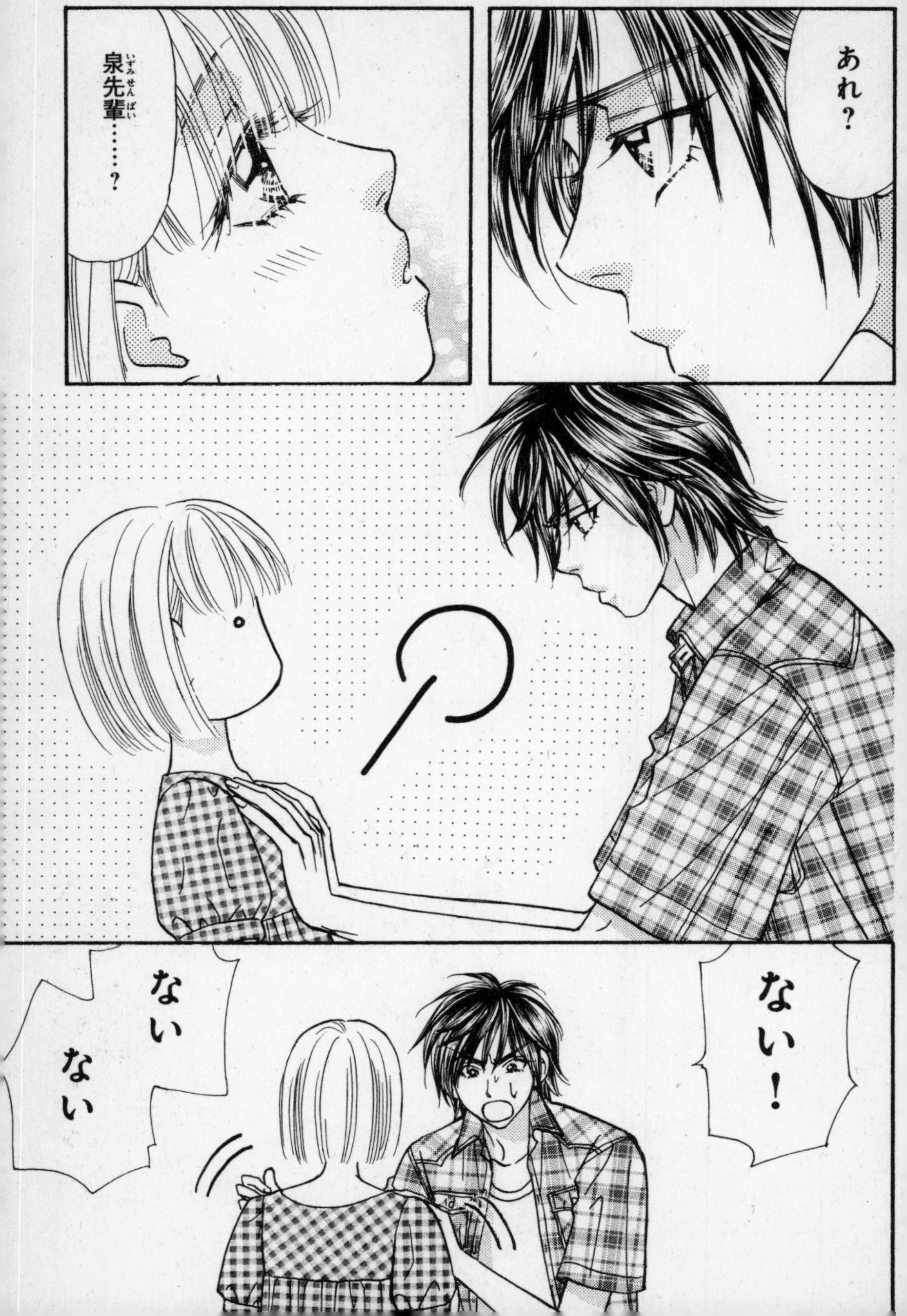
あれ？
泉先輩……？
ない！
ない ない ない

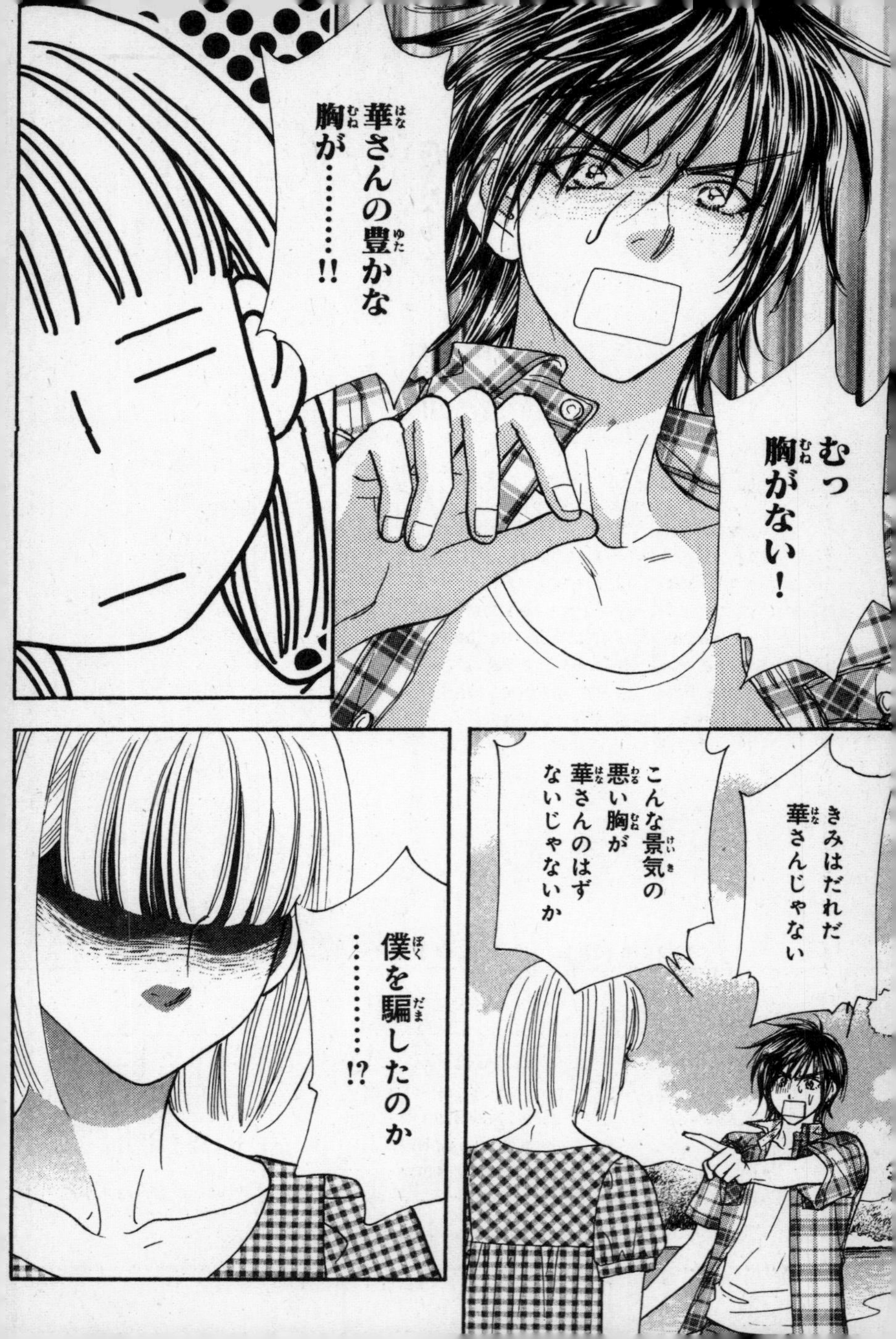
華さんの豊かな胸が……!!
むっ胸がない!
きみはだれだ華さんじゃない
こんな景気の悪い胸が華さんのはずないじゃないか
……僕を騙したのか……!?

STORY BY SURT LIM
ART BY HIROFUMI SUGIMOTO

A DEL REY MANGA ORIGINAL

Exploring the woods, young Kasumi encounters an ancient tree god, who bestows upon her the power of invisibility. Together with classmates who have had similar experiences, Kasumi forms the Magic Play Club, dedicated to using their powers for good while avoiding sinister forces that would exploit them.

Special extras in each volume! Read them all!

VISIT WWW.DELREYMANGA.COM TO:
• Read sample pages
• View release date calendars for upcoming volumes
• Sign up for Del Rey's free manga e-newsletter
• Find out the latest about new Del Rey Manga series

RATING   T AGES 13+

 DEL REY MANGA デルレイ

The Otaku's Choice.™

KITCHEN PRINCESS

STORY BY MIYUKI KOBAYASHI
MANGA BY NATSUMI ANDO
CREATOR OF ZODIAC P.I.

HUNGRY HEART

Najika is a great cook and likes to make meals for the people she loves. But something is missing from her life. When she was a child, she met a boy who touched her heart— and now Najika is determined to find him. The only clue she has is a silver spoon that leads her to the prestigious Seika Academy.

Attending Seika will be a challenge. Every kid at the school has a special talent, and the girls in Najika's class think she doesn't deserve to be there. But Sora and Daichi, two popular brothers who barely speak to each other, recognize Najika's cooking for what it is—magical. Could one of the boys be Najika's mysterious prince?

Special extras in each volume! Read them all!

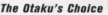

BY MACHIKO SAKURAI

A LITTLE LIVING DOLL!

What would you do if your favorite toy came to life and became your best friend? Well, that's just what happens to Ame Oikawa, a shy schoolgirl. Nicori is a super-cute doll with a mind of its own—and a plan to make Ame's dreams come true!

Special extras in each volume! Read them all!

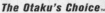

Papillon

BY MIWA UEDA

BUTTERFLY, SPREAD YOUR WINGS!

Ageha is a shy tomboy, but her twin sister Hana is the ultimate ultra-glam teen queen. Hana loves being the center of attention so much that she'll do anything to keep Ageha in her shadow. But Ageha has a plan that will change her life forever and no one, not even Hana, can hold her back. . . .

• From the creator of *Peach Girl*

Special extras in each volume! Read them all!

TOMARE!

止まれ

[STOP!]

You're going the wrong way!

Manga is a completely different type of reading experience.

To start at the *beginning*, go to the *end*!

That's right! Authentic manga is read the traditional Japanese way— from right to left. Exactly the opposite of how American books are read. It's easy to follow: Just go to the other end of the book, and read each page—and each panel—from right side to left side, starting at the top right. Now you're experiencing manga as it was meant to be!